* *

AMERICA AND THE MAKING OF AN
INDEPENDENT IRELAND

**GLUCKSMAN
IRISH DIASPORA**

THE GLUCKSMAN IRISH DIASPORA SERIES
Edited by Kevin Kenny
Associate Editor Miriam Nyhan Grey

America and the Making of an Independent Ireland: A History
Francis M. Carroll

America and the Making of an Independent Ireland

A History

Francis M. Carroll

NEW YORK UNIVERSITY PRESS
New York

NEW YORK UNIVERSITY PRESS
New York
www.nyupress.org

© 2021 by New York University
All rights reserved

References to Internet websites (URLs) were accurate at the time of writing. Neither the author nor New York University Press is responsible for URLs that may have expired or changed since the manuscript was prepared.

Library of Congress Cataloging-in-Publication Data
Names: Carroll, Francis M., 1938– author.
Title: America and the making of an independent Ireland : a history / Francis M. Carroll.
Description: New York : New York University Press, [2021] |
Series: The Glucksman Irish diaspora series | Includes bibliographical references and index.
Identifiers: LCCN 2020015047 (print) | LCCN 2020015048 (ebook) |
ISBN 9781479805655 (hardback) | ISBN 9781479805693 (ebook) | ISBN 9781479805679 (ebook)
Subjects: LCSH: United States—Foreign relations—Ireland. | Ireland—Foreign relations—United States. | Ireland—Politics and government—1910–1921. | Ireland—Politics and government—1922–1949. | Self-determination, National—Ireland—History—20th century. | Ireland—History—Autonomy and independence movements. | Irish question. | Home rule—Ireland—History—20th century. | Nationalism—Ireland—History—20th century.
Classification: LCC E183.8.I6 C37 2021 (print) | LCC E183.8.I6 (ebook) |
DDC 327.73041509/041—dc23
LC record available at https://lccn.loc.gov/2020015047

LC ebook record available at https://lccn.loc.gov/2020015048New York University Press books are printed on acid-free paper, and their binding materials are chosen for strength and durability. We strive to use environmentally responsible suppliers and materials to the greatest extent possible in publishing our books.

Manufactured in the United States of America

10 9 8 7 6 5 4 3 2 1

Also available as an ebook

CONTENTS

List of Abbreviations	vii
Prologue: Changed, Changed Utterly	ix
1. America and the Irish Rising of 1916	1
2. America, the War Crisis, and the Irish Problem, 1916–1918	13
3. The 1919 Paris Peace Conference, the American Commission on Irish Independence, and Self-Determination for Ireland	36
4. Money: The Sinews of War, 1919–1921	64
5. Ireland in the Eye of Public Opinion: The American Commission on Conditions in Ireland, 1920–1921	89
6. American Aid for Ireland, 1920–1922	111
7. The Emergence of the Irish Free State and American Diplomatic Recognition, 1921–1927	142
8. President William T. Cosgrave Comes to the United States, 1928	165
9. Secretary of State Frank B. Kellogg Comes to Ireland, 1928	184
Epilogue: Ireland and America	199
Acknowledgments	203
Appendix 1. The Meeting of John Quinn's Delegation with A. J. Balfour on 4 May 1917	205
Appendix 2. Documents Submitted and Witnesses at the Senate Foreign Relations Committee Hearings on the Treaty of Peace with Germany	213

Appendix 3. American Commission on Conditions on Ireland: Hearings and Witnesses before the Commission in Washington, DC   217

Appendix 4. Report on Secretary of State Frank B. Kellogg's Visit to Dublin in August 1928   221

Notes   225

Bibliography   263

Index   277

About the Author   293

Illustrations follow page 81

LIST OF ABBREVIATIONS

AARIR	American Association for the Recognition of the Irish Republic
ACRI	American Committee for Relief in Ireland
AFSC	American Friends Service Committee
AIHS	American Irish Historical Society
BDFA	*British Documents on Foreign Affairs: Reports and Papers from the Foreign Office Confidential Prints, Series C, North America, 1919–1939*
BL	British Library, London
CO	Colonial Office
Cong. Rec.	*Congressional Record*
DBFP	*Documents on British Foreign Policy*
DIFP	*Documents of Irish Foreign Policy*
DO	Dominion Office
FO	Foreign Office
FRUS	*Foreign Relations of the United States*
FOIF	Friends of Irish Freedom
HUL	Harvard University Library
IRB	Irish Republican Brotherhood
LC	Library of Congress, Washington
NAI	National Archives of Ireland, Dublin
NARA	National Archives and Records Administrations, College Park
NLI	National Library of Ireland
NYPL	New York Public Library

NYT New York Times
PWW *Papers of Woodrow Wilson*
Parl. Deb. *Parliamentary Debates*
RG Record Group, State Department Papers
TNA National Archives, Kew
UCDA University College Dublin Archives
UML University of Michigan Library
YUL Yale University Library, Manuscripts and Archives

Prologue

Changed, Changed Utterly

Ireland and America. Would Ireland have acquired self-government and independence without America? In the one hundred years since the 1916 Easter Rising, we can seriously assess the extent to which the Irish American community, the American public, and, eventually, the American government provided aid and support for the Irish nationalist struggle, from 1916 through the 1920s. Of course, the determination and physical courage of the Irish people themselves were crucial in the Easter Rising, as well as in the reemergence of Sinn Féin, the War of Independence, the Civil War, and the creation of the Irish Free State. The Easter Rising in the midst of World War I was the turning point for Ireland, as well as for Britain and, ultimately, for the United States. The postwar world was not the same; this was a new era. Yeats was right—everything was "changed, changed utterly." When Ireland stepped forward, America was prepared to help.

The celebration of the one-hundredth anniversary of the 1916 Easter Rising has renewed discussions about that formative event in Irish history. A century's distance provides a degree of objectivity that was not possible when the half-century was celebrated in 1966; then, many participants were still alive, perhaps the most prominent being Eamon de Valera, the senior surviving commandant from 1916 and president of the Irish Republic. Not surprisingly, the anniversary was very much a triumphalist celebration, of the very people who had set in motion the events that led to the modern independent Irish state.[1]

By 2016, fifty years later, a new generation had come of age, a high proportion of which had never known Ireland outside the European Union, much less as a part of the United Kingdom. The Easter Rising, among other significant events, was still revered as the beginning of their Ireland. But, with membership in the United Nations and the European Union, peacekeepers in global trouble spots, and connections around the world, Ireland can look back at 1916 in a broader historical framework. The enormous number of Irishmen who volunteered and fought in the British Army in World War I, well in excess of the Irish Volunteers, is one example; the large number of civilian casualties in Dublin in the Easter Rising is another. In this context, it should be acknowledged that the Rising and much of Ireland's subsequent struggle to achieve self-government—not to mention acceptance in the international community—depended on the assistance of the United States.

The centennial celebrations in New York in April 2016 emphasized the United States' enormous contribution to the Rising. Five of the 1916 Proclamation's seven signatories (Thomas J. Clarke, Patrick Pearse, James Connolly, Seán Mac Diarmada, and Joseph Mary Plunkett) had toured or lived or worked in the United States. Indeed, the proclamation itself, justifying the right of the Irish people to insurrection, declared the Rising to be "supported by her exiled children in America." US backing of the revolutionaries—the Irish Republican Brotherhood, the Irish Volunteers, and the Irish Citizen Army—laid much of the groundwork for the Rising. In the stark words of Joseph J. Lee, "No America, no New York, no Easter Rising."[2]

But was there more to the American dimension of the Irish struggle for independence? Would the unresolved matter of Irish self-government jeopardize the American commitment to the Allied cause as the country entered World War I in 1917? Was it possible for the United States to call for self-determination for Ireland, along with the countries of Central Europe, at the Paris Peace Conference in 1919? Could the Irish community in America raise enough money to help fund the Dáil Éireann government after it had declared independence? Might liberal America call attention to, and protest against, the cruelties of the Anglo-Irish War as waged by the Black and Tans? Would Americans generally support relief efforts in Ireland following the Anglo-Irish War, as they had in Belgium and Central Europe in the wake of World War I? Once the Irish Free State was established, ought the United States to extend the first-ever diplomatic recognition to a British Dominion? And, finally, would the United States, as a great power, make overt gestures of friendship to the young Irish government? For the next decade, the relationship between the two countries was complicated, deep-rooted, and multilayered, as this book demonstrates.

※

American support for the Irish struggle for independence did not end with the Rising. But what could private citizens—in this case, the "exiled children in America"—do, either individually or collectively, to promote the independence of an aspiring nation? Indeed, what could members of Congress and the leaders of the government do if they also hoped to maintain normal "friendly" relations with Great Britain? International law and custom had to be observed; Britain was the leading world power of the early twentieth century and a key ally in the war. The US government had to be cautious. Only sixty years earlier, during the American Civil War, the British government had casually allowed private individuals to build and supply Confederate naval vessels that caused enormous damage to the American merchant fleet. In 1871, an arbitration tribunal found the British government to have been negligent and therefore responsible for damages amounting to some $15,500,000. While there were limits to what America could do to help Ireland achieve independence, the "Irish question" remained a pertinent issue for Americans for almost two decades. As Lawrence J. McCaffrey has pointed out, it should be kept in mind that, in the early twentieth century, the Irish American community still labored under an ethnic and religious liability in a largely Anglo-Saxon and Protestant culture, and the nationalist yearning was, to some extent, a reaction to a sense of alienation.[3] Eventually, however, Americans at many levels of society were engaged in the Irish struggle, including the most recent Irish immigrants, establishment eastern liberal elites, stereotypical Irish American serving girls, and even the president of the United States. Indeed, the liberal progressive exposure of conditions in Ireland, together with the public endorsements of both presidents Warren G. Harding and Calvin Coolidge, were a vindication. The Irish question had become an urgent one in American public life.

Years ago, the distinguished scholar Nicholas Mansergh cautiously asserted that "it was this twofold support, diplomatic and financial, that rendered American backing for Ireland in 1919–21 of great, though probably, despite British views to the contrary, not of decisive importance."⁴ Since Mansergh's seminal work was published, crucial papers in government archives in Ireland, Britain, and the United States have been opened, and sophisticated monographs written. This book questions Mansergh's assertion and demonstrates that, at every stage, from the home rule movement through the 1916 Rising to the world of international diplomacy in the 1920s, the United States performed a crucial role in, and was a major contributing force to, the achievement of Irish sovereignty.

☘

As this book will show, the United States, from at least 1914 to 1928, played a dynamic part in Ireland's emergence as an independent state: providing relief after the Rising, urging the British government to implement some form of Irish self-rule, working to obtain a hearing for Ireland at the Peace Conference in Paris after World War I, and raising substantial funds for the Dáil Éireann government. The United States mounted a major relief effort in the aftermath of the War of Independence, generated widespread public support for Ireland through a public investigation of the country's wartime conditions, extended early diplomatic relations to the Irish Free State, welcomed the head of an Irish government to Congress and the White House, and sent a US secretary of state on an official visit in 1928—all concrete efforts with profound results. By the 1920s, most of Ireland was an independent state, and the United States had strongly contributed to its making.

1

America and the Irish Rising of 1916

Once or twice in a century, events grip a nation or a people and things are never the same again. These do not have to be great victories or triumphs, as the Alamo, Pearl Harbor, John F. Kennedy's assassination, or 9/11 would illustrate. For Ireland, the 1916 Rising was just such a turning point. Yeats understood it shrewdly: "A terrible beauty was born." Everything seemed to go wrong; the weapons did not arrive; the leadership was a self-appointed and self-divided clique; the operations were canceled and then rescheduled for the next day; British intelligence knew much of what was going on; the uprising was crushed within a week; the elected Irish members of parliament regarded the entire affair as treachery; everyone regarded it as a disaster. And yet everything was changed utterly. Within two years, the Irish Parliamentary Party was repudiated at the polls, and the survivors of the 1916 Rising and their colleagues were elected to represent much of the country. It was a remarkable political turnaround. There would be no going back to the political world that existed before the outbreak of the Great War.

When the Irish Volunteers and the Irish Citizen Army marched up O'Connell Street on Easter Monday, 24 April 1916, and seized the General Post Office (GPO) building, Patrick H. Pearse stood and read a proclamation announcing to an astonished public the creation of the Irish Republic, established by a Provisional Government formed by the Irish Republican Brotherhood (IRB) and the Volunteers and the Citizen Army. This was, to be sure, an Irish declaration of independence, justifying the armed action and explaining the intentions behind it. Of particular interest is Pearse's statement that the rebellion was "supported by her exiled children in America." This was more than just a gesture to Irish Americans, or an expression of hope that the association with America in the context of World War I might offer protection. The "exiled children" had already played an important role in the events leading up to the 1916 Rising—in the physical force movement, in the Irish Ireland movement specifically, and in Irish nationalism generally. Arguably, one might say that Ireland's "exiled children" had been standing by since the eighteenth century.

☘

By the 1910 Census, there were 4,504,360 Americans who had either been born in Ireland or had at least one parent born in Ireland. It was estimated that third- and fourth-generation Irish Americans numbered as many as 20,000,000, or about 21 percent of the total population of 91,972,266 people. These statistics meant that the "exiled children" in the United States constituted an enormous potential resource for any political or cultural movement in Ireland. Even if only a fraction of people with Irish origins could be enlisted to support a cause or contribute to an organization, it would represent an enormous groundswell. In other words, there were two Irelands: the four million people living in Ireland, and the great diaspora of people of Irish origins living abroad, the vast majority of whom were in the United States.

From colonial times up to the eve of World War I, this immigrant community had taken part in American life and, from at least the 1860s on, had been generous and influential in supporting nationalist activities in Ireland. After the particularly turbulent 1890s, with the Charles Stewart Parnell divorce scandal and Parnell's death, the split in the Irish Parliamentary Party, and the defeat of William Ewart Gladstone's Home Rule Bill, the new century seemed to present new opportunities. A reunified and reinvigorated Irish Parliamentary Party attracted great numbers of Irish Americans who joined the United Irish League of America and rallied behind John Redmond and his party. As a result of the two general elections of 1910, the Liberals and the Conservatives (then known as the Conservative and Unionist Party) were tied in the House of Commons with 272 members each; the Irish Party, with 84 members, held the balance of power. John Redmond and his lieutenants, John Dillon, T. P. O'Connor, and others, toured the United States, Canada, and Australia, raising hundreds of thousands of dollars to finance elections and pay salaries to members without private incomes. "You have the race at home and abroad solidly, sincerely, and almost unanimously with you," judge Martin J. Keogh wrote to Redmond from New York in May 1912, when the Home Rule Bill passed its second reading in the House of Commons.[1] It is fair to say that Irish Americans, after all the trials and calamities of the nineteenth century, wanted results and were prepared to back a winner. By 1914, however, in the face of Unionist defiance in the north of Ireland, the Liberal government's indecision at Westminster, and the outbreak of war in Europe, Irish American support for Redmond and the Irish Parliamentary Party began to evaporate. William Bourke Cockran, the distinguished congressman from New York, wrote to a friend in England in March 1914, with perhaps more foresight than he realized: "If a revolt [against Redmond] were started in Ireland, I think the Irish in America would support it to a man."[2] The suspension of the Home Rule Bill, the war, and Redmond's urging of Irish enlistments in the British Army destroyed enthusiasm for the United Irish League of America, and, ironically, by 1915 Redmond had to send money to the United States to keep the United Irish League (UIL) of America alive.

Of course, not all nationalists in Ireland and the United States supported the Irish Parliamentary Party and the prospect of the successful enactment of the Home Rule Bill. For some, the powers were too modest; for others, Ireland still remained within the British Empire, Many considered the Parliamentary Party corrupt, but for a serious cadre home rule was simply not a republic. In the United States, the Clan na Gael constituted the leading antagonists to the Irish Parliamentary Party, the Home Rule Bill, and John Redmond. The Clan was founded in New York in 1867 for a specific purpose. When the Fenian movement disintegrated as a result of both military failures and internal divisions, the Clan na Gael emerged as a secret society for Irish Americans with republican revolutionary sympathies could join. "Camps" were originally created in New York, Jersey City, Buffalo, Boston, and Philadelphia, but the organization quickly spread across the United States. The Clan had a troubled history, beset by scandals and faction fights and a serious split for almost twenty years. However, it was reunited in 1900 under the leadership of John Devoy. Called "the greatest of the Fenians" by Patrick Pearse, John Devoy had been a chief organizer for the Fenians in Ireland, was imprisoned in 1866, and allowed to emigrate to the United States in 1871, where he devoted the rest of his life to Irish republicanism. Devoy never married, lived a Spartan existence in a single room in a New York City rooming house, and worked as a journalist until 1903, when he founded the *Gaelic American*, which would become the most militant Irish American nationalist newspaper. Single-minded, irascible, and increasingly deaf, Devoy emerged as the unyielding leader of the Clan na Gael.[3] As the twentieth century unfolded, the Clan found itself confronted with the apparent success of the Irish Parliamentary Party and home rule, and the prospects for a republican revolution looked bleak. In 1910, Chicago's Revolutionary Directory member John T. Keating wrote, "Ten years of struggle, and we are reaching what seems to be the end." He agreed with Devoy that more "mere negative policy . . . will kill us if too much prolonged."[4] Under the circumstances, it was difficult for a secret society to recruit new members, raise money, and formulate a practical policy program.[5]

All was not lost, however. Perhaps most important, the Clan was instrumental in keeping the IRB alive as a functioning organization. By 1910 the IRB had declined from as many as 40,000 members down to a rather sleepy 1,500 or 2000, spread across Ireland and Britain. The Clan sent about £600 (about $3,000) a year, sometimes more, to the Supreme Council in Dublin, which gave it some working funds. It also sent new people, which served to reinvigorate the leadership of the organization. The most important of these was Thomas J. Clarke, who had been jailed for fifteen years in England for revolutionary activity, worked for Devoy in New York on the *Gaelic American*, and in 1907 returned to Dublin, where he was co-opted into the IRB's Supreme Council. IRB historian Leon O'Broin attributes the organization's revival to the initiative Clarke provided, particularly in pushing forward new leaders.[6] Others who became prominent were Patrick McCartan, a protégé of Joseph McGarrity of Philadelphia, and Diarmuid Lynch, who had been active in US Irish-language and Irish-dancing circles.[7] The Clan also sent representatives to the IRB meetings in Ireland once a year and brought over Irish representatives to their own annual conventions. All of this cemented the links between the two organizations and particularly strengthened Clarke's efforts to draw into key positions forward-thinking young men such as Bulmer Hobson, Denis McCullough, Seán Mac Diarmada, the latter of whom represented the IRB at the Clan convention in Atlantic City, New Jersey, in October 1912.[8] Patrick H. Pearse spent several months in the United States in early 1914, raising money for his school, St. Enda's, while also building relations with Irish American leaders as diverse as John Devoy and Joseph McGarrity, as well as John Quinn and Morgan J. O'Brien. It should not be forgotten, either, that James Connolly lived for several years in the United States, largely preoccupied with labor recruitment, although he was neither a member of the Clan nor of the IRB until January 1916, when he committed the Irish Citizen Army to the plans of the Military Council.[9]

The Clan na Gael also supported many of the Irish Ireland groups that were equally opposed to the Irish Parliamentary Party and the home rule it pursued, included Sinn Féin, the Gaelic League, the Gaelic Athletic Association, the Abbey Theatre, and St. Enda's, among several other organizations attempting to reinvigorate Irish life through a reinvention of, and an immersion in, some form of uniquely Irish life. During the 1890s and the first twelve or so years of the twentieth century, these groups stood precariously outside Ireland's political mainstream, which was dominated by the Irish Parliamentary Party. For funds, audience, status, and, in some cases, leadership, these groups and individuals—in many instances including IRB members—turned to the Irish in the United States. The list is impressive: Maud Gonne, John MacBride, Douglas Hyde, Lady Gregory, William Butler Yeats, Francis Sheehy-Skeffington, Thomas Ash, Bulmer Hobson, Patrick H. Pearse, and Sir Roger Casement, to name the most famous. John Quinn, a successful New York lawyer and art patron who was not in the Clan, and Daniel F. Cohalan, a New York Supreme Court judge, played key roles in arranging tours for these groups and individuals as they made their way across the United States, telling their stories and gathering support.[10] In fact, John Devoy complained that Clan members were spending too much time "raising money for the [Gaelic] League, to the neglect of our own work."[11] The audiences these people performed for tended to be linked to the Clan, as they themselves tended to be linked to the IRB. What historians have made clear is that much of the recruitment for the revolutionary nationalist movement came out of these Irish Ireland organizations, which the Clan na Gael helped to carry on during the years before World War I.

As the Irish Home Rule Bill appeared assured of enactment, Unionists throughout the United Kingdom, and particularly in Ulster, presented a seemingly defiant front. The creation of the Ulster Volunteer Force, under the leadership of Sir Edward Carson, in January 1913, provided a conspicuous precedent for the creation of the Irish Volunteers, in defense of nationalist principles, in November. Eóin MacNéill of University College Dublin, who proposed the force at the public meeting in the Dublin Rotunda, was chosen commander in chief. By May 1914, the Volunteers numbered about one hundred thousand. Although Mac-Néill headed the Irish Volunteers, members of the IRB occupied key places in its organizational structure. The Clan was slow to react to this new situation, but by June the membership demanded some action. The American Provisional Committee, Irish National Volunteers, was formed under the leadership of Clan member Joseph McGarrity of Philadelphia. They established a fund and by the end of the month were able to send MacNéill $5,000 with which to buy weapons—support that was immediately jeopardized by John Redmond's demand that, as the leader of the elected representatives of the Irish people, he should have a position in the Volunteers' governing body. For the physical-force people in the IRB and the Clan, giving the hated Redmond a voice in the Volunteers was painful but politically inescapable. As fate would have it, Sir Roger Casement came to the United States in July 1914 as the representative of the Provisional Committee of the Irish Volunteers, to raise money. Casement, a distinguished retired member of the British Consular Service with a worldwide reputation as a humanitarian, had been part of the group that organized the purchase of 1,500 rifles in Germany and their transportation to Howth Harbor and Kilcoole. He was able to convince John Devoy and other members of the Clan leadership that the IRB had not lost control of the Volunteers, although he warned his friends not to let any of the money get into the hands of Redmond's supporters.[12]

The outbreak of World War I in August 1914 changed the nature of Casement's mission in the United States and the role the Clan leadership could play in Irish affairs. Casement's growing disillusionment with the British government over home rule, together with the strong anti-

British sentiment of Clan leaders, made for a powerful combination. Casement's international prestige and his claim to speak for the Irish Volunteers made him effective in raising funds and generating support. Casement even met Theodore Roosevelt, who thought him "charming." However, the Clan had larger plans for Casement. The Clan and other Irish American groups had worked with German Americans in years past to fight any treaties or measures that seemed to promise closer Anglo-American relations; when World War I started, Irish- and German American cooperation began immediately. Large rallies were held in New York, Philadelphia, Chicago, and St. Louis, with Irish leaders such as John Devoy, Jeremiah A. O'Leary, and Shaemus O'Sheel denouncing Britain's role in the war and attacking John Redmond's efforts to encourage Irishmen to join the British Army. Together with recruiting issues, the fate of the Home Rule Bill—passed, given royal assent, but postponed—was a catastrophe for the parliamentarians in the United States. The United Irish League of America was virtually closed down, and many of its members, disgusted, turned to the Clan. In Ireland, of course, Redmond's speech led to the secession of the original Irish Volunteers from the so-called National Volunteers created in the summer, thus assuring IRB control over the loyal members.[13]

When the war broke out, talks began right away between Devoy, Casement, and various members of the German Embassy, including Captain Franz von Papen, the military attaché. By 24 August 1914, Devoy, Casement, and several others met with the ambassador, Count Johann Heinrich von Bernsdorff, and members of his staff, at the German Club in New York. There, it was asserted that Ireland would, before the end of the war, attempt to overthrow the British regime; Devoy asked that Germany "supply the arms and a sufficient number of capable officers to make a good start."[14] Interestingly, his assertion seems to have been made some time before the IRB's Supreme Council came to a similar decision. The following day, Casement drafted a letter to the kaiser, sympathizing with Germany and wishing her success in the war, while drawing "Your Majesty's attention to the part that Ireland necessarily, if not openly, must play in this conflict and in every conflict where seapower is at stake," implying that Ireland would be involved.[15] The Clan executive signed the letter with Devoy's name first. This became part of a prolonged effort by Casement to get the German government to publicly commit to supporting an independent Ireland, which he did in 1915. Von Bernsdorff, meanwhile, advised his government in Berlin that if the war were expected to be prolonged he would "recommend agreeing to the Irish wishes."[16] Unmistakably, in view of these and subsequent events, the 1916 Rising in Dublin must be seen in the context of, and as part of, World War I.

It has not been possible to trace the origins of Casement's plan to go to Germany and organize an Irish battalion from among Irish prisoners of war. However, by late September 1914, Casement was writing to Joseph McGarrity about the project, and, on 5 October, at a meeting with Devoy, McGarrity, and Judge Cohalan, the decision was made that Casement go to Germany by way of Norway and be given $3,000 for his expenses. Having shaved off his beard to affect a disguise, and traveling with the passport of an American by the name of James E. Landy, Casement boarded the *Oscar II* on 15 October for Norway and Germany. Casement's failed attempts to recruit a battalion, his growing frustration with German authorities, his return to Ireland by submarine in 1916, and his subsequent trial and execution are all well known. From the perspective of the American role in the 1916 Rising, Casement's problems become secondary to those of attempting to coordinate German support with the plans for military action in Ireland. The Clan leadership—specifically, Devoy and Judge Cohalan—became the link between the IRB in Ireland, the German Embassy, and the German government.[17]

☘

Bulmer Hobson wrote in his memoirs that "in the autumn of 1914 . . . the Supreme Council of the IRB decided they would embark on an insurrection against the British Government before the European War came to an end."[18] He said that some members objected, but, being outnumbered, acquiesced. From that point on the matter of the insurrection concerned only a portion of the council. Within the leadership of the Irish Volunteers, a small group of executive members, as well as members of the IRB, began planning for the Volunteers' role in the exercise. The Clan sent money to the IRB: £2,000 in both September and November, and larger amounts later, totaling about $100,000. Devoy and the Clan in New York were informed regularly of events in Ireland through Tommy O'Connor, an IRB messenger who worked on a White Star passenger liner. The Clan also facilitated the movement from Ireland to Germany of couriers such as John Kenney; Michael Francis Doyle, the Philadelphia lawyer; and Joseph Mary Plunkett, an IRB member of the General Council of the Volunteers. Plunkett, who had earlier traveled to Germany to confer with Casement, sailed for New York in May 1915 to inform Devoy of the current plans for a rising and the state of negotiations with Germany.

Even so, it was not until about 5 February 1916 that John Devoy actually learned that the Rising would take place. In his memoirs, Devoy recounts meeting Tommy O'Connor in a New York restaurant and receiving a message from the IRB's Supreme Council in an unfamiliar code. O'Connor had a key to the code and helped Devoy decipher the message. When they got to the second line, which read, "Nobody but the Revolutionary Directory and the chief German representative must know the contents of this," Devoy took the message away from O'Connor, asked for the key himself, and decoded the note in the privacy of his office. The vital part of the message stated that the Rising was to take place on "Easter Sunday, April 23," and that the Germans were requested to "send a shipload of arms to Limerick Quay" between 20 and 23 April.[19] Devoy delivered the message to Captain von Papen the same day, and the Germans made arrangements for a ship—the *Libau*, sailing under the name of the Norwegian vessel *Aud*—to carry a cargo of old Russian rifles and ammunition to Fenit Pier; the Germans confirmed. Philomena Plunkett, the daughter of Count Plunkett and older sister of Joseph Plunkett, who had served as a courier, brought a subsequent message from Ireland on 14 April, changing the arrival date of the rifle-loaded ship to 22 April, the day before Easter, that was also delivered to von Papen in his office on Wall Street and sent to Germany. However, by that time, the *Aud* had already sailed and, without a radio, was beyond reach. The ship arrived off Tralee on Thursday, 20 April, and waited for a contact on shore until it was hailed by a ship of the Royal Navy and ordered to Cobh (Queenstown), where it was scuttled, thus depriving the Rising of a substantial supply of weapons. Casement and two others were landed by submarine on Banna Strand on Good

Friday, and Casement and one other were quickly arrested. Knowledge of these events prompted Eoin MacNéill to cancel the operations of the Volunteers planned for Easter Sunday, thus upsetting the intended military timetable.

On 18 April, US Secret Service agents raided the offices of the German military attaché in New York, in connection with acts of sabotage in the munitions industry, confiscating copies of the correspondence of Devoy, Cohalan, and the Germans concerning the Rising. Devoy was convinced that the Wilson administration turned copies of these documents over to British intelligence, but this was not correct. In the weeks after the Rising, the British requested from the State Department any relevant communications. The secretary of state refused the request. Actually, British intelligence was able to intercept German transatlantic cable traffic and decrypt the German codes, giving them much of the same information held by the US government.

Quite apart from these highly secret activities, the Clan also planned for the creation of a new public organization that could provide broad popular support for the Rising when it occurred. Invitations, signed by 350 prominent Irish American leaders, were sent out across the country in February for the first Irish Race Convention, to be held in New York on 4 and 5 March 1916—the largest meeting of the Irish American community in the United States at that time. Over two thousand people attended, their most important task being the founding of the Friends of Irish Freedom (FOIF). The key organizer and speaker was judge Daniel F. Cohalan, the successful New York lawyer and Supreme Court Justice, who wielded great influence in Democratic Party affairs.[20] Victor Herbert, the composer and grandson of painter and novelist Samuel Lover, was elected president, Thomas Hughes Kelly treasurer, and John D. Moore secretary. Clan na Gael members were well placed on the executive committee to shape the policies of the organization. The new society attracted people from all factions and groups (associate membership was created for already existing organizations), including many who had formerly supported the Irish Parliamentary Party and the United Irish League of America. No mention was made of the coming rebellion in Ireland—it was known to only three or four people—but, in retrospect, the large public organization was put together to provide support for Ireland when and after the Rising took place. The FOIF would become a major Irish American nationalist organization, continuing into the 1930s, and it did in fact rally Irish Americans in the aftermath of the Rising and particularly in 1919, after World War I.[21]

The 1916 Rising itself took place on Easter Monday. The small circle of IRB men within the leadership of both the IRB and the Volunteers planned it in such secrecy that key people such as Denis McCullough, the president of the IRB's Supreme Council, and Eoin MacNéill, the commander in chief of the Irish Volunteers, did not know what was coming until the middle of the week before the Rising itself. That, together with the capture of the *Aud* and the anticipated weapons from Germany, led to MacNéill's cancelation of the exercises on Easter Sunday, as planned. The result was that only a fraction of the Volunteers, together with the Irish Citizen Army, came out on Monday, 24 April, on the orders of the IRB's Military Council. Nevertheless, a message was cabled to John Devoy in New York—"Tom successfully operated today"—to signal that the Rising had begun.[22]

The 1916 Rising was an incredible organizational accomplishment for the IRB, the Irish Volunteers, and the Irish Citizen Army, despite all of its failures and missteps, and it would not have been possible without the support from the Irish community in the United States. The Clan na Gael had helped to reinvigorate and keep alive the IRB in the years prior to the outbreak of World War I in 1914. Encouraged particularly by John Devoy and Joseph McGarrity, a young generation rallied around Tom Clarke after his return to Dublin in 1907 (Diarmuid Lynch, Patrick McCartan, Bulmer Hobson, Denis McCullough, Seán Mac Diarmada), all with at least some American experience. The IRB and the Clan were ready when events unfolded in 1913 and 1914 to form a paramilitary organization in Ireland—the Irish Volunteers—in response to the creation of the Ulster Volunteers. Once again, the Irish American community sent money (at least $100,000) and support. Devoy and Cohalan remained the link between Germany and Ireland after Casement had sailed. As the IRB's plans for a rising matured, new people were drawn into the tight planning circle: Patrick Pearse, Joseph Mary Plunkett, and, finally, James Connolly. When the Rising took place and the Proclamation was signed and read, five of the seven signatories had lived in or toured the United States. Thomas Clarke and James Connolly had resided in America for several years, Seán Mac Diarmada and Joseph Mary Plunkett had traveled to the United States on IRB business, and Patrick Pearse had toured the United States to raise money for his school and became increasingly involved in nationalist political activities. Only Thomas MacDonagh, poet and teacher at Pearse's school, and Éamonn Ceannt had not been to the United States. Among the leaders of the Rising, the American influence of Ireland's "exiled children" was enormous.

Militarily unsuccessful and crushed by British forces by the end of the week, the Rising was generally condemned in both Ireland and the United States in its immediate aftermath. Nevertheless, the executions of the signatories of the proclamation, and several others—sixteen in all—carried out two or three a day for several days, together with the arrest and internment of several thousand nationalists across the country, led to a dramatic shift in public opinion both at home and abroad. It was, in the words of Maurice Walsh, the beginning of "the unravelling of empires provoked by the First World War."[23] Across America, protest meetings were held, many of them organized by the FOIF, with speakers from both the Irish American and the general community, and editorials increasingly critical of British actions were published. Shane Leslie, a home ruler then in the United States, observed shrewdly that the Irish "remembered Robert Emmet and knew where they stood."[24] Unhesitatingly, the "exiled children in America" once again gave their support.

2

America, the War Crisis, and the Irish Problem, 1916–1918

The Easter Rising came as a complete surprise in the United States to all but John Devoy and a select circle of the Clan na Gael. The shock kept the Rising an issue for the American public throughout the remainder of 1916, even though this was an election year in the United States, and the international situation was becoming increasingly grim. By early 1917, however, relations between the United States and Germany had deteriorated over issues like the sinking of the *Lusitania*, submarine warfare, and the Zimmerman telegraph. Nevertheless, once the United States went to war with Germany in April 1917, the unresolved matter of the Irish government became an obstacle in the process of forging a close working relationship between the United States and Britain. The voice of Irish America needed to be heard once again. However, as John Quinn assured Maud Gonne, "you need have no worry about American opinion, because it is now irrevocably on the side of Ireland."[1]

Mainstream American newspapers condemned the Rising as foolish and, indeed, blamed the Germans. The arrest of Sir Roger Casement drew attention in connection with the Rising in Dublin. On 26 April the *Christian Science Monitor*'s headlines ran: "Sir R. Casement Taken Prisoner by British. Riots in St. Stephen's Green—Sinn Fein Movement Believed to Be Implicated in Conspiracy," and the *New York World* announced: "Uprising in Dublin Quelled.[2] The *New York Times* declared that it was all over: "Troops Crush Revolt in Dublin, Take Post Office Seized by Rioters; Many Killed in Street Fighting." The historian Robert Schmuhl points out that in the Saturday, 29 April issue of the *New York Times* the paper carried eighteen separate articles focused on the Rising.[3] The *New York World* commented on Casement and his links to historical figures such as Wolfe Tone and contemporary actors like Sir Edward Carson. Many US papers saw the Rising as a betrayal of John Redmond and home rule. In fact, in the immediate aftermath of the Rising, meetings were held in New York, Boston, and Chicago, endorsing Redmond.⁴

As the news began to spread across America that British forces were executing the leaders of the Rising, public opinion began to change dramatically. The *Washington Post* questioned the British procedures, observing critically that the Irish leaders "had been tried by a drumhead court-martial, found guilty and sentenced in a trice and shot at sunrise"—that is, neither the rules of war nor civil procedures had been followed. "Are the 'rivers of blood' at last dammed?" asked the *New York World*.⁵ Many also noted, by contrast, Britain's statesman-like handling of the South African rebels a generation earlier. Prominent non-Irish figures in the United States were drawn into this controversy—Charles McCarthy, the Wisconsin progressive; A. Lawrence Lowell, president of Harvard University; Nicholas Murray Butler, president of Columbia University; Willard Straight, publisher of the *New Republic*; and former president Theodore Roosevelt made both public and private statements criticizing the executions. William Dean Howells, then an imposing American literary figure, commented in the *Nation* that "the shooting of the Irish insurrectionists is too much like the shooting of prisoners of war." Britain's moral position in the war was, Howells feared, diminished by this act of "Schrecklichkeit" (frightfulness). Liberal journals such as the *Nation* reasoned that the executions were a "mistake" and certain to turn the leaders of the Rising into "martyrs" in the traditions of Tone and Emmet. The *Nation* also pointed out that several of the leaders of the Ulster revolt of 1914 were now members of the British government.⁶ A large protest meeting was held in New York at Carnegie Hall on Sunday, 14 May. At least five thousand people filled the building, and several thousand stood outside on Seventh Avenue to hear speakers such as New York congressman William Bourke Cockran and Father Francis P. Duffy, later famous as the chaplain of the Sixty-Ninth New York Regiment, speak of their shock at the execution of the Irish prisoners who had surrendered. Bainbridge Colby, a distinguished lawyer and John Quinn's former partner who eventually became Woodrow Wilson's secretary of state in 1920, argued that Britain's behavior in Ireland was as bad as Germany's in Belgium, and that Britain's current actions had discredited her claim to be a defender of small nations.

Quinn, who also spoke at the meeting, wrote privately that the executions were "the greatest diplomatic blunder that England has committed since the war," and he also thought they were a more serious misstep "than the Germans made when they sank the Lusitania" because "it has made it impossible for England to pose as the champion of small nations"—one of Britain's leading propaganda arguments in the war.[7] Similar meetings were held in Lowell and Westfield, Massachusetts; New Haven, Connecticut; Providence, Rhode Island; Rochester and Hoboken, New York; Chicago, Illinois; and again in New York City.

All of these newspaper accounts and protest meetings were essentially reactions to the events in Ireland. Gradually action began to be taken in the United States, the first being to look after the welfare of Americans who had been caught up in the Rising and sent to hastily constructed prison camps in Frongoch, Wales. Appeals were made to President Wilson and the State Department in regard to the arrests of John J. Kilgallon (a young man from Far Rockaway, New York, who was a student at Pearse's school, St. Enda's) and Jeremiah (Diarmuid) Lynch (who had become a US citizen while living in New York between 1886 and 1907) for participating in the Rising.[8] The US consul in Dublin, Edward L. Adams, asked British authorities about Kilgallon and Lynch and also Edward (Eamon) de Valera, whose wife in Dublin had made representations to the consul because her husband was born in New York. Adams reported that all three had been arrested and sent to prison in Wales, but not executed. Historians have disagreed as to whether the intervention by the US consul was influential, or if these men simply benefited from their names being low on the list of prisoners.[9] When appealed to directly, President Wilson responded with carefully worded statements. "My natural sympathies are with men struggling for freedom, and concerning whose sincerity as patriots, seeking solely the welfare of their country, cannot be questioned," he assured the Knights of St. Patrick in San Francisco. "I have done everything, so far as representations go, to provide for their humane and just treatment."[10] The interests of Americans in Ireland had indeed been looked after, but Wilson's statement implied more than what diplomatic custom permitted.

The Rising and its consequences became an issue in Congress by early May. On 5 May, senator William E. Borah of Idaho read into the *Congressional Record* an editorial from the *New York Sun* supporting Redmond and home rule, and just over a week later he criticized the court-martials as "midnight judgments." Congressman Leonidas C. Dyer introduced a resolution on 12 May, calling on the British to recognize the rebels as "prisoners of war" rather than "criminals." Similar resolutions were introduced by congressmen Thomas Gallivan of Chicago and Murray Hulbert of New York.[11] Congressman Jeff McLemore of Texas spoke strongly on 16 May about the Rising, criticizing Ireland's British administration and praising the rebels and their alliance with Germany. McLemore had earlier introduced a controversial anti-Ally resolution that would have forbade Americans from sailing on belligerent vessels.[12] Several days later, on 17 May, senator John W. Kern from Indiana introduced a resolution calling on the secretary of state to investigate Americans arrested in the events surrounding the Rising and to look after the welfare of Americans in Ireland, which sparked a correspondence between the White House and the State Department, although the conclusion was that the US consuls in Ireland were already carrying out these duties. The resolution was adopted without opposition on 2 June.[13]

A larger and more controversial matter was the fate of Sir Roger Casement. His earlier humanitarian efforts in Africa and South America gave him a status in the United States that none of the other participants in the Rising could claim, and the fact that he would be tried for treason in a London court invited commentary and intervention. The Philadelphia labor lawyer and Democratic Party politician Michael Francis Doyle, acting on behalf of Agnes Newman, Casement's sister, who lived in the United States, sought the assistance of the State Department in joining the barristers defending Casement. Inasmuch as Casement was a British subject, Wilson was aware that he himself could not intervene, although he did arrange for the State Department to give some assistance to Doyle. The State Department told Doyle that it could not contact the Foreign Office directly, but assured him that the US ambassador in London, Walter Hines Page, "undoubtedly will notify the authorities of your relation to the case."[14] On the strength of this endorsement, foreign secretary Sir Edward Grey, asked home secretary Sir Herbert Samuel, to allow Doyle to join Sergeant A. M. Sullivan and George Gavan Duffy in defending Casement.[15] In the end Casement was convicted and sentenced to hang, raising the question of whether clemency would be extended. In Britain, at least, the surreptitious release of Casement's diary, revealing his homosexual preferences, undercut any movement to save his life, but the diary was not widely circulated in the United States.[16] Even before Casement's sentencing, On 20 June, senator James E. Martine of New Jersey introduced a resolution asking for a "stay of execution" for Casement until new evidence could be brought forth, and the measure was sent to the Foreign Relations Committee, over the objections of Senator Martine, who predicted that it would "sleep the sleep of the righteous" in committee and never be reported for a vote.[17] Clearly, the chairman of the committee, William J. Stone, was not satisfied with the resolution, and no action was taken. Indeed, several senators criticized the language of the resolution as diplomatically inappropriate. The matter came to the floor of the Senate on 25 and 29 July, when senator Key Pittman of Nevada introduced a new resolution asking "that the Senate [express] the hope that the British Government may exercise clemency in the treatment of Irish political prisoners, and that the President be requested to transmit this resolution to the Government."[18] After some debate, the Pittman resolution was passed on Saturday morning, 29 July, by a vote of forty-nine to nineteen, with thirty abstentions. The resolution was sent to the White House, referred to the State Department by 11:00 a.m. on 2 August, and cabled to the US embassy in London by 1:00 that afternoon. Although Ambassador Page was actually at sea, the resolution was delivered by chargé d'affaires Irwin B. Laughton on Thursday morning, 3 August, the very day of Casement's execution. The foreign secretary indicated that he and members of the British government were already fully aware of the passage of the resolution from both newspaper accounts and the British ambassador's reports, and Grey promised to show the resolution to the prime minister.[19] Casement was hanged that morning nonetheless. Grey later wrote to Edward M. House, President Wilson's special emissary, that "we are not favourably impressed by the action of the Senate in having passed a resolution about the Irish prisoners though having taken no notice of outrages in Belgium and massacres of Armenians," ignoring the reality of a population of twenty million people of Irish extraction in the United States.[20] While ineffective in the end, the resolution indicated that the Senate regarded the British executions of the Irish prisoners, including Casement, as excessive and a mistake— a strong indication that Irish matters were a public issue in the United States.

As America reacted to the 1916 Rising and the executions that followed, the toll of the Great War weighed heavily on the Irish and British alike. The Tenth (Irish) Division, including the famous D Company of the Seventh Royal Dublin Fusiliers (the "Pals" regiment), had suffered heavy casualties the year before at Suvla Bay on the Gallipoli peninsula in Turkey. A British force of about 9,000 at Kut Al Amara in Mesopotamia surrendered to the Turks on 29 April, as the Rising itself was coming to a conclusion. An even greater blow would fall on 1 July, roughly two months after the Rising and two days after Casement's sentencing, at the beginning of the Battle of the Somme. It was the worst day in the history of the British army, with over 19,000 killed and over 57,000 injured. The Thirty-Sixth (Ulster) Division—made up substantially from the prewar Ulster Volunteer Force—took the brunt of the opening of the Somme offensive in France, suffering 5,500 casualties in the first two days. As Thomas Bartlett has argued, the Battle of the Somme was as much a "blood sacrifice" for the Unionists as the Rising was for nationalists.[21]

Extensive private efforts to save Casement were also attempted. As early as 4 May, in conversation with British ambassador Sir Cecil Spring Rice, Baltimore archbishop James Cardinal Gibbons very delicately advised that the British not execute Casement. To do so, he cautioned, would simply be "manufacturing martyrs" for the extreme elements in the United States.[22] Later in July, New York lawyer John Quinn drafted a twenty-four-page letter urging clemency and arranged for some twenty-five prominent "pro-Ally" people to sign it, including ten lawyers, four editors, a former cabinet member, a New York State judge, a Columbia University professor, and several businessmen, among them Irish American figures James Byrne, William D. Guthrie, John D. Crimmins, Victor J. Dowling, and Lawrence Godkin, as well as American establishment figures Frank Crowninshield, former attorney general George D. Wickersham, Arthur B. Davies, Allen Dawson, Professor Frank H. Giddings, Frederick J. Gregg, Fairfax Landstreet, Howard

Mansfield, Colonel Robert Grier Monroe, and George F. Parker, among others. Spring Rice cabled this letter to Sir Edward Grey, explaining who the signatories were and their importance as spokespersons.[23] The president of the Negro Fellowship League of Chicago appealed to the British government that Casement's life be spared out of consideration for his earlier service to Africans in the Congo. Henry Cabot Lodge—who of course knew everybody—wrote directly to Grey, explaining that it would be a mistake to execute Casement and that Britain's friends hoped he would be spared, while Britain's enemies wanted an execution. American newspapers, although critical of the Rising, regarded the earlier execution of the prisoners as well Casement as a mistake.[24] The *New York Times*, which had been very scornful of the Rising, featured a four-page lead article on Casement by John Quinn in its Sunday Magazine on 13 August. Quinn stated very clearly that he had worked with Irish cultural and literary nationalists for years, but in the war he supported the Allies and regarded Germany as a threat to Western culture. In this he differed with Casement, although he knew and respected him as a man of honor and courage. In 1913 and 1914 the British government had acquiesced in Ulster's defiance of the law, threat of rebellion, and flirtation with Germany, and the government had thereby set in motion the sequence of events that led to the creation of the Irish Volunteers, the suspension of the Home Rule Bill, and the 1916 Rising. Quinn emphasized that "fair-minded Americans felt that Ireland's honorably-won struggle [for home rule] had been defeated by the Ulster treason," and he pointed out the irony of the current situation: Casement's loyalty to Ireland resulted in Britain convicting and executing him for treason, while Sir Edward Carson's and F. E. Smith's apparent loyalty to Ulster, which brought the country to the brink of civil war in 1914, resulted in British politics promoting them to positions in the government. Quinn held Germany equally responsible for Casement's tragic fate: "If England was pitiless," he concluded, "Germany's act was infamous."[25] Quinn had made a powerful statement outlining the Irish situation that was read by a large, broad audience. Ambassador Spring Rice reported to the Foreign Office that "our cause for the present among the Irish here is a lost one."[26]

The efforts of both the American government and private individuals to appeal for clemency and moderation for the treatment of those captured after the Rising was only partially successful. One positive accomplishment was the raising of money to assist in rebuilding portions of Dublin and to provide support to families who had lost loved ones, either to death or prison. The celebrated Irish tenor John McCormack organized a benefit concert; he sought the practical support of New York mayor John Purroy Mitchel (the grandson of the Young Ireland rebel John Mitchel), and banker and art patron Otto Kahn, who made the Century Theater available for the evening of 23 May. Between eight and nine thousand dollars were raised, and the event was attended by such notables as President Wilson's daughter Margaret and Wilson's advisor Colonel Edward M. House.[27] Cardinal John Farley of New York served as patron of a major concert at Carnegie Hall on 27 May featuring Victor Herbert and commemorating those executed after the Rising. An Irish Relief Fund Committee was created with cardinals James Gibbons, John Farley, and William O'Connell and archbishop William Walsh of Dublin as honorary officers, and Thomas Addis Emmet as president; George G. Gillespie, chairman; Thomas Hughes Kelly, treasurer; and John D. Moore, secretary. By midsummer they had raised over $100,000.[28] In July the committee sent John A. Murphy, a Buffalo lawyer and Clan member, and John Gill, a New York labor leader, to Ireland to administer the relief funds. This delegation coordinated efforts in Dublin with the Irish National Aid Association and the Irish Volunteer Dependents' Fund, and later in July, the relief committee sent a second installment with its treasurer, New York banker Thomas Hughes Kelly, and Massachusetts journalist Joseph Smith, who were detained in Liverpool and prevented from sailing to Dublin. Efforts by the State Department were unsuccessful; Scotland Yard regarded Gill as "merely a Sinn Fein in disguise" and Smith as "an agent of the German Government." Cardinal Farley wrote to Wilson, thanking him for the government's efforts. Historian Bernadette Whelan concludes that, in the Irish relief effort and several other matters, "the Wilson government had intervened positively in Irish affairs."[29]

Fundraising for Irish relief continued throughout 1916. Kate Feighery has outlined how Catholic churches in New York collected substantial sums of money each Sunday. A high point was reached with the Irish Relief Fund Bazaar in Madison Square Garden from 14 to 22 October 1916. The bazaar attracted a great deal of attention with its striking poster depicting the wounded James Connolly being shot by a British firing squad, which was displayed prominently in subway stations across New York, among other places.[30] An elaborate affair, the bazaar featured Gaelic pipers, singers, choral groups, circus acts, and comedians. Seán Mac Diarmada's sister had a booth at the bazaar. Speakers included Nora Connolly, James Connolly's daughter, and the poets Joyce Kilmer and Peter Golden. The German American community strongly supported the event, which did play into the growing international tensions of the time. In that regard, the exhibit at the bazaar of the first working submarine, called the Fenian Ram, developed by the Irish American John P. Holland, seemed to reinforce solidarity with the current German submarine campaign. Significantly, the bazaar raised $45,000 for Irish relief.[31]

As the 1916 U.S. election campaign season began to unfold, the question arose as to whether Wilson could retain the loyalty of the Irish American community, a crucial element of the Democratic Party coalition in 1912. Had Wilson been sympathetic and supportive of Irish aspirations, or callously indifferent to Irish suffering? Wilson was always controversial, not least among many Irish Americans. Historian Robert Schmuhl points out that Wilson, with two grandparents born in Ulster, had very good Irish antecedents, to which he referred from time to time.[32] However, Wilson was never a participant in an Irish American organization, and as president was very careful not to complicate relations with Britain by making strong statements about Ireland. He made occasional comments to his private secretary, Joseph Tumulty, favoring home rule for Ireland or criticizing the obstructionist tactics of the Unionists, but he generally refrained from stating such views publicly. Would his relatively bland remarks satisfy his Irish American constituency?

Members of the Clan na Gael and, increasingly, of the FOIF, as well as various German American groups, had worked to forge an alliance between Ireland and Germany in 1916. James K. McGuire's books *The King, the Kaiser, and Irish Freedom* (1915) and *What Germany Could Do for Ireland* (1916) were typical in their extravagant confidence that Germany could secure Ireland's future.³³ While each party wanted the "ethnic vote," most of the candidates running for national office deplored the so-called "hyphenate" influence as sacrificing American interests in favor of the aspirations of the hyphenate's former homeland. For Wilson the hyphenate issue came as a direct challenge when Jeremiah A. O'Leary, a New York Irish American, president of the American Truth Society and editor of the anti-British paper *Bull*, published a biting letter to the president in the *New York Times* on 30 September 1916, stating, "Your foreign policies, your failure to secure compliance with all American rights, your leniency with the British Empire, your approval of war loans, and the ammunitions traffic, are issues in this campaign." O'Leary challenged Wilson on the direction of the campaign: "Anglomaniacs and British interests may control newspapers, but they don't control votes. . . . When, sir," he went on, "will you respond to these evidences of popular disapproval of your policies by action?"³⁴ Wilson hit back at O'Leary, the militant Irish Americans, and other pro-German ethnic groups, with a public rebuke: "I would feel deeply mortified to have you or anyone like you vote for me. Since you have access to many disloyal Americans and I have not, I will ask you to convey this message to them."³⁵ Commentators and historians have seen Wilson's public denunciation of O'Leary as a major event in the campaign. Wilson had repudiated the physical-force Irish Americans like O'Leary, Devoy, and Cohalan and was reelected in 1916. He had probably retained the support of most of the Irish American community, but he was also reminded that the Irish question had not gone away.

This alleged disloyalty of Irish- and German Americans and other immigrant groups, encompassed in the term "hyphenate," was widespread. Unlike Wilson, former president Theodore Roosevelt felt free to deal with the hyphenates and the importance of the Irish question directly; he had a long history of interest in Irish affairs and as early as 1905 had strongly supported university chairs of Irish studies, the Irish cultural revival, and the idea of Irish home rule. However, he resented the intrusion of Irish affairs in American politics and foreign relations, such as the Irish-German cooperation in 1916. Although acknowledging his own German and English family origins, Roosevelt wrote in journal articles in 1916 that "I do not believe in hyphenated Americans. I do not believe in German-Americans or Irish-Americans; and I believe just as little in English-Americans." He reasoned that "we Americans are a separate people," and argued in another article that the hyphenate was "an enemy to this country."³⁶ Roosevelt was even more direct in 1917, arguing that a "blind hatred of England" made some Irish Americans "disloyal to America." In an article titled "The Hun Within Our Gates," he claimed that German Americans had helped to finance extreme Irish American nationalists, contrary to American interests. Even the title of his collected articles is revealing: *The Foes of Our Own Household*.³⁷

The dramatic return to Germany's policy of unrestricted submarine warfare in January 1917 led to the declaration of war by the United States on 6 April. Wilson hoped to avoid war, but his confidential foreign affairs advisor, Colonel Edward M. House, took tentative steps to align the United States with the Allies—specifically, Britain. In early March, House and the British intelligence officer in New York, Sir William Wiseman, drafted a paper for the meeting of the Imperial War Conference to be held later in London. The memorandum covered a number of issues that troubled Anglo-American relations, Irish affairs being one of them: "The Irish question is one of the greatest obstacles to a good understanding," it asserted. Reasonable Irish Americans would support the implementation of Irish self-government by the end of the war, but "would not expect the British to listen to Irishmen of the type of Devoy and O'Leary," Wilson's antagonists. Sympathy for Irish self-government, the memo went on to say, derived "its greatest strength by the fact that reasonable honest citizens of the type of John Quinn feel so strongly about it." House noted that Wilson had read the memo and considered it "a fair statement."³⁸ It was a signal to the British from Wilson and House that meaningful American support for Britain during the war would be difficult with a resentful Irish American community. Would Wilson do anything regarding Ireland? Historian Stephen Hartley asserts that America going to war allowed Wilson to raise the issue of Ireland with the British.³⁹

In this context, it is significant that on 10 April, just five days after the declaration of war, Wilson asked secretary of state Robert Lansing to instruct the US ambassador in London, Walter Hines Page, to raise the Irish matter privately with the prime minister. Page should explain to him that "the only circumstance which seems now to stand in the way of an absolutely cordial cooperation with Great Britain by practically all Americans who are not influenced by ties of blood directly associating them with Germany is the failure so far to find a satisfactory method of self-government for Ireland." This was a remarkably forceful warning to the British that full American participation in the war effort would be in part dependent on a solution to the ongoing domestic Irish problem. Wilson also suggested that this sentiment in the United States extended well beyond what might be regarded as Irish American constituencies, as could be seen in the debates in Congress over the war resolution. Implementation of Irish self-government "would absolutely divorce our citizens of Irish birth and sympathy from the German sympathizers here with whom many of them have been inclined to make common cause."[40] In his instructions to Lansing, Wilson made the additional comment that "if a way could be found now to grant Ireland what she has so often been promised, it would be felt that the real programme of government by the consent of the governed had been adopted everywhere in the anti-Prussian world."[41] This was a remarkably strong moral judgment about Britain's handling of the Irish problem. And, of course, it was all the more revealing of Wilson's attitude in the context of Britain's claim to be fighting in the war in defense of small nations. Would the unresolved Irish question cloud the war effort in the United States?

Page was able to report back directly to the president a week later that he had talked with David Lloyd George, who told him that he was "glad that the President had instructed me to bring the subject up." The prime minister, who led a coalition government formed in December 1916 that was dominated by Conservatives, told Page he had been worrying about American opinion and the Irish home rule problem but was "doing his best." He urged Wilson to talk with Arthur J. Balfour, the foreign secretary, who was leading a British mission to the United States—the first sitting cabinet member to visit America. Balfour was a former prime minister and former Irish chief secretary, and a major figure in the Conservative Party that had fought home rule before the war, but Irish nationalists remembered him as "Bloody Balfour."[42] If he could be persuaded to support some form of Irish self-government it would be of great help: "The Prime Minister feels sure of a good result of a frank explanation to him by the President," the Ambassador assured Wilson.[43] In another conversation, Page noted Lloyd George's despair of making progress with the Unionists. Pointing to Sir Edward Carson, the center of Ulster resistance to home rule before the war and then first lord of the admiralty, the prime minister said, "Madmen, madmen—I never saw such a task." When Carson approached, Lloyd George said, "I've been telling the Ambassador, Carson, that we've got to settle the Irish question now—in spite of you."[44] Carson skillfully changed the subject to naval matters. Lloyd George mentioned Balfour again to Page, and indeed the cabinet instructions to Balfour leading the mission to the United States were to "make special inquiry" and report to the war cabinet about "the importance of the Irish question in connection with our relations with the United States."[45] In fact, both the British Embassy and the government were anxious that Wilson would make a public statement about Ireland in the context of the American entry into the war. Wilson assured Tumulty that on the matter of Irish home rule he was "doing a number of things about this which I hope may bear fruit."[46]

Balfour did lead the British mission to the United States in late April and May, the intended purpose of which was to negotiate direct American support for the war effort and preferably the engagement of American troops in Europe, but of course the Irish question was unavoidable. He arrived in Washington on 22 April and the next day was introduced to Wilson by Secretary Lansing for the first of at least four meetings with the president. This formal greeting was followed on 30 April by a private dinner at the White House, after which Balfour talked with Wilson and Colonel House about the war for over two hours. On 1 May, Balfour reported to the Foreign Office that "neither the President nor any Member of the Government has said a word to me about Ireland."[47] However, on 5 May Robert Lansing drove to Gunston Hall, south of Washington, DC, where Arthur Balfour and Sir Eric Drummond joined him, to talk out of the range of reporters. Among other issues, Lansing, prepped by Tumulty, talked frankly about the American government's problem with the Irish question. Noting that the sympathies of the American people ran more in favor of France than Britain, Lansing told Balfour that "the failure of his government to respond to the intense longing of the Irish for the freedom of Ireland from British rule by conceding to them a measure of independence made thousands of Irish-Americans bitter enemies of Great Britain." These sentiments created serious problems, "with which our government found it difficult to cope." Lansing specifically urged the British government to "do something to remove this hostility of persons of Irish blood and of their American sympathizers." While the setting may have been informal, these remarks by the secretary of state were an unmistakably frank charge to the British foreign secretary. Balfour assured Lansing he would "lay the matter before his government when he returned to England."[48] After he returned to Britain, Balfour did report to the cabinet on 23 June about his mission to the United States, but downplayed the seriousness of his meetings with Wilson and Lansing. "The President never referred to it [the Irish question] at all; the Secretary of State never referred to it officially," he said, minimizing, if not dismissing, Lansing's specific remarks. He did go on to say that Americans were "deeply concerned that no solution has yet been found for this ancient problem," and that it remained "the one obstacle which stands in the way of close friendship between their country and ours"—in short, closer Anglo-American relations in the war.[49] However, this report contained no sense of urgency, and no mention that the secretary of state had actually urged a settlement of the Irish problem. Perhaps this was asking too much of this old conservative. In his memoirs, Lansing would muse on the ironic coincidence of discussing how to protect all rights and interests in an Irish settlement at the eighteenth-century home of George Mason, the principal author of the American Bill of Rights.

Even before the Lansing meeting, Sir Horace Plunkett and Shane Leslie had met with the British embassy and Balfour's staff and made arrangements for a deputation of Irish Americans to meet with Balfour in order to impress upon him the need for a settlement. John Quinn, who had emerged as the most respectable and well-placed Irish American spokesman of the moment, put together a distinguished group to meet the leader of the British mission in Washington on 4 May. As Quinn told Theodore Roosevelt, the British need for close American participation in the war effort created "a great chance for England to make a generous [Irish] settlement."[50] The deputation included Morgan J. O'Brien, the former presiding judge of the Appellate Division of the New York Supreme Court and vice president of the recent New York constitutional convention; Colonel Robert Temple Emmet, a descendant of Robert Emmet's brother and a West Point graduate, a regular army officer and Medal of Honor winner; Lawrence Godkin, a leading New York lawyer and son of the publisher of the *New York Evening Post*; and John F. Fitzgerald, the former mayor of Boston and a former congressman (also grandfather of future president John F. Kennedy). A mix of Catholics and Protestants, they all enjoyed some standing among home rule nationalists, and they took the view that Ireland had fairly earned home rule by parliamentary procedures; that "Ireland had won her innings," and that it should be implemented; that Ulster Unionist obstruction had been outrageous, and that Unionists should be given various guarantees, but that the exclusion of several Ulster counties was unacceptable and a "betrayal." Unionist acceptance of a home rule government, they argued, was a sacrifice that had to be made as a war measure. Quinn made the point that "the Irish question had now in a sense become an American question," and that the failure of an Irish settlement was "the one outstanding obstacle to complete and cordial relations between the people of this country . . . and Great Britain." These cordial relations were crucial, he noted, in the context of latent pro-German sympathies among the "radical Irishmen here." Balfour responded that over the past fifty years British governments had introduced progressive reforms in Ireland, thereby removing many of the complaints about British rule. He was "not much impressed," he said, by the argument that Ulster would suffer economically or that there would be religious persecution under a home rule government, but that the desire of Ulster Unionists to remain as they were was hard for Britons to ignore. The meeting went on for about two hours and was conducted in a friendly manner, Quinn noted with some satisfaction, and Balfour assured the group that he would convey their views to his government.[51] He wrote to Lloyd George the following day that the deputation spoke "with great moderation" but urged "very strongly how desirable it was in the present crisis to promote unity in the United States by a settlement of the Irish question." They supported implementing home rule, but felt that the partition of Ireland would not be an acceptable solution. Almost as an addendum, Balfour noted that

Shane Leslie had confided to him that Irish American opinion would accept the exclusion of parts of Ulster as a last resort.[52] This "Most Secret" comment, more "congenial to his own views," as Catherine Shannon has observed, worked to minimize what the deputation had actually told him (see appendix 1).[53]

Balfour also met with many other American leaders and was warmly received, despite the anxiety of the British Embassy. With the approval of a delegation of Irish American politicians, he was invited to address both the House and Senate, the first foreigner to do so since the Irish home rule leader Charles Stewart Parnell in 1880. In a special gesture, President Wilson attended and joined the reception line. Later, congressman Medill McCormick, brother of the publisher of the *Chicago Tribune*, gave Balfour a dinner, which included among the guests a number of Irish American politicians. In his late June report, Balfour made an ominously accurate assessment: "If no settlement arises out of the present proposals I fear the extremists, who are now silently watching the course of events, will again regain the upper hand and do their utmost to cause dissention and mistrust between the United States and Great Britain."[54] However, as with his meeting with Lansing, he did not convey the urgency of the concerns of either the American government or of leading Irish American spokesmen.

During the period of Balfour's visit, the matter of Ireland's form of government was a matter of constant public discussion. Congress introduced numerous resolutions asking the British government to take steps to provide some form of self-government, and various petitions and memorials were printed in the *Congressional Record*. Congressman James A. Gallivan of Massachusetts prepared a telegram to the British prime minister urging that home rule be put into operation as soon as possible; that cable was signed by 140 other congressmen and sent on 22 April.[55] On 22 April, twenty-seven prominent Irish Americans had cabled John Redmond that the partition of Ireland "would be deeply deplored by American citizens of Irish birth or descendants of Irishmen."[56] Major American newspapers such as the *New York Times*, the *New York World*, the *Washington Post*, the *Literary Digest*, and the *Christian Science Monitor* ran extended articles about the Irish question and the amount of its support in the United States. Lord Northcliffe, the press baron who owned the *Times* of London, working through his representative in the United States together with John Quinn, arranged for a series of letters by prominent Americans to be published in the newspaper expressing opinions on the Irish question.

The first series appeared in the *Times* on 26 April, led by former president Theodore Roosevelt, who said bluntly, "I most earnestly hope that full Home Rule will be given to Ireland," although Ireland must remain in the British empire through a federal structure such as that of the United States; resolution of the Irish problem in such a fashion would be of "immense advantage" to the empire in the war and after. Quinn wrote to Roosevelt thanking him for his letter, saying, "It was the right statement at the right time," and noting, "All Irishmen owe you a great debt of gratitude."[57] Cardinal Gibbons, speaking as a Catholic leader in a largely Protestant country, was confident that the freedom of all denominations in Ireland could be protected by constitutional guarantees. Former president William Howard Taft, president emeritus of Harvard University Charles W. Eliot, president of Columbia University Nicholas Murray Butler, New York mayor John Purroy Mitchel, former Democratic Party candidate for president Alton B. Parker, former chief justice of the New York Supreme Court Appellate Division Edgar M. Cullen, and former US attorney general George W. Wickersham all expressed similar views: that an Irish government within the British empire could work, that minority interest could be protected, and that both the empire and the war effort would be strengthened.[58]

The following day, 27 April, the *Times* published letters from another distinguished group of Irish Americans—Robert E. Dowling, Victor J. Dowling, John F. Fitzgerald, Robert Temple Emmet, Maurice Leon, Charles Stewart Davison, and archbishop John Ireland—reinforcing the importance to both America and Britain of a just settlement of the Irish home rule question.[59] Michael J. Jordan wrote to Redmond on 7 May, reporting the successful executive committee meeting of the United Irish League of America, which had been quiescent since the beginning of the war. Jordan related with some enthusiasm that he "learned also from a man high in authority [probably Joseph Tumulty] that President Wilson is straining every nerve to see that the Home Rule Bill goes into effect."[60] Shane Leslie, from a prominent Anglo-Irish family, a cousin of Winston Churchill with very good connections in Washington and New York, assured Redmond that "the English are beginning to realize that without you there can be no true or lasting entente between this whole country and Great Britain."[61] In the midst of the American entry into the war, the problem of how to satisfactorily resolve the Irish problem was very much an issue at many levels of American society.

☘

On 16 May, Lloyd George sent letters to the leaders of the several Irish parties, offering either immediate home rule (although with six counties of Ulster excluded) or a "convention of Irishmen of all parties for the purpose of producing a scheme of Irish self-government."[62] John Redmond, perhaps emboldened by the American support for an undivided Ireland, rejected immediate home rule with partition, but supported a constitutional convention. The creation of the Irish Convention, to meet at Trinity College Dublin, was publicly announced by Lloyd George on 21 May. In the minds of many, the proposal of an Irish Convention to work out and agree upon a new constitution for Ireland, somewhat on the model of the American Constitutional Convention in Philadelphia in 1787, seemed to be an ideal solution. Sir Horace Plunkett was selected as chairman, and although some have criticized him for his leadership skills, no better person could have been chosen to satisfy American opinion. A younger son of Lord Dunsany, Plunkett had ranched in Wyoming in the 1880s with Theodore Roosevelt, and in more recent years he had returned to the United States regularly for health treatments, thereby maintaining contacts with a wide cross-section of figures in American public life. As Shane Leslie has vividly noted, "From America Sir Horace Plunkett sped to Dublin to assume the chairmanship of the Irish Convention."[63] Both Sinn Féin and Irish labor refused to attend, and the Ulster Unionists were reluctant participants, but, altogether, ninety-one delegates met in Dublin. It is sometimes argued that the convention was merely a diversion thought up by Lloyd George to mollify the United States, while the more crucial problem of building the relationship to pursue the war was worked out. Certainly, President Wilson was kept informed of the workings of the conventions, as Plunkett, particularly sensitive to the American dimension, sent him copies of the periodic secret reports that he wrote for the king. R. B. McDowell's thorough study of the Irish Convention reveals that the British government had been preoccupied since the Rising with the issue of how to implement some form of Irish self-government that would be tolerably acceptable to all parties. However, no mention of American influence pushing the British government to take action appears in his book, despite what is now known of President Wilson's message to Lloyd George, the various meetings with Balfour during his mission to Washington, all of the letters and articles the newspapers on both sides of the Atlantic, and the fortuitous choice of Plunkett as chairman.[64]

Few figures in American public life have had interests as wide-ranging as Roosevelt. His many well-placed Irish and British friends—Sir Horace Plunkett, Ambassador Sir Cecil Spring-Rice (who served as best man at Roosevelt's second wedding in 1884), and John Quinn come to mind—gave him good information and strong opinions about the Irish struggle for self-government. As the war crisis intensified, the unresolved Irish question and open dissention in Ireland became increasingly vital issues for Roosevelt and for other Americans. Through Quinn's efforts, Roosevelt had contributed the lead letter to the *Times* of 26 April 1917, expressing approval of home rule for Ireland and asserting that it would strengthen Britain and the Empire.[65] By midsummer Quinn was working with Roosevelt once again. In Ireland, George Russell (Æ), the writer who had been part of Plunkett's staff in Ireland's agricultural cooperative movement, was appointed to the secretariat of the Irish Convention. To explain the workings and the potential of the convention, Russell wrote an article for the *Irish Times*, which was published as a pamphlet titled *Thoughts for a Convention: Memorandum on the State of Ireland*, a copy of which he sent to Roosevelt. The former president was intrigued and on 6 August sent a long commentary back to Russell. He liked Russell's idea of a Convention, but disagreed with the process that Russell suggested for obtaining the approval of the various Irish constituencies. Roosevelt urged that the convention work independently and confidentially, and that it present the Irish population with a completed draft of a constitution to be accepted or rejected, as had the American Constitutional Convention in 1787. To reinforce his arguments, Roosevelt also sent a copy of the delegates' manual for the recent New York State Constitutional Convention. Roosevelt approved of Russell's pamphlet overall, however, and told him that it should also be published in the United States, even suggesting that he might reprint it himself. Russell's reasoned arguments and measured tones, Roosevelt thought, would counter the poorly informed and often biased opinions on Ireland being published in many American newspapers.[66]

Since the summer of 1916, John Quinn had emerged as a leading spokesman for the moderate Irish American nationalists, and he was in touch with Roosevelt, Plunkett, Russell, and others involved in Irish matters. Quinn also had received Russell's pamphlet, as well as a copy of Sir Horace Plunkett's speech "A Defence of the Convention," and he was determined to publish them both in the United States in a deliberate attempt to shape American opinion along the lines of moderate nationalist thinking and to prepare the public for a home rule solution for Ireland. He also acquired Roosevelt's 6 August letter to Russell and recognized it as a persuasive American perspective on the Irish problem. A small book began to take shape articulating Irish, British, and American points of view. In Quinn's hands, much of the two chapters "Sinn Fein and the Dublin Insurrection" and "The American Point of View" were drawn extensively from Roosevelt's letter to George Russell. Although Quinn made some changes in syntax and in some instances softened the language, a comparison will immediately reveal Roosevelt as the source.[67] Thus Roosevelt's understanding of the problem of Irish self-government became the "American Point of View." Thanks to his long friendships and correspondence with people such as Plunkett, Spring Rice, Lady Gregory, and Yeats, Roosevelt was remarkably well informed. George H. Brett of Macmillan in New York agreed to publish the materials as a book if Quinn wrote an introduction. Quinn spent two days dictating what would eventually run to 94 pages in his 183-page book.[68]

The Irish Home Rule Convention was published by Macmillan in September 1917. Through Quinn's work, it made a major effort to shape opinion in the United States, Ireland, and Britain and win support for a moderate home rule solution to the Irish problem in the midst of the war. Would it have been more effective if Theodore Roosevelt's name had been on the title page along with those of Plunkett, Russell, and Quinn? Quinn wrote to a friend that he hoped arguments in the book to extend some form of self-government to Ireland without delay would persuade the British, specifically Lloyd George and Balfour, that "Great God, we have got to do it this time, for America expects it." This was asking a lot. After all, with the exception of the war crisis and American support for the Allies, the merits of Irish self-government and Unionist objections had been debated for years. Quinn was sure that there was nothing in the text to offend either an Englishman or an Ulsterman, but he determinedly wanted to undercut "the stupid pro-German Irish in this country."[69] He sent the book to some two hundred influential people in the United States, Ireland, and Britain; Theodore Roosevelt thanked him for his copy of "that capital little book."[70] It was Quinn's last major effort on behalf of Ireland.

The Irish Convention struggled through late 1917 and into 1918 without bridging the fundamental gap between the southern nationalists who wanted a Dublin government for all Ireland and the Ulster Unionists who wanted no part of it. In fact, there were divisions even among the nationalists. While progress was made in establishing something of a working relationship between the nationalists and the southern unionists, this was not enough to create overwhelming majority support for the recommendations before the convention. For Lloyd George, preoccupied with the war crisis, the persistent Irish problem was a perilous distraction. He warned Plunkett in February 1918 that if there were "acute" disagreement the recommendations of the convention would be "held over for determination after the war," but he admitted to Andrew Bonar Law in mid-January that giving in to the exclusion of parts of Ulster from the jurisdiction of a Dublin government would be seen in the United States as "sacrificing the interests of the War to that of a small section." American opinion—and, specifically, that of the Irish in America—was crucial for the support that the British and the Allies needed as the specter of the spring offensives in France got closer. "The Irish in America would be more rampageous than ever," he warned Bonar Law, "and Wilson's position, embarrassing enough as it is now with Germans and Irish on his flank, would become untenable. The Irish are now paralyzing the War activities in America," he said with some exaggeration. But his conclusion was not too far wide of the mark nevertheless: "If America goes wrong we are lost."[71] Lord Northcliffe, just back from his organizing British purchasing missions in the United States, told Plunkett that sympathy for Irish self-government had interfered with his war efforts: "I wanted copper," Northcliffe related to Plunkett, "Thomas F. Ryan gave me cigars a foot long but no copper until the Irish question is settled. I want steel—I am blocked by Farrell, and so on. Irishmen everywhere."[72] As 1917 turned into 1918, it appeared that a compromise put forward by Lord Midleton might win widespread support, but as time went by the prospect of agreement became more and more remote. In the end, the Ulster delegation issued a proposal to keep all nine northern counties outside the jurisdiction of a Dublin parliament, while the controversial customs provisions—the mark of practical control of the country's economy—was passed with such a slim majority as to undermine its workability. Because of the considerably less-than-unanimous results of the Irish Convention, the government did not overrule the Ulster unionists or, indeed, act on the convention's final report.[73]

The work of the Irish Convention was effectively preempted by the war crisis. The spring offensive by the Germans had resulted in dramatic advances along the front in northern France and tremendous casualties among British forces—some three hundred thousand between March and April. The government's solution was to extend conscription to men as young as seventeen and as old as fifty-one, but to justify this expansion the government felt it had to include Ireland, for the first time. This would clearly provoke resistance in Ireland, but would it be even more of a problem in the United States? Balfour telegraphed Colonel House on 2 April, laying out the issue and noting that extending conscription would unite nationalists and the Church and probably result in "serious disorder and possibly, even, bloodshed." He asked House for his opinion on the "effect [of conscription] on the conduct of the war viewed from America." House consulted with Wilson and replied to Balfour that the president felt that in the circumstances conscription in Ireland would "accentuate the whole Irish and Catholic intrigue which has gone hand in hand in some quarters in the country with German intrigue."[74] New conscription legislation was introduced in the House of Commons on 9 April 1917.

As foreseen by Balfour, House, and Wilson, the threat of conscription pulled Sinn Féin, the Irish Parliamentary Party, and the Catholic hierarchy together in a unified show of public opposition. The government, as if taking a hint from Wilson's concern about possible Irish-

German collusion, announced the discovery of a "German plot" on 11 May and arrested many of the leading Sinn Féin figures, including Eamon de Valera. It was a gesture that convinced few. The US consul in Cork, Charles M. Hathaway Jr., reported that the claim of German involvement was "merely a piece of Government chicanery." Indeed, he explained to the State Department that this was a transparent attempt to "vilify Ireland and discredit the Irish cause abroad so as to relieve the British Government of the handicap of foreign sympathy (and particularly American sympathy) with Ireland's lack of freedom and self-determination."[75] Hathaway was uncomfortable with the active involvement of the Catholic Church in these political matters, but clearly understood both Irish nationalist resistance to conscription and the intentions of the British government.

Conscription either created a whole new political dynamic in Ireland, or simply accelerated a new political process that had actually begun earlier, with the first successful challenges made by Sinn Féin in the several by-elections where the Irish Parliamentary Party candidates were defeated. Furthermore, conscription drew the Church into line with Sinn Féin, and although the Irish Party MPs withdrew from Westminster and joined protests to defy the government, they seemed increasingly irrelevant. In this new crisis, the government ignored the proposals of the Irish Convention. Would the immediate implementation of the sort of home rule proposed by the convention—or embraced in the Home Rule Act already on the statute books—have redeemed the situation? In the end, President Wilson's opinion and advice, the urgings of Secretary Lansing, the writings and efforts of Theodore Roosevelt and John Quinn, as well as the worrying of Lloyd George and Lord Northcliffe, bore no fruit; more immediate pressures and expediencies moved the British government. American opinions were not paramount, nor were the efforts of President Wilson or former President Roosevelt, even in the war crisis, when Britain and the Allies needed all the support from the United States that they could get.

3

The 1919 Paris Peace Conference, the American Commission on Irish Independence, and Self-Determination for Ireland

World War I was a particularly distressing experience for the Irish American community. Their loyalties to the United States, to Irish nationalism, and to the Allied cause were often pulled in seemingly irreconcilable directions. However, Irish Americans and nationalists in Ireland seized upon President Wilson's rhetoric about war aims to secure the principle of self-determination for struggling nationalities. In his famous Fourteen Points speech to Congress on 8 January 1918, Wilson spoke of the "freest opportunity of autonomous development" for Central European minorities; in his earlier message to Pope Benedict in August 1917, he said that "peace should rest upon the rights of peoples, not the rights of Governments."[1] Speaking in February 1918 to a joint session of Congress, Wilson was even more specific: "National aspirations must be respected; peoples may now be dominated and governed only by their own consent. 'Self-Determination' is not a mere phrase. It is an imperative principle of action, which statesmen will henceforth ignore at their peril."[2]

Would Wilson be able to bring these ideas into effect, and would they apply to Ireland? His secretary of state had serious misgivings. "The more I think about the President's declaration as to the right of 'self-determination,' the more convinced I am of the danger of putting such ideas into the minds of certain races," Robert Lansing wrote in his diary. "What effect will it have on the Irish," as well as other nationalities, he queried? "Will it not breed discontent, disorder and rebellion?" On the concept of self-determination, he concluded, "The phrase is simply loaded with dynamite. It will raise hopes which can never be realized."[3] However, on the basis of these war objectives, the Irish could reconcile their loyalties to the United States and the Allies as well as to Ireland, setting aside—momentarily, at least—their misgivings about the British government. When the Armistice was declared on 11 November 1918, Irish Americans felt that it was now up to President Wilson to redeem at the Peace Conference these pledges that had justified participation in the war. Ronan Brindley and Michael Hopkinson have pointed out that public opinion in Ireland held that Wilson, the Peace Conference, or the League of Nations would resolve Irish claims for self-government—what Erez Manela has called the "Wilsonian Moment." As Eamon de Valera was later to say in Dáil Éireann, when entering the war the United States had "given their nation as a guarantor of the principles of Self-Determination and of the League of Nations so that the rules of justice and right should be established as the basis of their relations with each other instead of the rules of force and might."[4] Indeed, this was a view held by minorities around the world. It was imperative, therefore, that the opportunity of the Peace Conference, like the opportunity of German intervention in the 1916 Rising, not be lost.

Poignantly, Wilson himself had misgivings. As he sailed to France for the Peace Conference in December 1918, he confided in George Creel, the progressive journalist and head of the wartime Committee on Public Information. Creel recorded a scene together on board ship, looking out to sea: "The President stood silent for quite a while, and when he turned to me at last his face was as bleak as the gray stretch of sunless water." Wilson thanked Creel for successfully popularizing America's war aims of self-determination and the rights of small nations, going on to say, "But I am wondering if you have not unconsciously spun a net for me from which there is no escape. It is to America that the whole world turns today, not only with its wrongs, but with its hopes and grievances." The president listed a number of the world's needs and problems, noting that people will suffer tyrants patiently but demand immediate change when liberated. "What I seem to see—with all my heart I hope that I am wrong," Wilson cautioned, "is a tragedy of disappointment."[5]

As soon as the Armistice was declared, Irish American spokesmen—including Catholic bishops, archbishops, and cardinals—began appealing to President Wilson to use his influence at the Peace Conference to bring about the realization of Irish nationalist aspirations. Several resolutions were introduced in Congress, resulting in public hearings on 12–13 December, with over sixty witnesses and the publication of the transcript as *The Irish Question*. The resolution that eventually emerged asked the Peace Conference to "favorably consider the claims of Ireland to the right of self-determination."[6] Although it passed in the House, the resolution failed to come to a vote in the Senate before that chamber adjourned. Wilson replied to an appeal by senator Thomas J. Walsh of Montana that he appreciated "a proper solution to the Irish question," but he would have to find his way at the Peace Conference, although he would use his "influence at every opportunity to bring about a just and satisfactory solution."[7] Wilson's replies were polite but vague; he was aware of the problem, and he would do what he could. However, according to Sir William Wiseman, Wilson had assured him that "he would not allow IRELAND to be drawn into the Peace Conference."[8]

Meanwhile, Irish American nationalists, who had found themselves under suspicion during the war because of their pre-1917 attachments to Germany, began rehabilitating themselves and the idea of Irish nationalism in the United States. "Self-Determination for Ireland Week" was organized in New York, and on 10 December over twenty-five thousand people met at Madison Square Garden to hear Cardinal William O'Connell of Boston speak of "self-determination" and to urge, "Let that application begin with Ireland." Politicians were petitioned and resolutions were introduced in Congress. All of these efforts—particularly the latter—provided Irish American nationalists with effective platforms. Both the Clan na Gael and the Irish Progressive League held national meetings in New York in early January 1919 to reevaluate their objectives in view of the end of the war and the Peace Conference. Even more important was the overwhelming victory of Sinn Féin candidates in Ireland in the December 1918 general election. British electoral reform legislation had increased the number of eligible voters in Ireland from about seven hundred thousand to over two million, many of them young and with no loyalty to the Parliamentary Party. John Quinn had seen this coming; as early as July 1917 he commented on the third successful by-election that year: "The last victory of the Sinn Féiners, that of de Valera over [Patrick] Lynch, for Willie Redmond's seat, seems to demonstrate that the parliamentary party is a shell and hopelessly out of touch with Ireland generally."[9] Sinn Féin turned the political situation in Ireland upside down, winning seventy-three seats and reducing the once-dominant Irish Parliamentary Party to a mere seven seats (the Unionists also won twenty-six seats).[10] Acknowledgment and affirmation were due to those elected as Sinn Féin members of Parliament meeting in Dublin as Dáil Éireann on 21 January 1919, and of their declaration of independence.[11] Across Europe, revolutions were taking place and new nations were coming into being—the "unraveling of empires provoked by the First World War," as Maurice Walsh has called it.[12] Ireland also claimed a place in this new world, and Sinn Féin pledged to send a delegation to the Peace Conference to secure the self-determination of which Wilson had spoken. The liberal progressive journal *New Republic* understood the connection: "When President Wilson put the weight of America behind the idea of self-determination, the full political aspiration of the majority of the Irish was completely renewed," and it ascribed the resounding electoral victory of Sinn Féin in December to this goal. "Morally the case of the Irish people is invincible," the journal concluded.[13]

In an attempt to emphasize the unity of all Irish groups, the Clan na Gael and the FOIF called for the Third Irish Race Convention to be held in Philadelphia on 22 and 23 February 1919 and to include delegates from all factions of the Irish American community.[14] Moderates balanced militants; even the revered Cardinal Gibbons participated. To complement the Catholic clergymen, Presbyterian and Anglican ministers, as well as a Jewish Rabbi, were made part of the program. Non-Irish politicians also participated. The convention cabled support to Dáil Éireann, financed the Irish National Bureau in Washington, and launched the Irish Victory Fund, a major fundraising campaign.[15]

The convention coincided with Wilson's hasty trip back to the United States from Paris to dispose of pressing legislation prior to the adjournment of the Sixty-Fifth Congress. Alarmed by the rumor that Wilson regarded the Irish question as purely a domestic problem for Great Britain, Irish Americans were not conciliated by a denial from Wilson's private secretary, Joseph P. Tumulty. A committee appointed by the convention to speak to the president was made up of prominent Irish Americans who called on Tumulty at the White House. Tumulty subsequently warned Wilson of the dangers to the Democratic Party, and to his presidency, in ignoring the Irish, and claimed that their strength had grown. "During the past few days," Tumulty said, "men of all races have come to me, urging me to request you to see the committee." Because he himself was not a "professional Irishman," he cautioned that a refusal would play into the hands of US extremists. When Tumulty suggested that Wilson meet the committee of twenty-five for a few minutes after his speech at the New York Metropolitan Opera House on 4 March, the evening he was to sail again for France, Wilson agreed.[16]

The meeting in New York on Sunday evening did not go smoothly. Wilson refused to accept Judge Cohalan as a part of the delegation. Judge John J. Goff pleaded with the president to "present to the Peace Conference at Paris the right of Ireland to determine the form of government under which she shall live." Wilson was reported as saying that he could not express an opinion on Irish matters, but that he was "in thorough accord with the aspirations voiced by the Judge and had been for a long time." Frank P. Walsh, who had served under Wilson, referred to president's message to Congress on 7 April 1917 in which the president said that the United States was entering the war to insure "the rights and liberties of small nations," and he asked Wilson to use his position at the Peace Conference to see that an Irish delegation could present its case. Bishop Peter Muldoon of Rockford, Illinois, also urged the president to support an Irish settlement. Careful not to speak directly to the Irish situation, Wilson said in regard to Ireland, "I will have to use my best judgment as to how to act."[17] At the end of the meeting, which lasted twenty-five minutes, Wilson shook hands with the members of the committee before leaving to board the passenger liner *George Washington* for France. The president's physician, Admiral Grayson, noted in his diary that Wilson "heard the committee courteously but made no promises."[18] The delegation was very displeased and adjourned to the McAlpine Hotel to confer with the spurned Judge Cohalan.

Once on board ship, Wilson told Ray Stannard Baker that he had no right to interfere. But once the League of Nations was established, the Irish question could be openly discussed. Wilson complained to Baker, "They were so insistent . . . that I had hard work keeping my temper." By the time he reached France, his mood had not improved; he told one of the American staff members of the peace delegation,

David Hunter Miller, that his first impulse had been to tell the Irish Americans "to go to hell."[19]

☘

The importance of the Irish question had been driven home to Wilson as the result of his meeting and the simultaneous Irish agitation in Congress. The House passed Joint Resolution 357 on 3–4 March 1919, in the waning hours of the session, urging the Peace Conference to "favorably consider the claims of Ireland to the right of self-determination," and both chambers received numerous petitions from Irish American groups.[20] Anything Wilson might have hoped to do for Ireland at the Peace Conference had been thwarted by the many demands made in the negotiations. The historian Arthur Walworth has asserted that Wilson did talk with Lloyd George about Irish matters shortly after returning to Paris, pointing out that neglecting an Irish settlement would generate opposition to any treaty, as well as to the League of Nations.[21] Moreover, events in Ireland had changed rapidly during the time he was abroad. Prompted by the agitation among both the Irish American community and the Irish themselves, Wilson sent George Creel—at the time Wilson's personal troubleshooter, investigating problems in Europe—to Ireland for a new appraisal of the Irish situation.[22]

Creel met with many prominent Irish figures in Dublin, including Michael Collins and Harry Boland, and found them to be more reasonable in their demands than many Irish Americans. On his way back to Paris he managed a three-hour meeting with Lloyd George, who he said "fairly bubbled with enthusiasm over the 'rights of small peoples,'" but was sending troops into Ireland.[23] Creel was able to convey his impressions to the prime minister, although without impact. By 1 March, Creel sent his report to Wilson, explaining that the Sinn Féin victory in 1918 had been virtually complete. Sinn Féin represented all of Ireland except for four counties in Ulster, where they formed large minorities. He said the old Irish Parliamentary Party and home rule were thoroughly repudiated, although, in his judgment, the leaders of Sinn Féin were not at that time completely serious in their demands for an Irish republic. He wrote that Lloyd George "blandly dismisses the whole matter by professing his entire willingness to grant any settlement Irish leaders will agree upon," which Creel said was "buncombe" because there had been substantial agreement for the past four years. Nonetheless, if the British government would now institute Dominion status with county options for Ulster, it would be "accepted as a satisfactory adjustment of the situation." However, he warned, "if it is not done within the next two months, sentiment in Ireland and America will harden in favor of an Irish republic." Creel concluded his report shrewdly and quite prophetically: "The agitation has really not started yet in the United States, but as it gains strength it will be the dominant factor in our political situation, and the determining factor in any international arrangement involving Great Britain."[24] Wilson read the report by 20 March, but his answer was noncommittal: "The suggestions of your letter are very valuable indeed, and you may be sure will remain in my mind."[25] Nonetheless, Creel was convinced of Wilson's sympathy for Ireland.

☘

The meeting on 4 March between Wilson and the committee from the Irish Race Convention had been unsatisfactory for both parties. Wilson had refused to commit himself to support Irish self-government at the peace conference, and the officers of the convention and the committee of twenty-five felt that further measures must be taken. They appointed a subcommittee of three to go to Paris with the title of the "American Commission on Irish Independence." The committee selected three distinguished Irish Americans from their own number—Frank P. Walsh, Edward F. Dunne, and Michael J. Ryan.

FRANK P. WALSH

> The leader of the commission, and the most important and forceful member. A well-known labor lawyer, Walsh had worked with Wilson and supported his bid for the presidency as early as 1910. Walsh achieved national stature in 1913–15 when President Wilson appointed him chairman of the Industrial Relations Commission.[26] The commission held hearings across the country exposing terrible working conditions in post–Civil War industrial America, with Walsh publically grilling such powerful tycoons as John D. Rockefeller Jr. Walsh emerged as a crusading reformer and a prominent progressive, and he helped to enhance President Wilson's reformer image in the process. Wilson appointed Walsh again in 1918 to the National War Labor Board as

joint chairman with former president William Howard Taft and to the War Labor Conference Board. Walsh's selection by the Irish Race Convention as chairman of the American Commission on Irish Independence capitalized on his national reputation as a dynamic reform leader as well as on his links to Wilson, and the likelihood that Wilson would listen sympathetically to Walsh's arguments. Walsh's many critics charged him with being a radical agitator and opportunist; unquestionably, he brought to the Irish movement a great deal of ability, energy, and optimism. Although not previously active in Irish affairs, he became one of the most prestigious figures in the nationalist movement in the 1920s.[27]

EDWARD F. DUNNE

The commission's second member. Born in Waterville, Connecticut, Dunne was educated at Trinity College Dublin and held an LL.B. degree from Union College of Law in the United States. After a successful career as a lawyer in Chicago, Dunne was appointed circuit court judge in Cook County, Illinois, and then elected mayor of Chicago. He was also reform governor of Illinois from 1912 to 1917. Aside from the several U.S. senators of Irish descent, Governor Dunne was the highest elected official to be identified with the Irish nationalist movement in the United States. Although he had not previously played an active role in Irish American activities, he, too, brought national prestige to the commission.

MICHAEL J. RYAN

The third member of the commission, began political life as Philadelphia city solicitor in 1911 and from 1915 to 1919 served as public service commissioner. Of the three members of the commission, Ryan's prominence had grown out of his participation in the Irish American nationalist movement. He had been president of the United Irish League of America for years, which placed him at the head of the powerful organization of constitutional nationalists during the agitation for home rule prior to 1914. Ryan disagreed with John Redmond over Irish support of the British in World War I; his pro-German position—as well as his disengagement from the repudiated home rule politicians—made Ryan an acceptable figure for Irish American nationalists of many shades of opinion with links to the past as well as the present.

The commission sailed from New York on the last day of March 1919. Their specific objectives were threefold: first, to obtain safe conducts for Eamon de Valera, Arthur Griffith, and Count George Noble Plunkett, to travel to Paris as representatives of Dáil Éireann; second, to plead the Irish case themselves before the Peace Conference if unable to secure safe conducts for the Irish delegation; and, third, to work for the recognition of the Irish Republic. Upon their arrival in France on 11 April, they were met by Major de la Chappelle on behalf of M. Tardieu, the French foreign minister, and by Sean T. O'Ceallaigh and George Gavan Duffy, the Dáil Éireann envoys in Paris.[28] Through the kindness of the American journalist Lincoln Steffens, Walsh was introduced to Ray Stannard Baker, then director of the press bureau for the American Commission to Negotiate Peace, who also received all official correspondence for President Wilson and agreed to assist them in arranging an interview with Wilson. That same day, 14 April, Walsh met William C. Bullitt, who was in charge of the Peace Commission's current intelligence department. Bullitt, who was fully informed about the Irish Race Convention and the unsatisfactory meeting between Wilson and the committee, offered to contact Lloyd George's confidential secretary, Philip Kerr, and to talk with him about Walsh's mission. The following day Bullitt reported to Walsh that Kerr had told him Lloyd George would probably give the Irish delegation passports to come to France, but that he would never agree to have them appear before the conference. That afternoon, Walsh met with Colonel Edward M. House, the president's confidential advisor on foreign affairs and a commissioner plenipotentiary to negotiate peace, who said he was familiar with the home rule situation in Ireland through his friend Sir Horace Plunkett and that he also knew the republican arguments. House was cordial, and Walsh made arrangements to meet with him again in a few days.[29] Walsh could take pleasure in the prospects of the success of his commission and the chances of the Irish delegation.

On the encouragement of Baker and Bullitt and the strength of these successes, Walsh, Dunne, and Ryan sent a letter to President Wilson, stating whom they represented and outlining the purposes they hoped to accomplish in Paris. In regard to the Irish delegation, they told Wilson, "If these gentlemen were furnished safe conducts to Paris so that they might present their case, we feel that our mission would be, in the main, if not entirely accomplished." They appealed to the president "to obtain from Lloyd George, or whomsoever may be entrusted with the specific details of such matters by the British government" safe conducts for the Irish delegation, adding, conspicuously, that millions of Americans would be appreciative of such a service. Through his secretary, the president replied that he would like to see Walsh that afternoon.[30]

Wilson's willingness to meet with Walsh on 17 April may have been prompted by the reports he had received from George Creel and others that the Irish leaders were more moderate than they seemed and that the resolution of the whole problem was a possibility, if the leaders of Sinn Féin and the leaders of the British government could be brought together for talks. The agreeable cooperation of the American Peace Commission indicated a confidence in the possibility of success. In Walsh's words, Wilson told Walsh that "he had had two exhaustive interviews with Lloyd George on the subject; that in these interviews he had urged upon Lloyd George the necessity of an early settlement of the Irish question," but, Wilson went on to say, these meetings were inconclusive and "unsatisfactory" because the prime minister said the Irish themselves would have to work things out.[31] Of necessity, these talks had been unofficial, and the only possible subject for him to discuss officially with the British was peace with Germany. After peace was achieved, however, he proposed he would say to Lloyd George that the Irish in America were all united and "intense" over the issue of Ireland's government, and that if the Irish question were not settled, it would seriously affect both British American and British colonial relations. Wilson's promise to speak in the League of Nations about the threat of the Irish question put pressure on Lloyd George to solve the Irish problem before that occasion arose. No doubt the commission would have liked to receive a stronger commitment, but the president told Walsh that he had spoken with Lloyd George about resolving the Irish crisis and was willing to do so more forcefully at a later date. Walsh recorded in the commission's journal that the president had agreed with Walsh's views and that "he [Wilson] talked and acted as though we had a common purpose in the matter of having the Irish Republic recognized."[32] This reassuring talk with the president, together with the promising meetings with other members of the Peace Commission, marked a major turnaround from the opera house meeting a month earlier.

House, meanwhile, had talked with Lloyd George and was able to inform the commission what they had also learned from Bullitt: that

Lloyd George would probably allow the Irish delegates to come to Paris for talks, although not before the Peace Conference itself. House demonstrated American interest in the Irish question by showing Lloyd George some typical resolutions sent to the government by groups in the United States. Through House and Sir William Wiseman, arrangements were made for the commission to meet Lloyd George, probably for the purpose of making preparations for the Irish delegation. Busy at the Peace Conference itself, Lloyd George twice postponed his meeting with the commission, at which point it was suggested—by whom is a matter of some disagreement—that the commission should make a trip to Ireland to examine the situation for themselves.[33]

The commission thought a trip to Ireland was a good idea; it would allow them an opportunity to meet with the leaders elected in December 1918. Walsh, Dunne, and Ryan arrived in Dublin on Saturday, 3 May 1919. They were met first at Holyhead by a delegation led by William T. Cosgrave and Joseph McGuiness, and then at Kingstown (now Dun Laoghaire) by Eamon de Valera and others and driven to the Mansion House in Dublin, where they were received by the lord mayor. They proclaimed to the press the goals of their mission—that they had come to Ireland "to confer with President de Valera upon the question of securing international recognition of the Irish Republic at the Peace Conference."[34] They also described their conversations in Paris with President Wilson, Colonel House, and Sir William Wiseman, and they strongly implied that their trip to Ireland had the approval and support of both Wilson and Lloyd George. The following day, after attending services at the pro-cathedral with de Valera, Countess Markievicz, and others, the commission traveled to Glendalough with Sinn Féin leaders. On Monday, 5 May, Governor Dunne and Ryan left for Belfast, where Ryan was quoted as saying that they were "out to get an Irish Republic" and that they would not "compromise" with any other form of government. Dunne and Ryan then went on to Cork on Wednesday, 7 May, and the following day met in Limerick with bishop Michael Fogarty, as well as several other members of the hierarchy. In these meetings, the members of the commission spoke freely on matters of Irish independence, on an Irish republic, on the American model of republicanism, on the Allied war aims concerning self-determination, and on the powers the Dáil government derived from the 1918 election.[35]

Back in Dublin on Friday, 9 May, the commission addressed the third session of Dáil Éireann in the Mansion House. After generous introductions, all three Irish Americans addressed the Dáil, emphasizing the parallel between Ireland's current struggle and America's in the 1770s. Walsh and Dunne commented on President Wilson's enunciation of war aims and of the US commitment to apply them to Ireland as well as to the nations of eastern Europe. Walsh emphasized that their mission was to not to tell the Irish people what to do, but to facilitate an Irish delegation's trip to the Peace Conference. "Our mission here and its spirit . . . is to press the Irish question," Walsh asserted, concluding, "I cannot believe that that request can be denied." Referring to the December election triumph, Governor Dunne declared, "The nation has spoken, and you have decided on a Republic." Ryan assured the Dáil that "never in the history of the Irish People in America has there been such union as there is today" in support of Irish independence.[36] The three American commissioners congratulated the Dáil and Irish people and the assured them of success. They did not mince words.

All of this, perhaps not surprisingly, produced a strong reaction. Later on Friday, following the Dáil Session, armed Dublin police and British Army troops massed outside the Mansion House, ostensibly looking for escaped convicts. This military demonstration effectively delayed from 5:30 to 9:55 p.m. a reception that had been planned to honor the American commission, to which some 1,500 people had been invited. The following day, the commission was also denied permission to inspect Mountjoy Prison. However, when they produced their diplomatic visas and argued strongly that the British prime minister had urged them to investigate conditions in Ireland, they were allowed in. They were similarly refused permission to enter the military district in the Westport area in County Mayo and were turned back by soldiers on 11 May. They returned to Dublin the next day, and that evening Dunne and Ryan left for London. Walsh and secretary Patrick Lee were driven to Armagh to talk with Michael Cardinal Logue, before Walsh too left to return to London. On the evening of Friday, 16 May, after two weeks away, the delegation returned to Paris. During the course of these events, the commissioners made many speeches in which they described their purpose at the Peace Conference and the degree to which their visit to Ireland had been worked out through the leaders of the British and American governments. They openly expressed their views on the need for Irish independence, the failures of British rule in Ireland, and the support of the American people for the Irish cause. Sean T. O'Ceallaigh, Dáil envoy in Paris, reported that the commissioners were "charmed beyond measure" by their reception in Ireland and that Walsh "has told us that he is prepared to devote himself to the work of pressing Ireland's cause in America."[37]

The press reaction in Britain, however, was immediate and explosive. The London newspapers reported on 5 May that the commission had arrived in Ireland, and by the following day they were expressing concern. The *Times* questioned Lloyd George's judgment in allowing the commission to go to Ireland at all, and the *Morning Post* stated defiantly, "There is no Irish Republic and there is no President de Valera; but there is a rebel faction in Ireland which is allowed the most extraordinary license by the Government, and it is to give strength and countenance to this rebel part that the Irish-Americans have come over." By 9 May the *Globe* had printed headlines that read: "Impudent Yanks Flaunting 'Irish Republic' Before Our Eyes." There was growing concern that the presence in Ireland of the Irish American Commission was an event that was being manipulated by Irish leaders and that it would be wrongly interpreted by the Irish people and world opinion.[38] Upon the commission's departure from Ireland, the *Times* concluded that "the Irish-American delegates . . . have done more political harm in one week than British statesmanship can expect to undo in many months."[39]

All of this provoked a predictable debate in Parliament. On 14 May, Andrew Bonar Law, a Conservative Unionist acting as deputy prime minister, was asked in the House of Commons whether the Irish American commission was "accredited by the American Government." Bonar Law said that Lloyd George had simply wanted the three Irish Americans, as private citizens, to see for themselves the conditions in Ireland, and that he had intended to meet with them after their return to Paris in order to have an "opportunity of putting the British case." In view of the present circumstances, this meeting would no longer be possible.[40] A similar exchange took place in the House of Lords on 22 May, when

Viscount Midleton, a spokesperson for southern Irish Unionists, asked if the Irish Americans had not traveled to Ireland with some authority, because they were permitted to go to parts of Ireland where public meetings had been forbidden. Lord Birkenhead, the Lord Chancellor, replied that Lloyd George had presumed they would be more discreet and responsible than they proved to be, and that he was quite opposed to what they had in fact done. Birkenhead did not think responsible Americans would take seriously what the Irish Americans had said in Ireland about a republic.[41] This public debate in the press and in Parliament spelled the end of the commission's prospects for getting the Irish leaders to Paris.

While the commission was only halfway through its visit to Ireland, Lloyd George wrote to House, complaining that he had permitted the commission to go to Ireland on the understanding that they were responsible men who wanted to impartially investigate the conditions there. "To my amazement," he wrote, "I now find these gentlemen, so far from investigating the Irish problem in a spirit of impartiality, announced on arrival in Dublin that they had come there to forward the disruption of the United Kingdom, and the establishment of Ireland as an independent Republic." Furthermore, Lloyd George stated, they were taking part in demonstrations with these same Irishmen who had been attempting to aid Germany. He told House that the British government could not permit these activities to go on.[42] House replied that the commission had not specifically wanted to go to Ireland "to study conditions on the spot," nor had they even wanted to meet with Lloyd George, but that they simply wanted the British to receive de Valera, Griffith, and Plunkett.[43] Lloyd George wrote back that he had been given an altogether different understanding from both House and Sir William Wiseman, and, that being the case, he decided to cancel the proposed interview. He also said that, in view of the present situation, he would inform the viceroy in Ireland to take whatever steps "necessary in the interests of peace and order."[44] Thus, when Walsh applied to the military authorities later in the same day to go to Westport, he found to his surprise that his permission to travel freely in Ireland had been greatly restricted. The *New York Times* Paris correspondent reported that the British authorities were "incensed" at the commission stirring up trouble in Ireland. The London papers reported that House had said he would no longer serve as "intermediary between the Commission and the British Government in Paris."[45]

❧

When the commission sailed for Ireland, it had seemed on the verge of success in its mission to get the Irish delegation to Paris. Through the efforts of Bullitt, House, Wiseman, and Kerr, as well as the subtle pressure of President Wilson, Lloyd George had seemed willing to allow the Dáil delegation to come. When the commission returned, the situation had changed completely. It is difficult to say what prompted them to speak publicly in Ireland with such complete disregard for the delicacy of the situation, but, regardless of the reason, the change in attitude in Paris marked the failure of the commission's primary purpose. Either their own weakness and inexperience or the shrewdness of the British in perceiving that they would undo themselves saved Lloyd George from having to come to grips with the Irish question at the Peace Conference.[46]

When the commissioners returned to Paris, they immediately met with Colonel House and wrote to secretary of state Robert Lansing in an attempt to reopen channels of communication. The following week the commission wrote a similar letter to Wilson, which also expressed surprise that the trip had offended the British, who had arranged the visit; House, they said, had given them reason to believe that Lloyd George would grant safe conducts for the Irish delegation. Wilson discussed the letter with Lansing, who wrote to the commission on 24 May that while there had been British and American cooperation in allowing the three members of the commission to travel to Ireland and attempt to secure permission for the delegation to come to Paris, it had all been done unofficially. Because of the notoriety of the trip, that method was no longer feasible; "certain utterances" had been made that caused the "deepest offence to those persons with whom you were seeking to deal." Lansing concluded that, in view of these facts, new attempts to talk with the British authorities about the Irish delegation "would be futile and therefore unwise."[47] This forceful letter from the secretary of state, drafted in consultation with House and the president, was intended to terminate the commission's work. In fact, Ryan, who had some disagreements with the other members of the commission, left Paris for the United States on 24 May. Walsh and Dunne, however, tried to retrieve the situation by further arguing their case. They talked with House, who told them that much damage had been caused by the press coverage. The commission also sent a short note to Lansing on 26 May and a longer one the following day. Henry White, one of the five US commissioners plenipotentiary to the Peace Conference, reported to senator Henry Cabot Lodge that the Irish Americans had obviously not sought to make their appeal an official concern of the American Peace Commissioners until after their private efforts through House had failed, and he denied any responsibility for their lack of success. White, a former career diplomat, had no sympathy with the intrusion of Irish affairs into the Peace Conference, which, as he put it, had "nothing to do with making peace with Germany and Austria."[48]

Later, Walsh and Dunne sent letters to each of the five members of the American Peace Commission, demanding a hearing for the Irish delegation. Walsh forwarded to Wilson over thirty cables from Irish American organizations demanding the same thing. Walsh argued also that Article X of the League Covenant served as a threat both to aspiring nations like Ireland and to world peace. Failing to elicit a positive response, Walsh and Dunne next demanded that they themselves be given an interview with the American Peace Commissioners. The effect of this request was the unanimous advice of the four commissioners to their chairman, Wilson, that no interview should be given. When secretary-general Joseph C. Grew so informed them, Walsh and Dunne replied to Grew that the Peace Commission seemed to mistake this request for a hearing of the Irish delegation.[49] They had learned that the British had "definitely denied safe conducts" to Ireland's representative, and they were now attempting to carry out their alternative plan of appealing on Ireland's behalf themselves. While they did not actually represent the Irish people, they claimed to have been commissioned by a national convention of over five thousand democratically elected delegates from hundreds of thousands of organized Irish Americans, whose role it was to speak for the twenty million people of Irish descent in the United States; on their behalf, the commission demanded to be heard. They also sent an official communiqué to Georges Clemenceau, president of the Paris Peace Conference.[50] No reply was received.

With these rejections, Walsh and Dunne gave up hope of actually getting the Irish delegation to Paris. On 6 June, Walsh had an interview with Secretary Lansing, but he used a new set of tactics. He repeated the old arguments, but more important, he submitted to Lansing a copy of the report that he and Dunne had written about their trip to Ireland, which dealt at great length with the treatment of political prisoners and the excesses of the military establishment there. The language of the report was quite inflammatory and obviously designed to appeal to public opinion rather than to diplomats. Walsh asked Lansing to send a copy in the diplomatic pouch to Congress, and he himself mailed copies to the other participants at the Peace Conference, as well as to King George V, Andrew Bonar Law, Lord Birkenhead, and three major London newspapers.[51] Certainly this represented a turn away from a practical effort to bring the commission to Paris and toward an attempt to sway public opinion. These activities annoyed President Wilson intensely. When Ray Stannard Baker said that Walsh and Dunne were in his office every day, Wilson replied that he did not know how long he could keep himself from condemning their "miserable mischief-making." He said, "They see nothing except their own small interest."[52] When Tumulty in Washington attempted to warn Wilson of the resolution in favor of Irish self-determination, which was passed by the Senate, the president shot back, "I have tried to help in the Irish matter but the extraordinary indiscretion of the American delegation over here has almost completely blocked everything."[53] Wilson later sent a second cable to Tumulty in which he explained how Walsh, Dunne, and Ryan had made it virtually impossible for the Peace Commission to do anything for Ireland. He told Tumulty, as he later told Walsh, that they had "practically cleared the way for the coming of the Irish representatives to Paris" when the incidents surrounding the three Irish Americans in Ireland had ended that possibility. He could not see how anything more could be done without threatening Anglo-American relations. Tumulty replied that he understood, but that he hoped that the president would not allow these mistakes to prejudice his judgment "against Ireland."[54]

Despite his irritation, Wilson, under considerable pressure, did agree to meet with Walsh and Dunne one more time. The 11 June meeting started with an awkward discussion of the inability to obtain safe conducts for the Dáil Éireann delegation to come to the Paris Conference. Walsh argued that denial of freedom to come to Paris illustrated the "captivity" in which Ireland was held by the British and the "blockade" that had been put around the island. Wilson acknowledged that "no small nation of any kind has yet appeared before the Committee of Four," and that the conference had limited itself to countries that had actually been involved in the war. Walsh urged that a "guerilla" war was going on in Ireland. As for dealing with the Irish situation, Wilson asked, "Why should this whole thing be left to me?" Walsh replied that Wilson was the commanding figure at the Peace Conference and, he said with poignant irony, "because it was you who raised the hopes in the hearts of these people that they could come to you." He read out extracts from Wilson's wartime speeches that spoke of the rights of people to self-determination. These words, Walsh said, had inspired millions of people, many of whom might be killed attempting to achieve some form of self-government. "You have touched on the great metaphysical tragedy of today," Wilson replied. "When I gave utterance to those words I said them without the knowledge that nationalities existed, which are coming to us day after day."[55] Wilson knew of the Irish problem, of course, but he was limited by others at the conference who did not have the same objectives as he. When pressed by Walsh, Wilson shot back, "Now Walsh, if it is your intention to go back to America and try to put me in bad, I am going to say when I get back that we were well on our way to getting Mr. de Valera and his associates over here, we were well on the way, when you made it so difficult by your speeches in Ireland that we could not do it; that it was you gentlemen who kicked over the apple cart."[56]

Wilson effectively turned the tables on Walsh and his colleagues, clearly arguing that the indiscretions of the American Commission on Irish Independence had ruined the prospect of bringing an Irish delegation to Paris. This may have gone beyond what the British were prepared to consider in 1919, but it was a powerful rebuttal of Walsh's accusation of the president's failure to live up to his wartime goals. Wilson then eased up somewhat and told Walsh and Dunne, "I want to say to you that I have the deepest sympathy for Ireland and her people and her cause. I know I speak for others when I say that all we could do unofficially we have been doing and will do." Wilson concluded the interview with an observation that might be understood as a comment on his experience at the Peace Conference: "I came here with very high hopes of carrying out the principles as they were laid down. I did not succeed in getting all I came after. I should say—I should say that there was a great deal—no, I will put it this way—there were a lot of things I hoped for but did not get."[57] The meeting ended with Governor Dunne in tears.

One thing that Wilson got but had not hoped for was an Irish resolution from the Senate. Working together with Judge Cohalan, senator William E. Borah of Idaho, a leading member of the of the Foreign Relations Committee, introduced a resolution on 29 May asking the American Commission to Negotiate Peace to make arrangements for the Irish delegation to present their case at the Peace Conference. The resolution was reported back to the Senate on 5 June and amended on the floor by senator Henry Cabot Lodge of Massachusetts, the chairman of the committee. The final version of Senate Resolution 48 read as follows:

> Resolved, That the Senate of the United States earnestly requests the American Peace Commission at Versailles to endeavor to secure for Edward de Valera, Arthur Griffith, and Count George Noble Plunkett, a hearing before said peace conference in order that they may present the cause of Ireland.
>
> Resolved further, That the Senate of the United States express its sympathy with the aspirations of the Irish people for a government of its own choice.[58]

The measure was passed on 6 June by a vote of sixty to one and was cabled immediately to Wilson. The president, in consultation with his fellow American Peace Commissioners, concluded that the resolutions should simply be forwarded without comment to Georges Clemenceau, the president of the conference, which Lansing did. No reply was returned. However, the passage of the resolution and its timing served as a warning to Wilson of the dangerous linkage between the matter of Irish self-government and the fates of the peace treaty and the League of Nations.[59]

Walsh and Dunne were not satisfied with Wilson's explanation of the problems of the Peace Conference. They sent a series of letters to the peace negotiators, in increasingly belligerent tones, calling attention to public opinion about Ireland, presenting memorials and resolutions passed by the American Federation of Labor, and, most important, referring specifically to the Borah resolution on 6 June. They demanded to know what the Peace Conference had done and was doing, personally and officially, to obtain recognition for Ireland. On the advice of Lansing, Henry White, General Tasker Bliss, and Christian Herter, Grew wrote to Walsh and Dunne that the resolutions had been sent to conference president Clemenceau, who determined what items were brought.[60] Grew's letter virtually ended the commission's attempts to gain a hearing for the Irish delegation. On 27 June they sent another letter to Clemenceau, asking him to consider the crisis in Ireland and allow the Irish delegation to come before the conference. This letter was never answered. Walsh and Dunne returned to New York on 8 July and went immediately to confer with Irish leaders, including de Valera, who had traveled to the United States. Governor Dunne set to work writing a booklet entitled *What Dunne Saw in Ireland*, which restated much of the commission's report but made the argument that both the British and American governments were aware of the commission's political objectives before suggesting that it visit Ireland.[61]

In order to forestall the somewhat unfair criticism of the American Peace Commission, as well as to protect his own position with the Republican Party, Henry White, still in Paris working on parts of the treaty, wrote to Secretary Lansing, and later to Lodge, that he had learned that Sean T. O'Ceallaigh felt the Irish had no real complaint about their treatment in Paris: "The Irish Delegation here had no grievance against the President or any of us, feeling that we had done all that could be expected; and that of course . . . they had got all the publicity they wanted and had no discourteous treatment on our part to complain of."[62] Lodge replied that the Irish complaints could not be dismissed as mere publicity. The Irish Americans, he said, had reported the courteous treatment they received from the Peace Commission, but the point was that they had not been able to accomplish their mission. As for Walsh and Dunne, Lodge later wrote to White, "I assure you that these are not men whose testimony can be whistled down by the wind whatever you may feel about the Irish."⁶³

In US liberal circles, the feeling grew that the Irish question had to be addressed. Even Wilson's admirer and strong supporter George Creel wrote extensively about America's war aims and Ireland. In July 1919, just four months after leaving the president's service and completing his mission to Ireland, Creel published *Ireland's Fight for Freedom*, which provided a well-researched, nationalist interpretation of Irish history, with a photograph of Eamon de Valera as its frontispiece. Although he did not mention Wilson, the Senate resolution, or the peace treaty, he did make a clear statement of the commitment of the United States to the war aims of "self-determination" and the "rights of small peoples," which meant that "the Irish question had some very vital American aspects, and that its settlement was immeasurably the largest contribution that England could make to the common cause." Moreover, in a thinly disguised reference to the Versailles Treaty and the League of Nations, Creel asserted, "Make no doubt that the Irish vote [in the United States] will be a *block vote* [Creel's emphasis] against England and all things English as long as the Irish question is allowed to persist." And he concluded that when the Irish and the Irish Americans "ask that pledged principles of justice be applied to Ireland, America will find it difficult indeed to refuse."⁶⁴ This was an ominous warning indeed as the peace treaty came before the Senate Foreign Relations Committee for approval.

During the winter of 1919, while President Wilson was in Paris, the Sixty-Sixth Congress, elected in 1918, came into session. The Senate Foreign Relations Committee was now under the chairmanship of the Republican Henry Cabot Lodge, who was largely unsympathetic to Wilson and the treaty being drafted in Paris. The Irish American nationalists, along with a number of other disappointed ethnic groups in the United States, thus became the natural allies of the Republican senators in opposing Wilson and the treaty. This was clearly seen in the Senate's passing the Borah resolution on 6 June.⁶⁵ When, therefore, the Senate Republicans began planning their opposition to the Versailles Treaty in July and August, they enlisted the assistance of the disillusioned and embittered Irish American nationalists, among others. The American Commission on Irish Independence formed an important nucleus in the Irish American delegation of some 115 people led by judge Daniel F. Cohalan, which testified before the Senate committee hearings on the treaty for most of Saturday, 30 August. As Hopkinson argues, "The failure in Paris drove Irish-American opinion into the arms of the opposition to the League of Nations in the US."[66]

Judge Cohalan started the proceedings, asserting that he spoke for some twenty million Americans of Irish descent, and submitted a number of documents, including the 21 January 1919 Dáil Éireann declaration of independence. He talked about American foreign policy principles, such of freedom of the seas and the Monroe Doctrine, arguing that the Versailles Treaty and the League of Nations would undercut them and leave the United States subordinate to the British Empire. An independent Ireland would ensure freedom of the seas, he claimed, and protect the independence of the western hemisphere. As Michael Doorley points out, "Cohalan cleverly linked American security interests to Irish independence." Cohalan had Patrick J. Lynch, clerk of the Indiana Supreme Court and Appellate Court, submit a memorial with 189 signatures from Irish Americans all over the United States urging the rejection of the Versailles Treaty.[67] Cohalan then introduced the American Commission on Irish Independence: Walsh, Ryan, Dunne, and John Archdeacon Murphy (the commissioner in Paris in July and early August). Walsh admitted that he had been a supporter of President Wilson and his war aims but was shocked by and disappointed with the secretive manner in which the negotiations in Paris took place. He submitted to the committee all of the commission's unproductive correspondence with officials at the Peace Conference together with the record of the 11 June conversation between Wilson, Walsh, and Dunne. The passages from the commission's diary directly quoting Wilson's defensive responses caused a sensation. Wilson admitted that "no small nation of any kind has yet appeared before the Committee of Four," and that to do so would require unanimous consent of the four great powers—essentially the "secret diplomacy" criticized in his Fourteen Points speech. When pressed about the war aims regarding the rights of small nations, Wilson lamented in words now often quoted: "You have touched on the great metaphysical tragedy of today." As for self-determination, Wilson admitted, "when I gave utterance to those words, I said them without the knowledge that nationalities existed, which are coming to us day after day."[68] These sensational admissions became powerful weapons, often quoted and used against Wilson in the fight to defeat the Versailles Treaty. Ryan, Dunne, and Murphy recounted what they saw in Ireland and their frustrations in Paris. W. W. McDowell, the lieutenant governor of Montana, told of Eamon de Valera's visit to his state, and Daniel C. O'Flaherty of Virginia spoke about the nonsectarian support for Irish independence. Congressman William Bourke Cockran gave a long and impassioned discourse on the history of British misrule in Ireland, concluding, "Peace must be established in Ireland before it can be made permanent throughout the world."[69] People that could not attend had twenty-five additional submissions presented to the committee. The Senate Foreign Relations Committee hearings gave the Irish American nationalist community a platform to voice their resentment at the failure of President Wilson, despite the efforts he had made officially and unofficially, to deliver some form of self-government to Ireland (see appendix 2).[70]

The Senate hearings continued throughout August 1919, with growing criticism of the Versailles Treaty. Republican Party senators, who in the majority controlled the committee, began introducing reservations, which among other things weakened the American role in the League of Nations. President Wilson's addresses to Congress as well as his other attempts to work with the senators had not successfully rallied support for the treaty. Wilson's solution was to go directly to the people. On 3 September, Wilson left Washington on the presidential train for a cross-country tour, visiting cities large and small. He gave forty speeches in twenty-one days, to cheering audiences of thousands. On 25 September, in Pueblo, Colorado, he made one of his most stirring appeals for support for the treaty and the league. But he also called up a sinister specter of disloyalty to the United States by the critics of the treaty:

> I have perceived more and more that men have been busy creating an absolutely false impression of what the treaty of peace and the Covenant of the League of Nations contains and means. I find, moreover, that there is an organized propaganda against the League of Nations and against the treaty proceeding from exactly the same sources that the organized propaganda

proceeded from which threatened this country here and there with disloyalty. And I want to say—I cannot say it too often—any man who carries a hyphen about with him carries a dagger that he is ready to plunge into the vitals of this republic whenever he gets a chance. (applause) If I catch any man with a hyphen in this great contest, I will know that I have caught an enemy of the republic. My fellow citizens, it is only certain bodies of foreign sympathies, certain bodies of sympathy with foreign nations that are organized against this great document, which the American representatives have brought back from Paris.[71]

This was a biting indictment. With the Irish American community being the largest hyphenate group in the country, it was inescapably clear that the president saw these critics as disloyal to the American republic. But it was also clear that Wilson and the Democratic Party had lost the Irish American vote. This was the president's last public speech about the treaty. Later that evening his health deteriorated, and the tour was canceled. Less that a week later, on 1 October, Wilson, back in Washington, suffered a massive, incapacitating stroke.

As predicted throughout 1917 and 1918, the failure of the Peace Conference to deal with Irish claims had profound consequences. Shortly after the Senate Foreign Relations Committee hearings, Frank P. Walsh reported to Sean T. O'Ceallaigh in Paris that "the Senate Committee was very favorable and sympathetic to our cause, and individually and collectively they told us how much we were strengthening the fight." Walsh asserted strongly that "if it were not for the Irish effort [the] Covenant of the League of Nations would have gone through, Article X. and all."[72] The hearings of the committee were published in the *Congressional Record*, and the correspondence and report of the American Commission on Irish Independence was separately printed and widely distributed. Daniel T. O'Connell at the Irish National Bureau in Washington told senator William E. Borah that they had distributed seventy-five thousand copies of these hearings and asked that Borah mail out another five thousand, using his franking privileges.[73] The FOIF also produced a number of leaflets and brochures urging the defeat of the treaty and the league, arguing that they constituted a British conspiracy that threatened American freedom of action. The treaty came before the Senate on 19 November and was voted on three times, twice with reservations and once without, and failed each time to obtain a two-thirds majority. The *Gaelic American* celebrated the defeat with the bold headline: "Senate's Action a Splendid Vindication of Americanism."[74] Judge Cohalan wired Senator Borah the very next day, saying "Heartiest congratulations," and assuring him that this was the "greatest victory for [the] country and liberty since [the] Revolution." Borah replied thanking Cohalan for his important contribution: "You have rendered in this fight a service which no other man has rendered or could have rendered." Borah went on to praise "the Irish people who have helped to make this great fight."[75] Despite the adverse vote in the Senate, there was a reluctance to accept that the United States would not ratify the Versailles Treaty or join the League of Nations. A fourth vote was scheduled for March 1920, but during the interval opposition had grown and still more reservations to the treaty were introduced. On 17 March, senator Peter C. Gerry of Rhode Island introduced a reservation in which the United States consented to the treaty while affirming the principle of self-determination and "sympathy with the aspirations of the Irish people," as expressed in the Borah resolution.[76] Efforts were made to add amendments that would weaken and broaden the reservation, but they were defeated. The final reservation reads as follows:

> In consenting to the ratification of the treaty with Germany the United States adheres to the principle of self-determination and the resolution of sympathy with the aspirations of the Irish people for a government of their own choice adopted by the Senate June 6, 1919, and declares that when such government is attained by Ireland, a consummation it is hoped is at hand, it should promptly be admitted as a member of the League of Nations.[77]

This was a strong statement, but it also reflected something of a hollow victory, inasmuch as the treaty, including the Gerry reservation, among several others, again failed to obtain a two-thirds vote. Commentators then and historians since have argued that many of these late resolutions were intended to guarantee that the treaty would be defeated.[78] Nevertheless, the Gerry reservation was one more reminder that until the Irish matter was satisfactorily resolved it would remain a dangerous and disruptive element in American affairs.

In Ireland, the Senate's June resolution was seen in less cynical terms. Here was a public appeal by the upper chamber of the legislature of a great power expressing the hope that the Peace Conference would satisfy Ireland's claims for self-government. The Dáil expressed its gratitude in the form of a motion: "It is therefore resolved: That the elected Government of Ireland be and is hereby directed to convey the thanks of the Irish Nation to the Congress of the United States." The motion further stated that Ireland had no territorial ambitions, but only wished "to live in cordial peace with, and as one of, the Free Nations of the World." The motion added an additional barb, referencing Great Britain and the American Revolution and noting that "the ties of blood and friendship which subsisted between both nations [Ireland and America] in the days of their subjection to one common oppressor [Britain] have endured and are indissoluble."[79] The motion passed unanimously.

☘

Altogether, the record of the American Commission on Irish Independence was impressive, in view of the private capacity in which it worked. Together with the Dáil envoys in Paris, the commission's activities made the Irish cause a major public issue. "In Paris the most clamorous of all the nationalist groups was a Sinn Féin delegation from Dublin, pressing a demand that Ireland's case be judged by the peace conference," George Creel wrote, and "side by side with them stood a highly vocal committee from the United States [the American Commission on Irish Independence], claiming to speak for the fifteen million Americans of Irish birth or descent, and no less insistent than the Sinn Féiners that Erin's revolt against British rule was a proper subject for consideration by the Big Four."[80] The attempts of the Irish Americans and Irish leaders to move the question of Irish self-determination out of the domestic jurisdiction of the United Kingdom and onto the world stage of the Paris Peace Conference were not misguided.

The commission failed in its objective to arrange for the delegation to come to Paris. But had there ever really been a chance? Lansing, House, and President Wilson especially later talked as though it had been certain the British government would allow the Irish leaders to come to Paris, until the Irish American commissioners "kicked over the apple cart." In the wake of the commission's trip to Ireland, spokesmen for the British government, sensitive to the volatile issue on their hands, said that Lloyd George had never intended to let the Irish representatives come to Paris and that he only agreed to meet the commissioners in order to give them a lecture. The question would appear to be unanswerable. The British government did permit a delegation of Egyptian nationalists, who had earlier been held in detention on Malta, to come to Paris, but the Egyptians, unlike the commission, saw no one of importance at the Peace Conference. In retrospect, it would seem inconceivable that an Irish delegation would have been permitted an opportunity to present the Irish case before the Council of Four or the Council of Ten. However, it would have given de Valera, Griffith, and Count Plunkett a chance to meet privately with Lloyd George. One cannot speculate too far on the possible fruits of such talks. An Irish delegation led by Sean T. O'Ceallaigh and George Gavan Duffy did get to Paris, where they talked briefly with Colonel House, General Bliss, and Herbert Hoover, but they were denied official contacts, particularly with the British.[81] Ultimately, de Valera, Griffith, and Lloyd George did not meet for another two years, after all the bloodshed and destruction of the Irish War of Independence. Although diplomatic efforts did not meet with success, they moved closer to their objective, and closer to the people in power, than any similar small national group at the conference. With the publicity they generated, they made the Irish cause a major public issue.

The negative impact of the commission's failure was to turn Irish American opinion against President Wilson and the Versailles Treaty. Although historians today would argue that several factors led to the treaty's defeat, Wilson's devoted admirer and close associate George Creel later stated that it was the unresolved Irish question that closed the door to the treaty and shattered the possibility of US participation in the new world order created in Paris. "More than anything else, perhaps, this was responsible for the treaty's rejection," Creel concluded.[82] Wilson would have agreed. As William E. Dodd, a University of Chicago professor soon to help edit an edition of the Wilson papers, wrote to a friend after having lunch with the president early in 1921, Wilson spoke with "insistence that the Irish had wrecked his whole programme for the adoption of the work at Paris. 'Oh, the foolish Irish,' he would say. 'Would to God they might all have gone back home.'"[83] Of course, by this time, Wilson, still suffering from his stroke and having seen the Versailles Treaty defeated and his policies rejected in the 1920 election, was a shattered and embittered man. But, certainly, Irish American hostility over the failure of Wilson and the Paris Peace Conference to deal with Irish self-government was a major factor in the rejection of the treaty and the League of Nations. The warning about the consequences of failing to resolve the Irish question seemed to have been borne out.

4

Money

The Sinews of War, 1919–1921

The pace of events moved rapidly in the aftermath of the Great War. Public attention was, understandably, focused on the peace negotiations in Paris, the fate of the defeated Central Powers, and the promise of the League of Nations. However, as the weeks turned into months and winter turned to summer, it became clear that the great aspirations of the Irish American nationalists and the Irish themselves for self-determination and the guarantee of the rights of all small nations would not be implemented through the peace conference. Independently, the Sinn Féin candidates who won the election in December 1918 did not go to Westminster to take their seats in Parliament, but instead met in Dublin at the Mansion House as Dáil Éireann, and on 21 January 1919 declared their independence, proclaiming Ireland a republic. This assertion of an independent government required that the Dáil provide some government services, challenge the continued British occupation of the country, and seek international diplomatic recognition. Indeed, over the next twenty-four months, the conflict between Dáil forces and the Crown unfolded into the War of Independence, or the Anglo-Irish War. All of this required substantial amounts of money. On 1–2 April, amendments to the constitution were put in place and the Dáil government was reorganized. Eamon de Valera, having recently escaped from Lincoln Jail in England in February, became *Príomh-Aire*, or prime minister (the position now termed *Taoiseach*, or leader, in Irish), and seven other executive offices were confirmed. Significantly, Michael Collins moved to Finance from Home Affairs.[1] Collins, who is remembered primarily for his military role in the War of Independence, had worked in banking and the brokerage business in London for ten years before returning to Ireland in 1916, and so was a fitting choice for Finance's crucial portfolio.

When the Dáil met again on 10 April, de Valera stated bluntly, "It is obvious that the work of our Government cannot be carried on without funds." He announced that the government would therefore soon issue a loan for £1,000,000 sterling, £500,000 to be offered immediately, £250,00 in Ireland and £250,000 abroad. On 19 June, the arrangements for the internal loan were announced and de Valera, the Most Rev. Dr. Michael Fogarty, the bishop of Killaloe, and James O'Mara, a Limerick businessman, were named as the trustees.[2] Bond prospectuses were issued in the summer of 1919 for the internal loan, and sales of the Sinn Féin bonds began. Despite the fact that British forces inflicted heavy punishments on anyone caught either promoting or purchasing the bonds, by the summer of 1921 some £370,165 worth had been sold in Ireland—what Arthur Mitchell calculates to have involved 150,000 purchasers, or about 15 percent of Irish households.[3] This was an incredible success. How well would the sale of bonds abroad—largely in the United States—compare?

The original intention was that the Dáil would authorize an external loan of up to £250,000 for sale in the United States, with an initial offer of $1,250,000 worth of bonds. However, in May, the American Commission on Irish Independence visited Ireland. Frank P. Walsh, Edward F. Dunne, and Michael J. Ryan all warmly supported the idea of a bond issue and urged that a higher target figure be considered As a result, de Valera and Collins sent instructions on 19 May to the three Dáil members in the United States—Patrick McCartan, Diarmuid Lynch, and Liam Mellows—to undertake the preparatory work for an Irish bond issue, but to not circulate a prospectus until they had talked with a special envoy, Harry Boland, also a member of the Dáil, who was being sent to join them. A suitable bank was to be found to handle the arrangements and to underwrite the issue, and someone of appropriate standing in both the Irish and the financial communities should direct the issue. By late May it also seemed clear that the Peace Conference was not going to recognize Ireland's claims for independence or self-government. Sean T. O'Ceallaigh, the Dáil envoy in Paris, who was in consultation with the American Commission on Irish Independence, wrote to de Valera on 24 May:

> As I have already said our American friends [Walsh, Dunne, and Ryan] are satisfied the fight must be transferred to the United States, and they are pre-

pared to do their share in making the issue a burning one. For that reason we are of the opinion that it would be useful if you could go to the States as soon as it is definitely known that we have been turned down here, and that all hope of achieving anything through the Peace Conference has vanished.[4]

Although his departure from Ireland in the midst of the War of Independence would be criticized, by June de Valera had decided to lead a mission to the United States himself. On 17 June, just five weeks after the members of the American Commission on Irish Independence had visited and addressed the Dáil, acting president Arthur Griffith announced that, with the advice of the cabinet, de Valera had gone abroad.[5]

※

The story of de Valera's career and of his eighteen-month American mission in 1919–20 is well known. However, writers generally focus on two aspects of de Valera's trip: the unsuccessful efforts to obtain diplomatic recognition for the Irish Republic from the US government, and the calamitous split in the Irish American nationalist movement.[6] De Valera must share part of the blame for these two disasters; nevertheless, his mission was successful in at least one respect—in raising money for the Dáil Éireann government. Altogether, between 1919 and 1921, nearly six million dollars were raised—over seventy-four million in contemporary dollars—which was more money than the Irish American nationalist movement had ever previously collected for any purpose. This was a signal achievement, especially considering that it was accomplished in the face of both the split in the Irish American movement and the growing disapproval of the United States.

De Valera was smuggled on board the White Star liner SS *Lapland* as a stowaway and had an uncomfortable trip to New York, where he was met by Harry Boland. Still traveling incognito, he met with leading figures in the Clan na Gael, such as Joseph McGarrity, as well as senator William E. Borah in Washington and Cardinal Gibbons in Baltimore, before visiting his mother (who had remarried and was now Catherine T. Wheelwright) and her family in Rochester, New York. On 23 June, de Valera dramatically presented himself to the American public as the president of the Irish Republic in the Waldorf-Astoria Hotel in New

York. He told the crowd of over three hundred people, "From today I am in America as the official head of the Republic established by the will of the Irish people, in accordance with the principles of self-determination."[7] At a press conference he said that Ireland hoped for American aid in the struggle for independence, and he later announced that one of the major sources of aid was to help finance the Dáil government. What de Valera specifically hoped to do in America was to sell bonds in the name of the Republic of Ireland. Once he began to confer with Irish American leaders, he increased the amount to be raised. Through the urging of Joseph McGarrity of Philadelphia, $5,000,000 was selected as the target, but on 20 August $25,000,000 was authorized by the Dáil, at de Valera's request. This enormous figure would have both propaganda and practical value.[8] When the time came for the actual sale, a more realistic figure could be selected for the bond issue, but a ceiling of $25,000,000 gave de Valera the freedom to attempt to sell everything the market would bear.

The whole matter of selling Irish bonds in the United States met with some formidable difficulties. First, there were the objections raised by the leaders of the FOIF, which had led the Irish nationalist movement in America since the collapse of home rule during World War. I The Friends, led by Judge Cohalan, had started the Irish Victory Fund at the Irish Race Convention in February 1919. The drive to raise money for the fund was only at mid-course by the summer of 1919. Furthermore, the use of the fund became a matter of increasing controversy among both Irish American and Irish leaders. De Valera, Joseph McGarrity, and others wanted most of the Irish Victory Fund to be sent to Ireland for the use of the Dáil; others, such as Judge Cohalan and John Devoy, wanted most of the money to be used by the FOIF in the public relations battle in the United States, to win support for Ireland and to oppose President Wilson and the League of Nations. De Valera later commented to the cabinet in Dublin that "the F.O.I.F. organization . . . was quite simply inadequate for such a task," but that was only part of the problem.[9] Although the disagreement was never completely resolved, the Friends did agree to terminate the Irish Victory Fund by late August 1919 after raising $1,005,080 (roughly $12,908,091 in today's dollars). They were also willing to finance some of the expenses of the de Valera mission ($26,748), and they did purchase $100,000 worth of bonds in order to help de Valera's organizers get the campaign started. The Friends had also financed the American Commission on Irish Independence in Paris earlier in 1919 ($19,073), as well as the Dáil envoys in Paris ($20,000), and later in the fall they sent $115,000 in cash to the Dáil.[10]

The second obstacle, about which Judge Cohalan was particularly sensitive, was the legal problem of an unrecognized government or regime attempting to sell its bonds to the American public. In international law, the Irish "Republic" did not exist. Therefore, as an investment, bonds issued in its name had no standing. Such securities sold under the name of government "bonds" contravened investment protection laws ("blue sky laws") in many states. Several committees wrestled with the problem of how to sell the issue and still stay within the law, as well as how to handle the banking arrangements. Martin Conboy, a leading Irish American lawyer in New York, concluded that it would be possible to sell them, but he advised that this should be confirmed. Franklin D. Roosevelt, formerly assistant secretary of the navy under President Wilson and, later in 1920, Democratic Party candidate for vice president, had returned to his law practice at Emmet, Marvin, and Roosevelt; he met with de Valera and confirmed that funds could be raised through the sale of "bond certificates."[11] This solution of calling the instruments "bond certificates" would enable the purchaser to exchange the certificate at par for a gold bond issued by the Dáil "one month after the Republic has received international recognition." Banks, however, would not underwrite the issue, but merely allow the money to be deposited. This meant that the sale of the issue could not be conducted through the normal securities market, but would have to be done through the efforts of the Irish Americans and de Valera's staff.[12] In late August, Judge Cohalan, Thomas Hughes Kelly, William Bourke Cockran, Richard F. Dalton, and John D. Moore finally agreed to this procedure. Given the prominence and the legal expertise of his opposition, it is fair to say that only someone with de Valera's stubbornness and prestige—as senior survivor of the 1916 Rising and president of Dáil Éireann—could have overcome the objections to his plan. He and many others felt these objections did not stem from a desire to protect the investing public or to stay on the right side of the law so much as they did a desire to keep fundraising (and, thus, control of the Irish American nationalist movement) in the hands of the current leadership of the FOIF.[13]

De Valera's problems with the leadership of the Clan na Gael and the FOIF raised serious concern about the extent to which these organizations could be expected to work efficiently to sell bond certificates across the United States. To be sure, de Valera had a great many supporters, but he could not afford any mistakes. The solution was inspired: de Valera turned to the American Commission on Irish Independence, which had enjoyed a great deal of publicity through its activities in France and Ireland, rather than to any of the existing Irish American organizations. Moreover, since returning to the United States, the members of the commission had given spectacular testimony at the Senate Foreign Relations Committee hearings in Washington on their experiences at the Paris Peace Conference and thus were now well known within the Irish American community; they had also discussed the Dáil Loan with de Valera earlier in Dublin. Frank P. Walsh, the chairman of the commission, enjoyed a certain public stature and, more important, got along with de Valera. De Valera was anxious as to whether the members of the commission would agree to serve, and indeed he met with some hesitation on the part of all three members. De Valera reported to Arthur Griffith on 13 July that he was "trying to get the Walsh-Ryan-Dunne Commission to take it over." Walsh rallied his colleagues by appealing to their sense of duty, arguing that in the circumstances only the commission could do the job.[14]

The commission opened their headquarters in New York City at 411 Fifth Avenue on 23 August 1919 and became the national organizers for the bond certificate drive. Work began in September to build a national network to do the selling; state organizations were created across the country and city chairmen appointed in the large metropolitan centers. These leaders and their staffs were to utilize the members of local Irish groups such as the Friends, the Ancient Order of Hibernians, the Irish Progressive League, the Knights of Columbus to do the actual canvassing and sales. If separate sales forces were required, they could be created when and where needed.[15] Harry Boland, a member of the Dáil and Irish envoy to the United States, was appointed secretary to national chairman Walsh, and de Valera wrote to Griffith requesting that James O'Mara be sent over to direct the sales of the bond certificates and to organize the national campaign. As 1919 came to an end, Boland concluded O'Mara "had things in fine shape." Certainly, O'Mara is given credit for appointing the state chairmen and city and district offices that created a national campaign organization. Handbooks, promotional literature, and letters of advice poured out of the New York headquarters to inform and guide the organizers across the country. Arrangements were made to deposit the funds in the Guaranty Safe Deposit Company, the Central Union Safe Deposit Company, the Garfield Safe Deposit Company, and the Harriman National Bank. Prominent people such as Captain Robert Montieth, known in Irish circles for his service in Sir Roger Casement's brigade, and Peter Golden, poet and leader of the Irish Progressive League, were hired as organizers.[16]

De Valera was vital to the success of this campaign. He made several trips across the United States exploiting his role as "President of the Irish Republic," preparing and informing Irish American communities. In early July he toured the northern states, to the Pacific coast and back, speaking to rapturous crowds of as many as fifty to seventy thousand people and conferring privately with Irish American groups about raising money for the Irish government. In late August he went south, into Maryland and Virginia, and then back east, to New York, Pennsylvania, Ohio, and Indiana. By October and November he was ready for another cross-country tour that would take him through the Irish centers of the Midwest and the Pacific coast. Sean Nunan, Patrick McCartan, Harry Boland, and James O'Mara, among others, accompanied him for parts of his trips. Speeches, parades, receptions, and special church services were arranged, and at every opportunity de Valera and his party spoke both publicly and privately with local Irish American groups, civic officials, and churchmen. It was painful and sometimes humiliating work, but it created a loose organization. Once again, it was often the prestige of the Irish president that attracted support from the disparate and quarrelsome Irish American groups. As Sean Nunan would later claim, "He made a tremendous impression wherever he went and laid the ground for the organization of the Bond Certificate drive."[17]

By early 1920, most of the organization for the bond certificate drive had been completed. A decision was reached to set a public goal of

$10,000,000, with an anticipated target of raising at least $5,000,000. The bond certificates would bear an interest rate of 5 percent, to be paid when exchanged for gold bonds drawn on the Irish treasury, and they were to be sold in denominations of $10 to $10,000. Fenian bonds, sold in the 1860s, would be acceptable for exchange for bond certificates—an ingenious historical touch that linked generations. US government liberty bonds were also to be exchanged for bond certificates, until the Treasury Department protested. The security of all the money was to be protected by the honor of the trustees of the Dáil Loan—de Valera, a member and president of the Dáil; James O'Mara, also a member of the Dáil; and the Most Rev. Michael Fogarty, bishop of Killaloe. A combination of the three had to authorize and sign for any withdrawals from deposits in American or Irish banks. The prospectus announced that the purpose of the loan was to support the Dáil consular service, the development of Irish industries, and the creation of a land mortgage bank to reverse out-migration by assisting people to acquire farms.[18] No mention was made of the acquisition of weapons to prosecute the War of Independence, inasmuch as that would have violated American neutrality law.

☘

By early 1920 the public campaign was ready to begin, and on 17 January the bond certificate drive opened. "An appeal will be made to Americans who love liberty, and who desire to see it triumph in Ireland, for subscriptions to the Bond-Certificates of 'The Irish Republic,'" and the purchase would assist "the ELECTED government of the Irish people to restore Ireland to her Strength, her Health, her Beauty, and her Wealth."[19] De Valera was escorted to the New York City Hall by an honor guard from the old, storied "Fighting Sixty-Ninth" Regiment. Mayor John H. Hylan bought the first bond certificate from President de Valera in a ceremony in which de Valera was also given the Freedom of the City, and "Irish Loan Week" was declared in New York City. At that same moment forty thousand canvassers in the metropolitan area began soliciting sales. According to one spokesman, a million people throughout the United States were ready to sell the bond certificates. This was an exaggeration, but it captured the enthusiasm of the moment. De Valera spoke the following day, along with many other Irish American leaders, at a three-hour event in the Lexington Opera House, where $2,400,000 were pledged, giving the drive a very strong start. The New York Clan na Gael alone brought in $600,000, and the borough of Brooklyn raised $150,000 on the first day. The next week de Valera was invited to Albany as the houseguest of governor Alfred E. Smith, and he addressed the New York Assembly, which subsequently passed a resolution endorsing the bond certificate drive. Within three weeks, claims were made that most of the New York quota of $3,000,000 had been pledged.[20] Archbishop Patrick J. Hayes of New York sent $1,000, together with a very gracious letter. "After a very satisfactory conference with Mr. Eamon de Valera, President of the Irish Republic," he wrote, "I am convinced that his program for agricultural, industrial, and commercial development of Ireland is entirely practical and constructive," and the archbishop went on to say, "America surely will not refuse her moral support to Ireland."[21] This letter was printed and used by congressman William Bourke Cockran, the New York state chairman. In the rest of the country, the drive went well, although perhaps not as spectacularly as in New York. But Edward L. Doheny—the very wealthy California oil tycoon who, within months, became the president of de Valera's new organization, the American Association for the Recognition of the Irish Republic (AARIR)—purchased $10,000 worth of bond certificates. By March, de Valera reported to Griffith that "the subscriptions to the Bonds are proceeding fairly satisfactorily."[22]

All was not smooth sailing for the bond certificate drive, however. Several sets of problems developed. The growing antagonisms within the Irish American nationalist movement, for one thing, could not help but affect the drive. De Valera's unfortunate interview with the *Westminster Gazette* and the *New York Globe* in February 1920 generated loud criticism among those demanding complete independence for Ireland. He had suggested that Britain might negotiate a kind of foreign policy arrangement for Ireland similar to that which the United States had with Cuba, even mentioning the Platt Amendment, which gave the United States the authority to intervene in Cuban affairs under certain circumstances. The Cuban analogy caused a storm of protest and did a great deal to bring the faction fight out into the open. De Valera wrote to Griffith on 23 March, "It is very important that there should not be an open rupture until the Bond drive were over at any rate."[23] However, through this and several other incidents, de Valera became the central figure in the polarization of the nationalist movement in America. Connecticut state chairman James J. Splain quarreled continuously with the national organizers. "He [de Valera] doesn't know America, and apparently some of those who are directing him don't know America," Splain grumbled to Frank P. Walsh.[24] Iowa state chairman W. P. Slattery held a similar view of de Valera's staff. "As for the choice between Mr. Harry Boland and Judge Cohalan, give me Cohalan," he wrote to Walsh.[25] Manhattan borough vice-chairman John D. Moore thought the affluent Irish Americans had been alienated, and only the "least wealthy" had subscribed to the drive. The overall effect of these sentiments on the success of the bond certificate drive is difficult to estimate, but one example may be suggestive: as late as 23 July, 1920, the bond certificate drive had not been started in Detroit, Michigan, because of the struggle within the nationalist movement. "Of course we've known the split would come," wrote Mrs. Peter Golden on 16 February 1920, "but too bad it had to come during the bonds."[26]

The sale of the bond certificates encountered obstacles from outside the Irish community as well. A Boston publisher and bookseller wrote to President Wilson asking if the proposed exchange of US government liberty bonds for Irish bond certificates constituted a tacit endorsement by the US government of the Irish issue. "If not," he wrote, "how long is this raising of funds for the purpose of attack upon a friendly government to be permitted."[27] Secretary of the treasury Carter Glass wrote back that the government discouraged any attempts to transfer or exchange liberty bonds or other government notes for any reason. In fact, the Treasury Department claimed it had no knowledge of the "so-called Irish bond issue."[28] However, by early February 1920, secretary of agriculture David F. Houston wrote to Frank P. Walsh, threatening that the campaign to exchange US securities for Irish bond certificates would have to stop.[29] Walsh, for his part, had already sent specific instructions to all campaign chairmen, warning them to always use the term "bond certificate" and never simply say "bond."[30] Clearly, the technical distinction between the two was lost on most of the public, which usually referred to them as "the Irish bonds." De Valera wrote to Walsh in September 1919 that he wanted subscriptions "only from those who seek to serve a good cause, not from those who want immediate pecuniary profit."[31] This caveat was echoed by the official announcements of the state chairmen, such as William Bourke Cockran, but it was a subtlety the public probably did not take into account.[32]

♣

Despite the criticism and the problems caused by the split within the Irish American nationalist movement, the bond certificate campaign was an enormous success. During 1920 and part of 1921, some $5,123,640 worth of Irish bond certificates were sold in the United States. The campaign officially closed in October 1920, but money continued to be collected well into 1921, as people completed the pledges they had made earlier.[33] On 17 August 1921, the Dáil passed a vote of thanks to the American people for the funds raised for the first loan. On a motion introduced by de Valera and seconded by Michael Collins, the Dáil expressed "the gratitude of the Irish nation to the people of the United States of America for the warm support they have always given to the cause of Ireland and particularly for the generous subscription to the First Loan of the Irish Government, and we furthermore declare that each Bond Certificate purchased in the United States will be redeemed in due course by the Irish nation."[34] This was both a thank-you and a promise, and it was passed unanimously.

After eighteen months in the United States, de Valera returned to Ireland in December 1920, and elaborate arrangements were made to protect the funds in New York banks and to provide for appropriate withdrawals. Without loan trustees de Valera and James O'Mara actually together in the United States, withdrawals could be authorized by any one of three combinations of chosen individuals: John J. Hearn and Harry Boland, Joseph McGarrity and Sean Nunan, or Joseph McGarrity and John J. Hearn. Boland was a member of the Dáil and the secretary of the campaign, and Nunan had been de Valera's secretary in the US; Hearn was from Connecticut and a leading figure in the campaign and the AARIR, and McGarrity was a key Clan na Gael member and supporter of de Valera in the split. When Boland returned to Ireland, his powers were transferred to Stephen O'Mara. This O'Mara, the mayor of Limerick, succeeded his brother James as a trustee of the loan.[35]

In the summer of 1921, after the talks between de Valera and Lloyd George had begun, plans for a second loan campaign were started.

Harry Boland reported on the steps being taken to get a drive underway. Stephen O'Mara and Frank P. Walsh were to head the campaign, and O'Mara proposed moving headquarters from New York to the offices of the Irish Mission at the Munsey Building in Washington, DC. The Dáil Éireann authorized a new loan of £500,000 in Ireland and $20,000,000 in the United States. This loan followed the same legal forms and general description in the United States as the earlier one. The Second Loan served several purposes: a continued source of funds was, of course, a major objective, but the Dáil government also wanted to send a signal to Lloyd George that it could raise large amounts of money in the United States to further finance the War of Independence if the peace talks broke down—"to keep the [Irish] question a live issue," as Harry Boland put it.[36] Furthermore, successful Irish agitation in the United States during the Washington Naval Conference, where the British hoped for an accommodation with the United States on the issue of naval rivalry, would give Lloyd George added motivation to settle the Irish problem.[37] Therefore, with peace talks in progress since July, this second bond certificate drive was opened only in the District of Columbia and Illinois and ran from mid-October to December, until the Anglo-Irish Treaty was signed. Nevertheless, the campaign raised $622,720 before it was called off. Thus the total revenue generated by the two bond certificate campaigns in the United States was an impressive $5,746,360.[38] In current dollars that would be worth roughly $74,964,895—a very significant amount of money.

More than five and a half million dollars was the largest amount ever raised in the United States by the Irish American nationalist community. De Valera's determination to raise the funds through some form of financial instrument was of significance, both for practical reasons and for reasons of public image, and should not be underestimated. The Dáil representatives had failed to get an audience at the Paris Peace Conference, and the hope of extracting diplomatic recognition from the US government through congressional lobbying had turned out to be wildly unrealistic. International law and custom simply did not allow a third party like the United States to intervene in the circumstances that prevailed in Ireland from 1919 to 1922. Nevertheless, the

Dáil government worked diligently to ensure that Ireland carried out all of the roles of an international legal person, a de jure regime, a legitimate nation-state. For this reason, as well as the need for revenue to operate the Dáil government, the bond certificate drive was important both symbolically and practically: it projected the image of Ireland as a player, and it raised the revenue to allow Ireland to play.

Indeed, in practical terms, the sale of the bond certificates in the United States as well as the sale of bonds in Ireland provided the monies that financed the Dáil government, sustained Irish Republican Army operations, maintained the so-called Sinn Féin courts, and paid the Irish representatives in European capitals and several American cities. Sean T. O'Ceallaigh, who had been a Dáil envoy at the Paris Peace Conference and to Italy, gave a generous thanks to the United States in his remarks to the Dáil on 28 February 1922. Responding to a financial report detailing the revenue raised by the first and second Dáil loans, O'Ceallaigh said, "We who are in this Dáil, now that we have a statement of the amount of money coming from America, should express our very deep gratitude to America for the way she has supplied us with funds. Were it not for that assistance the recent fight would have been an impossible one. We owe a deep debt of gratitude to the people of America for what they have done for Ireland."[39] Countess Constance Markievicz urged that these sentiments be placed in a motion, which the acting speaker accepted, and was seconded by James N. Dolan and minister of finance Michael Collins and, in the absence of any opposition declared, adopted. The American bond certificates made an enormous contribution to the achievement of Irish independence and the creation of the modern Irish state.

The Anglo-Irish Treaty signed on 6 December 1921, ending the War of Independence and providing for the creation of the Irish Free State should have resolved the social and political tensions of the past several years in Ireland and normalized the finances of the Dáil government; the affairs of the first and second Dáil Éireann loans should also have been terminated. However, the Anglo-Irish Treaty generated new tensions, culminating in a split in the Dáil and the Sinn Féin Party and the subsequent civil war. The unexpended monies raised in the United

States and Ireland became valuable assets claimed by both sides, with the possible potential of determining which side might emerge successful in the conflict.

Informal agreements not to use these monies for political purposes had been made in the spring, but, after hostilities broke out between pro- and antitreaty forces, these arrangements were seriously strained. Under the original practice, any one of three loan trustees could make withdrawals from the accounts. By the summer of 1922, none of the trustees were in the United States, but several individuals had been given power of attorney and were thus able to make withdrawals. Furthermore, some of the monies had been invested in commercial bonds that paid regular interest merely on the presentation of a coupon, without requiring any identification or authorization. Problems emerged first in the United States, where tensions arose between Matthew Garth Healy, who had been given power of attorney by trustee Stephen O'Mara, and Timothy A. Smiddy, who was the fiscal agent of the minister of finance Michael Collins. Smiddy, who had been an advisor to Collins, was sent to the United States in March to replace Harry Boland. Smiddy was anxious that unauthorized withdrawals were being made. In September 1922, acting on legal advice from the prestigious New York law firm of Stetson, Jennings, and Russell, Smiddy sought a court injunction to obtain control of $2,500,000 of Irish bond certificate funds still in New York banks.[40] The injunction issued by the courts froze the monies in the banks and deprived the republicans of access to them during the most critical period of the civil war and in the dark days immediately thereafter.

Although, in Dublin, de Valera and O'Mara had by now been replaced as loan trustees, the secretary to the trustees, Daithi O'Donoghue, refused to facilitate transfer of loan funds to the Dáil attorney general. On 19 November, Bishop Fogarty and the two new trustees, Richard Mulcahy and Richard Hayes, obtained a writ from the Irish High Court to show why the Munster & Leinster Bank should not turn over the loan fund in its possession. This became *Fogarty and Others v. O'Donoghue and Others* and went to trial on 22 July 1924.[41] The defense argued that the Provisional Government and the Irish Free State had been created by the Southern Ireland Parliament, which was itself a function of the Government of Ireland Act of 1920, and had no claim to the Dáil Loan monies, whereas the trustees of the loans had been appointed by the Second Dáil, which, they asserted, had never expired and under whose authority the original trustees still had the right to control the monies. On 31 July, the High Court gave the Dáil government custody of the monies, arguing that the Third Dáil was as legitimate as the Second Dáil, which, furthermore, had approved the Anglo-Irish Treaty on 7 January and set in motion the election of the Third Dáil. One of the defendants, Stephen O'Mara, appealed the decision to the Irish Supreme Court, which on 17 December 1925, upheld the lower court decision. Justice FitzGibbon agreed with the lower court that the procedures through which the Second and Third Dáila were elected and convened and by which they selected loan trustees were perfectly legitimate. As for whether the Irish Free State, a British Dominion, could claim funds raised for an Irish Republic, Justice Meredith argued that the law only protected the security of the return of monies *loaned*, not the use to which they were put, unlike monies *given* for a specific purpose; therefore, the status of the Free State as a claimant was irrelevant. Justice Johnston also validated the legitimate authority and claim of the Third Dáil and the Irish Free State, citing several cases in which the United States successfully claimed assets of the Confederacy after the American Civil War.[42] In the end, all loan funds were deemed to revert to the Irish Free State's minister of finance.

The case in New York took a different turn. The Free State lawyers asked that the New York court accept the Irish Supreme Court decision and award the funds to the plaintiffs on the basis of res judicata. However, the court ruled that the case at bar in New York was now sufficiently different. On 25 November 1925, the New York court had granted motions to allow two bondholders' committees to intervene in the case on the basis that both the plaintiffs and the defendants claimed to represent the intentions of the original purchasers of the bond certificates. The "Hearn Committee" was headed by John J. Hearn of Westfield, Connecticut, a strong ally of de Valera who at one time held de Valera's power of attorney on bond certificate matters. The committee argued that the Irish Free State was not entitled to the funds, that the funds were intended for an Irish Republic, and, failing their being awarded to an Irish Republic, that they should be returned to the individual bond certificate purchasers. The "Noonan Committee," chaired by Bernard Noonan, held that the Irish Free State was entitled to the monies, but asked the court to require the Free State to adhere to the original purchase agreement to exchange the bond certificates for bonds drawn upon the Irish government. The case, *Irish Free State, et al. v. Guaranty Safe Deposit Company, et al.*, went to trial on 7 March 1927 and lasted for two weeks; de Valera himself gave testimony for two and a half days. The defense argued that a British Dominion could not succeed an independent Irish Republic, that the Irish Free State was the legal successor to the British regime in Ireland, and that the purchase of the bond certificates amounted to a gift specifically for an Irish Republic. The defense concluded that the Second Dáil had never been legally dissolved and therefore still had a legal claim to the monies it had raised. The plaintiffs claimed that the Second Dáil had negotiated the Anglo-Irish Treaty, in due course approved it, and set in motion the election of the Third Dáil and the creation of the Irish Free State, making the Free State the legal successor to the Irish Republic, with a proper claim to the bond certificate money. The plaintiffs also cited the cases following the American Civil War, whereby the United States government took possession of Confederate assets.[43] Judge Curtis A. Peters handed down his decision on 11 May, concluding that the Dáil government never constituted a de facto government in Ireland, being unable to drive British forces out of any significant part of the country. The terms of the Anglo-Irish Treaty made no reference to the Dáil, but rather established the Provisional Government through the machinery of the Southern Ireland Parliament, created by the Government of Ireland Act of 1920 enacted by the British Parliament. In Judge Peters's opinion, the Irish Free State had no claim to the money. The judge also denied the defendants' claim, concluding that the original terms of the sale of the bond certificates on behalf of an Irish Republic, to be exchanged for gold bonds upon international recognition of the Irish Republic, could no longer be fulfilled.[44] Judge Peters, having rejected the arguments of both the plaintiffs and the defendants, essentially accepted the reasoning of the Hearn Committee and ordered that the money be returned to the original purchasers.

A receivership apparatus was set up to contact the bond certificate holders across the United States and return to them the portion of their purchases still in the New York banks. By February 1933 the claims of some 70,000 people, out of 303,587 original purchasers, were paid $2,539,783, or about $.58 for every dollar subscribed. As the money was being disbursed, an irregularity was discovered in the claim of the FOIF. The FOIF had lent the bond drive $100,000 in 1919 to get the campaign started. It was agreed that they would be given bond certificates for that amount, but the actual certificates were not delivered until the representatives of the Irish Free State took over the loan documents. The claims of the FOIF were subsequently challenged and, when this dispute went to court, denied. The FOIF appealed the case to the New York Supreme Court, Appellate Division and on 24 June 1931, the court found that the agreement of the $100,000 loan overrode the peculiarities of the deliverance of the bond certificates themselves.[45] However, members of the Hearn Committee and supporters of de Valera then went to court hoping to force the FOIF to return the monies they received to the subscribers to the 1919 Irish Victory Fund. The court held that the money subscribed to the Irish Victory Fund had been a free gift, not a gift in trust, and therefore could be properly retained by the Friends for their use.[46] It was not until early 1933 that the last New York monies were paid out by the receivers.

The position of the Irish Free State government in all of this remained complicated. In 1924, even before the Irish courts awarded the unexpended money to the government, the Irish government passed the Dáil Éireann Loans and Funds Act, committing itself to repaying all of the First and Second Dáil Éireann Loan money in both Ireland and the United States. Spokespersons for the Irish government made repeated assurances that all of the money would be fully repaid. However, in September 1927, the *Irish World* announced that purchasers could turn in their certificates to raise money for the *Irish Press*, the newspaper that de Valera intended to start in Dublin. De Valera had left Sinn Féin in 1927, formed a new Irish political party, Fianna Fáil, and brought his supporters into the Dáil. The prospect of this money passing directly into the hands of the opposition gave the Free State government reason to delay repaying the spent portions of the bonds. Frank P. Walsh and John T. Ryan, representing the bondholders' committee, attempted to enlist the support of the State Department to hurry the Free State along in repaying the full amount of the bond certificates. Although willing to mention the matter to William T. Cosgrave during his visit to Washington in early 1928, the department refused to use its good offices in this complicated international situation.[47] By late 1927 and early 1928, de Valera again toured the United States, raising money for the *Irish Press* and asking people to turn over to him their bond certificates as convenient contributions. With the help of money from US supporters, de Valera was able to put the *Irish Press* into operation in 1931 and win the 1932 general election. One of de Valera's first orders of business was the announcement that the government would repay the remainder of the bond certificates. On 16 December, the government approved the repayment of $1.25 for each dollar subscribed (less $.58 already paid by the receiver), which amounted to a yield of 25 percent. Appropriations had to be passed by the Dáil, and insufficient time was allowed for claimants to submit their papers, with the result that further measures needed to be passed. This gave rise to raucous exchanges in the Dáil, with one opposition member calling the measure "*Irish Press* bill, second edition."[48] The last payments were made in 1936. A total of $2,487,651 was paid out to some 112,119 claimants. Both the raising of the money and its complicated repayment a decade later were remarkable achievements. Of even greater importance was the fact that the First and Second Loans provided the funds that kept the Dáil Éireann government functioning during the critical years of 1920 and 1921.

Casement and Devoy: Sir Roger Casement (left) came to the United States in the summer of 1914 to build support for the Irish Volunteers, but, following the outbreak of World War I, he worked with John Devoy (right) and the Clan na Gael leaders to forge an alliance with Germany. *Credit: Joseph McGarrity Collection, Digital Library@Villanova University.*

A. J. Balfour and Robert Lansing: Secretary of State Robert Lansing (right) led the official delegation to Union Station in Washington, DC, on 22 April 1917, to greet A. J. Balfour (left), British foreign secretary and leader of the British mission to coordinate Allied war efforts. Two weeks later they would meet privately for an extensive talk about the Irish problem. *Credit: Library of Congress.*

American Commission on Irish Independence: The American Commission on Irish Independence toured Ireland from 3 to 16 May 1919, during which time they met with leaders of Dáil Éireann. Front row, left to right: Count George Noble Plunkett, secretary for foreign affairs; Edward F. Dunne, commissioner; Eamon de Valera, president of Dáil Éireann; Michael F. Ryan, commissioner; Frank P. Walsh, commission chairman. Back row, left to right: Father Michael O'Flannigan; Arthur Griffith, secretary for home affairs; Laurence O'Neill, Lord Mayor of Dublin; and Dr. Cosgrove. *Credit: Irish Independent Archives.*

Bond certificate drive: The opening in New York of the Irish bond certificate sales campaign on 17 January 1920. The young saleswomen are shown with brochures and sales forms. *Credit: Author's collection.*

The American Commission on Conditions in Ireland: The American Commission on Conditions in Ireland held its hearings at the Hotel Lafayette in Washington, DC. Shown here are the five commissioners: from left to right, Senator David A. Walsh, James A. Maurer, Jane Addams, vice-chairman Dr. Frederick C. Howe, and chairman L. Hollingsworth Wood. *Credit: Author's collection.*

Protests against British policies: Street protests in the United States against British military action to suppress the Irish struggle for independence in 1920 or 1921. The signs contain veiled references to the League of Nations, American aims in World War I, Turkish atrocities during the war, and the tradition of the American Revolution. Protests and agitation like this stimulated public concern about conditions in Ireland and the need for relief during the Anglo-Irish War. *Credit: Author's collection.*

American Committee for Relief in Ireland: The American Committee for Relief in Ireland sent a delegation to Ireland from 12 February to 31 March 1921 to assess the needs for assistance during the War of Independence. The delegation members were: chairman Clemens J. France, secretary Samuel Duff McCoy, R. Barclay Spicer, Oren B. Wilber, William Price, Philip W. Furnas, and John C. Baker. *Credit: British Pathé.*

Opening relations in Washington: Timothy A. Smiddy presented his credentials as minister plenipotentiary to president Calvin Coolidge on 7 October 1924, thus opening diplomatic relations between the United States and the Irish Free State. Smiddy is shown here at the New Year's Day reception at the White House on 1 January 1925. *Credit: Author's collection.*

Representation in Dublin: Frederick A. Sterling was the first diplomat sent to Dublin to open an American legation. Sterling (left) is shown here with governor-general T. M. Healy (center) and executive council president William T. Cosgrave (right) at the Vice-Regal Lodge following Sterling's presentation of his credentials on 27 July 1927. *Credit: British Pathé.*

Cosgrave's visit to America: President William T. Cosgrave undertook an extensive visit to the United States and Canada from 20 January to 3 February 1928. The tour began with Cosgrave (left) meeting New York mayor James J. "Jimmy" Walker at City Hall within minutes of getting off the ship. *Credit: British Pathé.*

Cosgrave in Washington, 1928: (from left to right) President William T. Cosgrave, secretary of state Frank B. Kellogg, and Irish Free State minister Timothy A. Smiddy in Washington, DC, during Cosgrave's visit in 1928. *Credit: Author's collection.*

Kellogg's visit to Ireland: Following the signing of the Kellogg-Briand Peace Pact in Paris, secretary of state Frank B. Kellogg and William T. Cosgrave sailed to Ireland on the USS *Detroit*, arriving at Dún Laoghaire on 30 August 1928 for a five-day visit. Seen here ascending the steps of the Royal Irish Yacht Club are (front row, from left to right) Cosgrave, Kellogg, and a representative of the governor-general, followed by minister Frederick A. Sterling, and other members of the welcoming party. *Credit: British Pathé.*

5

Ireland in the Eye of Public Opinion

The American Commission on Conditions in Ireland, 1920–1921

Throughout 1919 and 1920, the struggle in Ireland between the forces of the Dáil Éireann and the British government increased in intensity and scope. A full-scale guerilla war developed: the Anglo-Irish War, or the War of Independence. Crown forces attempted to suppress the insurrection while the Irish Volunteers (Irish Republican Army, as they became) attempted to defeat British efforts. The cost of this conflict in both property and people became increasingly alarming. Meanwhile, in the United States, the Irish nationalist movement split into two irreconcilable factions.[1] Nevertheless, American support was seen as crucial for the survival and success of the Dáil government. Frederick T. F. Dumont, the US consul in Dublin, who was not sympathetic to the Irish independence movement, reported to the State Department at the end of 1919 that the movement was "kept very much alive by reports of the great progress the cause of Irish freedom is making in the United States." He pointed out that "every expression favorable to Sinn Féin is given the greatest publicity," and that "exaggerated accounts of his [de Valera's] receptions are published" in the local press, which sustained the movement.[2] In 1920, as the conflict intensified, something had to be done to raise public awareness in both Ireland and the United States of the atrocities resulting from the Irish conflict, as well as to divert attention from the divisions within the nationalist movement.

One of the most successful means of drawing attention to the Irish struggle was a proposal to create an American Commission on Conditions in Ireland that would investigate the reported atrocities. Both sides in the conflict would be asked to present evidence, and private individuals would be permitted to relate their experiences in ostensibly impartial and nonpartisan hearings. The commission would have significant informational and publicity value and, furthermore, appear to replicate the famous Bryce Commissions: the British investigations of German atrocities in Belgium in 1914 and the massacre of Armenians in Turkey. An Irish commission would have a particularly important effect on domestic and international public opinion, still very much moved by the memory of World War I.[3]

♣

The idea of a public investigative commission for Ireland was conceived by Dr. W. J. M. A. Maloney, who would play an increasingly significant role in the Irish nationalist movement in the United States. Maloney was born in Edinburgh in 1882 of Irish parents, trained in neurology at Edinburgh, Paris, London, and Munich and in 1911 moved to New York, where he married Margaret McKim, the daughter of the famous architect Charles Follen McKim. When war broke out in 1914, Maloney volunteered as a medical officer in the British army and was discharged after being seriously wounded at Gallipoli. Disillusioned by his experiences in the army and offended by the ruthless suppression of the Easter Rising, Maloney became increasingly active in Irish nationalist affairs in the United States. By sheer happenstance, Maloney was also related by marriage to Oswald Garrison Villard, the editor of the liberal New York weekly journal the *Nation*. Villard, the son of the railway and newspaper tycoon Henry Villard and Helen Frances Garrison Villard, the daughter of the abolitionist William Lloyd Garrison, was a leading advocate of liberal causes. The *Nation* had supported self-government for Ireland and was strongly critical of the British suppression of the 1916 Rising, particularly the execution of its leaders. Thus, the *Nation* was a logical liberal-leaning organization to initiate Maloney's project. In addition, William MacDonald, a former Brown University professor and a writer and editor for the *Nation*, had traveled in Ireland in the early summer of 1920, interviewing leading nationalist figures, and he brought to Villard his impression of what was happening. Maloney persuaded Villard to use the pages of the *Nation* to form a national blue-ribbon committee that would choose a smaller body to actually investigate the situation in Ireland. "Maloney wielded the laboring oar and deserves the credit," Villard would acknowledge. "It [the Commission] would never have gone at all but for him and would have perished in the early days but for his enthusiasm and determination."[4]

On 29 September 1920, the *Nation* reported that invitations had been sent to form a committee of one hundred that would appoint a commission to investigate "the charges and counter-charges of atrocities in Ireland." The project was publicly promoted in the pages of *The Nation*, which strove "to emphasize the entirely non-partisan and non-political character of the proposed investigation."[5] The editors assured readers that the journal's role was merely to facilitate the organization of the committee and would not exert its influence on the proceedings or the investigation. By October, well over a hundred and fifty people had agreed to serve on what was subsequently called the "Committee of One Hundred Fifty." A large number of political leaders agreed to servve: ten US senators, including Henry F. Ashurst of Arizona, Hiram H. Johnson of California, and Robert M. La Follette of Wisconsin; five congressmen, six state governors, and seventeen mayors, including Frank J. Hague of Jersey City and John F. Hylan of New York. Some thirteen prominent writers and editors and at least eleven academics signed on, including W. E. B. Du Bois, editor of the *Crisis*; William Randolph Hearst; William Allen White, editor of the *Emporia Gazette*; David Starr Jordan of Stanford University; and Robert Morss Lovett of the University of Chicago. A substantial number of clergymen of all denominations lent their names, including four Catholic bishops and twelve Protestant bishops. Ten labor leaders joined, as well as a number of figures in American public life, such as Henry H. L. Dana of Columbia University, who had been active in the People's Council of America for Democracy and the Terms of Peace; Fiorello H. La Guardia, then an alderman, later mayor of New York, and a strong New Dealer; Dudley Field Malone, former assistant secretary of the treasury; Amos Pinchot, a leading progressive and brother of Gifford Pinchot; and Raymond Robbins, formerly head of the American Red Cross Mission to Russia during the Russian Revolution. To be sure, the committee also included some leading Irish Americans, such as senators James D. Phelan and David I. Walsh, congressman William F. Mason, as well as Cardinal Gibbons, Martin Conboy, and John Milholland, among others. Of even greater public relations value was the large number of Americans who were not of Irish extraction. Altogether, it was an impressive group of left-leaning, socially activist, upper-middle-class elite from all parts of the country and many walks of life—the very sort of people who would have regarded the Irish and Irish Americans with some disdain a generation earlier.[6] Even before the commission got started, one prominent Irish American, John D. Moore, wrote encouragingly to Villard, "My belief is that the investigation will do no end of good."[7]

☙

The committee met on 1 November and elected from their members a smaller panel of five (later expanded to eight) that would be called the American Commission on Conditions in Ireland. The commission members were a distinguished company of nationally prominent figures.

L. HOLLINGSWORTH WOOD

The chairman, L. Hollingsworth Wood was a prominent Quaker and partner in the New York law firm of Kirby & Wood and a founding member of the American Civil Liberties Union, the American Friends Service Committee, and the National Urban League, of which he was president for twenty-six years. Wood was also active in peace work, civil rights, and race-relations activities and served as chairman of the board of Fisk University.

DR. FREDERIC C. HOWE

The vice-chairman, Frederic C. Howe was an author and a lawyer with a PhD from Johns Hopkins University. He had been active in urban reform and economic affairs in Cleveland and more recently was commissioner of immigration of the Port of New York, a key federal government patronage appointment, where he worked with Irish immigrants. He had also been an advisor to the American delegation at the Paris Peace Conference, after which he served as president of the League of Small Nations.

JANE ADDAMS

A major figure on the commission, Jane Addams initially served as the chairperson. Addams was widely known as the country's leading social reformer and sociologist, and as the cofounder in 1889 of Hull House, the first settlement house in the United States. Addams was actively involved in a variety of organizations, such as the National Conference of Charities, the International Congress of Women, the Women's Peace Party, the International Committee of Women for Permanent Peace, the Women's International League, and the American Union Against Militarism. Together with Hollingsworth Wood, she was also a founder of the American Civil Liberties Union. She worked with the American Friends Service Committee in Germany in 1919 in establishing a relief program. In 1931 Addams was awarded the Nobel Peace Prize.[8]

JAMES A. MAURER

Maurer was a progressive labor leader and president of the Pennsylvania State Federation of Labor. A strong socialist, Maurer had served in the Pennsylvania legislature, where he voted against a measure supporting the break in relations with Germany in 1917.

MAJOR OLIVER P. NEWMAN

Major Newman, journalist, lecturer, and sociologist, was a founder of the Social Unit Organization and vice president of the National Community Board. President Wilson had appointed Newman to the board of commissioners of the District of Columbia, but he resigned to serve in the US Army in France during the war.

REV. NORMAN M. THOMAS

Presbyterian minister, lecturer, and editor of the *World Tomorrow*, Rev. Thomas was a leading figure in the "Social Gospel" movement in the United States. Thomas preached against participation in the war and joined the Socialist Party of America in 1917. He is remembered today as a perennial socialist candidate for president.

SENATOR GEORGE W. NORRIS

Norris was a Republican senator from Nebraska who had served five terms in Congress and five in the Senate. Something of a radical progressive, he had supported Theodore Roosevelt in the 1912 election and opposed entry into the war in 1917, being one of the six senators to vote against the declaration of war against Germany. Norris emerged after the war as an "Irreconcilable" and opposed the Versailles Treaty and the League of Nations.

SENATOR DAVID I. WALSH

Senator Walsh, lawyer and politician, had been the first Irish Catholic to serve as governor of Massachusetts. Walsh had supported women's suffrage and the work of the Anti-Death Penalty League, and he had opposed the showing of the racialist stereotypes in the popular motion picture *The Birth of a Nation*. Walsh was the only Irish American among the commission members, but he had not been active in Irish nationalist affairs.[9]

This was a formidable body of people who would be recognized across the country. Although of a distinctly liberal, if not a radical, cast of mind, they were in keeping with the *Nation*'s readership. While none of these commission members had a record of support for Irish nationalist activities, their pacifist, socialist, civil-liberties, and anti-imperialist opinions made a pro-Irish attitude among them probable. These eight members would actually hold the public hearings at which witnesses would testify.

The commission had a staff, called the secretariat, to look after the mechanics of its work. William MacDonald, who had served first as secretary of the Committee of One Hundred Fifty, became the secretary. Royal W. France agreed to be treasurer; Albert Coyle was made the official reporter to transcribe the hearings; and Harold Kellock was in charge of publicity. The commission's affairs of were disentangled from those of the *Nation*. MacDonald wrote to Villard asking for clarification about the relationship between the *Nation*, the Committee of One Hundred Fifty, and the commission. Villard replied that the commission was autonomous, to be limited only by its own finances; it could alter its own composition or that of its staff, assume responsibility for its own expenses, and undertake such projects as it saw fit without consulting either the *Nation* or the Committee of One Hundred Fifty. The *Nation* made a public appeal for contributions to finance the work of the commission, at least to pay the transportation and accommodation costs of witnesses coming from Ireland. Villard told MacDonald that, starting the next day, 28 October 1920, Royal W. France, the treasurer, would be authorized to write checks as an officer of the Committee of One Hundred Fifty.[10]

Money was a problem even at that early stage. MacDonald had sent anxious notes to both Villard and France, saying that funds were limited, and that if the committee did not allocate money immediately, Maloney would have to pay expenses out of his own pocket. Once these details were taken care of, the commission began to function with greater assurance.[11] On 6 November 1920, both the commission and the committee transferred their headquarters from the *Nation*'s offices in New York to the Hotel LaFayette in Washington, DC. Villard told the commission that most of the money that had been raised by *Nation* had come from Irish sources in the United States, and he hoped that, as the commission began to hold its public hearings, money would begin to come in from liberal-minded people.[12] What Villard did not tell the commission (and indeed may not have known himself) was that

Maloney had worked out a plan with Irish leaders then in the United States—Eamon de Valera, Harry Boland, and Patrick McCartan—to have the Irish mission finance the commission if money from other sources was not forthcoming. McCartan's memoirs disclose that the Irish in the United States were behind the creation of the commission to a far greater extent than was realized. McCartan suggests that de Valera was cool to the idea of an independent body judging Irish as well as British military activities, although he asserts that Maloney finally prevailed and convinced the Irish leaders that the commission could not fail to serve Irish interests. Maloney's memorandum on the subject argued in favor of the commission and the importance of the Irish mission financing it if no one else would. He said that, even with as many as ten hostile witnesses, the commission would inevitably be favorable to the Irish nationalists. Moreover, an impartial account of British activities in Ireland might inhibit British operations until there was a change in the British government or until world opinion was moved. "The main object to be kept in mind," Maloney wrote bluntly, "is that the Commission is merely a mask to place the Irish case before the tribunal of the civilized world." The Irish, he felt, could not lose in such an enterprise, and, with the liberal composition of the commission, he was correct in his view.[13]

British officials, while they seemed unaware of the commission's Irish origins, clearly understood the pitfalls presented by such a group. When British ambassador Sir Auckland Geddes learned of the project, he cabled the Foreign Office that it was "obviously designed to embarrass us as naturally no evidence can be forthcoming from this side."[14] Geddes thought that anyone who attempted to present the British side should be discouraged from doing so, but he also felt that it would be a mistake to prevent such people as Muriel MacSwiney from attempting to leave Ireland, since that story would be more damaging than anything she could say.[15] In response to a letter from MacDonald asking for British cooperation in the commission's investigations, the Foreign Office finally decided that it would not assist in any way, but "no one will be refused a passport to the United States on the ground that he or she desires to give evidence on either side."[16] The difficulties that various Irishmen did have in obtaining British passports seemed to contradict these assurances. In response to MacDonald's letter, Geddes replied "that nothing will be done by the British Government to encourage the holding of this inquiry or to assist witnesses to appear before the committee."[17] US ambassador to Britain John W. Davis was clearly uncomfortable about the commission's intervention in Irish affairs. When Sir Horace Plunkett asked his advice after being invited to testify, Davis told him, "I thought [the] Com[mission] not calculated in either composition or method to accomplish any good."[18]

Before the commission began its hearings, at least one idea was tested and drew an unequivocal response from British authorities. Vice-chairman Frederic C. Howe wrote to Villard in early November about sending a delegation to Ireland to investigate conditions. "I feel," Howe wrote, "that it [the commission] should widen out into bigger fields than we planned and become a more active agency." Three commission members were selected for this mission—Newman, Maurer, and Thomas—and two new people were also added: Robert Morss Lovett, dean of the University of Chicago, and Arthur Gleason, author and labor expert.[19] Geddes cabled the Foreign Office this new request and recommended that the commission members be permitted to proceed, although as private persons. After some discussion, the Foreign Office referred the matter to the Irish Office, which vigorously rejected the proposal. Sir Hamar Greenwood, the Irish Chief Secretary, said he had already prevented Archbishop Mannix of Australia from entering Ireland, and he was a British subject. "I certainly object," Greenwood wrote to the Foreign Office, "to any foreigner or foreign comtee. meddling in Irish affairs in Ireland."[20] Greenwood's opinion in the matter was final; MacDonald was told that the visas would not be granted.

The subject of travel to Ireland by members of the commission did not end here. Within a week, a letter was sent to the secretary of state from senators George W. Norris, Thomas J. Walsh, Joseph I. France, Robert M. LaFollette, Joseph E. Ransdell, David I. Walsh, Asle J. Gronna, George E. Chamberlain, Duncan N. Fletcher, and J. N. Shields, several of whom were involved with the commission's formation, asking that the secretary of state lodge a formal protest with the British government because of the unusual procedure of refusing passage to the commission members. The denial of permission was, among other things, a "violation of the right of free communication between the liberty-loving people of two democracies": a suppression of the right to free speech and a threat to the good relations between the two countries. After all, they pointed out, the British had sent missions to the United States.[21] Norman Davis, answering for the secretary, replied that the US government had no right to demand the admission of its nationals into another country, and that the State Department had opposed such demands when made by the Japanese government on behalf of its nationals. As to the similarity of the British missions to the United States, Davis wrote, "their mission was evidently very different from that of the persons who desire to investigate conditions in Ireland."[22] Senator Thomas J. Walsh replied to Davis, indignantly, that such restrictions for Americans were contrary to the usual practice accepted by most nations.[23] The State Department made no further reply, and the matter finally died in January 1921, when the commission concluded its hearings.

The commission's declared purpose was to ascertain the truth about what was happening in Ireland. In the words of acting chairman Frederic C. Howe at the opening session, "It [the commission] plans to learn as nearly as possible just what the conditions in Ireland are and what brought them about. It plans to conduct a series of public hearings in Washington. It will hear witnesses who present themselves representing English and Irish opinion."[24] In order to do this, the commission had invited both Irish and British leaders to send spokesmen to testify. British authorities had decided not to participate. The Irish mission in the United States said that, while it approved of the idea, it could not in a time of war single out private citizens, for fear of British reprisals. The commission then simply sent invitations to a large number of people in Ireland and the United States who had either figured in or been affected by the fighting in Ireland. Ostensibly for their protection, the Irish mission requested that all witnesses receive legal counsel, and the commission provided Frank P. Walsh and Basil M. Manly of the American Commission on Irish Independence, assisted by Dudley Field Malone and Michael Francis Doyle. These attorneys both advised the witnesses and asked them questions of the witnesses to help them prepare their responses, along with the commissioners themselves. Whatever the objectivity of the commission's eight members, the questions and comments of Walsh, Manly, Malone, or Doyle—whose partisanship was never denied—certainly influenced the resulting testimony.[25]

☘

The commission held its first hearings at the LaFayette Hotel in Washington, DC, on 18–19 November 1920. There was some anxiety about what would transpire. Although a good number of people had been invited to testify, it was not certain whether anyone would appear. With newspaper reporters expected in large numbers, a lack of witnesses would have been a public-relations disaster. In fact, to the great relief of the commission's members, two Irishmen and six Americans with experiences in Ireland presented themselves. Denis Morgan, chairman of the urban council of Thurles, told the commission of acts committed in his community by Crown forces, relating how he and his family had been subjected to great personal danger and indignities as his house was riddled with bullets and he was subsequently arrested and held in England. He reported that the local creameries had been destroyed, and that the town hall in the neighboring Templemore was burned.[26] On the second day, John Derham, town councillor of Balbriggan, described the British reprisals, which resulted in the burning of his house and pub. "It was burned to the ground, and not a vestige left," he reported. A portion of the village, including the homes of his neighbor and some twenty others, were destroyed on 21 September. Derham also described the destruction of the textile factory: the mill was "totally destroyed; one hundred thousand pounds loss," he said. "It is owned in London. The manager is an Englishman. There is nothing in a political line there."[27] Two other important witnesses were Francis Hackett and his wife, Signe Toksvig, both of whom were editors of the progressive journal the *New Republic*. Hackett had also written about conditions in Ireland for the *New York World* and was the author of *Ireland: A Study in Nationalism*. The Hacketts, who had visited Ireland, provided grim reports of British attempts to suppress the nationalist movement. Four other Americans who had traveled in Ireland and lived with relatives there gave accounts of dangerous and unpleasant encounters with British authorities in the Irish countryside. All together, these testimonies lent credibility to the work of the commission. Publicity officer Harold Kellock held a successful press conference for about two hundred Washington reporters.[28] The first hearings were a triumph (see appendix 3).

The second hearings, which were held on 8–10 December 1920, were certainly among the most important of the commission's efforts and in some ways the most spectacular. The principal witnesses were Muriel MacSwiney and Mary MacSwiney, the widow and sister, respectively, of the late lord mayor of Cork. In circumstances that had been well reported by the American press, Terence MacSwiney had died on 25 October as the result of a seventy-four-day hunger strike in protest of his arrest by British authorities. The two young women made an appealing spectacle as they described Terence MacSwiney's personality and long vigil. Mary MacSwiney spoke for one entire session and part of a second, giving her view of Irish history and the struggle to preserve Irish nationalism and Irish Catholicism in the face of British oppression, and making the point that the executions of the 1916 rebels had made the country "consciously" republican.[29] Muriel MacSwiney told of her husband's several arrests and then the ordeal of the hunger strike that led to his death. She had accompanied him at his court-martial and kept a vigil with him in hospital in London. Villard recalled vividly in his memoirs the dramatic impression she made: "Muriel MacSwiney, the Lord Mayor's widow, turned out to be the ideal person for the role she was called upon to play. No one could have been more charming or more tactful or quicker to understand the situation. Young, slim, pretty, with lovely gray eyes, dressed in deep mourning, she was greeted at the steamer by a committee representing *The Nation* and the commission and escorted by a procession of 10,000 people to the St. Regis Hotel."[30]

Muriel MacSwiney also spoke of her husband's periodic arrests for nationalist activities during their courtship, before the 1916 Rising. In fact, the MacSwineys had been married while Terence was in an internment camp in England, in June 1917. Released later in the year, he was again in prison when elected to the Dáil in the 1918 general election. Free for about a year, he was elected lord mayor of Cork following the assassination of Thomas MacCurtain in March 1920. Arrested in August 1920, he went on the hunger strike that led to his death at Brixton Prison in October. She had only half an hour with him before he died.

"I think he may have known me that day, because he smiled a little bit when I kissed him. I do not know, but I think he did," she recounted. "And so I did not see my husband again until after his death."[31]

Four other witnesses were former members of the Royal Irish Constabulary. They told lurid stories of the escalation of the campaign to destroy the Sinn Féin Party and the nationalist movement. Each speaker had his own experiences about the decline of the constabulary, the disillusion of the old members, and the great alienation that resulted from the enlistment of Englishmen, many of them ex-soldiers, on the force—the so-called "Black and Tans."[32] The picture that emerged was one of government-sponsored reprisals and officially sanctioned brigandage. Underscoring that very point, the sensational news came of the burning and destruction of parts of the business district of Cork on 11 December by British Army units. Nothing could have pushed the activities of the commission into newspaper headlines more effectively. The *New York Times*'s front page on 13 December read: "Cork Swept by Incendiary Fires; Property Loss Estimate, $15,000,000.[33] Nevertheless, the testimony of the MacSwineys and the Irish policemen had certainly been impactful. Muriel MacSwiney became a major spokesperson in the United States for an Irish republic, and Mary MacSwiney even had a meeting with Warren G. Harding.

Two more sets of hearings were held in December. Lawrence Ginnell, a former member of Parliament and then a member of the Dáil, told the commission how years of British rule in Ireland had been disastrous for the country. Susanna Walsh and Anna Walsh described in detail one of the most infamous incidents in the Anglo-Irish War, when they saw their brother-in-law Thomas MacCurtain, the late lord mayor of Cork, die before their very eyes after gunmen, presumed to be British soldiers, had broken into his house in the middle of the night of 20 March 1920 and shot him. The first actual English witnesses were women: Annot Erskine Robinson and Ellen C. Wilkinson, representatives of the British Branch of the Women's International League. They had originally been denied visas by the US consul in Manchester, who told them, "We are not encouraging inquiries in America into the state of affairs in Ireland." After an overnight trip to the consulate general in London, they obtained their visas. They told the commission about the political, economic, and social relationship of Ireland to the rest of the United Kingdom and argued that, for economic reasons, it was contrary to the interests of the establishment in Britain to allow Ireland to control its own affairs. Robinson toured Belfast and Lisburn and witnessed the destruction caused by the sectarian riots at the Belfast shipyards and the Lisburn linen mills. Of Lisburn she said, "I should say that one house out of three had been destroyed. Some of them were simply heaps of stone, and from other houses the walls and windows were gone. The picture was one of absolute devastation. It reminded me of pictures I had seen of the northern district of France after the German invasion."[34]

Wilkinson traveled with two Quakers through parts of southern Ireland, visiting Dublin, Limerick, Galway, Tuam, the coast of County Clare, Mallow, and Cork. She reported seeing many burned-out farms and creameries, and, when she was in Cork City in mid-October, she witnessed British troops shooting at buildings indiscriminately after dark. Wilkinson made caustic remarks about the failure of either the British Red Cross or the American Red Cross to come to Ireland's aid, and she also submitted a report on conditions in Ireland prepared by the Women's International League, which concluded, "This state of affairs can lead only to the economic ruin of Ireland and great economic injury to Great Britain; to a still more disastrous moral injury to Great Britain and to her reputation in all the world." The report urged that a truce be established, British troops withdrawn, Irish prisoners released, and the country "placed in the hands of Irish local elected bodies, thus creating conditions under which Irish people may determine their own form of government."[35] Ruth Russell, an American who had traveled to Ireland writing for the *Chicago Daily News*, similarly described the nature of the Anglo-Irish conflict in terms of class and economic divisions. Paul J. Furnas, who had been an American delegate to the World Congress of Friends, gave to the commission a damning report, widely circulated in Britain, on conditions in Ireland drafted by a three-man committee headed by John H. Barlow, sent by the London Yearly Meeting of the Society of Friends, condemning the British government's policy in Ireland and urging that the British public recognize that only the Irish could govern themselves. Several other Americans who had recently returned from visiting family in Ireland told of their misadventures as well.[36]

Lord mayor of Cork Donal O'Callaghan, who succeeded MacSwiney, was the highlight of the fifth hearing on 13 and 14 January 1921. O'Callaghan had been in the newspapers even before he addressed the commission. He left Ireland as a stowaway with no passport and when he arrived at Newport News, Virginia, was denied entry to the United States. He claimed status as a seaman, which would allow him a period of time to remain there, during which he could theoretically sign on a new ship. Since his name did not appear on the crew list and he had told the immigration authorities that his employment was lord mayor of Cork, the "seaman" device was a bit transparent.[37] Nevertheless, it did allow him to address the commission and several other groups in the United States, where he was able to describe in great detail the dimensions of the war in County Cork. He outlined the extent to which elected officials in Cork were harassed and intimidated by both army troops and the Black and Tans; after the murder of lord mayor Thomas MacCurtain in March 1920, he and other officials never slept in their own homes. "I sleep in a different place each night," he told the commissioners, although his duties required his "being in the city hall and being in the court house" by day.[38] O'Callaghan said his own house was raided by Crown forces eight times. The regular night raids eventually led to the spectacular burning of sections of Cork City on 12 December 1920. After the newspaper coverage of the fire just a month before, he was a spectacular witness. "About nine o'clock military cars drove through the town very wildly and recklessly and a number of shots were fired," driving people off the streets, he said. Fires broke out in various parts of the city, destroying the town hall, the Carnegie Library, and many commercial buildings. The fire brigade, attempting to put out the fires, "were fired upon that night," he reported, and their "hose was cut in one case."[39] The lord mayor estimated that the damages to Cork City were between three and four million pounds. O'Callaghan also brought with him a number of sworn statements from people describing incidents of harassment, destruction, or injury caused by Crown forces. As with the MacSwineys, O'Callaghan achieved something of celebrity status in his travels and public appearances in the United States, which certainly did not hurt the commission.

A Galway merchant and five other Americans also testified at this session. Four of the Americans were merchant seamen who had no connections or interests in Ireland; their ship had simply put in at what was then called Queenstown, and they had gone ashore for a few hours' leave. They all reported harassment and injury at the hands of British soldiers in Cork. Not only did they claim to have been beaten and robbed, but that they had been singled out because they were Americans. The fifth American was Peter J. MacSwiney, the brother of the late Terrence MacSwiney, who confirmed the sailors' accounts and related his own experiences of harassment by soldiers and police while visiting in Cork.[40]

The sixth hearings, on 19 and 21 January 1921, were the commission's last. Frank Dempsey, chairman of the urban council of Mallow, described living conditions in the existing state of war, and J. L. Fawsitt, the so-called consul general of the Irish Republic in New York, gave a general account of the effects of British policy in Ireland over the past several generations, as did Louie Bennett, secretary of the Irish Branch of the Women's International League, and Caroline Townshend, an Anglo-Irish woman who was an officer of the Gaelic League.[41] Much of the value of this testimony was in the recounting of the witnesses' personal experiences in the conflict in Ireland, much of it focused on the personal suffering or injury they endured or observed. However, there were also detailed descriptions of the long struggle for Irish self-government, the betrayal of home rule by successive British governments, the intransigence of Ulster Unionism, the political success of Sinn Féin in elections across the country, the wide acceptance of the workings of the Dáil Éireann government, and the inexcusable and senseless violence of the Black and Tan forces of the British government, particularly in destroying sources of income, such as creameries. This testimony was a burning indictment of the British government's attempts to suppress the political independence claimed by the Irish people.

With the hearings over, the commission turned to producing its two reports for public information. In fact, widespread accounts of the commission's activities had appeared in American newspapers during the autumn of 1920 and January 1921, and especially in the pages of the *Nation*, which also published transcripts of the testimony in weekly installments.[42] Chairman L. Hollingsworth Wood set to work writing a draft of the report. According to Patrick McCartan, this draft became a long discourse on Irish history and not the kind of evidence-based document that was required. In his memoirs, McCartan suggests that Maloney wrote the report largely by himself, and that this was accepted by the other commission members; certainly, it was a comprehensive statement of their efforts and the problems they had overcome. It presented a short history of the Irish question, described the nature of British forces in Ireland, and outlined the effects of their efforts to suppress the nationalist movement, and it included many pictures of destroyed buildings in Ireland, some correspondence of the commission, and assorted other documents. *The American Commission on Conditions in Ireland: Interim Report* was published in late March 1921 in cooperation with the Benjamin Franklin Bureau, the Dáil Éireann's information agency in the United States. The publication was subsidized by Irish funds in both America and Britain and either sold almost at cost or distributed free. Some three thousand copies were also distributed in France, Belgium, and Switzerland, where much was made of it in the newspapers.[43]

The "Conclusions" section of the *Interim Report* was the most important part of the document, and it was there that the commission made an unequivocal judgment about the situation in Ireland. It declared, "We find that the Irish people are deprived of the protection of British law, to which they would be entitled as subjects of the British King. They are likewise deprived of the moral protection granted by international law, to which they would be entitled as belligerents. They are at the mercy of Imperial British forces which, acting contrary both to all law and to all standards of human conduct, have instituted in Ireland a 'terror.'"[44] The commission lists seven areas in which British policy and military action created damage, terror, and loss of life in Ireland, going on to state specifically that the British government had placed forces in Ireland numbering at least 78,000 men, many of whom were inexperienced and uncontrollable; that these forces had been responsible for widespread destruction of both private dwellings and places of employment; that Crown authorities had on the basis of military proclamations carried out reprisals on individuals and communities; that this "terror" had failed to "re-establish Imperial British civil government in Ireland"; and that, despite all of this effort by the British government, "[the] majority of the Irish people having sanctioned by ballot the Irish Republic, give their allegiance to it, pay taxes to it, and respect the decisions of its courts and of its civil officials."[45]

This was, of course, a ringing denunciation of British policy in Ireland. Whatever the original commitment of the founders of the commission to its "non-partisan and non-political character," the report pulled no punches as to whom it regarded as responsible for conditions in Ireland. Both Villard and the text itself lamented that it had not been possible to obtain any statements or commentary representing the British government's position, nor had a delegation from the commission been allowed to go to Ireland. When Hollingsworth Wood attempted to deliver a copy of the report to President Harding personally, the State Department advised against a meeting and instructed Wood to simply send a copy to the White House.

The British government issued a rebuttal on the very day the *Interim Report* was released, which Ambassador Geddes said successfully refuted the claims of outrage in Ireland. The *New York Times* quoted the embassy as asserting that the report and its conclusions were "based entirely on the evidence of *ex parte* statements by persons admittedly holding extreme views." The report, the embassy held, painted a picture of Ireland devastated by ruthless and uncontrollable British forces, whereas the country was "the most prosperous part of the United Kingdom and probably the whole of Europe."[46] However, questions also were raised in parliament by the old Irish Parliamentary Party MP, T. P. O'Connor, who asked if the government had taken account of the charge in the *Interim Report* that "British forces in Ireland have indiscriminately killed innocent men, women, and children" and engaged in the wanton destruction of property. Sir Charles Henry, answering for the Irish chief secretary, dismissed the report, as did Geddes, as having been compiled by people of "extreme views," and that the commission had "no official character" and therefore needed no official response from the government.[47] The liberal journal the *New Republic* acknowledged the British complaint that the hearings had been one-sided, but it asserted that "there is also no doubt in the mind of any one who has followed Irish events closely that the commission's bill of indictment against British military occupation is in general a true one," concluding that until the troops were withdrawn there would be no hope of peace.[48] In the face of ongoing criticism, the *Nation* declared that "its editors believe that it has been a public service to bring out the facts and to concentrate the responsibility" for the outrages in Ireland. Commenting on the report, Villard, justifying the intervention into the Irish conflict, referred to the conclusions of the former editor of the *London Daily News*, A. G. Gardiner, "that there are three parties to the Irish problem, the Irish, the English, and the Americans."[49] Villard shared with Norman Thomas that the report was "a most excellent piece of work," and he was confident "it will stand better and better as time passes." Jane Addams later claimed that the *Interim Report* was "never contradicted."[50]

The final report, *Evidence on Conditions in Ireland*, was published in July 1921. Unlike the *Interim Report*, this volume made no attempt to offer any conclusions or judgment about the events of the Anglo-Irish conflict. The transcripts of witness statements would speak for themselves. Assembled by Albert Coyle, the reporter to the commission, *Evidence on Conditions in Ireland* ran to over one thousand pages, consisting almost entirely of the transcriptions of witness testimony, together with a number of documents and papers submitted by people and organizations that could not attend. *Evidence on Conditions in Ireland* stands as a massive record of personal accounts by both civic officials and private citizens about the impact of the war in Ireland.

In some respects, the publication of the final report was anticlimactic. The commission had moved too slowly and ponderously; events in the spring and summer of 1921 rushed ahead of the testimony about the experiences of the previous summer. Lloyd George and de Valera had begun talks by the time the final report was ready for the public. The bad timing of its publication exacerbated the commission's financial problems. The *Nation* had been separate from the commission, but Villard had not wanted to lose touch altogether; the journal printed transcripts of the hearings, for instance, with the commission to pay the cost of printing. Villard sent urgent letters to chairman L. Hollingsworth Wood, demanding that the bills be paid. Wood argued that the publicity of the commission's work should have stimulated The *Nation*'s sales sufficiently to cover the costs. Villard insisted that the reverse was true, in part because of Wood's insistence that the relevant issues be printed in numbers larger than usual.[51] By May 1921, Wood wrote to Frank P. Walsh, chairman of the American Commission in Irish Independence, telling him of the commission's plight: current printing bills amounted to $1,900, and the commission had only $5000 in the bank. Maloney had previously lent some $10,000 of his own savings and could not be approached for more money. Wood feared the sale of the *Interim Report* would probably not cover its costs, because the Benjamin Franklin Bureau had, without reimbursing the commission, published a special issue that it distributed for free.[52]

There were other problems as well. The commission had stirred up a hornet's nest of controversy that dated right back to its inception. Senator John Sharp Williams of Mississippi was indignant at having been asked to participate on the Committee of One Hundred Fifty, while James Brown Scott of the Carnegie Endowment for International Peace refused to interrupt his vacation. Others such as W. A. Neilson, the president of Smith College, resigned from the committee because he felt that without "a fair distribution of witnesses," the original objectives of the commission could not be achieved.[53] To the complaint that the witnesses were all pro-Irish, Villard responded that there had been ample opportunity for the British argument to be made, but no one came forth. Much of the criticism was directed at Villard; indeed, the public generally referred to it as "Villard's Commission" or "The *Nation*'s Commission," rather than by its proper name, which resulted in Villard receiving a fair amount of criticism and abusive mail questioning his right to initiate an investigation into the domestic affairs of a former ally, or the capacity of a private body such as the commission to conduct an objective investigation. Irving Winslow, secretary of the Anti-Imperialist League, of which Villard was a founding member, wrote, "The wicked effect of the diatribe called a 'Report' is however leavened by the audacious over-reaching extravagance."[54] The *New York Times* quoted his defense of these criticisms: "Those of us here who have been most warmly urging an early solution of the Irish trouble do so primarily because we are interested in keeping the peace between England and the United States."[55] The *Nation* also published the report of the British Labor Party's investigation into conditions in Ireland, and pointed out that these British criticisms of the government's Irish policy were even stronger than those of the American commission. Villard's biographer, Michael Wreszin, notes that these were just the sorts of issues this outspoken liberal enjoyed. To Villard's dismay, however, protest over The *Nation*'s involvement resulted in many canceled subscriptions. In fact, Villard commented, "our report had a much better reception in England than it did here."[56]

Even the Irish American community was not altogether pleased. The anti–de Valera faction in the United States, led by the newspaper The *Gaelic American*, condescendingly referred to it as "Captain Maloney's Commission" and said that not only did the very people involved "preclude . . . the possibility of any really effective work being done," but also that the commission was merely a device to divert public attention away from the tragic split in the Irish American nationalist movement, which may in fact have been true.[57] The *Irish World* had little good itself to say about the commission. On the other hand, John D. Moore, the former national secretary of the FOIF, wrote dismissing the criticism of The *Gaelic American* and The *Irish World* and assured Villard, "The investigation will do no end of good."[58] The combination of financial problems and the general controversy created difficulties that the commission had not foreseen the previous September. In May 1921, writing about Villard, Maloney, and himself, L. Hollingsworth Wood complained to Frank P. Walsh that "altogether the three main movers in this enterprise are feeling pretty unhappy."[59] Villard confided to Jane Addams that he was "utterly sick about it" and sorry that he had asked her to serve on the commission.[60] Certainly Villard was shocked by the strong criticism he received from his non-Irish readers.

Nevertheless, the work of the commission stands out as a major effort to keep the calamities in Ireland before the public eye in late 1920 and early 1921. The importance of the parallel between the so-called Bryce Commission on Atrocities in Belgium and the American Commission on Conditions in Ireland cannot be emphasized too strongly as a factor in public opinion. Nor should it be overlooked that, prior to the formation of the Committee of One Hundred Fifty, very few Americans who were not of Irish descent had lent their names or talents to any activities in Ireland (other than those making periodic statements for political purpose). The Committee of One Hundred Fifty enlisted the support of a distinguished group of Americans from across the country. Similarly, the eight members of the commission itself were people of stature in American public life. One hundred years, later several names are still remembered because of their influence in shaping the liberal-progressive tradition in twentieth-century America. That the political composition of the commission was distinctly liberal or left-of-center makes it no less important. Certainly the British government could not avoid the fact that Irish matters were jeopardizing relations with the United States; at the British cabinet meeting on Christmas Eve, 1920, after just four sets of hearings by the American Commission on Conditions in Ireland, the danger was noted that "further compromising incidents [in Ireland] . . . might even attain such gravity as to bring on us the intervention of the United States of America."[61] The situation looked no better a month later, when Lloyd George commented to Bonar Law that the ambassador to the United States had sent "a most gloomy account of the situation in America and," Lloyd George went on to say, "in the interests of peace with America I think we ought to see De Valera and try to get a settlement."[62] Bonar Law was less convinced, and the government's decision to open talks with de Valera was months away, but clearly the prime minister was alarmed that the deteriorating situation in Ireland was seriously damaging Britain's public image . By May, Winston Churchill seemed to agree with the prime minister, commenting in a cabinet meeting that "we are getting an odious reputation; poisoning our relations with the United States."[63] Jane Addams was convinced that the commission's work was helping to shape events: "We think that the report of our Commission has been instrumental in bringing about a change of sentiment among the English themselves."[64]

With the passage of time, Villard came to believe that the commission's efforts to expose to America the cruel and inexcusable actions of British forces in Ireland were necessary and justified. Norman Thomas wrote to Villard some years later that he thought the work of the commission had a "useful part in getting [the] Black and Tans out of Ireland."[65] In his memoirs, Villard quotes at length from a letter from Albert Shaw, editor of the *Review of Reviews* and after whom the Shaw Lectures on Diplomatic History at John Hopkins were named, in which Shaw said to Villard, "It took rare courage to assume a sponsorship for an organized American inquiry into the conditions prevailing in Ireland." The work of the commission "turned the scales," and, as a result, Shaw concluded, "Mr. Lloyd George realized that the time had come for a truce to be followed by an arrangement far more favorable to Ireland than had been proposed in the home rule programs of Parnell and Gladstone."[66] These were stirring affirmations of the wisdom of Villard's willingness to rise above the criticism and work to initiate the American Commission on Conditions in Ireland. Villard was prepared to accept public praise for the commission's efforts. Historians today would argue that several elements were at play prompting Lloyd George to seek a truce, but Villard, and all those involved in the commission, could take satisfaction in the fact that their work had been vindicated and made a significant contribution to ending the Anglo-Irish War.

6

American Aid for Ireland, 1920–1922

By 1920 the Anglo-Irish War had assumed dramatic proportions. Stories about the exploits of British forces Black and Tans appeared regularly in the press. These accounts prompted the creation of the American Commission on Conditions in Ireland, with the result that by late November 1920 witnesses began testifying at public hearings. Such incidents as the destruction of Balbriggan and the burning of Cork stirred the concern that parts of Ireland were suffering ravages of war comparable to what Belgium and France had recently endured. The response of the Irish American community—and the American public generally—was to offer assistance. Eventually, the newly created American Committee for Relief in Ireland raised over five million dollars, rivaling the success of the Dáil bond certificate campaign itself. Once again the American government became involved in Irish problems.

Earlier efforts had been made to provide relief after the 1916 Rising. A large fundraising bazaar in New York in October 1916 and the Irish Relief Fund and the Irish Volunteer Dependents' Fund assisted in that crisis. Now, in December 1920, the Irish-American Club of Philadelphia sent to Cork a ship loaded with 1,700 tons of food and clothing. The two US organizations that usually responded to disasters and famines were the Quakers and the American Red Cross; as early as mid-November, the London Quakers cabled an appeal to Clarence E. Pickett, the executive secretary of the Board of Young Friends Activities in the United States: "Meeting Sufferings Committee undertaking relief work in Ireland[.] Would welcome American cooperation."[1] Pickett, who had been in London in the summer and knew about the growing concern over the scale of distress and destruction in Ireland, wrote in turn to James A. Norton, one of the officers of the American Friends Service Committee, suggesting that the American committee was the appropriate body to engage in any American Quaker relief in Ireland. Pickett was aware of the potential political difficulties—the Irish problem has "a political color to it for Americans," as he put it—but he thought there was a potential for good: that "it could be done by the Service Committee in such a way that there would be no undue hindrance to the effect of the work on that account."[2] Norton replied that the Service Committee would consult with the London Quakers, but he cautioned, the Service Committee was presently committed to work in Germany, Austria, Serbia, Poland, and Russia. Pickett urged that this opportunity should not be missed. As a nonpolitical organization, he said, "we can really figure as an agency of reconciliation in Ireland."[3] To what extent the American Quakers might have facilitated any sort of reconciliation or peace settlement in Ireland is impossible to say.

The destruction of part of Cork City on the evening of 11 December 1920, by Crown forces accentuated the urgency of the situation. On 14 December, Irish Quakers began inquiring about aid. James G. Douglas, a prominent businessman and Dublin Friend, contacted L. Hollingsworth Wood—a New York lawyer, member of the American Friends Service Committee, and, significantly, chairman of the American Commission for Conditions in Ireland—about the possibility of relief from the United States. "English Friends commencing relief. Irish group assisting. Money required urgently, also some workers," he wrote.[4] Certainly the Dublin Friends were hopeful of American support, but the American Friends were increasingly wary of other relief efforts, which they felt had been recruiting Friends by trading on the Quakers' reputation. Executive secretary of the Service Committee Wilbur K. Thomas cabled John H. Barlow at Friends House in London on 29 December. Barlow had led a commission of English Friends to Ireland for two weeks in September and October and produced a scathing report about the destruction and suffering caused by the war. Thomas said that Irish Americans were "asking for Friends workers and support of [the] Friends Service Committee," and they were promising "large sums of money" for relief.[5] Thomas sought Barlow's advice. On 29 January 1921, Barlow replied: "Financial cooperation welcome[;] personal help doubtful."[6] In response to a query from the American Red Cross, the executive secretary of the American Friends Service Committee replied in late January 1921, "We have been contributing through our English and Irish Friends toward the relief of suffering for some time." Or, as Thomas put it to another Quaker: "Such funds that come to us earmarked for Ireland, we are turning over to the English Friends for their work, but we are not as yet at least making any special appeal for this work."[7] When Samuel Graveson wrote on behalf of the London Friends in March 1921 to chairman of the American Friends Service Committee Rufus M. Jones, urging that the American and English Quakers collaborate on a reconstruction project in Ireland, Jones replied, "It does not seem possible for Friends in America to do very much directly at present. Our money is pledged to work already arranged. We have not been able to secure any funds for this distinct purpose. If a way opens for us to assist we shall be glad to do so."[8] The American Friends, unlike their Irish and English counterparts, were not able to become officially involved, although they were fully committed to relief operations in eastern Europe in 1920 and 1921.

When Cork City was burned the night of 11 December 1920, lord mayor Donal O'Callaghan cabled the American Red Cross, "Urgently request help [from] American Red Cross [to] relieve distress consequent on burning and sacking of City of Cork."[9] Actually, the Red Cross had received a number of US appeals for aid to Ireland, but this was the first from someone of authority in Ireland itself. Red Cross national director Livingston Ferrand, sensitive to the political implications of American relief, consulted with the State Department, the British embassy, and the British Red Cross. The State Department warned of the danger of "the Red Cross involving America in a national controversy foreign to our interests." On the basis of a report from the British Red Cross director that no one was without shelter as a result of the destruction, replies to inquiries were that no action could be taken.[10] This drew sharp comments from Irish American spokespersons such as Mrs. Peter Golden of the Irish Progressive League, who complained that the American Red Cross had not been so inhibited in Cuba, Belgium, or Serbia. The *Nation* was equally scornful of the caution of the Red Cross: "But when Cork lies prey to the flames, Irish villages by the dozen are laid waste, and the Bishop of Cork appeals to the American Red Cross for help, our Red Cross pauses gravely and politely to inquire of the British Red Cross whether, in its opinion, the appeal of the Irish bishop should be heeded."[11] The journal also commented that Herbert Hoover had not sought German permission for relief in Belgium. Appeals to the secretary of state for advice were also turned aside. Officialdom could not be moved at this stage.

The remarkable Dr. W. M. J. A. Maloney ultimately set the relief operation in motion. His first attempts to organize a relief ship for Ireland in 1920 had not seemed very promising; he had earlier consulted with US Federal Food Commissioner Alfred W. McCann about putting together a large shipment of food and was told that the first shipload to Belgium during the war had cost $247,000.[12] To raise the necessary funds would take careful organization. The *Nation*, which was fully engaged in the American Commission on Conditions in Ireland, observed that "help must soon be sent from America for the wounded, the destitute, and the suffering," and concluded, prophetically, that a new organization must be created to accomplish this.[13] Maloney, according to Patrick McCartan, organized a dinner at the Commodore Hotel in New York on 4 December 1920, at which one of the guests, New York lawyer (and former judge in the Philippines) Richard Campbell noted that California oil millionaire Edward L. Doheny had come into town that very day. Neither Campbell nor Maloney knew Doheny, but they asked senator David I. Walsh, a member of the American Commission on Conditions in Ireland, to arrange a meeting with Doheny, which he did. The next morning, at the meeting, Doheny, a generous philanthropist and recently elected president of de Valera's new AARIR, wrote a check for $10,000 and agreed to underwrite the amount needed to send a fully loaded relief ship to Ireland.[14] This was a very promising beginning.

Maloney subsequently organized a luncheon at the Banker's Club of New York on 16 December, to broaden the base, and Doheny agreed to preside. Invitations were sent to a long list of prospective participants—businessmen, industrialists, and professionals, for the most part. The burning of Cork five days before guaranteed Maloney a sympathetic audience. Armed with this news and a cable from James G. Douglas to Hollingsworth Wood appealing for assistance ("English Friends commencing relief. Irish group assisting. Money required urgently, also some workers"), Maloney proposed that a national organization be created in the United States to raise money and to coordinate and direct relief in

Ireland. Both Doheny and Senator Walsh spoke strongly in support, and the guests enthusiastically accepted the new plans.[15] Herbert Hoover, then a private citizen but the celebrated administrator of relief in Belgium and eastern Europe during the war and soon to become secretary of commerce, replied to a cable that same day, "I shall be only too delighted to cooperate with them in any way possible and suggest that they should investigate the reports as to starvation among children in Ireland that we may take any measures necessary and possible."[16] Hoover's name was an important asset in building U.S. support for Irish relief.

By 29 December, the executive committee of the new American Committee for Relief in Ireland was made up of twenty-three distinguished Irish Americans, many of whom had attended the Banker's Club luncheon. The chairman was judge Morgan J. O'Brien, presiding justice of the Appellate Division of the New York State Supreme Court; the secretary was judge Richard Campbell, a New York lawyer; and the treasurer was John J. Pulleyn, president of the Emigrant Industrial Savings Bank and a director of the New York Life Insurance Company and the County Trust Company. Other members of the executive committee included senators James D. Phelan, David I. Walsh, and Thomas J. Walsh; bishop Michael J. Gallagher; as well as Thomas Fortune Ryan, Nicholas F. Brady, Edward L. Doheny, Lawrence Godkin, John Quinn, and L. Hollingsworth Wood, all of whom had been active in Irish affairs. They set to work immediately to make a national appeal for funds and to create a broadly based organization to collect them. Doheny advanced the committee $250,000 to get started. On 7 January 1921, Judge O'Brien, through Wood, cabled $25,000 to the trusted Dublin Quaker James G. Douglas, which was deposited in the Bank of Ireland.[17]

The creation of the organization was of crucial importance for reasons both of practical necessity and shrewd public relations. The enterprise was meant to parallel the vast civilian relief activities carried out during and after World War I, initially in Belgium, but subsequently throughout much of Eastern Europe and Asia Minor. Just two years after the war, the equation of British action in Ireland with German destruction in Belgium served as a very powerful public relations device. Thus, the relief operations would have the economic importance and humanitarian impact in Ireland that its organizers expected, but also political implications in America and Britain that they could only have hoped for.[18]

Maloney suggested that the committee send a delegation to investigate the actual conditions in Ireland and to see how relief operations could be most effectively handled. The committee approved his proposal and in January appointed a delegation of eight, several of whom were members of the Society of Friends with prior experience in European relief activities.

CLEMENS J. FRANCE

> The group was led by Clemens J. France, former executive secretary of the Port of Seattle and a brother of senator Joseph I. France, of Maryland, and Royal W. France, treasurer of the American Commission on Conditions in Ireland. France had served as an officer in the war.

R. BARCLAY SPICER

> The former head of the Friends Service Committee to the Baltic States and a member of the Friends Reconstruction Unit in France, Germany, Serbia, and Poland. Spicer had also been the editor of the *Friends Intelligencer* and chairman of the Extension Committee of the General Conference of Friends.

OREN B. WILBER

> Wilber was the owner of a dairy and creamery and a member of the New York Yearly Meeting of Friends who represented the American Friends Service Committee at the 1919 Conference of Friends in Dublin.

WILLIAM PRICE

> Price served as an advisor on architecture and building.

PHILIP W. FURNAS

> A housing expert, Furnas had served two years with the Friends Relief Unit in France.

JOHN C. BAKER

> Baker was a farm implement dealer who had served on the American Friends Unit in France in agricultural reconstruction.

WALTER C. LONGSTRETH

> Longstreth was a lawyer and settlement worker.

SAMUEL DUFF MCCOY

> McCoy was an author and journalist who had served with the American Red Cross and who functioned as the secretary to the delegation.

Altogether it was an able delegation, previously without Irish nationalist affiliation but closely identified with earlier relief work. Indeed, the public descriptions of the delegation focused on the Quaker persuasion of the several members, leading to protests from the American Friends Service Committee. Committee executive secretary Wilbur K. Thomas wrote to both the State Department and the American Red Cross to explain that the Society of Friends had "nothing to do with the organizing of this group [the American Committee for Relief in Ireland]," and that such involvement as it had with Irish relief was through the English Quakers.[19] The American Friends Service Committee feared that this new relief organization, whatever its claims, was dominated by an Irish Americans political agenda. Nevertheless, the delegation sailed on 29 January 1921, for England and Ireland, where talks began with the Friends relief committees in both countries and with the Irish White Cross.[20]

Led by Clemens J. France and Samuel Duff McCoy, the delegation went first to London, where they met and talked with both US ambassador John W. Davis and Irish chief secretary Sir Hamar Greenwood, who was skeptical and noncommittal about their relief projects. Arriving in Dublin on 12 February, the delegation followed the ambassador's advice and consulted with US consul Frederick T. F. Dumont, who took them to Dublin Castle to meet with Sir John Anderson, the undersecretary for Ireland, and General Sir Neville Macready, then commander in chief of British forces in Ireland. The delegation claimed to be nonpolitical and nonsectarian and stated that their purpose in Ireland was merely to provide American relief funds to "the men and women in Ireland who were in distress and, further, the [American] Committee had in view the carrying out of a program of industrial reconstruction." General Macready said he had no objection to any relief efforts in the peaceful parts of Ireland; however, any efforts in the areas of the country under martial law would be "in direct conflict with the policy of the British Government." In General Macready's words, he hoped to "bring these people to their senses."[21] Macready suggested that the delegation first go to Belfast and the north to examine conditions there, and he and Anderson would decide later about visits to other parts of the country. Consul Dumont also talked privately with

Anderson's assistants Mark Sturgis and A. W. "Andy" Cope about the "American Quaker Relief Mission," as they styled it. Sturgis concluded, "Properly guided they can do much good if they rebuild and feed and *do not give money*," and he also noted that for political purposes relief efforts would be "a good safety valve for American-Irish money, better than S[inn] F[éin] if we can prevent SF from capturing them" (emphasis in original). Several days later Sturgis observed, again in conversation with Dumont, that "the Quaker folk seem to be proceeding on the right lines but will want shepherding."[22] So Dublin Castle did not regard the delegation as entirely hostile.

The delegation made a productive tour of the north, meeting with a variety of people, including the military authorities. After nearly two weeks passed without any further word from Macready or Anderson, the delegation decided to proceed to Cork. Consul Dumont warned them that they traveled in Ireland at the pleasure of British authorities, but they reasoned that Macready had not specifically denied them permission. Once in Cork they met with the deputy lord mayor, with US consul Charles M. Hathaway Jr., and with General Sir Peter Strickland, the commanding officer in the martial law area. Strickland, surprisingly, proved to be most accommodating and gave the delegation permission to travel through parts of the area by car and raised no objection to the proposed efforts for commercial reconstruction and relief for distressed individuals.

When the delegation returned to Dublin, a meeting was arranged for 12 March with General Macready, Sir John Anderson, chief of staff brigadier general J. Brind, undersecretary for the Belfast area Sir Ernest Clark, Anderson's senior assistant Mark Sturgis, and several other officials. The delegation explained their assessment of the need for the reconstruction of commercial facilities that had been destroyed, resulting in widespread unemployment, which in turn created a need for personal relief. Macready and Anderson gave their "unqualified approval," yet expressed some reservations. As reported by the delegation, General Macready said

> he would have no objection to the Irish White Cross distributing such funds for the feeding of school children in Dublin and Cork; that he would have no objection to the distribution of such funds by the Irish White Cross

for reconstruction work in Balbriggan, which was the request made by the Archbishop of the diocese. He was quite frank, however, in stating that monies transmitted by the American Committee [for Relief in Ireland] to [James G.] Douglas and turned over to the White Cross, which were thereafter distributed to individuals in the martial law areas, would inevitably in his opinion go to the support of men and their dependents who were in active opposition to the British Government's military policy. He stated that if large sums were so distributed it was quite probable that the Crown forces would place a ban upon the operations of the Irish White Cross.[23]

Thus the delegation actually obtained conditional approval to distribute relief, but several objections remained. General Macready singled out one problem specifically: How could relief for individual suffering arising out of the conflict be separated from the possibility of subsidizing individuals active in the war or their family members? No solution was formulated. The other major problem was the Irish White Cross, which General Macready at one point described as "a Sinn Féin organization" that listed Michael Collins and Arthur Griffith among its officers. The delegation argued that the Irish White Cross was a broadly based organization that drew support from a representative mix of the Irish population, including many business and church leaders representing diverse political and religious views, a portion of whom might be expected to have nationalist sympathies. The British officials clearly had mixed feelings about the White Cross; while they did authorize it to disburse relief funds in some circumstances, they also maintained reservations about it. This was a delicate situation, given the possibility of British authorities obstructing the Irish White Cross, and, in his memoirs, James G. Douglas later noted that Clemons J. France served as a line of communication between the two. Douglas expressed great respect for the delegation and their effectiveness: "It has been my great privilege to form a friendship with Mr. France & Mr. McCoy & with my co-religionists who accompany them," he reported to Judge O'Brien. "I have the highest opinion of their ability & of their tact in what has been no easy task here," he wrote, adding that their report will be "of much value to you & to us."[24] In fact, by May an agreement was worked out between the lord mayor of Dublin and Anderson to allow a committee of Dublin businessmen to distribute relief. Sturgis recorded in his diary that rebuilding damaged facilities such as creameries and engaging businessmen would be "useful not only for re-establishing Irish industry but also on a job of this sort [business] men who otherwise might not meet have a chance to do so and to become coherent."[25] The *Report of the Irish White Cross* shows that in fact substantial amounts of relief monies were distributed in the martial law areas of Cork, Kerry, and Tipperary counties, although it does not indicate whether this was done before or after the truce that went into effect on 11 July 1921. Actually, the largest expenditures were in Belfast (£362,356) as the result of the disturbances there, compared to those in Cork (£170,389).[26]

Altogether, between 12 February and 31 March, the delegation visited ninety-five damaged or destroyed villages and towns and concluded that at least 600 structures needed substantial reconstruction. Based on their own observations and from conversations with people in the distressed areas, as well as from the advice of other relief organizations in Ireland, the delegation compiled a report for the American Committee for Relief in Ireland, estimating the type and amount of relief needed. In the judgment of the delegation, the destruction was widespread throughout the country: over 150 towns and many rural farms suffered damage. 90 percent of the affected buildings were private property, for which no resources for reconstruction were readily available. The greatest damage had been done to private dwellings, farms, shops, and creameries, in that order; of that group, the delegation concluded the most important to be creameries, 55 of which had been put out of operation, thus affecting some 15,000 dairy farmers and jeopardizing approximately £1,000,000 in annual income. The total value of property destroyed was estimated at $20,000,000 and the actual replacement costs at $25,000,000. In addition, the delegation reported that there were 25,000 families (or approximately 100,000 men, women, and children) out of work, without housing, or in some way destitute as a result of the country's conditions of war.[27]

With an assessment from their delegation in Ireland, the executive committee began building up a national organization in America and a campaign to raise money for the relief work. The committee turned to Herbert Hoover, the recognized expert on overseas war relief, who strongly recommended the appointment of Captain John F. Lucey, who had been one of his principal officers in Belgium. Lucey became the national director, with responsibility for proposing a blueprint for relief operations and organizing the fundraising drive. James A. Healy, who had also worked under Hoover, was made assistant secretary to the executive committee.[28] Between January and March, the committee set up the National Council, a large blue-ribbon committee composed of politicians, judges, educators, labor leaders, social workers, churchmen, and editors, as well as a large number of businessmen and professionals. A deliberate effort had been made to recruit people who were not of Irish extraction in order to validate the claim that the project was nonpartisan. Judge O'Brien became the chairman, which numbered 179 members, with some forty dignitaries appointed honorary vice-chairmen, including twenty state governors, as well as three former cabinet members: Josephus Daniels, Franklin K. Lane, and William G. McAdoo. Other distinguished members were General Charles G. Dawes, banker and future vice president; Henry Morgenthau, former ambassador to Turkey and critic of the Armenian massacres; Pierce Butler, Associate Justice of the Supreme Court; Patrick J. Hurley, later President Hoover's secretary of war; Alfred E. Smith, governor of New York and presidential candidate in 1928; James Cardinal Gibbons of Baltimore, who died shortly after appointment; William Cardinal O'Connell of Boston; two editors, William Randolph Hearst and Henry Watterson; Jane Addams, the leading social worker and member of the American Commission on Conditions in Ireland; David Starr Jordan, first president of Stanford University; Samuel Gompers, founder of the American Federation of Labor; Bernard Baruch, financier and advisor to presidents; and George M. Cohan, the popular songwriter.[29]

The executive committee built a second-tier structure to function at the state level and sent out instructions on putting together a state campaign. Elaborate organizations were established for each of the states, with special headquarters created for New York City and Washington, DC, and a special branch for the Canal Zone in Panama. The size of these organizations depended on the size of the state; typically, they included working officers, a state director, state treasurer, chairman of a publicity committee, and honorary members who were generally people of distinction in the state—sixteen state governors, nine senators, thirty bishops, several university presidents, war heroes, and public figures. Each state would also have representatives on the National Council. The chairman should be "an active, energetic, popular man with a capacity for leadership," and the vice-chairman the "most active woman in the district, who can attract to herself the services of most of the women living there."[30] They were to work with existing societies, such as the Knights of Columbus and the Ancient Order of Hibernians. The entire structure was put together between late December 1920 and March 1921 and all the more impressive because it not only raised the money—it stayed out of the tangled relationships of the other overtly political groups of Irish American nationalists. By early March Captain Lucey was able to report to Herbert Hoover that the organization "is shaping up along splendid lines, and the character of [the] men identified with [the] movement in all states justified your endorsing it."[31] The *Nation* editor Oswald Garrison Villard took some satisfaction that the work of the commission he had helped to initiate had contributed to the creation of a relief program. "It is gratifying to note that the American Committee for Relief in Ireland, which in a sense grew out of the interest aroused by *The Nation's* Commission, is hard at work and has already cabled large sums of money for immediate relief in Ireland," he wrote in early 1921.[32]

The executive committee launched the national campaign to raise funds launched on St. Patrick's Day, 17 March 1921. In fact, work had begun in January to publicize the need for relief and raise such funds as would enable the committee to start sending money to Ireland before the organization was complete. But on 17 March "A Summons to Service" was issued "To all Americans," calling for assistance and declaring that the people of Ireland were "suffering to a still greater degree even than Belgium during the great war. Property is being everywhere destroyed, houses and homes wrecked and devastated, and the aged and infirm, the women and children, are the chief sufferers. . . . We are not concerned with the causes of this suffering, our appeal is solely humanitarian, absolutely non-sectarian, and strictly non-political."[33] It was a ringing cry familiar to many Americans, who vividly remembered wartime relief operations.

Perhaps even more important than the appeal itself were the endorsements that accompanied it. The new president himself, Warren

G. Harding, gave strong support to the committee. On 26 March, he wrote to Judge O'Brien:

> I wish you the fullest measure of success not only in the great benefit performance at the Metropolitan Opera House on April 3rd, but in every worthy effort to make a becoming contribution on the part of our people to relieve distress among the women and children of Ireland. The people of America never will be deaf to the call for relief in behalf of suffering humanity, and the knowledge of distress in Ireland makes quick and deep appeal to the more fortunate of our own land where so many of our citizens trace kinship to the Emerald Isle.[34]

This was a powerful and unprecedented public endorsement from the president that no Irish organization had ever before received in the United States. The president's words, of course, were widely publicized in major newspapers, such as the *New York Times*. Other public figures, such as vice president Calvin Coolidge, secretary of commerce Herbert Hoover, and secretary of war J. Wingate Weeks, wrote the committee letters of encouragement. Cardinal Gibbons also made a passionate appeal: he wrote that "the sad plight of the destitute in Ireland appeals to our common sentiments of humanity," and it should move Americans all the more because of the contribution of people of Irish origins have made to the United States. "Let us pay some small portion of our debt to the Irish by practical sympathy in their sufferings," he said, urging the Catholic Church in America to be particularly helpful and generous.[35] All of this would have significant implications for Anglo-American relations; indeed, the British Embassy issued an immediate statement on 30 March, declaring that Ireland "has never been more prosperous," and that "widespread misapprehension appears to exist in regard to the necessity of raising funds from American sources for relief work in Ireland." Any possible need, the embassy insisted, could be supplied "from British sources."[36]

Although the report from the delegation that went to Ireland estimated that $25,000,000 would be needed to rebuild destroyed property, the executive committee of the American Committee for Relief in Ireland was not so optimistic as to think that it could raise such a large amount. They agreed upon the more modest figure of $10,000,000 as the target for the fund drive and together with the state committees arrived at the quotas that each state should meet in order to achieve the national goal. The final report of the American Committee for Relief in Ireland showed the quotas that were fixed, the actual amount raised, and the percentage of the target.[37]

The $10,000,000 target was, in fact, ambitious: the Irish Victory Fund organized in 1919 by the FOIF raised just over $1,000,000, and the Bond Certificate Drive of 1920 carried out for Dáil Éireann brought in $5,123,640.[38] However, the endorsements of President Harding, Vice President Coolidge, and Cardinal Gibbons helped enormously, and many celebrities lent their aid. On 3 April the famous Irish tenor John McCormack gave a benefit concert at the New York Metropolitan Opera House, followed by concerts in Boston and Chicago. Madison Square Garden was donated for a boxing match, raising over $65,000. On 26 May the National Committee held an extravagant fundraising dinner at New York's Hotel Astor , where the guest of honor was Laurence O'Neill, the lord mayor of Dublin. The US Catholic Church made its resources available, from the leaders of the hierarchy down to the parish guilds. With the patronage of the Most Rev. Patrick J. Hayes, the archbishop of New York, the archdiocese collected over $110,000. Bishop Michael J. Gallagher of Detroit (also president of the FOIF) urged members of his diocese, quoting Cardinal Gibbons, to give generously to the American Committee for Relief in Ireland. He compared Ireland's plight with that of Belgium during the war, noting that this relief effort was "entirely non-political" as well as "nonreligious, or rather all-religious," and was supported by Catholics, Protestants, and Jews. Numerous Irish American groups—such as the Ancient Order of Hibernians, the Knights of Columbus, the Friends of Irish Freedom, and the American Association for the Recognition of the Irish Republic—gave their support. Even the American Red Cross, which had earlier thought that conditions in Ireland did not warrant its intervention, contributed $100,000. Altogether, in several months, a very substantial $5,069,194 was raised. Ireland's "exiled children" had stepped forward, and they brought others with them. A reluctant British ambassador had to admit that "this particular form of propaganda has proved, in this country, more effective than any other hitherto attempted by the Irish agitators."[39]

Meanwhile, the committee hoped to work with the American Friends Service Committee, as Herbert Hoover had urged. In early March Judge Campbell and Captain Lucey met in Philadelphia with Wilbur K. Thomas, secretary of the Friends Service Committee, to discuss a working arrangement. Campbell and Lucey proposed that food, clothing, and funds should be distributed by "some form of joint control" under the direction of the American Committee for Relief in Ireland, the American Friends Service Committee, and Hoover himself. Lucey asked Hoover to contact Thomas and explain "just how you wish the alleviation of the acute suffering . . . should be carried out." Hoover, who had just days before been made secretary of commerce in the new Harding administration, replied cautiously, "I cannot however in justice to the large duties I have accepted in the government undertake direction of extended relief activities," although he assured Lucey, "I have every confidence in your ability to handle this problem."[40] This was not an arrangement that would satisfy the Quakers. Judge Morgan J. O'Brien, the chairman of the American Committee for Relief in Ireland, wrote immediately to Hoover, worried that joint action with the American Quakers might not materialize without the prestige of Hoover's participation. He reported that the "Friends are dissatisfied with [the] present arrangements," and urged Hoover "to suggest some plan of joint control of distribution to Mr. Wilbur K. Thomas" of the Friends Service Committee. Hoover praised the idea of relief for Ireland as an "American work of mercy," but he clearly would not involve himself while also secretary of commerce.[41] He did write the next day to secretary of state Charles Evans Hughes the next day, praising Lucey and the American Committee for Relief in Ireland and noting that he had suggested that the committee work with the American Quakers in distributing relief in Ireland: "I believe it would be in everybody's interest if the British authorities would be willing to accept the Friends Service Committee, the official organization of the Quaker Church doing relief work in almost every country in Europe and well-known to the British Government for their pure objectivity, and give them complete freedom of action in Ireland."[42] He asked Hughes to raise this with the British ambassador. A week later Hughes reported that he had discussed the matter informally with Sir Auckland Geddes, who was sure the authorities would be agreeable to the Friends Service Committee distributing relief in Ireland, although he thought they should work with the British Friends Service Committee. This remarkable concession seems to have never been followed up.

In the end, the executive committee decided not to undertake the distribution of the money in Ireland itself. L. Hollingsworth Wood, a member of the executive committee, contacted James G. Douglas to consult about distributing the relief money in an objective, nonpolitical manner. It was clear that there was no national organization in Ireland capable of carrying out this scale of relief; the British Red Cross could not as such function in Ireland while the British government was pursuing its military operations, and the American Red Cross was unwilling to become directly involved. A new organization had to be created. Therefore, by 15 January 1921, Douglas talked with lord mayor of Dublin Laurence O'Neill; George Russell, Æ from Plunkett House; and James McNeill, the brother of Eoin MacNeill, about how to proceed. The new organization, the Irish White Cross, came into being on 1 February, and people of distinction from all walks of life were invited to join its General Council: for example, leading nationalists Arthur Griffith and Michael Collins, as well as people outside the nationalist community such as Captain David Robinson, DSO, and Trinity College Dublin professor E. P. Culverwell. The support of the Irish churches was essential, so His Eminence Michael Cardinal Logue was made president, and the General Council included two Catholic archbishops, two Church of Ireland bishops, the Chief Rabbi of Ireland, the former president of the Irish Methodist Conference, six Irish Quakers, and one English Quaker. Douglas himself became a trustee and treasurer. In their initial statements, White Cross organizers declared that "the appeal which we make to-day is not made in the name of any section of a people, but in the name of humanity; no political distinctions exist in suffering, and none must exist in its relief."[43] Douglas confided in Hollingsworth Wood, commenting on the remarkable objectivity and representative character of the organization:

> The British authorities are furious because we have actually persuaded men who they call the "murder gang: to give their names in support of a body

including pacifists like myself and also including Protestant Bishops and Unionists. They give as an excuse for not making peace that they will not make peace with these men and it upsets their plans when English people see that Bishops and Quakers & others are willing to associate with them. Consequently as they dare not openly suppress the White Cross they are trying to break it up by sending untrue statements to the U.S.A. to frighten the U.S.A. committee.[44]

The American Committee for Relief in Ireland never wavered in their confidence in the Irish White Cross, although British denials of any need for relief in Ireland did find an audience in the United States.

The funds raised by the American Committee was sent through Douglas, who turned the money over to the White Cross. The disbursement of money in Ireland by the Irish White Cross was made in two categories indicated by the American Committee delegation in its report for March 1921: "Personal relief as a result of unemployment, injury, or loss of a bread winner," and "Reconstruction relief as a result of property damaged or destroyed." To these was added a third category, "Specialized forms of relief," which provided assistance for feeding school children, support for the Infant Welfare Society, hospital and hotel facilities, and various special circumstances. The general criterion used by the White Cross was that the suffering or damage be traceable in some way to the conflict in Ireland and that there be no other available source of assistance.[45] By these standards and through these categories the White Cross distributed approximately £1,351,069 of aid money across Ireland. Miscellaneous sources such as Canada, England, Scotland, the United States, and Pope Benedict XV accounted for £164,167 9s. 7d., of which the White Cross raised £62,643 19s. 2p. in Ireland itself. The total revenue of the Irish White Cross was £1,374,795 1s. 10d. However, the report of the Irish White Cross shows that the overwhelming proportion of its revenue came from the American Committee for Relief in Ireland.[46] Indeed, it could be said that the committee's contribution effectively financed the actual relief work of the White Cross, while the remaining contributions paid for the administrative costs. Funds were sent on a fairly regular basis from 7 January 1921, until the summer of 1922.[47]

The American Committee for Relief in Ireland was conspicuously successful. As a result, it influenced events beyond the reconstruction of creameries or the feeding of children. Perhaps it was unrealistic to think that relief operations on such a scale could avoid getting involved in politics. Of course there was the distinct possibility that its founders—especially people like Maloney—understood full well the political potential of this sort of operation, with large amounts of money subscribed from across the country and public support from the very highest sources. Letters of endorsement from President Harding and Secretary Hoover and others seemed to indicate something close to government support, rather than simply good wishes. British ambassador Sir Auckland Geddes, armed with views of the British government about conditions in Ireland, went to see the new secretary of state, Charles Evans Hughes, on 31 March 1921, to discuss Ireland and the position the administration intended to take toward it.[48] Hughes assured Geddes that "the president's attitude with regard to Ireland is that there must be no interference by the United States in a purely British internal affair," and that, to emphasize this position, the government had forbidden the marching of soldiers or sailors in St. Patrick's Day celebrations. Geddes reported to the Foreign Office that Hughes was "considerably perturbed" about the president's letter to the American Committee for Relief in Ireland, even though it had been prompted by humanitarian instincts. The ambassador himself had an opportunity to talk to the president a few days later in a long private meeting. President Harding said he was "sorry" that his letter was understood as "supporting the Sinn Féiners," and asked Geddes if there was anything he could do to be helpful in the situation. Geddes replied that he could make a clear public statement that the United States had "no political interest in Ireland" and would not support extremists. The president replied, "I could not say that politically, it would be impossible, but it is true."[49] Neither could Harding retract the letter, so, despite his private assurances to Geddes, the president's public position on relief in Ireland remained unchanged. Although Harding's assurances to Geddes would have been welcomed, the secretary of state would bring up the Irish question again.

The actual distribution of relief in Ireland also raised anxiety in the American government. When the delegation returned to the United States in April 1921, its secretary Samuel Duff McCoy met with G. Howland Shaw, the secretary of state's executive assistant. McCoy stated that the American committee had intended to carry out its relief efforts through the Irish White Cross, which was already functioning in Ireland. British authorities gave limited approval but raised objections because of the nationalist affiliations of some White Cross leaders, which threatened the reliability of the Irish White Cross being able to carry out the American Committee's relief projects. McCoy suggested to Shaw that the State Department distribute the funds the committee had raised, as it had done to some extent in Belgium during the war; this action by the department ought to satisfy British scruples about the impartiality of relief administration, he said, and would be justified by the Belgian precedent and by the interest and involvement of the president and the vice president, among other members of the administration. Shaw recommended that the secretary of state discuss the proposal with the British ambassador in order to ascertain the views of that government.[50]

The views of the British government about American relief were not favorable. In early April, Irish Parliamentary Party member T. P. O'Connor queried Parliament whether in view of the destruction of parts of Cork City and the "relief of distress," as he put, "to which, among others, President Harding has contributed," the British ambassador in Washington would be asked to correct or withdraw his statements that there was no need for relief in Ireland. Sir Charles Henry, answering for the Irish chief secretary, reiterated that there was no need for relief because Ireland "has never been more prosperous than at the present time." He went on to say that any disturbance "was directly due to Sinn Fein rebellion." These, he said, were "self-made grievances for American consumption."[51] Sir Auckland Geddes in Washington, who had followed the progress of the American Committee for Irish Relief with growing concern, stated boldly that the "situation here with regard to Irish affairs is assuming an aspect which is in my judgment more menacing than it has been in my experience of this country."[52] Secretary Hughes and Geddes had talked on 4 and 5 May, and although Hughes made no aide-mémoire of his conversations, it is possible to get a reasonably clear picture of what transpired from Geddes's cable to the Foreign Office, which took the form of an unofficial query about possible British reaction to McCoy's proposal. Geddes, noting all the public figures who had lent their names to the relief effort, observed that "now that these distinguished persons have caused money to be collected and an immense sentimental interest in helping women and children in Ireland to be created, they are somewhat at a loss to know what to do next." Thus, something of a political need to distribute relief funds had been created, the circumstances of which would result in a contest between American public opinion and British sovereignty in Ireland. In any such contest, Geddes asserted, the Irish nationalist leaders would be the winners. The State Department was caught in the middle, having previously maintained that "Ireland and Irish questions are an integral part of an internal question of [the] United Kingdom." However, "on the other hand to refuse to move is to bring on the heads of the government the wrath not only of the Irish, but of all, and they are many, who have subscribed to the fund under the impression that [the] president and vice-president, when they endorsed [the] appeal, knew what they were talking about."[53]

Ambassador Geddes saw three clear dangers: first, if the State Department did nothing it would become the focus of all the anti-British and the pro-Irish elements in the United States, and they would be likely to demand and get the resignation of Hughes; second, the department might officially make the proposal to distribute the relief, only to be refused by the British government, in which case Anglo-American relations would be gravely threatened; and, third, the department might make the proposals and have them accepted by the British government, in which case Britain would have surrendered a considerable degree of sovereignty in Ireland and placed herself on what would inevitably become a collision course with the United States. Geddes concluded that the immediate anti-British reaction to either of the first two alternatives would be serious, reporting that the "secretary of state seems to believe that if there is opposition to [the] proposals of [the] American Committee for Relief in Ireland a majority will be found in both houses of Congress in favor of recognition of an Irish republic." Geddes saw no really satisfactory solution to such a nightmarish dilemma and advised the Foreign Office to refuse to discuss the question of relief officially with the department, but to open talks directly with the American Committee for Relief in Ireland, thus taking the topic off the level of state-to-state negotiations and allowing the situation to be managed by some reliable group like the British Red Cross.[54]

Sir Auckland Geddes's three cables were circulated to the cabinet, and on 9 May foreign secretary Lord Curzon submitted a memorandum, which was to be the basis of cabinet talks the following day, about how the government should respond. After consulting with the Lord Lieutenant in Ireland and the Irish chief secretary, Curzon asserted that "the American proposal is in the main political in character, constitutes an unwarrantable interference with the government of a foreign state, would be indignantly rejected had it been made in analogous circumstances to the American government, and ought to be firmly though politely refused."[55] The cabinet agreed, authorized Curzon to send his letter to Geddes saying so, and concluded "that there is not the smallest need for relief in Ireland."[56] Curzon wrote to the ambassador, stating that Ireland had emerged from the war more prosperous than any belligerent country; that the American Committee's statistical information about distress in Ireland was wrong; that any distress was in fact the result of people refusing aid for political reasons; and that the "only funds [for] which there is apparently any substantial difficulty in keeping replenished, are those needed for carrying on the campaign of murder and terrorism." For these reasons, there was no need for any foreign relief mission in Ireland, however generously offered. Any such organization would be "without legitimate occupation" and would inevitably become involved in local affairs, replacing the duly constituted authorities. The real result of such relief operations would be to become entangled in the Irish political situation and to "prolong the state of rebellion and hinder that reconciliation and peace which is devoutly desired by the great majority of the Irish people."[57] It was a stinging rebuttal.

The subsequent meeting between Hughes and Geddes on 23 May was inconclusive. Hughes understood the British government's message that the American Committee's proposals were "entirely unacceptable," but the secretary replied that, while such a decision was entirely the prerogative of the British, the ambassador should indicate to his government the extent to which anti-British feeling would be aroused in those who had contributed to the committee for purely humanitarian reasons. Furthermore, if the secretary and the department did not appear to act, these contributors would very likely "appeal to the president," thus creating a still more awkward situation.[58] Hughes voiced many of the concerns expressed in Geddes's earlier letter to the Foreign Office, and Geddes's report of his conversation also reiterated the difficulties that would flow from total British rejection of all of the American Committee's proposals, not the least of which the possible passage by Congress of a resolution "in favor of recognizing [the] independence of [the] Irish Republic." As carefully as he could, the ambassador again suggested a compromise plan for the distribution of relief in Ireland under some kind of British auspices. Although this notion had some support within the Foreign Office, the government would not hear of it.[59] As the historian Bernadette Whelan has concluded, "Throughout spring 1921, Ireland remained a principal cause of tension in US-British relations."[60]

Meanwhile, by late March 1921, the State Department had begun to receive information about conditions in Ireland from Frederick T. F. Dumont, its consul in Dublin, which contradicted Samuel Duff McCoy's report. Dumont sent three dispatches during the early spring months, challenging the need for relief. He questioned the reliability of the American Committee's delegation of experts, who, he suspected, had been rather naïvely exploited by the Irish White Cross. That organization, he argued, was dominated by people with undeniable links to the Sinn Féin movement, as the British asserted.[61] As for the present conditions in Ireland, Dumont said that he had assisted at the Johnstown flood, the San Francisco earthquake, and the retreat from Caporetto in Italy during the war, and he knew what disaster looked like. Indeed, he argued, Ireland had never been more prosperous. Drawing on statistics from the Irish Agricultural Organization Society, Dumont attempted to show that in 1920 joint-stock banks and post-office savings and trustee savings accounts held much more money than in 1914. He argued that substantial amounts of interest were being paid in Ireland on British government bonds, that the current marriage rate was the highest on record, and that the immigrants that he saw daily were better dressed and carried better luggage than ever before. In fact, the need for relief was manufactured to serve other purposes, the most important of which was the subsidy of people involved in the Anglo-Irish War. "It can be stated with confidence," Dumont wrote, "that they [the American Committee for Relief in Ireland funds] are to be used to relieve the treasury of Sinn Fein . . . permitting it to devote its funds entirely to the forwarding of the revolutionary movement in Ireland."[62] Dumont's view of Ireland and of the need for relief was not markedly different from that of the British government. This attitude of the American consul was clearly understood by the leaders of the Dáil. De Valera wrote to Harry Boland in the United States concerning Dumont, "I wish we had a more a sympathetic man," and Michael Collins complained that the consul "gets his views on the situation from our enemies here."[63]

Dumont's views, however sincere, must be considered in the context of the reports and assessments of conditions in Ireland by uninvolved observers such as the British Labour Party Commission, the British Friends Service Committee, regular accounts in the newspapers, the findings of the American Commission on Conditions in Ireland, and the statistics produced in the reports of the American Committee for Relief in Ireland and the Irish White Cross. The minutes of a May meeting of the English and Irish Friends spoke directly to the kinds of doubts of Dumont and others: "We desire to record our satisfaction that so many members of the Society of Friends are prominently identified with the Irish White Cross and that its work is being carried on non-party and non-sectarian lines. The aim of the White Cross to administer relief mainly by the reconstruction of factories and creameries and by other means for providing employment meets with our entire approval."[64] The statement went on to welcome any support the American Friends and others might give. These reports provided persuasive evidence of the substantial measure of destruction resulting from the fighting. Furthermore, the letters of gratitude and testimonials printed in the final report of the Irish White Cross bear consideration: nine Catholic bishops; thirty-one parish priests; the Catholic archbishops of Dublin, Cashel, and Tuam; and Cardinal Logue all sent their thanks to the American Committee for Relief in Ireland for relieving the suffering they saw and experienced. As for subsidizing the rebellions, James G.

Douglas, some years later in his memoirs, stated categorically, "not one penny ever reached the funds of the IRA."⁶⁵ These opinions uniformly assert that the need for assistance in Ireland was incontrovertible, and they cannot be dismissed out of hand

Nevertheless, Dumont's reports came as rather a shock to the department. His first letter, of 22 March, found its way to the president's desk. Harding's reply of 30 April to Hughes was a masterpiece of understatement: "I need not say, in making acknowledgement, that I hold it to be a highly interesting document."⁶⁶ The department cabled Dumont and the other consuls in Belfast and Cork asking for further reports on conditions in Ireland and the need for relief operations, causing a flurry of correspondence. The secretary of state himself later wrote to Dumont asking for details concerning the transfers of money from the United States to Ireland and commending the consul for his recent operations.⁶⁷ No doubt the secretary was not comforted by G. Howland Shaw's information that Hoover had withdrawn his support. Captain Lucey also stepped down as the committee's national director in April, to pursue, as he said, his own business interests (but with the comment that the committee was "doing the very best it could"). Shaw, however, attributed his departure to a growing anti-British tone in the committee's proceedings.⁶⁸ Nevertheless, it should be kept in mind that Hughes's discussions with Geddes about the American Committee's relief proposals took place over seven weeks after Dumont's first dispatch had been sent and three weeks after the president had seen it. Thus, whatever suspicions the department may have had about the relief proposals as a result of Dumont's reports, they did not inhibit the secretary from raising the matter with the British ambassador and linking the question of relief in Ireland to a resolution in Congress in favor of the recognition of the Irish Republic.

For the State Department, the Irish question was by no means the most serious problem confronting the United States and Britain. Anglo-American naval rivalry and the possible renewal of the Anglo-Japanese Alliance were the two issues that dominated newspaper editorials, congressional debates, and departmental discussions in 1921. In this context, Japan more than Ireland was seen by many as the principal irritant to positive Anglo-American relations. After World War I, particularly with the elimination of German and Russian fleets in the Far East, the United States increasingly saw Japan as its only naval rival in Asia, and the Anglo-Japanese Alliance as being directed exclusively at the United States. This resulted in a resumption of capital-ship building after the war by all three powers, as well as a campaign on the part of the United States to get Britain to terminate its alliance with Japan when it came up for renewal in 1921.[69] From the British point of view, the US naval building program directly threatened their traditional position of naval supremacy, while the United States' criticism of the Japanese treaty challenged what had become its basic policy in the Far East.[70]

The proposal that the State Department administer relief in Ireland thus took on increased significance when the tension provoked by the Anglo-Japanese alliance renewal approached a climax. On 23 June 1921, two months after the last meeting on the relief question, Hughes told the British ambassador rather pointedly that the renewal of the alliance would provoke the rallying of all anti-British elements in the United States. One specific result would be a debate in Congress on a resolution calling for the recognition of the Irish Republic. In the words of Hughes's aide-mémoire;

> The secretary also told the ambassador that he had been advised that a resolution for the recognition of the Irish Republic would be introduced in Congress; that the resolution in the secretary's opinion would not pass but that it would be debated; that undoubtedly in the debate any relation between Great Britain and Japan could be seized upon by the enemies of Great Britain as indicating an attitude of disregard of what were believed to be the interests of this country, and would be made the most of, while action on the part of Great Britain indicating a desire to support the policy in the Far East to which this government was committed, would give great aid and comfort to those who were opposing such a resolution.[71]

This was exactly what Sir Auckland Geddes had warned the Foreign Office would result from a failure to make some accommodation with the department on the Irish relief question.[72] Hughes himself now held out the specter of it happening. Others had certainly seen the connection of the relief movement and collateral support for the recognition of the Irish Republic. Frank P. Walsh had observed the trend with pleasure early in February: "Relief meetings are being held all over the country, non-political and non-sectarian, every one of which turns into a splendid demonstration for the republic, and a fierce demand for its recognition by this country," he noted, seemingly oblivious to the contradictions in his observations.⁷³ One might also add the notoriety that Britain received as a result of the work of the American Commission on Conditions in Ireland and regular newspaper coverage. As mentioned earlier, even Winston Churchill admitted in cabinet that "we are getting an odious reputation; poisoning our relations with the United States."⁷⁴

Did the secretary's remarks to Geddes, together with the earlier relief proposals, constitute an implied threat that the US government would intervene in Ireland in some way unless Britain broke off the Anglo-Japanese Alliance? Several historians have so concluded. Stephen Roskill asserts quite frankly that Hughes "used support for Irish independence as a weapon to force Britain to liquidate the alliance," and Jean-Baptiste Duroselle concludes that the secretary "threatened that if the Anglo-Japanese treaty were renewed, the United States might well recognize the new Republic of Ireland."⁷⁵ Hughes's biographer, Merlo Pusey, has said that the possibility of a congressional resolution being passed was used by the secretary as an argument in favor of Britain's abrogating the Japanese alliance.⁷⁶ L. Ethan Ellis makes the same point and describes the process as one "in the course of which delicate threats were exchanged."⁷⁷ It is indisputable that, beginning in early May, Hughes had linked first the relief proposals and then the renewal of the Anglo-Japanese treaty with the possible passage in Congress of a resolution on recognition of the Irish Republic, at the height of the Anglo-Irish War. Moreover, these exchanges in May and June 1921 were, as Whelan points out, the first time when a secretary of state had mentioned the Irish question to a British official since Robert Lansing's talk with A. J. Balfour in May 1917.⁷⁸ There were at the time several resolutions before Congress that dealt with Irish issues, and no one could forget that the Senate had passed a resolution in 1919, urging that an Irish delegation be heard at the Paris Peace Conference, and in 1920 a reservation to the Versailles Treaty, expressing sympathy for Irish self-determination. In view of these circumstances, the British government and ambassador could not afford to take the secretary's warnings lightly.

By 11 July 1921—the date the truce that ended the fighting in the Anglo-Irish War and ultimately led to the treaty came into effect—major events were taking place in the Anglo–Irish–American world. Lloyd George had invited the Americans to a conference on Far Eastern affairs, to which Charles Evans Hughes countered with an invitation to a conference on naval arms limitations. Significantly, also on 11 July Lloyd George announced to the House of Commons that he accepted "with the utmost pleasure" Hughes's invitation, with the goal of "friendly relations with the United States."79 This became the Washington Conference, which resolved the questions of both naval rivalry and Far Eastern security. Secretary Hughes had been prepared to use every available resource to obtain British cooperation on these questions. In this context the discussion between the two governments about the possibility of the United States' intervention in the distribution of relief in Ireland and the Harding letter had been useful for US policy: in a sense for the first time, it showed that the US government might be prepared to take some kind of action in regard to Ireland that would be contrary to British interests. This was the very anxiety that Lloyd George had expressed to Bonar Law in January.80 Whatever the State Department's anxieties may have been about the validity of Consul Dumont's allegations, they were beside the point. The talks themselves had given the department leverage, which Hughes was prepared to use, together with the issue of recognition by Congress, when negotiating with the British on a question of vital importance for US policy: the renewal of the Anglo-Japanese Alliance.

For the State Department, the truce in Ireland and the opening of talks between Lloyd George and de Valera in July 1921, coinciding with the agreement to hold the Washington Conference, relieved them of any further responsibility for intervening in the Irish crisis—relief operations, arms, congressional resolutions, whatever. But relief operations did continue in Ireland, despite the suspension of payments by the American Committee to the Irish White Cross between July and August 1921. Indeed, in August, Hollingsworth Wood urged that advantage be taken of the truce to get to work reconstructing creameries, factories and villages. Payments resumed in September, when it was feared that in a breakdown of the Irish peace talks the British government might effectively prevent additional monies being sent. Key members of the executive committee—treasurer John J. Pulleyn and secretary Richard Campbell—seized the opportunity to make an inspection of the relief operations in Ireland. In late October and November 1921, James G. Douglas made a brief trip to the United States to report to the American Committee for Relief in Ireland and to thank the people of the United States for their generous support. He travelled to New York, Boston, Pittsburgh, Chicago, Milwaukee, St. Louis, and Washington, meeting with key figures in the fundraising effort and speaking before numerous groups, by whom he was very warmly received.[81] Had the peace talks broken down, the groundwork would have been established for renewed fundraising. In fact, the relief work in Ireland went ahead without pause for the rest of the year and continued after the Anglo-Irish Treaty was signed in December 1921.

When the terms of the treaty were published in the United States, the American Committee cabled its congratulations to de Valera and the Dáil government, adding that the American people "earnestly hope for the ratification of the treaty by Dáil Éireann." The executive committee sent copies of the message to the state organizations with the suggestion that they send the same or similar telegrams to the Dáil. The request was made, the executive committee said, in order "to emphasize our earnest desire for Irish unity."[82] It was also the first effort of the American Committee for Relief in Ireland to support the new Irish Free State.

Within two weeks of the signing of the treaty in London, Clemens J. France, the American Committee for Relief in Ireland representative in Dublin, reported the growing split in the Dáil between the Griffith-Collins and the de Valera factions. France personally favored the latter and shared its distrust of the British government, though he outlined a plan by which the committee could support the Irish Free State, which they observed had the "great approval of the majority of the Irish people." France pointed out that the United States could play an important role in consolidating the gains promised by the treaty, by opening a consulate-general in Dublin that would be separate from the diplomatic mission in the United Kingdom. Such a move would serve as a kind of diplomatic recognition and help to develop meaningful commercial ties.[83] In mid-January, France and James G. Douglas wrote to the executive committee that the present situation was particularly volatile, and that the funds currently directed to distressed individuals should be diverted into creating employment in order to insure social and economic stability: "If the people in Ireland find themselves getting back to work, the Irish government will hold the great majority which is now in its favor. It might lose that majority if the present stagnation in agriculture and industrial pursuits continues." They warned that "the next three or four months will determine to a large extent the success or failure of the new Irish government."[84] They recommended that in order to place the resources of the American Committee in support of the Irish Free State the policy of direct relief to the individual victims of the Anglo-Irish War be stopped and a new policy of job creation and job placement be initiated. Inasmuch as the program of direct relief had served, in part at least, to subsidize the families of participating members of the Irish Republican Army and thereby support the Irish war effort, this decision to support employment represented a significant break from the committee's previous operations and policy. Thus, by stabilizing the economic situation, the American Committee for Relief in Ireland attempted to strengthen the Irish Free State and to discourage the movement toward civil war. The effectiveness of these efforts is difficult to estimate. The *Report of the Irish White Cross* shows that considerably more was spent on "personal relief" (£788,215/14/5) than on "reconstruction" (£234,063/0/0).[85]

The work of the American Committee for Relief in Ireland was vitally important and surprisingly successful. The committee created a special new US organization and in a matter of some three months raised a remarkable amount of money—$5,069,194 (roughly $66,130,837 in current dollars). Had the conflict in Ireland and the fundraising campaign continued further into 1921 and 1922, it is worth considering whether the target goal of $10,000,000 might have been reached. The committee also attracted the support of a large number of people not previously—or at least recently—involved in Irish nationalist activities, including such non-Irish public figures as President Harding.[86] It was important because it actually financed the major task of reconstruction and subsidy in Ireland in a time of great crisis. Beyond these achievements, however, it is clear that the American Committee for Relief in Ireland played a political role that they did not altogether foresee. The Dáil delegation to negotiate the end to the Anglo-Irish War, led by Arthur Griffith and Michael Collins, wrote a warm letter of thanks to American Committee for Relief in Ireland in October 1921, offering their "profound gratitude" on behalf of the countrymen for the "generous assistance sent to Ireland for the relief of suffering, loss and misery incurred by the Irish people in their struggle for national independence." They went on to emphasize that "it is not only that the material aid you have organized has been of incalculable benefit, you and your friends have helped to sustain the spirit of our people, and to make them realize that your great nation stood beside them with encouragement, sympathy and hope in the terrible ordeal undergone in the efforts to save their national institutions and the very fabric of their national life from destruction."[87] This was a heartfelt recognition of the aid and support that was rendered by the American public.

How often Secretary Hughes mentioned the affairs of the American Committee in his talks with the British ambassador in the spring of 1921, and whether this added more pressure on the British to settle with the Irish, is very hard to determine. The timing of these talks, coinciding with the announcement of the Washington Naval Conference and the opening of the Irish peace negotiations—the two major Anglo–Irish–American events of 1921—may have been merely a coincidence. The US consul in London reported that he had been told "by one who should know" that Lloyd George was anxious about the influence of the Irish in Australia, South Africa, and the United States, and that he therefore "decided that efforts must be made by him to obtain a settlement of this centuries-long problem."[88] While the available documents do not provide concrete answers, the sequence of these events strongly suggests that the work of the American Committee for Relief in Ireland significantly influenced the British government's decision to open talks with the Irish.

Eamon de Valera, a leading participant in these events, was convinced. Ten years later, when he was again heading an Irish government, de Valera had his secretary, Kathleen O'Connell, write to a prominent Irish American leader, asking for help from the US government in his dealings with Britain. Miss O'Connell wrote that de Valera "says that when the late President Harding was in office pressure from friends of ours got him to make strong representations to Britain, saying that there could be no accommodation with regard to the matters that Britain was then anxious about unless the Irish question was satisfactorily settled. He believes that this had not a little to do with Lloyd George's offer of negotiations."[89] It is significant that de Valera, a shrewd political operative, considered Harding—and the American Committee For Relief in Ireland that he had endorsed—to have been a powerful factor in moving the British to a resolution of the Irish situation in 1921. Certainly the British could not completely ignore American interest in Irish affairs, as the war and the Peace Conference had earlier shown, but the public involvement of the American president in an Irish "humanitarian cause" raised the stakes dramatically.

— 7 —

The Emergence of the Irish Free State and American Diplomatic Recognition, 1921–1927

With the Anglo-Irish Treaty in July 1921, American opinion reflected the shift from military to political efforts to resolve the Irish question. British attempts between 1919 and 1921 to legislate a modest form of Irish self-government in the north and the south through the Government of Ireland Act (1920) had been generally scorned by nationalist sympathizers whose demands had by now far exceeded these proposals.[1] The success of the Sinn Féin candidates in the Irish election of 1921 and the burning of the Customs House in Dublin seemed to emphasize the failure of British policy. Consequently, both Irish Americans and Americans in general regarded the truce and peace negotiations as evidence of Britain's willingness to grant Ireland some degree of sovereignty. News of the Anglo-Irish Treaty in December and creation of the Irish Free State strengthened the belief that the struggle was over and that Ireland was free. The Civil War won relatively little support in the United States, despite the efforts of republican advocates; in fact, it was almost as great a source of disillusionment to many Irish Americans—who had dreamed of a happy and prosperous Ireland freed from Britain's grip—as it was a source of satisfaction to some Americans, who regarded it as proof of the deficiencies of the Irish character. George Gavan Duffy, one of the negotiators of the treaty and since January the Dáil Minister for Foreign Affairs, submitted a report on Irish foreign policy on 21 June 1922, the day of the new general election and a week before the outbreak of the Civil War. He spoke specifically about the potential of the Irish Free State as a Dominion, its possible role in the League of Nations, and its opportunities as a sovereign state in the international community. First on his list of countries with whom Ireland should open diplomatic relations was the United States: "Washington is the Capital of the only country where we can strongly and directly influence official action on a large scale," he wrote. "And

England will always fear our influence in the U.S.A., if we take the trouble to organize and direct it."[2] Clearly, the Irish Free State occupied a new position: a Dominion in the British Commonwealth. But was this a sovereign nation-state, or a British colony? And how would the US government respond to it?

Irish American nationalist agitation decreased significantly as the result of the truce between British and Irish forces on 11 July 1921. The truce was regarded as an admission of defeat by the British in much the same way that most Americans regarded the Armistice in 1918 as the surrender of the Germans. Even during the preliminary talks, the *Sinn Feiner* featured the headline: "Irish Republic Triumphs, Britain Moves for Peace.[3] For most Irish American leaders, who may have had a clearer understanding of the delicacy of the situation, the truce imposed a degree of restraint that they had never found necessary, with the result that the summer of 1921 saw a marked lull in nationalist activities.[4] The *Gaelic American* continued to warn its readers that de Valera was about to betray the Irish Republic for some kind of home rule, and Judge Cohalan cabled Bishop Gallagher, urging him to make a statement that "there must be no surrender of [the] republic in Ireland" and warning of Lloyd George's trickery. However, neither the Clan na Gael, which held a highly secret convention in Boston on 4–5 July, nor the FOIF, which directed its energies toward creating an anti-British foreign policy, initiated any major programs during the remainder of the year.[5] The AARIR was also inactive, although it called for congressional action to force Britain to pay her debts to the United States and warned of British development of naval stations in Ireland that it felt could only be used against the United States.[6] In the circumstances surrounding the talks between de Valera and Lloyd George, even the most innocent gestures of goodwill could be misinterpreted. William Bourke Cockran introduced a resolution in Congress in July that expressed the desire that the negotiations lead to a "complete reconciliation" between the "English government and the Irish people." He was given a stern scolding by Mary MacSwiney, still in the United States, for weakening the Irish negotiating position by not referring to the Irish government.[7] Perhaps to avoid these problems exactly, none of the resolutions introduced in Congress during the spring that had given the State Department such concern were pressed and no further resolutions introduced until late autumn, when it was felt that they might strengthen the hand of the Irish negotiators in London.[8]

☘

Irish American leaders expressed a mixture of caution and optimism. Even before the truce was declared, Basil M. Manly commented to Frank P. Walsh that de Valera was negotiating with the British government "in magnificent style" and that Ireland was in a favorable position.[9] Walsh himself observed that he found "the Irish spirit very enthusiastic in America."[10] Senator Thomas J. Walsh was confident that "through the statesman-like efforts of President de Valera and his able associates a solution of their troubles . . . is at hand."[11] Despite their factional differences, both the FOIF and Clan leaders sent their congratulations to de Valera for his firmness in dealing with the British.[12] Nevertheless, Harry Boland wrote to de Valera from New York on 5 August that "our best friends here are of the opinion that now is the time when the $4,500,000 in the hands of the American Committee for Relief in Ireland should be thrown into Ireland and vigorous reconstruction begun."[13] Clemens J. France, representing the American Committee, also urged that relief funds be sent once again.[14] The committee complied at once and sent $472,062 on 2 September, to be followed by weekly remittances similar to those before the truce.[15]

In October, the agitation resumed vigorously through a second bond certificate drive in the hope of strengthening the bargaining position of the Irish delegation in London.[16] Stephen O'Mara was sent to the United States to replace his brother James in directing the second Dáil External Loan, which had been authorized for the amount of $20,000,000.[17] Despite the fact that this was twice the amount that of the first loan, the campaign opened on 15 November in Washington, DC, and Chicago, Illinois.[18] Departing from the policy of referring only obliquely to the use of the funds, O'Mara stated that the money would specifically be employed to resist aggression and to support the Dáil government.[19] In late October he explained to his Washington chairman, A. J. Barrett, how vital it was that the campaign be successful, in part because of the presence of a large British delegation at the Washington naval arms limitation talks. "Failure here will be quickly registered at Downing Street where the Irish Peace Conference sits," O'Mara wrote. "News of success will be as quickly borne there." O'Mara instructed Barrett to seek the support of wealthy Irish Americans and to emphasize "that one dollar now is of more importance and will be far more highly appreciated than ten times that amount when Ireland is free."[20] Frank P. Walsh wrote optimistically that the Irish in America could "raise fifty million dollars almost as easily as they raised eleven million [during the first loan and relief campaigns]," and Michael Collins later told the Dáil that the peace negotiators in London had been assured that the Irish Americans could supply "a million dollars a month" in the event that war resumed.[21] With the report of the signing of the treaty in London, the bond certificate campaign was called off after collecting over a half a million dollars.[22]

※

The signing of the Anglo-Irish Treaty in London on 6 December 1921, was as momentous an event for Irish Americans as it was for the Irish at home.[23] It was similarly regarded as an acceptable settlement, although it offered something less than a republic and reaffirmed provisions for the exclusion of parts of Ulster. At an important meeting of wealthy Irish Americans, AARIR leaders, and sympathetic politicians in Washington on 8 December to discuss methods of support for Ireland should the negotiations fail, a number of prominent leaders such as bishop Thomas Shahan and William Bourke Cockran spoke out in favor of the treaty. Senator Thomas J. Walsh observed that "it was the unanimous opinion that the agreement brought substantial freedom to Ireland and ought to be accepted," and he said that Irish Americans should not encourage the rejection of the treaty while they remained safe in the United States.[24] Although Boland and O'Mara expressed criticism of the treaty, they made it clear that they did not oppose it, and indeed they used the occasion to call off the second bond certificate campaign.[25]

Many of the national leaders of the AARIR also promptly endorsed the treaty. The AARIR's national president, Edward L. Doheny, stated that it cleared the way for harmonious Anglo-American relations, and one of the vice presidents said he was "delighted with the results of the

Irish peace negotiations."[26] Even knowledge of de Valera's disapproval of the treaty did not deter the AARIR's leaders. The state directorate met in Washington on 14 December and declared its "neutrality" regarding the issue, but several days later the national executive sent a cable to the Dáil "congratulate the government and the people of the Republic of Ireland on the magnificent struggle they have made for liberty and on the great progress they have already made towards its achievement," clearly hinting that they should accept what was at hand.[27] Frank P. Walsh probably spoke for many when he confessed his reservations about the treaty, although he thought that it was a "big step forward" and that "it puts mighty weapons in our hands for the final consummation of Ireland's complete independence."[28] Joseph Connolly, the Dáil's consul general in New York, reported to the Department of Foreign Affairs by mid-January that "the main body of opinion in so far as I can make out is in favor of the treaty and the main element who compose the minority is made up of those who are at the end of their tether without the Irish Cause to rant over," naming Joseph McGarrity and Dr. Maloney specifically.[29]

Despite this initial endorsement of the treaty, the AARIR leadership soon found itself badly divided. Even before the meeting of the national executive, a memorandum was drawn up outlining the reasons for keeping the organization going.[30] On 4 February 1922, members of the national executive met in New York City rather than at the national headquarters in Washington, but with fewer than twenty members present. The executive reversed their earlier position and extended their support to de Valera and the maintenance of the Irish Republic. They created an Irish Republic Defense Fund to which, according to Rossa F. Downing, all members of the AARIR were expected to contribute or face expulsion.[31] Many opposed this policy, which ran directly counter to the decision of the Dáil to accept the treaty, with the inevitable result that the leadership slipped into the hands of the more dogmatic republicans, and membership quickly declined. In fact, several days after this meeting, Doheny announced that he had not been informed of it beforehand and that, because of the Dáil's acceptance of the treaty and the creation of the Irish Free State, he found himself the president of an organization whose goals had been accomplished.[32] An angry national secretary protested immediately, disputing the appropriateness of Doherty continuing in office, considering his views.³³ Many of the members of the AARIR opposed the change in policy of the national executive and the tactics used to accomplish it. By mid-March Frank P. Walsh informed Stephen O'Mara that the organization was "absolutely shot to pieces," and Downing later confirmed that membership had declined to a mere 75,000.³⁴ The *Irish World*, which since the split in the Irish movement in 1920, had been the organ of the AARIR, rejected the treaty from the first; the paper bitterly denounced it, calling it "the Treaty of surrender," and, after news of its acceptance by the Dáil, announced that the "Irish Republic still lives."³⁵ The *Irish World* became an uncompromising spokesman for the republican position in the United States and started a slanderous campaign against the supporters of the treaty and the Irish Free State.

The reactions of the FOIF and the Clan to the treaty followed a different pattern. Diarmuid Lynch of the FOIF, Lawrence J. Rice of the Clan, and Judge Cohalan all immediately protested its provisions, especially those dealing with the Crown and British defense.³⁶ The *Gaelic American* announced that the Irish delegation had brought back mere "Home Rule within the Empire."³⁷ Holding its national convention on 10–11 December, the FOIF issued a statement that the organization did not endorse either the treaty or the Irish Free State, that their opinion had not been asked, and that they regarded any Irish acceptance of the treaty as a decision made under duress. They proclaimed "a free and independent Republic, separated from the Empire . . . is the only solution of the Irish national problem."³⁸ However John J. Splain recorded that most members of the convention felt that the Dominion status offered by the treaty was all that could be extracted from Britain at that time, because de Valera's actions in the United States in 1920 had compromised the position of the republic.³⁹ While condemning the treaty, the *Gaelic American* attacked de Valera for objecting to it, on the grounds that his compromises and blunderings had made it inevitable. By January 1922, the paper was beginning to support the Irish Free State and those in the Dáil who voted with the majority.⁴⁰ In mid-February, Devoy wrote to Michael Collins that "our best men here, under the existing conditions, favor giving the 'Free State' a chance to do what it can for Ireland," and he went on to condemn de Valera's presumed loyalty to a republic that he himself had destroyed.⁴¹ Increasingly the *Gaelic American* asserted that de Valera's republican followers had been duped and deluded, and that de Valera was encouraging civil war.[42] Judge Cohalan advised his friends to say that the Free State should be supported as a means to an end and that de Valera should be repudiated in favor of Collins.[43] On 28 March, the FOIF's national council published a statement on the conditions in Ireland, blaming de Valera for the disunity there and giving support to the Irish Free State, through which "very material advantages can be gained for Ireland."[44]

❧

Meanwhile, the growing disunity among the nationalist leaders in Ireland was dramatically revealed to the Irish in America in the form of two rival delegations sent to the United States on behalf of their respective factions. The Provisional Government sent James O'Mara, Piaras Beaslai, and Sean MacCaoilte (and, later, Denis McCullough) with instructions "to get in touch with political and other circles likely to be useful to this country"—in short, to win support among Irish Americans for the treaty and the Irish Free State and to raise money for the coming election.[45] Arriving on the same ship were Austin Stack and J. J. O'Kelly (to be followed shortly by Countess Markievicz and the sister of Kevin Barry), representing the antitreaty faction, whose purpose it was to raise money to fight the treaty's supporters and to marshal republican sympathy among Irish Americans.[46] An AARIR committee protested to Collins and de Valera that such a display of disunity would "prove disastrous here" and offered to divide equally all money raised by Irish Americans themselves.[47] However, neither side could afford to call back their delegations. In late February, Harry Boland had written to Frank P. Walsh that "we will require the support of all friends of the Republic in America now more than ever . . . and we will need a great deal of money to enable us to successfully place our case before [the Irish people]" in the coming election. The protreaty forces needed no money, he said, but wanted American support nonetheless.[48] Thus, both groups began touring the country, denouncing their opponents in Ireland with all of the malice and vituperation previously reserved for the British government. Stack and O'Kelly opened republican offices in New York and announced the creation of an election campaign fund, and O'Mara worked to cement an alliance with the

FOIF and the disaffected members of the AARIR in favor of the treaty as an immediate but temporary solution to the Irish problem.[49] This spectacle—made all the more serious by the *Gaelic American*'s allegations that de Valera was encouraging civil war in Ireland and by the *Irish World*'s accusations that Griffith and Collins (the leaders of the "Freak State") were traitors—severely demoralized the Irish American community.[50] Nevertheless, de Valera got the money for the election campaign, and Griffith and Collins received the support of Devoy and Judge Cohalan.

Very soon after, events in Ireland surpassed even this. The results of the June election were a clear majority for the treaty and the Irish Free State, which weakened (superficially, at least) the republicans' ideological position in the eyes of Americans. The *Gaelic American*, which had been predicting de Valera's collapse, jubilantly printed the headline "De Valera Decisively Beaten" and claimed that "routed in elections he seeks by Mexican methods to overcome the decision of the people by force."[51] The shelling of the Four Courts and the outbreak of the Civil War in Ireland were calamitous for Irish American morale. Observers were shocked and bewildered as Irish leaders—many of whom had traveled in America and were known to Irish Americans—died or were killed: Griffith and, later, Ginnell, from overwork; Collins, Boland, and Brugha, in action; Mellows, Childers, and O'Connor, by reprisals. John Quinn wrote to Douglas Hyde in disgust, "I would not shed the blood of a single Irish wolf-hound for the difference between a republic and a free state."[52] Archbishop Michael J. Curley of Baltimore returned from a trip to Ireland to announce that "de Valera is the [Pancho] Villa of Ireland"—a contemptuous reference to banditry in Mexico. bishop William Turner of Buffalo stated that 90 percent of the Irish people supported the Irish Free State.[53] In August 1922, W. J. M. A. Maloney and the Very Rev. Peter Magennis met in Ireland in with representatives of the Free State government and the republican forces and attempted to arrange a truce between them, but without success.[54] On 29 September, the national council of the FOIF met to denounce the Civil War with "horror and dismay," asserting that it was "a crime against Ireland and an outrage on the spirit of true democracy."[55] While some Irish American supporters of the Free State balked at the government's final policy of executing prisoners, the *Gaelic American* never flinched.[56]

Republicans in Ireland realized that, despite their control of the AARIR, their claim to the sympathy of the Irish American community was no longer strong. In fact, the leader of the AARIR once again clashed with the executive and had to be replaced. James E. "Red" Murray—a distinguished labor lawyer and later a liberal senator from Butte, Montana, elected in May 1922 to replace Edward L. Doheny, who had publicly supported the treaty—was forced out of office in August for attempting to use the AARIR to demand a reconciliation of the two factions during the Civil War rather than simply throwing the support of the organization behind the republicans. John F. Finerty was subsequently elected national president.[57] Nevertheless, the *Irish World* stoutly defended the republicans: it denied the significance of the June elections (because the so-called Independent candidates were merely antirepublicans in disguise), described the Irish government as an "illegal junta" created by the British, and called the Free State army "hirelings" and "Green and Tans."[58] Furthermore, republican delegations were sent to the United States to raise money to finance resistance in Ireland and to rally support. Muriel MacSwiney and Hannah Sheehy-Skeffington toured the country in an attempt to create an Irish Republican Soldiers and Prisoners Dependent's Fund, and, with judge John W. Goff as chairman and Frank P. Walsh as vice-chairman, they raised a substantial amount of money.[59] J. J. O'Kelly and Joseph O'Doherty were sent to the United States in the autumn to continue the Stack-O'Kelly-Markievicz mission of the previous spring, although even de Valera seems to have had little confidence in their winning assistance from Irish Americans at a national level.[60]

The reprisals carried out by Irish Free State forces in late 1922 and 1923 spurred some moderate support for the republicans that Lawrence Ginnell, the new republican envoy to the United States, and John F. Finerty, the tough new president of the AARIR, were able to exploit. Finerty, the son of a prominent Irish American nationalist leader, newspaper editor, and politician who was himself a lawyer for the US Railroad Administration, a federal agency of which he was deputy director, gave British authorities some considerable cause for alarm.[61] Even so, Irish American attempts to persuade Congress to pass resolutions deploring reprisals or extending diplomatic recognition to the republican government stood no possible chance of success. In fact,

Basil F. Manly advised Frank P. Walsh against any agitation in Congress because it would reveal the weakness of the republican cause in the United States.⁶² However, republican propaganda was distributed through the newly founded "Irish Legation Circular" that Ginnell directed, and Finerty used his administrative talents to rejuvenate the ailing AARIR.⁶³ Optimistic reports were sent back to Ireland about the possibility of raising money among Irish Americans for the republican cause, but it soon became clear to Ginnell that the present leadership of the AARIR was again badly divided, and a conference of the national leaders in March 1923 failed to generate encouragement for a new bond certificate campaign.⁶⁴ In November, the national office appealed to the republicans in Ireland for a loan of between $1000 and $2000 dollars to keep their doors open. On 27 December 1922, Ginnell ordered the seizure of the Irish "consulate" at 119 Nassau Street in New York in an attempt to obtain a list of the earlier bond certificate purchasers to whom requests for support might be directed. However, NYC police removed the republicans (who were led by Robert Briscoe) from the premises.⁶⁵ By the spring of 1923, the leadership of the AARIR was irreconcilably divided over the question of whether to expel the New York chapter because of its failure to contribute monetarily.⁶⁶ Internal dissension, along with Ginnell's death in April 1923 and the declining fortunes of the republicans in Ireland, prevented the effective rebuilding of the national organization.⁶⁷

Slowly and inconclusively, the Civil War in Ireland wound to an end in the spring of 1923, as more and more republican army leaders were killed or captured, until, finally, de Valera and Frank Aiken issued orders to cease operations and hide weapons. The *Irish World*, which in March had assured its readers that the Free State was on the brink of collapse, refused to admit that the republicans had been defeated and emphasized that de Valera had merely ordered a "cease fire," not a surrender.⁶⁸ Contemptuous of de Valera's efforts to negotiate, the *Gaelic American* fully supported William T. Cosgrave's government in its refusal to compromise or deal leniently with the republicans.⁶⁹ The arrest of de Valera, who came out of hiding to campaign in the August 1923 election, aroused appeals from diverse sources across the United States for American intervention to spare his life.⁷⁰ Senator Thomas J. Walsh spoke to both Secretary Hughes and President Coolidge about an American protest against his possible execution, and large public meetings were held in New York. These appeals broadened in 1924 to ask that clemency be extended to all Irish political prisoners, and a resolution to that effect was introduced in Congress.[71] Like Irish American leaders in years past, John F. Finerty tried to involve the American Red Cross, this time by requesting that it investigate conditions in Free State prisons.[72] But these efforts compared badly with the spectacular national agitation that had been provoked over the prisoners of 1916 or the hunger strike of Terence MacSwiney in 1920. The fact was that the Irish Free State formally came into existence in December 1923. Prominent Americans such as mayor John H. Hyland of New York, governor Channing H. Cox of Massachusetts, and archbishop Michael J. Curley of Baltimore, extended congratulations and expressed hope for the success of the new Irish Free State. Even president Warren G. Harding sent congratulations to Cosgrave, albeit through the British ambassador.[73]

Even before the Irish Free State was officially established on 6 December 1922, with the ratification of the constitution, the Cosgrave government was working to assert Ireland's independence. On 17 April 1923, it took a public step in that direction by applying for membership in the League of Nations, which had accepted British Dominions when it was established, and the Irish Free State was admitted on 10 September. President of the executive council William T. Cosgrave led a delegation, which was received with great applause, after which it was reported that "the floodgates of international eloquence were thrown open."[74] The Irish government saw the league as a platform from which its independence could be demonstrated to the international community. Ireland indeed took an active role and became a leader among the smaller powers in the 1920s.[75] Cosgrave also led a delegation to the Irish Free State's first Imperial Conference in London on 1 October 1923. These meetings became an increasingly important means through which the Irish Free State and like-minded Dominions such as Canada and South Africa could assert their independence while remaining members of the British Commonwealth, culminating in the Balfour Declaration in 1926 and the Statute of Westminster in 1931.[76]

Membership in both the League of Nations and the British Commonwealth were major steps in asserting self-government and independence. But did these associations establish Ireland as a sovereign state in the international community? This would appear to depend on Ireland establishing bilateral relations with a sovereign power, preferably outside the league or the Commonwealth. Who among the international community might extend diplomatic recognition to the Irish Free State? By 1922 and 1923 no Dominion in the British Commonwealth had ever received diplomatic recognition; indeed, the Dominions did not then have official representation among themselves. When, in August 1923, Timothy A. Smiddy, the Free State "general agent" (or trade representative) in the United States talked with William R. Castle Jr., the head of the State Department's Division of West European Affairs, about direct access without going through the British Embassy, he was told this could only be done informally, as with other Dominions such as Australia, but that this procedure "implied in no way any lack of courtesy to the Irish Free State."[77] British ambassador Sir Auckland Geddes reported to the Foreign Office that, as instructed, he had told "the State Department privately of this appointment and [made] it clear that Professor Smiddy claimed no diplomatic character."[78] For the Irish Free State to establish bilateral diplomatic relations with another sovereign state would be crucial and unprecedented.

Two schools of international law determined acceptance of a state as sovereign in the early twentieth century and influenced whether it was given diplomatic recognition by another international state. The *declaratory* theory held that a state was suitable for acceptance by the international community when it was self-governing, controlled its defined territory, had a stable government, and was willing to accept international responsibilities—in short, when a state regarded itself as independent, as indeed the Irish Free State increasingly did during the 1920s. The *constitutive* theory reasoned that acceptance as an international legal person depended on whether the state was given recognition by another international state.[79] Thus while the Irish Free State might well regard itself as a sovereign state under the declarative theory, diplomatic recognition by a great power such as the United States would irrefutably confirm it under the constitutive theory. International diplomatic recognition, therefore, was critical for the claim of sovereign independence by the government and supporters of the Irish Free State.

Actually, in the aftermath of World War I, Canada had worked out with the British government the formalities of establishing diplomatic relations with the United States in order to expedite the enormous amount of trade between the two neighbors. In September and October 1919, the Colonial Office and the Canadian government had agreed in principle to the appointment of a Canadian minister, but by 1923 and 1924 they still had not done so.[80] Working from Article 2 in the Anglo-Irish Treaty, which stated that the Irish Free State enjoyed the same relationship to the Crown and the British Parliament as Canada, the Cosgrave government set the process in motion to exchange diplomatic recognition with the United States. The Irish government representative in the US, Timothy A. Smiddy, visited Ottawa in February 1923 to consult about the possible opening of diplomatic relations. Although Smiddy was unable to meet with prime minister William Lyon Mackenzie King, he talked with two members of the government and several senior civil servants, but he came away with mixed opinions. Still, the Canadian government replied to the Colonial Office query by stating that they "cordially approve of the contemplated action of the British Government in arranging to meet the wishes of the Irish Free State to have in Washington a representative duly accredited to the United States Government."[81] Smiddy returned to Ottawa in May to meet specifically with Mackenzie King, who was reported as saying that the Canadian Parliament would be dealing with the matter of diplomatic representation. The Irish Free State would follow Canada's lead, the *New York Times* noted.[82] Indeed, as the British Ambassador was later to write: "in view of the decision reached in the case of Canada His Majesty's Government could not object to such an appointment yet they regarded it with some apprehension."[83]

On 19 October 1923, secretary to the executive council Diarmuid O'Hegarty wrote to Eoin MacNeill, who was in London on Boundary Commission business, pointing out that the British government had earlier mentioned in Parliament that procedures had been established to appoint a Canadian diplomatic representative to the United States. He emphasized to MacNeill that a Minister-Plenipotentiary at Washington would be of great value to us in many directions. In the first place it would add to the national dignity and be a manifestation to our people here that our status is what we claim it to be and not what the Irregulars [antitreaty republicans] pretend. This fact would in addition be made clear to our people in the United States and to dispel the misapprehensions which have been created by Irregular propaganda and thus close down a source of revenue or moral support to the Irregulars.[84]

So, opening direct diplomatic relations with the United States would accomplish several things: it would establish the Irish Free State as a recognized international legal person ("national dignity"); demonstrate to the Irish people that the Free State was independent ("what we claim it to be"); and similarly win over Irish Americans and reduce support for die-hard republicans ("dispel . . . Irregular propaganda"). The Irish government asked the governor-general to initiate procedures with the colonial secretary to make arrangements with the US government to appoint an Irish minister, emphasizing the need to expedite Irish financial and immigration issues. The British government moved slowly and consulted the other Dominions, and the Colonial Office was more cooperative than the Foreign Office in agreeing to diplomatic status. Joseph Walshe's comment is telling: "We invariably find that there is considerable delay in any matter in which the Foreign Office has to intervene and it is becoming more and more apparent that we have no friends there."[85] By June 1924, the US consul in Dublin reported that he just learned that "Mr. Fitzgerald [Minister for External Affairs] was informed in London that the Dominions had all replied to the appointment of an Irish Minister at Washington, that Canada and South Africa had heartily approved, that Australia had thought it might well be deferred—perhaps until after another Imperial Conference, and that New Zealand had objected vigorously." The consul assured the secretary of state that Fitzgerald was "urging prompt action on the matter."[86] There were also some questions about the kind of relationship an Irish minister would have with the British ambassador in the same capital. Very simply, the Irish minister would focus exclusively on Irish affairs and not be empowered to deal with British or general Commonwealth matters, and the British ambassador would not be responsible for the Irish minister. Ambassador Sir Esmé Howard wrote to Secretary Hughes on 24 June, stating that his government would prefer that the affairs of the Irish Free State be entrusted to an Irish legation. This Irish minister would be given powers that "would enable him to take charge of all affairs relating only to the Irish Free State." The secretary responded quickly that the US government "will be pleased to receive a duly accredited Minister Plenipotentiary of the Irish Free State."[87] Hughes also consulted with president Calvin Coolidge, relaying the ambassador's message and noting that "in matters falling within his sphere the Irish Minister would not be subject to the control of His Majesty's Ambassador."[88] By July the Irish government was informed that the United States government was prepared to accept as persona grata Timothy A. Smiddy as the Irish minister plenipotentiary.[89]

Smiddy was unusual among the leading figures of the Irish revolutionary generation. Rather than being shaped by the Irish-Ireland movement and serving in the events of 1916 or, later, in the formation of the Dáil Éireann, he was a technical expert, first recruited by Michael Collins to serve as an economic advisor to the treaty delegation in London in 1921. Trained in economics at University College Cork, he earned BA and MA degrees and studied in Paris and Cologne before returning to Ireland to become a professor of economics and, later, dean of the Faculty of Commerce at Cork. After the disagreements over the Anglo-Irish Treaty, Harry Boland, the Dáil envoy to the United States, returned to Dublin, and Collins appointed Smiddy as his representative on financial matters in the United States in the spring of 1922. It fell to Smiddy to take legal steps to secure for the provisional government the unexpended bond certificate monies in New York banks, leading to prolonged court cases. Once the Irish Free State came into existence, the government asked that Smiddy be accepted by the British Embassy and the State Department as a special agent to study "public administration" and to oversee the financial interests of the Free State.[90] In these capacities Smiddy urged the Irish government to see that his mission in the United States be given diplomatic recognition and raised to that of a legation. In fact, at the high point of agitation in the United States six years earlier, several resolutions came before Congress intended to force the president to extend diplomatic recognition to Ireland. Smiddy was able to meet with William R. Castle Jr., chief of the west European division of the State Department, although not with the secretary of state, as early as March and April 1922, and he reported home that Castle was "very sympathetic" and helpful.[91]

With the formal request from the British government to extend diplomatic recognition, the United States government was pleased to agree. Castle had already assured Secretary Hughes that Smiddy was "an intelligent, straightforward fellow," and Howard himself commented that "we should be able to understand each other."[92] The ambassador handed Smiddy his letters of credence on 29 September. On the afternoon of 7 October, Timothy Smiddy, minister plenipotentiary of the Irish Free State, presented his credentials to president Calvin Coolidge in the White House, and "complimentary speeches were exchanged."[93] It was a long-awaited moment in Irish and American history. Indeed, as Smiddy said in his address to the president, "to my country this occasion is of deep and historic interest," and he went on to emphasize that "for the first time in its annals there has been established diplomatic relations with another country." President Coolidge welcomed Smiddy and wished him well as he represented the Ireland to which, as he put it, "so many of our citizens are bound by the closest ties of relationship and sentiment."[94] These were not idle sentiments. The Irish Free State was the first British Dominion given diplomatic recognition, and ahead of the older Dominions, such as Canada, the oldest and the neighbor of the United States. Writing to Kevin O'Higgins later in October, Joseph P. Walshe, acting secretary of the Department of External Affairs, stressed the importance of establishing this relationship with the United States: "America is the only country with which our relations are entirely free and independent of any outside control," he argued, hinting at both the practical and the symbolic importance of this official contact beyond both the league and the Commonwealth. "The main accomplishment in our external relations is the establishment of a Minister Plenipotentiary in Washington," he concluded, with considerable satisfaction, two weeks after the ceremony.[95] Michael Kennedy has emphasized that, despite Irish participation in the League of Nations and the Commonwealth, the Irish Free State Legation in Washington "was Ireland's first *real diplomatic post*" (emphasis added).[96]

Smiddy's appointment was made at the rank of minister plenipotentiary: a position was created at this level so that a Dominion diplomat would not outrank the counsellor, the deputy head of mission at the

British Embassy. Several years later, when the United States and Canada opened diplomatic relations in 1927, the diplomats of the two countries were to be given the rank of envoy extraordinary and minister plenipotentiary. The United States in 1927 also appointed a diplomat to the Irish Free State at the same rank. In these circumstances the Irish government requested that Smiddy's rank also be upgraded to the status of envoy extraordinary and minister plenipotentiary. Thus the elements of diplomatic protocol were observed.[97]

There were some ironies to the ceremonies in the White House on 7 October. Instead of an extravagant celebration, with hosts of Irish American dignitaries witnessing the event and possibly even a benign British ambassador looking on, an extremely brief and modest ritual took place, with the president and minister giving short—and, in many ways, perfunctory—speeches. Outsiders were not invited. British ambassador Sir Esmé Howard, thought it better not to accompany Smiddy in order that the new minister not be compromised by too-close association with the British Embassy, which might have "led to attacks upon him from extreme elements of the Irish-American community."[98] The newspapers in large measure ignored the event. The front page of the *New York Times* featured an article on the fate of the boundary between the Irish Free State and Northern Ireland and described the presentation of Irish Minister in a short, bland article on page twenty-one.[99] Nevertheless, the ceremony did mark a major accomplishment for the new Irish Free State, which had achieved international bilateral diplomatic recognition from one of the world's great powers. This was of enormous symbolic importance in displaying to its constituencies both at home and in America that Ireland was in fact "a nation once again." This was also a milestone within the British Empire, demonstrating that a Dominion could conduct its own diplomatic relations. Indeed, much of Smiddy's work in the next several years would be devoted to speaking to groups and organizations across the United States, explaining that the Irish Free State was an independent, self-governing country while also a member of the Commonwealth.[100]

One immediate result of the extension of diplomatic recognition was the reorganization of the US consulates in Ireland. Although the United

States had had consulates in a variety of cities and ports in Ireland since the 1790s, by the mid-1920s there were consulates in Dublin, Cobh, and Belfast, with consular agents in Limerick and Galway, all of them under the jurisdiction of the consulate general in London. Dublin's had a staff of ten people, including a consul and three vice-consuls, and it generated a substantial amount of revenue through its normal business: some $66,000 was collected in visa fees during 1924, and, together with other fees, the consulate was able to sent $51,000 to the US Treasury after paying salaries. Dublin was a logical post to be raised to a consulate general. With recognition of the Irish Free State, together with the separate status of Northern Ireland, new arrangements were recommended. "It is believed that the office at Dublin should be raised to the status of Consulate General," the inspection report of the consul-at-large claimed in 1924. Moreover, "the [Irish] Government would immensely appreciate our establishing an office of that grade in the Irish Free State."[101] As Hughes wrote to President Coolidge on the day Smiddy presented his letter of credence, "It seems to me to be appropriate to elevate immediately the American consulate at Dublin to the grade of Consulate General, with supervisory jurisdiction over the other consular offices in the Irish Free State." The secretary also noted that this gesture would be "appreciated" by the Free State government, which was an understatement.[102] Charles M. Hathaway Jr., was a career diplomat and a Yale graduate with a doctorate in English literature who had taught at Adelphi College, Columbia University, and the US Naval Academy before joining the Foreign Service in 1911. He served as consul in Cork from 1917 to 1919 and returned to Ireland in 1924 as consul general in Dublin. Hathaway was instructed to carry out political reporting on events in Ireland until a legation was opened, which he did very effectively, and was regularly commended for the quality of his reports. The consulate general moved from Lower O'Connell Street to 34 Lower Abbey Street in 1924 and, with Assistant Secretary Castle's support, obtained offices at 15 Merrion Square in 1926. By 1926 the consulate general was one of the largest in the service, with a staff of twenty-seven, and one of the largest visa granting agencies in the world.[103] Hathaway left in 1927 and was appointed consul general in Munich. This consular activity was another form of recognition. The Belfast consulate, too, was elevated, but remained under the jurisdiction of London.

Whelan notes that part of the motivation of the State Department to upgrade the Dublin consulate to that of a consulate general was to avoid making a decision about the appointment of a minister. Given the American practice of political appointments, a certain logic suggested that the posting should go to a prominent Irish American. However, the acrimony that had riven much of the Irish American community since 1920 made such a decision politically awkward.[104] The result was that no decision was made until 1926, by which time Canada also asked to send a minister to the United States. In December 1926, Frank B. Kellogg, now secretary of state, inquired whether, in view of Irish and Canadian representation, the "appointment [of ministers to both the Irish Free State and Canada] would be acceptable to the British Government." The Foreign Office replied in early January 1927 that the Irish and Canadian governments "have learnt with much satisfaction of the intention of the President of the United States and that these appointments will be most agreeable."[105] The choice of minister to the Irish Free State was Frederick A. Sterling, a career Foreign Service officer, who—perhaps not accidentally—had been counselor of embassy in London when Kellogg was ambassador. He also had the advantage of not having any Irish American connections that might include political baggage. A Harvard graduate who had also studied law at Washington University, he had ranched for several years prior to entering the Foreign Service and spent some time in business. His diplomatic career took him to St. Petersburg and Beijing, and to the State Department in Washington as head of the Division of Western European Affairs during the war years of 1916–18. After the war he was posted to Paris from 1918 to 1921, to Lima from 1921–23, and to London from 1923 and 1927, as counselor of embassy in all three posts. Sterling's appointment as envoy extraordinary and minister plenipotentiary to the Irish Free State was a major career step for him as well as a gesture of seriousness in regard to Ireland, and he certainly took it seriously. Sterling assured the Department of External Affairs that he "intended to make the very most of his position to get Americans to take an interest in this country and to promote close relations between the two countries."[106] This was exactly what the Irish Free State government wanted.

Frederick A. Sterling, his wife, Dorothy, and their children arrived in Dun Laoghaire by ferry from Holyhead on 25 July 1927, and were met by a delegation. Diarmuid O'Hegarty and Joseph A. Walshe represented Cosgrave as president of the executive council and minister of external affairs, respectively, and Captain E. Butler represented the Free State Army, while consul general Charles M. Hathaway Jr. and secretary of the legation Wainwright Abbott accompanied Sterling as well. The party boarded the ship to welcome the Sterlings and escort them onto the pier. A crowd of some two thousand gathered as the No. 1 Army Band played "The Star-Spangled Banner," and a mounted honor guard of one hundred men from the Seventh Brigade of the Free State Army escorted them into Dublin and to their new accommodations in the former undersecretary's lodge in Phoenix Park.[107] On the morning of 27 July, Sterling, accompanied by Secretary Abbott, O'Hegarty and Walshe, and Captain J. C. O'Sullivan, aide-de camp to the governor-general, left the American Legation on Merrion Square in an entourage of motorcars. Proceeded by mounted troops, the party traveled by way of Nassau Street, College Green, O'Connell Street, and the North Circular Road to Phoenix Park, where they were met by four companies of one hundred men each from the Twenty-Seventh Battalion, Portobello Barracks, and the No. 1 Army Band, which played a bugle salute upon their entering the grounds of the governor-general's residence, the Vice-Regal Lodge. Arriving at precisely noon, the party was received by Cosgrave in his dual capacity and conducted into an adjoining ballroom and officially introduced to governor-general T. M. Healy.[108]

The reception of a diplomat was, by custom, a very formal occasion based on the presumption of one king embracing a brother monarch. Modern practice only modestly eased matters of dress and ritualistic language. But even through those formalities, sincere sentiments were expressed. Sterling, in the process of presenting his letter of credence, said that President Coolidge "charges me to convey to you and the Irish Free State Government his sincere wishes for your continued welfare and prosperity." The new minister went on to add pointedly, "The establishment of this new and important mission marks a happy development in the relations of the two countries, already bound closely together by ties of sympathy and kinship."[109] Sterling promised that he would work to strengthen those ties. Governor-General Healy responded warmly and generously, assuring Sterling that he took "great pleasure and satisfaction to have the honour of receiving the first Minister sent by the President of the United States to represent his great country in the Irish Free State," and he asked Sterling to convey to President Coolidge "our sincere appreciation of his good wishes for the continued welfare and prosperity of our country."[110] It was a very impressive ceremony that represented the culmination of the hopes and aspirations of the United States and Ireland, as well as an enormous amount of work by countless people over many years. Sterling reported to the State Department that his reception was handled with "efficiency and dignity" and conducted "in an atmosphere of cordiality, which was beyond my expectations." The new minister was conscious of the significance of his appointment as the first diplomatic representative in Ireland. "It was," he assured the department, "an evidence of the present status of the Free State—what they like to think is practically complete independence," as indeed it was.[111]

Edward J. Phelan, the chief of the diplomatic division of the International Labour Organization in Geneva, wrote to Desmond FitzGerald shortly after Sterling's appointment had been announced to "congratulate" him that a US minister had been named: "It is I think extremely important. It completes Smiddy's appointment, which was an anomaly so long as the U.S. did not reciprocate, and *it establishes our right of Legation beyond challenge*" (emphasis added).[112] The *Irish Times* similarly saw the creation of the American Legation as a "logical corollary to the dispatch of a Free State Minister to Washington, and places the diplomatic relations between that State and the United States on a completely new basis."[113] The US consul general observed that the elaborate ceremonies surrounding Sterling's arrival and the presentation of his credentials "were widely felt as a most significant event" across the country.[114] An American minister and legation in an independent Ireland: it was a symbolic victory. And it was much more of a publicly celebrated event than Timothy A. Smiddy's presentation of his credentials in Washington.

Arrangements had been made with the Free State government for Sterling and his family to stay in the former undersecretary's lodge in Phoenix Park, a short distance from the governor-general's residence. "Much struck with the beauties of the Park"; Sterling described the lodge as "spacious and attractive," enthusing that it was "like living in a beautiful countryside & yet only 10 minutes away by motor from the heart of the city."[115] The Lodge was subsequently regarded as the "most beautiful of all American legations"; Assistant Secretary Castle noted that, in making the house available, "the Irish [government] feel it was a great compliment [to the United States] to let you have it."[116]

The American Legation under Sterling was ably assisted by Wainwright Abbott, his secretary. After a distinguished record in the Great War, Abbott entered the Foreign Service in 1920. He left Yale in 1917 to join the Norton-Harjes Ambulance Service in France but soon enrolled in the Lafayette Escadrille, in which he served with distinction, being awarded the Croix de Guerre. He later entered the American army. After Dublin, Abbott was appointed first secretary in the embassy in London in 1930. He finished his diplomatic service as consul general in Belfast from 1949 to 1951.[117]

The appointment of Frederick A. Sterling as minister to the Irish Free State by the US government, the upgrading of the Dublin consulate to a consulate general, and the acceptance of Smiddy as the Minister from the Irish Free State, were very significant steps. These public acts by the United States government satisfied Ireland's need for symbolic international recognition and also smoothed the way for practical diplomatic and commercial relations. Moreover, these acts by the US government represented the tangible gestures of support for Ireland that had been sought since 1916. These were not Wilson's careful confidential expressions of goodwill, nor Harding's mild appeals for humanitarian assistance, but conscious and deliberate diplomatic actions. Despite the anxious moments leading up to the Anglo-Irish truce and the treaty negotiations, as well as the watchful waiting during the turbulence in Ireland, within less that two years of the establishment of the Irish Free State the government of the United States had moved publicly to extend to it international recognition. Indeed, the United States the first to extend recognition to Ireland and to a British Dominion. Within another three years, the United States opened its own legation in Dublin. Consul General Hathaway, reporting on these events to the secretary of state, commented on the warm feeling for the United States among the Irish and noted that "all of this has lain behind the very genuine welcome to the first American envoy and has *made it something far beyond the pleasurable reaction of national pride to the formal recognition of Irish status implied*" (emphasis added).[118] This was an emotional vindication as well as a major foreign policy triumph for the new Irish Free State. The United States had made a major contribution to the standing of the Irish Free State in the international community by extending diplomatic recognition in 1924 and sending its own envoy to Ireland in 1927. Irish membership in the League of Nations and the British Commonwealth had been important first steps, but they had been taken under the shadow of Great Britain itself. The conventional test of international sovereignty was diplomatic recognition by a great power. Here, the United States had stepped forward and acknowledged the Irish Free State. Not until 1929 did Germany, France, and the Vatican do the same.

8

President William T. Cosgrave Comes to the United States, 1928

One of the lingering problems plaguing the Irish Free State during the 1920s was the antitreaty republicans, who challenged the legitimacy of the state—the Irish "Freak" State, as they called it. Michael Collins claimed that the Anglo-Irish Treaty gave Ireland "not the ultimate freedom that all nations desire . . . but the freedom to achieve it."[1] Was this just self-deception? The fact that Ireland had joined the League of Nations and been given diplomatic recognition by the United States seemed to make no difference to some. In 1927, the Irish Ministry of External Affairs circulated a memorandum on precisely these issues: it outlined the significance of the Dominions individually signing the Versailles Treaty and joining the League of Nations, the equality among the Commonwealth partners at the 1926 Imperial Conference (which produced the Balfour Declaration formula of "equal in status"), independent representation at the recent Geneva Naval Conference, and the exchange of diplomats with the United States. "States of the Commonwealth will hold powers complete and exclusive in themselves, issued on the sole advice of their own Government" was the ministry's bold assertion of Dominion status. "Only independent sovereign states send and receive ministers."[2] As the 1920s unfolded, the Dominions and the Irish Free State functioned as legislatively autonomous, independent legal persons, both in law and in international practice. But did these technical arguments, which may have satisfied lawyers and political theorists, matter to people at home and in America? For a portion of the Irish community, the question of Irish independence remained. Would the dramatic diplomatic gesture of the Irish head of government's first official visit to the United States win over public opinion? It was in this context that William T. Cosgrave, the president of the executive council of Dáil Éireann, made a transatlantic voyage to the United States and Canada.

It fell to Cosgrave, as the head of the Irish government, to make the trip in order to demonstrate to both Irish and American constituencies that Ireland was now a sovereign nation and an accepted member of the international community. Not as well known as Griffith, Collins, or Eamon de Valera, William T. Cosgrave was born in Dublin on June 6, 1880, into a family of modest circumstances. He was educated in the local Christian Brothers schools, supported Sinn Féin as a young man, and in 1908 was elected as a Sinn Féin candidate to the Dublin City Council, where he became a major figure. In 1913 he joined the Irish Volunteers and served as an officer in the South Dublin Union in 1916. For this he was sentenced to death, although the sentence was commuted to life in prison; after being sent to Frongoch in Wales, he was released in January 1917 in the general amnesty. Cosgrave stood successfully as the Sinn Féin candidate for Parliament for Kilkenny City in a 1917 by-election and was returned again for Kilkenny North in the general election in December 1918. When the first Dáil Éireann got underway in 1919, Cosgrave was made minister of local government, and he became a key link between the Dáil and the local political network across the country. When Eamon de Valera brought the Anglo-Irish Treaty to the cabinet in December 1921, Cosgrave cast the decisive favorable vote. With the death of Arthur Griffith in August 1922, Cosgrave was appointed acting chairman of the Provisional Government, and, when Michael Collins was killed, he became president of the Dáil government and eventually president of the executive council, the prime minister of the Irish Free State. Thus it was left to Cosgrave to complete the drafting of the new constitution, get the Irish Free State government started, bring the Civil War to a close, deal with the Northern Ireland Boundary Commission, resolve the army "mutiny" question, manage the fragile financial position of the country, and establish Ireland as an independent state on the international stage.[3]

By the mid-1920s, the Cosgrave government was challenged by de Valera, who had withdrawn from Sinn Féin in 1926 and formed Fianna Fáil. In the June 1927 election, Fianna Fáil won forty-four seats, mostly at the expense of Sinn Féin; in August, following the assassination of Kevin O'Higgins, the strongman of Cosgrave's cabinet, de Valera and his party signed the oath of allegiance and entered the Dáil. Cosgrave, calculating that these dramatic events had worked to the advantage of his Cumann na nGaedheal party, called a second election in September 1927. He recovered his losses by securing a total of sixty-two seats. However, de Valera's Fianna Fáil party won fifty-seven seats and emerged as a serious political competitor. In the aftermath of two elections in 1927, de Valera announced that he would travel to America to raise money to fund his programs. The fact that he both challenged the legitimacy of the Irish Free State and drew much of his financial support from the Irish community in the United States pushed the government to focus on how that situation could be turned around.[4] In early December, Cosgrave talked over these matters with US minister Frederick A. Sterling, who would report that Cosgrave worried that de Valera was seen in the United States as the "true leader of Ireland" because he had been "the outstanding protagonist in America" in the recent struggle for independence. However, Cosgrave emphasized, de Valera did not now "represent either the majority [in Ireland] or the more intelligent or practical people of the Free State." The policy of the Irish government needed to be clarified in the United States, Cosgrave thought, and he was "turning over in his mind who could be sent there of his Party to explain to Irish sympathizers the true situation."[5] Could a tour of the United States by Cosgrave himself do the job?

In fact, minister Timothy A. Smiddy had encouraged the External Affairs Department to consider an official visit to the United States as early as July 1925. Smiddy wrote to minister for external affairs Desmond Fitzgerald that "the time is now ripe when a visit either from you or the President, or both, or by the Vice-President and you to the United States would be very effective." Smiddy had clearly thought through the possibilities: a warm welcome by the public, an opportunity for excellent publicity for the Irish Free State in the American press, and a platform for the leaders of the Irish government to publicize the progress that had been made in the country. "A visit would be opportune in March 1926," he suggested, "when a public reception could be given by the Legation here on the 17th of March to which the diplomatic corps, members of the U.S.A. Cabinet, representative Senators and Congressmen would be in invited," all of which would accentuate the independent status of the Irish Free State. In Smiddy's words, "It would expedite exceedingly the realization among all Americans of our real constitutional status."[6] For Cosgrave or FitzGerald, the years 1925 and 1926 were too much filled with the ramifications of the Boundary Commission failure, the important Imperial Conference, and participation in the League of Nations. In September 1925, minister of industry and commerce Patrick McGilligan led a party to the United States, where they attended a dinner hosted by the US secretary of commerce, Herbert Hoover.[7] This, however, was not a public event. The government also sent a delegation to the Congress of Inter-Parliamentary Union meeting in Washington, DC, but Smiddy himself had to do the cross-country tours to talk about the new Ireland.

☘

A timely invitation from Kevin Kelly, the secretary of the Irish Fellowship Club of Chicago, prompted a visit to the United States. Kelly, who was in Dublin in the autumn of 1927, talked with Cosgrave and Patrick McGilligan, the new minister for external affairs, and invited them to speak to his organization on St. Patrick's Day. By late 1927 many felt that an effort should be made by the Irish Free State government to emphasize bilateral relations with the United States and to cultivate support among the Irish American community. The Ministry of External Affairs was asked to brief the cabinet on this proposition. Secretary of the department Joseph P. Walshe prepared a memorandum for discussion at a cabinet meeting on 9 December, the day Cosgrave also met with Sterling. Walshe emphasized that this was an "opportunity . . . put into our hands," arguing that "the great body of Irish-American opinion worth having is positively on our side and it only requires a little nursing to become active . . . They want tangible evidence of our State's existence and nothing will bring it home to them more definitely than seeing the President or Vice-President received by President [Calvin] Coolidge in Washington and honored by the people who run the United States." This, he asserted, would have an enormously beneficial effect, by emphasizing the "tangible evidence of our State's existence": public diplomacy through speaking engagements in Chicago and elsewhere would provide an opportunity to call attention to the "independence and development of the Saorstát." It would also stimulate support for, and investment in, the Irish Free State. Walshe went on to note that the Vatican had successfully raised substantial amounts of money in the United States by courting wealthy Irish Americans who could just as well be approached by the Free State. He also included reassuring remarks from Smiddy, that the Irish Fellowship Club had in years past been addressed by such distinguished figures as former presidents William Howard Taft and Theodore Roosevelt, as well as by Patrick Cardinal O'Donnell.[8] The cabinet decided to send a delegation in January 1928, when the Dáil was not in session: President Cosgrave; Desmond FitzGerald, minister for defense; Diarmuid O'Hegarty, secretary of the executive council; Joseph P. Walshe, secretary of the Department for External Affairs; and Colonel Joseph O'Reilly, aide to President Cosgrave.[9]

The delegation faced problems in appealing to the Irish American community. Although many leading US figures had supported the Anglo-Irish Treaty and the Irish Free State—including John Devoy, editor of the influential *Gaelic American*; Judge Cohalan, a leader of Clan na Gael and the FOIF, as well as a power broker in both state and national politics; and even Edward L. Doheny, the California oil millionaire and former president of the American Association for the Irish Republic—there had nevertheless been holdouts. The powerful Irish American newspaper the *Irish World* had backed de Valera in 1920 and 1922 and bitterly criticized the Irish Free State. Furthermore, many "irregulars" (or republicans) had fled to the United States after the end of the Civil War in 1923, adding to the number of critics of the Irish Free State in the country. Eamon de Valera had found strong support among these groups, and the Irish government was also sensitive to the fact that de Valera would be touring the United States in late 1927 and 1928, appealing to bond certificate holders to turn their claims over to him in order to finance a new newspaper, the *Irish Press*.[10] The invitation from the Irish Fellowship Club presented Cosgrave with an opportunity to promote the Irish Free State in the United States, preempt de Valera's fundraising, and thank Americans for their earlier help rather than ask for more money.[11]

How would the American government respond to a visit by a delegation from the Irish Free State? It should be noted that an official visit to the United States by the head of a foreign government was quite unusual at this time. As late as 1928, no sitting head of a European great power had ever toured the United States, apart from specific negotiations of diplomatic matters. This was a ground-breaking event, and American officials were warmly receptive.[12] Frederick A. Sterling, the new American minister to the Irish Free State, was consulted immediately, and he cabled the State Department to make arrangements. William R. Castle Jr., now assistant secretary of state, talked with President Coolidge and Secretary Frank B. Kellogg on 17 December. Coolidge said he would be "glad to give a luncheon" for Cosgrave at the White House, and the secretary of state planned an official dinner. An elaborate itinerary was worked out for 23–26 January: several private meetings and a number of ceremonial functions. Minister Sterling recognized that in addition to giving President Cosgrave an opportunity to thank the American people, his visit would "enhance the prestige of the Free State" and also support "the stability of the country." Moreover, the visit would "counteract the influence which Mr de Valera exerts on a large section of the Irish-Americans in the United States," although Sterling assured the secretary that Cosgrave had "too much tact and sense of propriety" to bring Irish domestic politics to the United States.[13] Bernadette Whelan notes that American diplomats were generally sympathetic to the Cosgrave government and quite suspicious of de Valera.[14]

On 11 January, the Irish delegation set sail for New York on the White Star liner *Homeric*. Before their departure a celebratory dinner was held for them at Clery's Imperial Ballroom in Dublin, presided over by the outgoing governor-general, T. M. Healy. Over four hundred and fifty people—including many businessmen and professionals, as well as the members of the consular community—attended to wish President Cosgrave well. Cosgrave emphasized that the trip was not a political party exercise or a fundraising effort, but a way to conveys thanks to the American people for their support for Ireland. "It was in no small measure due to that practical sympathy and to their generous support in Press and from platforms that the long-drawn-out struggle for national independence was ultimately brought to a successful issue," he said to an appreciative audience, whom he assured he would encourage investment, trade, and tourism in Ireland. James G. Douglas, now a senator, echoed many of the president's sentiments and wished him every success. Commenting on Cosgrave's trip, the *Irish Independent* shrewdly observed that it would "have an important bearing on these relations."

The *Gaelic American*, a strong supporter of the Irish Free State, stated as early as December that the visit "is a wise, a timely, and a welcome move," whereas the Jesuit weekly *America* quoted Seán Lemass, a young member of the Dáil and an advisor to de Valera, as saying that the purpose of the trip was to "discredit" de Valera's mission and to "delude the Irish in America into thinking that independence is already won."[15]

The voyage to America was a difficult one. The *Homeric* was caught in severe winter storms and arrived two days late in New York City on Friday, 20 January. The ship was met in New York harbor by the municipal tugboat *Macom*, carrying an official party that included mayor's representative Grover A. Whalen, judge Daniel F. Cohalan, Timothy Smiddy, and several members of the Irish Legation. When the Irish delegation boarded the *Macom*, the band of the New York City Fire Department played "The Soldier's Song" and "The Star-Spangled Banner." With sirens blaring and whistles blowing, they were then escorted to the Battery by fireboats while the guns at the fort on Governor's Island fired nineteen salutes. Once ashore, the party was given a ticker-tape parade in an open car escorted by mounted police along a crowd-lined Broadway to City Hall. There, at 11:30 a.m., they were welcomed by mayor James J. Walker, himself the son of Irish-born parents, and Cosgrave—appropriately dressed for ceremony and spectacle, in morning clothes, silk hat, and gloves—was given a scroll of welcome. He also spoke in the council chamber: "I thank God I have lived to see this day—that Providence has been good enough in our time to give our people that recognition for which they sighed so long, and which New York, in the majesty and magnificence of its great heart, has extended to the representatives of my country today."

From the public gallery, a woman's voice broke into "The Soldier's Song" and then sang "The Star-Spangled Banner," which was followed by tumultuous cheering. It was an emotional moment. President Cosgrave then left for a brief audience with Patrick Joseph Cardinal Hayes at the archiepiscopal residence on Madison Avenue and at 2:45 p.m. boarded the private car of New York Central Railroad's president Patrick E. Crowley at Grand Central Station for the overnight trip to Chicago on the Twentieth Century Limited. The *New York Evening Post*'s headline read: " Wild Welcome Greets Cosgrave: City's Welcome to Irish Leader."[16] This was priceless good publicity.

On Saturday morning, 21 January, the presidential party was met at the LaSalle Street Station in Chicago by its flamboyant mayor, William Hale "Big Bill" Thompson, dressed in his characteristic fur coat and broad-brimmed hat, and driven to the Drake Hotel for a luncheon, followed by a reception at the Union League Club. President Cosgrave and his colleagues were then taken to meet Robert E. McCormick, the publisher of the *Chicago Tribune*, and viewed the city from the top of the Tribune Tower. That evening, Cosgrave gave his major address to the Irish Fellowship Club at the Stevens Hotel. Some 4,500 people attended the dinner: the "captains of industry, politics and the arts," as Keown has described them.[17] The Irish minister of defense, Desmond FitzGerald, and the American minister to Ireland, Frederick A. Sterling, made opening remarks, and read out best wishes from US vice president Charles G. Dawes. Courtesy of Radio Corporation of America chairman Owen D. Young, the proceedings were then linked to a national audience of millions, and judge John P. McGoorty introduced President Cosgrave, who said that it was to express the thanks of the Irish people for the support they had received from America that he had come. He spoke of the "high honour" it was "to be the bearer of Ireland's greetings and good wishes." Cosgrave said he wanted to tell Americans about the great strides that had been made in Ireland since independence: industry was being encouraged, and the budget had been brought under control and taxes brought down. The Shannon Electrification Scheme would, he said, provide power for both industry and agriculture. The work started years ago by the Land League was being completed, as over two million acres of farmland were being made available for small landowners through the present government. Efforts were also being made to better produce and market livestock, dairy goods, and poultry. Primary education was made compulsory, with the teaching of Irish intended to cultivate a national consciousness. Democracy, religious toleration, and peace were being established.

Cosgrave concluded with two main points: first, that "the Irish Free State is a sovereign state with all the powers, duties, and responsibilities inherent in sovereignty," responsible only to its own legislature—Dáil Éireann—and holding a position equal to that of the other Commonwealth nations and to Britain herself. Second, he encouraged investment and tourism, outlining what he saw as Ireland's promising economic potential and urging Americans to visit. "We want all of you who can do so, to come and see for yourselves," he said. "You can judge for yourself what use we are making of our freedom. You can see our sovereign parliament sitting untrammelled in the old town house of the family of Lord Edward Fitzgerald." Ireland, he insisted, had taken her place among the nations of the world, and he invited Americans, especially Irish Americans, to see the results for themselves.[18] The *Chicago Herald and Examiner* reported that the speech brought the entire audience to its feet, pointedly observing that "many of them were 'diehards' who came to the banquet thinking that Eamon De Valera's 'no compromise' platform was a better one than Cosgrave's"; winning over to the Irish Free State many of those "diehards" was certainly a major objective of Cosgrave's trip to America. "Throngs Hail Cosgrave" read the *Examiner*'s headline.[19] Chicago and the Irish Fellowship Club had given Cosgrave just the kind of public platform and media access to the Irish American community that the Irish Free State government wanted.

Both the Irish Legation and the State Department had created a schedule for Cosgrave in Washington to recognize Ireland's statehood and extend to Cosgrave the dignity his office deserved. It also provided a Secret Service agent to guarantee security, as there was some worry that "republicans" might cause trouble.[20] On Monday morning, 23 January, the party was met at Washington's Union Station by William R. Castle Jr., assistant secretary of state; J. Theodore Marriner, chief of the European Division of the State Department; William J. B. Macaulay, secretary of the Irish Legation; Colonel L. H. R. Pope-Hennessy, military attaché at the British Embassy; and several hundred others. Led by a cavalry escort, the party drove in the secretary of state's Packard to the Mayflower Hotel, where Cosgrave stayed in the presidential suite. A luncheon was arranged at the home of the assistant attorney general William J. Donovan, better known as the former colonel of the largely Irish American Sixty-Ninth Regiment of the New York ("The Fighting 69th") and head of the Office of Strategic Services during World War II. That afternoon Cosgrave was taken to the State Department to meet secretary Frank B. Kellogg and then across the way to the White House, where he was officially introduced to President Coolidge by Assistant Secretary Castle, and the two leaders spoke briefly about the finances of the Irish Free State. Later Cosgrave visited chief justice William Howard Taft, vice president Charles G. Dawes, and House Speaker Nicholas Longworth. That evening, the Irish party were the guests of honor at a formal dinner given by Canadian minister Vincent Massey that included British ambassador Sir Esmé Howard and his wife; senators George H. Moses, Arthur Capper, Thomas J. Walsh, and Key Pittman; Edith Bolling Wilson (widow of the late President Wilson), and Florence Jaffray Harriman (wife of the banker J. Borden Harriman), among others, as guests.[21]

Tuesday, the second day of the visit, started at 8:00 a.m., when President Cosgrave went horseback riding in Rock Creek Park, where he was joined by senator William E. Borah. Later that morning, Cosgrave was driven to Arlington National Cemetery, where he was met by brigadier general Herbert O. Williams and a guard of honor to lay a wreath on the Tomb of the Unknown Soldier. Then followed the highlight of the trip: an elaborate luncheon at the White House with President Coolidge and the First Lady. The thirty guests included cabinet members such as secretary of the treasury Andrew Mellon, secretary of war Dwight F. Davis, attorney general John G. Sargent, and secretary of commerce Herbert Hoover; and congressional leaders such as senators William E. Borah and Claude Swanson. Coolidge showed Cosgrave around the residence and pointed out some of the historical artifacts. Cosgrave later commented that Coolidge was "not only a charming host, but he displayed a broad knowledge of the progress of the Free State." Cosgrave was also able to tell the president that the appointment of Frederick Sterling as minister to Ireland had been an excellent choice.[22] None of the hallmarks of diplomatic work were fulfilled in this luncheon meeting—no treaty signed, no accord negotiated. no joint communiqué issued. Nevertheless, it demonstrated for both Irish and world opinion the acceptance of the Irish Free State and its government by the US political establishment: both what the Irish cabinet had hoped for in early December, and a public fulfillment of Irish American aspirations. The *New York Times* ran the byline "Cosgrave is Guest at White House," and the *Irish Independent* observed, "President's Honour to President."[23]

In the late afternoon, Cosgrave attended a reception at the home of Colonel L. H. R. Pope-Hennessy, the British military attaché and the son of the late Sir John Pope-Hennessy of Cork. A dinner was given in the Chinese Room of the Mayflower Hotel by Minister Smiddy that included Vice President Dawes, several cabinet members, and some distinguished Washingtonians. One State Department official called it a "beautifully arranged men's dinner."[24]

Wednesday morning started with a drive south of the capital to Mount Vernon, where President Cosgrave paid homage to the first president of the American Republic, George Washington. Lunch was arranged at the National Press Club, so Cosgrave could talk to overseas reporters about current affairs in Ireland. Over the course of the afternoon Cosgrave spoke seriously with William R. Castle Jr. and Green H. Hackworth, the State Department's chief legal officer, about the vexing question of the repayment of the bond certificates sold during 1920 and 1921 in the name of the Irish Republic. Castle and Hackworth had met earlier with Frank P. Walsh and John T. Ryan, who represented the Hearn committee of bond certificate holders, and heard their arguments that the Irish Free State was obligated to repay the money. Cosgrave gave assurances that the Irish government would honor the bonds, but asked advice as to how to avoid providing money for Walsh and others hostile to the Free State—the sole, albeit modest, issue of substance discussed during the visit to Washington.[25] In the mid-afternoon the Irish leader was taken to Capitol Hill for the second major event. At exactly 3:00 p.m., Congress adjourned, and President Cosgrave was brought to the floor of the House of Representatives by the leaders of the Republican and Democratic Parties to meet members of Congress, where he was introduced by House Speaker Longworth as the "right welcome guest of the United States," to applause. For almost twenty minutes, individual Congressmen were introduced to Cosgrave, after which he left a message of thanks to Congress, to be read out by the clerk.[26] Cosgrave and his party were next escorted into the Senate chamber by majority leader Charles Curtis, minority leader Joseph Taylor Robinson, chairman of the Senate Foreign Relations Committee William E. Borah, senior minority member of the Foreign Relations Committee Claude A. Swanson, and chairman of the House Foreign Affairs Committee Stephen G. Porter. President Cosgrave was introduced by Vice President

Dawes and given a seat to his right, after which the senators stood for an unprecedented ovation. The senators were offered an opportunity to meet the Irish leader, who was later asked to speak. He told the Senate, "I have come to extend to your President and to the people of America the thanks of my people for all that you have done for us during the last two hundred years, for the homes which you have extended to our people who have come here, and for the sympathy and support which you have been so gracious and so generous as to extend to my people." He said he was also reciprocating the visit that Benjamin Franklin had made to the Irish Parliament in the eighteenth century, during which Franklin said that both America and Ireland, "hand in hand, would achieve the freedom they sought." Both the senators and the crowd in the gallery warmly applauded.[27] The honor of speaking to the Senate that had years earlier been granted to Charles Stewart Parnell and recently given to A. J. Balfour and the king of Belgium.[28] The *Irish Times* wrote, "Congress Cheers Mr. Cosgrave," while the *Irish Independent*, which had sent its own correspondent, Frank J. Geary, ran the headline "Historic Event in Congress, Address to Senate by Mr. Cosgrave."[29] That evening, Secretary Kellogg and his wife held a formal dinner for the Irish party at the Pan-American Union: their major event in Washington. Among the fifty-six distinguished guests were General John J. Pershing, former secretary of state Robert Lansing, celebrated environmentalist Gifford Pinchot, and several cabinet members and senators. The dinner was followed by a reception at the splendid Dupont Circle home of Juliette Williams Leiter, the sister-in-law of US minister to Ireland Frederick Sterling. The luncheon at the White House, the address to Congress, and the secretary of state's formal dinner constituted precisely the kind of public recognition and acknowledgement for the Irish Free State that the government had desired, emphasizing the Irish Free State's foreign policy of special bilateral relations with the United States and the prestige accorded to the Irish government.[30]

On Thursday, Cosgrave met with the secretary of labor and a number of labor leaders, most of whom had Irish roots, and then had a private luncheon at the Mayflower. Later that afternoon, he received an honorary doctorate of law by the Catholic University of America. In the course of the ceremony, university rector bishop Thomas J. Shahan asserted that no visitor to the United States had been "awaited with keener anxiety" and "received with more cordial amity." In conferring the degree, archbishop Michael Joseph Curley of Baltimore said that "Ireland has taken its place among the nations of the world," and that, by the earlier meeting at the White House, the United States "through its chief executive has voiced its pleasure."[31] This was only the third honorary doctorate awarded by the university, the first two having been given to King Albert of Belgium and Désiré-Joseph Cardinal Mercier. The day—and the visit to Washington—concluded with a dinner held by the British ambassador and his wife, Sir Esmé Howard and Lady Isabella Howard, at their residence.[32] This was perhaps a controversial gesture, but, together with the earlier dinner at the Canadian Legation, it was intended to show that Ireland was a functioning member of the Commonwealth and that relations with Great Britain had been normalized. Altogether, the visit to the American capitol had been an unqualified success, projecting the image of the Irish Free State as a sovereign, independent nation-state.

President Cosgrave and his party left Washington for Philadelphia on the morning of Friday, 27 January. A visit to Philadelphia required visits to Independence Hall, the Liberty Bell, and Valley Forge, where Cosgrave paid honor to both American and Irish American heroes.[33] That evening, Cosgrave spoke at the Philadelphia Forum at the Metropolitan Opera House, where he was introduced by Michael J. Ryan, a long-time leading figure in the local Irish American community. The following day, the Irish leader also paid a courtesy call on Dennis Joseph Cardinal Dougherty, and that evening spoke with Professor Smiddy to a large audience at a dinner given by the Friendly Sons of St Patrick at the Bellevue-Stratford Hotel, once again presided over by Michael J. Ryan.[34] On Sunday, 29 January, the Irish party left by train for a brief stay in Atlantic City, and then a trip north to Montreal and Ottawa, for an official visit to the Canadian capital. Although a tragic train accident slowed their arrival in Ottawa, the government of William Lyon Mackenzie King welcomed President Cosgrave to Canada. The Irish party held private meetings with Mackenzie King and the governor-general, were hosted at a formal public dinner, and were brought into and given recognition by the House of Commons.[35]

On Wednesday, 1 February, President Cosgrave and his party arrived back in New York City at Pennsylvania Station, having traveled overnight in prime minister Mackenzie King's private rail car. Cosgrave had a variety of high-prestige functions to attend with major power brokers in the Irish American community and the New York establishment. With a mounted police escort, the party were first taken to the Biltmore Hotel and then to the Irish consular offices and the New York Stock Exchange in lower Manhattan. In the early afternoon, a luncheon was given by James A. Farrell, the president of the United States Steel Corporation, at India House, under the auspices of the Foreign Policy Association. Minister for defense Desmond FitzGerald told the businessmen in attendance that "Ireland is persuaded to do no more fighting," either now or in the future. President Cosgrave talked about the Irish economy, and Irish poet George Russell (Æ) who was one of the guests, spoke of the wisdom of the people who had emerged as Ireland's new leaders. After a courtesy call on the old Fenian John Devoy, whom Cosgrave had feted when the famous rebel returned to Ireland in 1924, the Irish party were the guests of Mayor Walker at a dinner for over a thousand people in the ballroom of the Biltmore Hotel. After-dinner talks, all broadcast on the radio, were given by Constantine McGuire, a foreign policy expert at the Brookings Institute, and Major Eugene F. Kinkead, a former congressman from New Jersey, as well as Mayor Walker and President Cosgrave. The following day, the Cosgrave party attended a luncheon given by the Bond Club of Wall Street at the Bankers Club, where Cosgrave spoke of Irish thrift and urged the two hundred financiers to invest in Ireland. The Irish delegation spent the afternoon visiting the gravesites of such Irish heroes as General Richard Montgomery, Thomas Addis Emmet, and William James McNevin. In the evening, the Irish party were the guests of honor at a dinner for about three hundred people at the Lotos Club on West 57th Street. Nicholas Murray Butler, the celebrated president of Columbia University, introduced both Cosgrave and FitzGerald. Butler, a leading commentator on international relations, said that the Irish Free State was "a nation in all respects equal in status to those other free and independent peoples with which it is associated as a member of the British Commonwealth of Nations."[36] Later in the evening, in front of a crowd of five thousand people, Cosgrave reviewed the famous old New York

"Fighting 69th" at their Armory on Lexington Avenue and attended a reception there.

On his last morning in New York, Cosgrave toured Columbia University and Grant's Tomb and then attended a luncheon at the Lawyers Club given by retired judge Daniel F. Cohalan, former head of the FOIF. Judge Cohalan praised Cosgrave warmly, stating that that he had "done a man's share in bringing his people so far forward on the road to independence and prosperity."[37] Judge Martin T. Manton also spoke, as well as President Cosgrave. Among the guests were former ambassador to Britain and Wall Street lawyer John W. Davis, former ambassador to Germany James W. Girard, international banker Otto Kahn, and several Supreme Court justices and city officials. Following the luncheon, Judge Cohalan and his wife gave a reception at their home on East 94th Street, providing an opportunity for the Irish dignitaries to meet prominent supporters of the Irish Free State. Cosgrave had hosted a luncheon for Judge Cohalan in Dublin in 1923, and these events were suitable occasions for these two political figures to reconnect. That evening the Irish party were then the guests of honor at a large banquet given by the Friendly Sons of St Patrick at the Hotel Roosevelt in Brooklyn, after which they were returned to the grand ballroom of the Waldorf-Astoria, to attend the eighty-eighth annual Emerald Ball, a fundraiser for Catholic charities that was a major social event for the Irish American community. President Cosgrave and Mrs. James M. Power led the grand march at this gala event.[38] It was a spectacular ending to three very successful days in New York City. The *New York Times* had already asked the rhetorical question "What guest could be more welcome to the majority of the American people?" and went on to praise Cosgrave as a leader whose political accomplishments had been "as difficult and brilliant as that of any contemporary statesman of Europe."[39] The *New York American* ran the headline "Cosgrave Honored at Many Fetes on Return to NY."[40] M. E. Hennessy of the *Boston Globe* observed that "he charmed everybody who met him."[41] Modest, soft-spoken, and down-to-earth, Cosgrave had moved easily among both establishment political and financial figures and in powerful Irish American circles, and he had filled the pages of newspapers and been seen by thousands. This was public diplomacy executed without a flaw.

President Cosgrave and his party left New York later that evening, Friday, 3 February, on the White Star liner SS *Olympic*, the sister ship of the ill-fated *Titanic*. Cosgrave had carried out a whirlwind tour of the United States and Canada, visiting six cities in two weeks, speaking to thousands of people, in particular several key Irish American communities and the hierarchy of the Catholic Church, and meeting the leaders of American business, finance, and government. Perhaps the leaders of government—President Coolidge, Secretary Kellogg, House Speaker Longworth—were the most important for the purposes of the Irish Free State government; their cordial meetings displayed the Irish Free State leaders on an international stage. Cosgrave cabled the White House that he was "deeply touched by the kindness and hospitality" offered by President Coolidge.[42] "Your President and Congress," Cosgrave said at one banquet, "by the gracious courtesy they have extended to us, have done my country an honor that can never be forgotten."[43] Ireland had appeared to "take her place among the nations of the earth," in the words that had stirred Irish nationalists for over a hundred years.[44] At home the Dublin newspaper the *Irish Independent* had gotten the point: the honors extended to President Cosgrave by the American government "will remove the last lingering doubts which may exist among a section of Irish-Americans as to the extent of the measure of independence which the Free State has secured," it pronounced. Going straight to the heart of the matter, the paper concluded, "Only the head of an independent Government could have been given this official welcome."[45]

☘

Was this public diplomacy a success? Were the Irish Free State government's expectations realized? Many people were certainly satisfied. Both President Coolidge and Secretary Kellogg had made generous public gestures of welcome to the Irish delegation. Congress had invited Cosgrave into its chambers. More could not have been expected. President Cosgrave sent a personal letter to Professor Smiddy, thanking him and the legation staff "for all your efforts to make our visit a success." For his part, Smiddy reported to Cosgrave that "your visit is doing much to kill any hostility among the sincere opponents of the Irish Free State. It is bringing home to everybody here the fact that we are an independent sovereign state." Smiddy reported his recent conversation with President Coolidge, who had told him, "Your President impressed me most favourably and I like him very much." This was a very welcome reassurance. Later, Smiddy added that the visit had "done a great deal to weaken the adherents of Mr de Valera," a connection that was certainly in the minds of members of the government.[46] Indeed, some months later Kellogg would tell Lord Cushendun that Cosgrave's visit had been "politically useful in America by counteracting the agitation of Irish extremist followers of de Valera."[47] Ambassador Howard, reporting to the Foreign Office in London, saw the visit of the Irish party as a triumph: "There can be no doubt, I think, that the visit has been a great success," he wrote. Later he concluded that "it may safely be said that the tour has been successful in its main object which was to bring home to the mass of Americans the fact that an autonomous country, known as the Irish Free State, actually does exist," noting that this publicity challenged the views that Eamon de Valera had promoted. Howard also talked with President Coolidge, who had been pleased with Cosgrave's visit and thought "the visit would do much good to the cause of the Free State generally."[48] American minister Frederick A. Sterling, now back in Dublin, reported the return of President Cosgrave and his party to Ireland and their triumphant reception by enthusiastic crowds testified to "the success of his American visit." Sterling went on to note that "no Irishman within Cosgrave's lifetime has been the recipient of so signal a mark of affection and esteem as that which Mr. Cosgrave was accorded."[49]

The perception of the Irish visit by the Irish American community as a success is more difficult to assess. Cosgrave and his colleagues certainly met hundreds of Irish American leaders and met thousands from the community, and they unquestionably made a good impression. Perhaps more important, Cosgrave was able to reconnect with such major supporters as John Devoy and Judge Cohalan. The *Gaelic American* noted that the visit "was a great success from every point of view," and Catholic weekly the *Commonweal* emphasized "the fact that Mr Cosgrave came here as the first regularly elected chief executive of his people," while the *Catholic World* provided a detailed description of the tour and printed in full Cosgrave's message to Congress.[50] The Irish newspapers were also supportive. "'Three Great Moments' for the Irish

People," wrote the *Irish Times*, and the *Irish Independent* commented on Cosgrave's "magnificently-successful visit to the United States and Canada."[51]

Of course, for the antitreaty republicans and many of the opposition in Fianna Fáil, Cosgrave's trip, despite all of the celebration and recognition by the American government and public authorities, was an empty gesture. The Irish Free State was not the country they wanted. W. P. Lyndon, an editor for de Valera's old organization the AARIR, and its former president, John F. Finerty, deprecated Cosgrave's visit. The *Irish World*, which had backed de Valera during the split in the Irish American nationalist movement in 1920 and again over the Anglo-Irish Treaty, was sharply critical of the Irish Free State. The paper had earlier called Cosgrave an "Imperial Agent" and largely ignored the Irish party's visit to the United States, apart from the fact that the Irish Free State government had not yet repaid the bond certificate holders. In February, while other newspapers were printing accounts of Cosgrave's triumphant return to Ireland, the *Irish World* reported that a "Mass Meeting in Dublin Flatly Condemns Cosgrave."[52] The Jesuit weekly *America*, which was clearly more sympathetic to de Valera, did concede that "a most hearty welcome was extended the President of the Executive Council of the Irish Free State, William T. Cosgrave." J. C. Walsh, a journalist with roots in the old home rule movement and nominally a de Valera supporter, wrote to his friend in Ireland James O'Mara, organizer of the bond certificate drives in 1920 and 1921, that although he found Cosgrave's dinner with the British ambassador symbolic of the subordinate status of the Irish Free State and Minister Smiddy insufferable, nevertheless Cosgrave "made a consistently good impression over here, and maintained his dignity very well."[53] All things considered, this was high praise, and a measure of how successful Cosgrave and his colleagues had been in representing an independent Ireland to the Irish American community.

☘

By his public meetings in New York, Chicago, and Philadelphia, and particularly his reception by President Coolidge and Congress in Washington, William T. Cosgrave had demonstrated the international status of the Irish Free State. Minister Smiddy assured Cosgrave of the "great importance and the opportunity it [the visit] furnished of making known to the average American our Constitutional status, and the use we are making of our freedoms. . . . Candidly, five years of well organized publicity would not attain such historical results."[54] The several levels of the US government played a consciously important role in this process, and, in doing so, enhanced the quest for "identity, legitimacy, symbolism, [and] status" described years later by Conor Cruise O'Brien as one of the essential missions of early Irish foreign policy.[55] "The propaganda value of Cosgrave's American trip was enormous," historian Ciara Meehan has concluded.[56] Through public diplomacy Cosgrave had emphasized the government's commitment to one of the pillars of Irish Free State foreign policy: bilateral relations with the United States. Seeing the meaning of the trip clearly, Desmond FitzGerald wrote that "for the first time the President of the United States, the Secretary of State, the American Government, the Senate and Congress were able to receive one who was not merely a popular leader . . . but the Leader of a State, one of the Comity of Nations, independent and internationally recognized."[57] This public acknowledgement of Cosgrave by the President and Congress constituted a significant gesture of American support for an independent Ireland. Indisputably, Cosgrave's visit placed the Irish Free State and both domestic and foreign policy on a new level. Ireland had indeed taken her place among the nations.

9

Secretary of State Frank B. Kellogg Comes to Ireland, 1928

The participation of the Irish Free State in the signing of the Kellogg-Briand Peace Pact—Ireland's first multilateral treaty signed with full powers—in Paris on 27 August 1928, and the subsequent visit to Ireland by US Secretary of State Frank B. Kellogg were major happenings in the life of the emerging new nation. The circumstances leading to US president William T. Cosgrave going to Paris to sign the treaty and Secretary Kellogg's trip to Ireland arose out of several unrelated events. Cosgrave, as noted earlier, visited the United States from 19 January to 3 February, 1928, and traveled to New York, Chicago, Philadelphia, and Washington, also making a brief trip to Ottawa. In private conversation, Cosgrave invited Kellogg to visit Ireland, and Cosgrave so warmed to the idea that he also raised the matter later with President Coolidge, who seemed agreeable.[1] Kellogg was in fact in the process of negotiating what would become a multilateral treaty that would hopefully "outlaw war." The signing of the treaty would bring him to Europe and make him available for a visit. Although the possibility seemed reasonable enough at the time, it would have been unusual in 1928. Robert Lansing, in 1919, as a member of the American Commission to Negotiate Peace, and Charles Evans Hughes, in 1924, in his capacity as president of the American Bar Association, had been the only secretaries of state to visit Europe while in office. Thus, such a trip, particularly a visit to Ireland, would have been quite extraordinary. However, no one in 1928 could have foreseen the diplomatic storm ahead. As a result, Ireland inadvertently became involved in the contretemps between the United States and Britain, which added a sharp edge to US recognition of Ireland's international stature as independent of Britain.

☘

Secretary Kellogg did not dismiss President Cosgrave's invitation out of hand, given Coolidge's approval, and the reports of his possible visit to Ireland began to travel the rounds of the diplomatic community. In April, Alanson B. Houghton, the US Ambassador to Great Britain, wrote to Kellogg, who had been ambassador to Britain from 1923 to 1925, urging him to visit England as well as Ireland. Later in the month, Frederick A. Sterling, the US minister to the Irish Free State and a friend of Kellogg since his service as counselor of the London embassy, also urged Kellogg to accept the official invitation that he understood would be made shortly. "It would be a great thing for this country," Sterling said, "if you could come as it has so long been considered a land of unrest & trouble, and a visit from an American Secretary of State will be a recognition of its stability."[2] Given the legacy of the Irish Civil War and the assassination of Kevin O'Higgins the previous year, this was a very relevant point. A state visit would be a major indicator of Ireland's full international acceptance. Sterling did go on to make one caveat: that a visit to Ireland should be accompanied by a visit to England, lest there be "any feeling that you are flouting them." This observation was not misplaced. On 12 May, Cosgrave himself wrote an official invitation to Kellogg and, recalling their earlier conversations, expressed the hope that the secretary would visit Ireland sometime in the summer. He offered Kellogg "a cordial welcome to our shores," and assured him that "we shall endeavor to make Mrs. Kellogg and yourself comfortable and render your stay pleasant and enjoyable."[3] Kellogg's response to these invitations was much the same: "Nothing would please me more than such a visit but I am afraid I cannot at present promise to go," he wrote to Cosgrave. "I am trying to negotiate the multilateral anti-war treaty."[4] These negotiations with the European powers prevented his leaving Washington. Furthermore, Kellogg confided to Sterling, he was sure that a visit to Ireland and Britain would make it difficult for him to refuse to also go to the Continent to negotiate with the foreign ministers of the great powers on the unresolved matters connected with the multilateral treaty. As a courtesy, he asked Sterling to hand deliver the letter to Cosgrave.[5]

Meanwhile, the Irish government recognized that the multilateral treaty then being negotiated was an international instrument with which they also wanted to be associated. The US and French governments had originally invited Great Britain to sign the treaty, but they did not extend invitations to the Dominions. On 8 May, the US minister in Ottawa reported a query by the Canadian undersecretary of external affairs whether Canada and the other Dominions would be individually invited to sign the treaty. Despite the fact that both Canada and the Irish Free State currently enjoyed diplomatic representation in Washington, Kellogg replied that this was a matter of British policy, adding that "the United States would warmly welcome Canadian participation in the treaty."[6] William Lyon Mackenzie King, the Canadian prime minister and minister for external affairs promptly wrote to the Dominions office: "If invited to participate, so far as His Majesty's Government in Canada is concerned, we would be prepared to sign [the] treaty." He went on to say that it was "essential that an explicit invitation covering Dominions should be extended by the United States Government."[7] Irish External Affairs had been kept informed of these discussions and on 14 May wrote to the Dominions office, "On receiving an invitation from the United States Government His Majesty's Government in the Irish Free State would be willing to participate in any negotiations which may be necessary for the conclusion of such a treaty." Moving quickly, the Irish Cabinet decided on 17 May to ask the British government to arrange an invitation to participate in the negotiations for "a multilateral treaty for the outlawry of war."[8] Two days later, the British foreign secretary informed the US ambassador that "on receipt of an invitation to participate in the conclusion of such a treaty, they [the Dominion and Indian Governments], no less than His Majesty's Government in Great Britain, will be prepared to accept the invitation."[9] Invitations to sign the treaty were sent promptly from Washington to Dublin and Ottawa on 22 May, and individual signing by the other Dominion and Indian governments was also arranged.[10] Minister of external affairs Patrick McGilligan replied on 30 May that "the Government of the Irish Free State warmly welcomes the action of the United States government in initiating this further advance towards the maintenance of general peace," and that it was pleased to be able to participate in the negotiations of the treaty.[11] Minister Sterling wrote to Secretary Kellogg that both the Irish press and the country were "enthusiastic" about the treaty and added, "Should the United States see fit, as now seems likely, to negotiate directly with the Free State on this matter, it would greatly please the *amour-propre* of the country and receive even more enthusiastic support, if it were possible."[12] In fact, the negotiations were largely limited to France and the United States. However, the British government wanted a reservation to the treaty that would allow the Dominions to come to the defense of members of the Commonwealth without being in violation of the treaty. The Irish Free State government, asserting its independence from British leadership, chose to sign the treaty without agreeing to any reservations.[13] The separate invitations and decisions to sign the agreement reinforced the independence and sovereignty of the Irish Free State and the other Dominions that had been asserted in the language of the Balfour Declaration in the 1926 Imperial Conference.

By the middle of July 1928, the final draft of the multilateral treaty to renounce war had been finally worked out. The signatories agreed to "condemn recourse to war for the solution of international controversies, and renounce it as an instrument of national policy," and they also pledged to settle all disputes between them by "pacific means."[14] Germany was the first to agree to accept the treaty, on 27 April, and in the next two months the five Dominions—Canada, Australia, New Zealand, South Africa, and the Irish Free State, and India—announced acceptance. Before the treaty could carry any international weight, however, the approval of the major powers was needed. On 14 July, France agreed; four days later, so did Britain. The Irish Free State also responded to the final draft of the treaty on 14 July . McGilligan wrote to Sterling, "The draft Treaty as revised is equally acceptable to the Government of the Irish Free State, and I have the honour to inform you that they are prepared to sign it in conjunction with such other Governments as may be so disposed."[15] Provisions now had to be made for the signing. As the health of the German foreign minister, Gustav Stresemann, was too delicate to permit a trip to Washington, Kellogg told President Coolidge that he had indicated to the French ambassador that he would be willing to go to Paris in the company of the European foreign ministers.[16] Over the next several weeks, arrangements were made for the signing of the Kellogg-Briand Pact—officially the General Treaty for the Renunciation of War as an Instrument of National Policy—in the famous clock room of the Quai d'Orsay in Paris on 27 August.

Kellogg's planned visit to Paris opened the door for the possible side trips to Ireland and England. While the arrangements were being made, Sterling cabled from Dublin on 22 July, congratulating Kellogg on his diplomatic triumph and urging him again to come to Ireland. In a letter, Sterling expanded on the idea of a visit to Ireland, pointing out that it "would be a great courtesy to the Irish Free State."[17] Kellogg's biographer David Bryn-Jones would later write that Coolidge had indicated to Kellogg that this would be a good opportunity to return Cosgrave's visit to the United States. Kellogg himself subsequently told the British foreign secretary that President Coolidge had "promised" Cosgrave a return visit, in part because Cosgrave's own tour of the United States had helped counter the influence of Eamon de Valera and the "Irish extremists" in America.[18] Kellogg consulted with his wife, Clara, who had hoped to see her friend Dorothy Sterling, and began to make arrangements. They would sail on the *Île de France* on 18 August and return home on the *Leviathan*, leaving Southampton on 4 September. This schedule would allow approximately a week to get from Paris to London, from London to Dublin, and from Dublin to Southampton. To facilitate their travel, the cruiser USS *Detroit* was put at their service.

Arrangements were made with Sterling to renew the Irish government's invitation to the secretary. Kellogg wanted to know whether Cosgrave was coming to Paris to sign the treaty, in which case they could travel to Ireland together on the *Detroit*. In fact, the usual procedure for the signing of a treaty was for the minister for external affairs to carry out the ceremony, but these plans were quickly reconfigured, clearly as a courtesy to Kellogg and Ireland's unique needs. McGilligan himself wrote to Cosgrave urging him to go in his place:

> [Ernest] Blyth [minister of finance] informed me of what the American Minister in Dublin told him and I am completely in agreement that under the circumstances you should make the journey to Paris and affix signature on our behalf to the Pact. The publicity that we will thereby secure will undoubtedly be of immense benefit and your presence in Paris will enhance the good repute we already enjoy with the Americans by reason of our unreserved and prompt reply to the Kellogg invitation [to sign the treaty]. So I urge on you that it is essential for you to go. If it seems almost assured, the Secretary of State returns to Dublin with you we are shown to the world as

specially associated with the Pact and specially favoured by America. Your association with Kellogg will put the crown on the good work already accomplished by your American trip. It is an opportunity not to be missed.[19]

McGilligan not only made a persuasive argument for Cosgrave to go to Paris and travel back to Ireland with the secretary of state, but he also stated very succinctly major elements of Ireland's foreign policy objectives: to cement the good relations Cosgrave had established with the secretary of state during his visit to Washington in January, to showcase the special position that the Irish Free State enjoyed in its bilateral relations with the United States, and to demonstrate to both domestic and world opinion that the Irish Free State was a fully sovereign and independent, nation-state participating in international affairs.

Kellogg, of course, had been ambassador to Great Britain from 1924 to 1925 before being called home to become secretary of state. The Kelloggs had many friends in Britain and had not been back in almost four year's time, which made a visit perfectly reasonable. Kellogg wrote to Ambassador Houghton, who was in the United States on holiday, making clear that protocol demanded that "I cannot well go to Ireland without also going to Great Britain," but that Houghton need not "cut short" his "vacation to go back to Great Britain to entertain Mrs. Kellogg and me just for a day or two."[20] Everything seemed to be in place for a two-day visit to both countries.

❧

At this point, an entirely unrelated incident intervened that threw the entire trip into doubt. President Coolidge had hoped to expand on President Harding's 1921 success with the Washington treaties in achieving an arms limitation agreement for capital ships. Coolidge proposed similar limits for cruisers, submarines, and auxiliaries, and, in 1927, invitations had been sent to signatories of the Five Power Pact to hold new naval arms limitation talks. France and Italy declined, but Great Britain and Japan joined the United States for negotiations in Geneva. However, it proved impossible for even the three countries to agree on the numbers of these classes of ships.[21]

In large measure, these problems hinged on the diverse functions of naval cruisers. The US Navy needed large cruisers that could stay at sea for some weeks and sail long distances, whereas the Royal Navy needed smaller cruisers to protect commerce and seldom sailed more than several days at a time from numerous naval stations in colonies around the world. These different needs put great strain on Anglo-American relations. The Geneva Conference broke up without agreement, but the League of Nations Preparatory Commission for the Disarmament Conference, which had been called into being in 1924, had undertaken talks on these matters in late 1927. By late June 1928, the British and the French privately came to a tentative agreement that seemed to mark an important shift by the British; it established limits on vessels of ten thousand tons with guns up to eight inches, but placed no limits for ships of six thousand tons and guns of six inches. This agreement was not made public until 30 July, when Sir Austin Chamberlain, the foreign secretary, inadvertently mentioned it in the House of Commons. The United States was not informed of the terms until the following day.[22]

The immediate reaction of the US government to this Anglo-French agreement was indignation and a certain level of outrage. To begin with, the agreement seemed to mark an abandonment of fairly consistent Anglo-American accord on naval matters and a shift to a new Anglo-French entente. Furthermore, it appeared to place limits on precisely the kind of cruisers that the United States needed—ten-thousand-ton vessels with six- to eight-inch guns—while leaving unlimited the number of cruisers the British, French, and Italians wanted—those under ten thousand tons with guns of six inches or less. Finally, the manner in which the agreement was made public seemed to Coolidge and Kellogg rather a slap in the face, as well as a diminution of the treaty to outlaw war that was to be signed in Paris some three weeks later.[23]

On 3 August, Kellogg reported to President Coolidge, on vacation near Superior, Wisconsin, that he had asked the British for an explanation. Coolidge also wrote to Kellogg on 3 August, and their letters may have crossed. Coolidge's letter was thunderous. In addition to telling the secretary to do nothing on the naval questions, he went on to comment, "I do not especially like the meeting that is to be held in Paris," which he thought might be an occasion "for some other purpose not yet disclosed" rather than simply the signing of the treaty.[24] Kellogg replied the following day: "I regret exceedingly that any inquiry was made of the British government," and promised not to raise the matter with the British until Coolidge was back in Washington and the two could confer more easily.²⁵

Furthermore, Kellogg went so far as to tell the president, "I am also very sorry that I agreed to go to Paris to sign the Treaty." In fact, he continued to make plans to go and told third assistant secretary William R. Castle Jr., that he would resign if forbidden to do so. Thus, as late as 16 August, Kellogg was not only still planning to go to Paris, but to London and Dublin also.²⁶ However, after talking to J. Reuben Clark, soon to be installed as undersecretary of state, who had just come from seeing Coolidge in Wisconsin, Kellogg changed his plans. On 17 August, the day before he was to leave, the secretary wrote to the president, "Mr. Clark told me what you said about England. It is entirely satisfactory to me. I have no desire to go anywhere and I wish to avoid as much as possible visiting any country except officially."²⁷ The trip to England was clearly off, and Kellogg dutifully reported that he had talked with Ambassador Houghton by telephone and told him, "My time was so short it was impossible for me to visit Great Britain." He informed the president that he would take the *Detroit* from Le Havre to Dublin and back to Cherbourg, where he would embark on the passenger liner *Leviathan* for the voyage home. Kellogg mentioned his obligation to Cosgrave, who had "changed his plans" to come to Paris as well as the long-standing invitation to Kellogg to visit Ireland.²⁸ Anglo-American relations, however, were in a state of turmoil, and the decision not to visit London was an unmistakable signal that enhanced the significance of to the decision to go to Dublin.

Thus, Kellogg went to Paris to sign the treaty at the Quai d'Orsay on 27 August, and Cosgrave also attended. Pageantry prevailed, as Swiss guards in medieval costumes assembled the heads of governments and foreign ministers of fifteen nations. Under the intense heat of the klieg lights used for filming the spectacle, Aristide Briand, Frank B. Kellogg, and Gustav Stresemann signed the treaty first. President Cosgrave was the tenth to sign. This was in fact one of the great diplomatic events in the interwar years.²⁹ The Kellogg-Briand Pact was the high point of Kellogg's career, for which he was later awarded the Nobel Peace Prize.

In the minds of many people in 1928, the apparent willingness of all of the world's powers to renounce war as an instrument of national policy seemed to mark a turning point in the history of civilization.[30] The treaty was seen as a major triumph for the foreign policy of the United States, as well as for the Irish Free State and for Cosgrave. This was the first multilateral treaty in which Ireland was included, and the first opportunity for Cosgrave to participate in a major international ceremony. The world observed Ireland take its place among the nations.

In these emotion-charged circumstances—after attending the social functions in Paris, being saluted by the Republican Guard, and put on a special train for Le Havre—Kellogg and Cosgrave boarded the USS *Detroit* on 29 August for an overnight trip to Dun Laoghaire. Elaborate preparations had been meticulously put in place for the observation of diplomatic protocol on the arrival of the official party in the Irish Free State. Flags decorated Dun Laoghaire, and cheering crowds lined the harbor walls and basin. Although the sun shone in town, the Irish Sea was covered with a light fog. Just before 11:00 a.m., as the mist lifted, the cruiser *Detroit* steamed into full view, and upon entering the harbor fired the first twenty-one-gun salute by a warship in Ireland's honor. From shore, nineteen guns replied, to pay respects to the US secretary of state. A motor launch came alongside with Mrs. Cosgrave, the American minister, and members of the Irish cabinet (dressed in silk hats and cutaways), who then went aboard to welcome Kellogg and Cosgrave. When the launch returned with the official party, the secretary's flag was lowered by the *Detroit* and the Irish Free State Flag hoisted to the mainmast.[31] A nation once again.

While an army band played, Kellogg and Cosgrave were taken past a guard of honor to the Royal Irish Yacht Club, where the secretary was welcomed by representatives of the suburban communities. Champagne was served, but, with prohibition the rule at home, the Americans abstained. A twenty-car motorcade took the official party into Dublin; all along the route, crowds cheered in the decorated streets. A cavalry escort in green uniforms joined the entourage at the Baggot Street Bridge, where a bugle fanfare was played, and Kellogg was taken to the Mansion House. Nine hundred soldiers lined Dawson Street, and an army band played the national anthems of both the United States and Ireland when the motorcade arrived. Kellogg was given the

Freedom of the City, which was memorialized on a scroll in English and Irish, in a silver casket. He signed the roll of Freemen and was told by Seamus Murphy, the chairman of the Dublin City Commissioners, that "no act which we have ever done has ever stirred within us so much pride, nor has any greater honor come to us than the opportunity of enrolling you as a Burgess of this city."[32] General Ulysses S. Grant, on his postpresidential tour, had been the only other American so honored.

Secretary and Mrs. Kellogg were then taken past still larger crowds in the center of Dublin to Phoenix Park, where they were to stay at the American Legation as guests of Minister Sterling and his wife. In the afternoon, Kellogg made a courtesy call on governor-general James McNeill, and in the evening the Kelloggs were guests of honor at a state banquet for over one hundred people held by President Cosgrave and members of the executive council at the Shelbourne Hotel. Kellogg told the dinner guests that he brought "greetings to the Irish people from the President of the United States."[33] President Cosgrave saluted Kellogg's great achievement in negotiating the peace pact and said, in that context, "We greet him here tonight as the most popular man in Ireland and the most popular man in the world."[34] Kellogg opened himself in reply to President Cosgrave: "I wish to thank you again for your wonderful reception. As I said today, I knew I would get a warm reception in Ireland. Everybody does. What a wonderful reception we have received! I shall remember it as the heyday of my life and, as I look back on it, it will be one of my brightest memories."[35] Kellogg's biographer would attest to this sentiment. After the dinner, a reception for about two thousand people was held at the Plaza Ballroom on Abbey Street. On Friday the Kelloggs had a quiet day at the legation, but they did visit Leixlip Castle, County Kildare, and were guests of Governor-General McNeill that evening at a dinner at the Vice-Regal Lodge for about thirty people. Later that night, the Sterlings held a reception and dance at the American Legation, where the famous tenor Count John McCormack sang and the band of the cruiser *Detroit* played.[36]

With most of the ceremonial functions completed, the secretary played golf with some of the officers of the *Detroit* and the legation staff on Saturday, 1 September. The Kelloggs later took a motor drive in County Wicklow, and in the evening Mrs. Kellogg went to a play at the Abbey Theatre as a guest of the playwright Lennox Robinson. On

Sunday, their last day, the Kelloggs and the Sterlings paid a call on the Cosgraves at their home in Templeogue, four miles from central Dublin. The trip to Ireland was a short visit—only three and a half days—but a great deal had been arranged.[37]

Monday, 3 September, saw the departure of the Kelloggs and elaborate ceremonies once again. The USS *Detroit* was brought around to the Alexandra Basin in Dublin harbor. A marquee had been set up and a military guard of honor paraded. The Kelloggs were driven to the quay at about 2:00 p.m. with the legation staff and representatives of both the government and the governor-general. In his parting statement Cosgrave said, "This visit, following the signature of the memorable Peace Pact, made a profound impression here, and it was an honor and a pleasure to us and the people of Ireland to receive you and Mrs. Kellogg in our midst."[38] Farewells were said, the national anthems were played, and the Kelloggs boarded the *Detroit*. As the ship moved slowly down the River Liffey and out of the harbor, crowds followed along the quay cheering. Kellogg, quite moved by all of this, stood on the deck and waved his hat.

These events did have significance beyond mere pomp and circumstance. At one level, the Irish participation in the signing of the Kellogg-Briand Pact was of major importance in the evolution of the independence of the Dominions within the Commonwealth. The self-governing Dominions, like the Irish Free State and Canada, were invited as individual nations to sign the treaty—the first major multilateral treaty, including the Versailles Treaty of 1919, in which the Dominions had played so independent a role. The *New York Sun* called attention to the way the Kellogg visit dramatized Ireland's independence: "When the guns of the Irish Free State fired their salute of welcome to the American Secretary of State aboard an American cruiser in an Irish port the significance of Dominion status in the British Empire was made clear and the consciousness of the reality of Ireland's position as a world Power took a firmer grip on the imagination of the onlooking nations."[39] The *Chicago Tribune*, the McCormick newspaper, noted also that the trip was "something more than the formal return of the visit of President Cosgrave," and the *New York Times* hinted at the symbolism of the occasion: "Ireland Delighted Over Kellogg Visit, Overjoyed at Tribute to Free State, Especially as He Did Not Stop in London."[40] Several months later Smiddy would report that Kellogg was still pleased with his reception in Ireland, but, more to the point, was grateful for Ireland's independent initiative: "He again said that the Irish Free State was one of the first countries to signify its willingness to sign his Treaty without reservations."[41]

Furthermore, secretary of state Frank Kellogg's visit Ireland was the first official visit of a foreign statesman to the Irish Free State. With all of the salutes and toasts and exchanges, this, too, signaled that the United States recognized the Irish Free State as a member of the international community. It was widely understood that this was a special gesture, for Kellogg chose to visit Ireland at pinnacle of his greatest prestige and of America's highest stature since the Paris Peace Conference of 1919. The chargé d'affaires at the American Legation in Dublin, Wainwright Abbott, reported that the visit was a "milestone in the history of the Free State." In Abbott's view, this was the first opportunity for Ireland to welcome "so distinguished a guest." The secretary of state's official visit "emphasized in a concrete way the autonomous status of the Free State in the British Commonwealth."[42] Abbott's comments reveal the sensitivity of American diplomats to the goal of the Irish government to assert the status of the country as a sovereign state. Even the *Times* of London acknowledged that the visit was an "advertisement in America for the Irish Free State's stability and progress."[43]

Was Kellogg's decision not to visit Britain, ostensibly for reasons of time, a snub? Despite his own denial to the British foreign secretary, the decision was deliberate. The Foreign Office itself remained quiet about the matter, but in the 1928 volume of the *Survey of International Affairs*, editor Arnold J. Toynbee drew the obvious conclusion that "Mr. Kellogg's action in visiting the Irish Free State, but not Britain . . . was popularly interpreted as an intimation that in this matter [the Anglo-French tentative naval agreement] American public opinion was in accord with the opinion of the Administration in Washington."[44] Indeed, British ambassador Sir Esmé Howard had to admit in his annual report to the Foreign Office that Kellogg's decision not to also visit Britain "was the subject of no little comment and speculation, the malevolent attributing it to a desire to slight Great Britain or to pique over the

Anglo-French compromise."⁴⁵ The failure of the Geneva naval arms limitation talks and the clumsy handling of the Anglo-French tentative agreements on ship classification, along with a number of other issues, had caused a steady deterioration of Anglo-American relations. This was the clear but unstated message expressed by Kellogg's visit to Dublin.

Cancellation of the trip to London was one signal, as was the visit to the Irish Free State and the prospect of a special relationship with the Cosgrave government. Other signals to the British were Kellogg's closer relations with Canada, including the week he spent on board the *Île de France* with prime minister William Lyon Mackenzie King before signing the peace pact, and the current American initiative to negotiate an arbitration treaty directly with Egypt. The United States had special relations of kinship and proximity with two of the Commonwealth Dominions and could conceivably develop special relations with others as well. Great Britain was being challenged in its own Commonwealth.⁴⁶

☘

The strain in Anglo-American relations reached a high point with President Coolidge's Armistice Day speech in November 1928, in which he seemed to call for US naval superiority. However, under the new Hoover administration, which took office in March 1929, Anglo-American relations began to mend. In the meantime, it was through Secretary Kellogg's trip to Dublin that the United States observed the protocol of an official return visit to Ireland. The visit was more than a mere official gesture; it was an assertion that the Irish Free State had been singled out in the foreign relations of the United States. This distinction seemed to bear out Patrick McGilligan's promise to Cosgrave, that the Irish Free State was "shown to the world as specially associated with the Pact and as specially favoured by America."⁴⁷ Once again, like Cosgrave's visit to Washington in January, Secretary Kellogg's trip to Ireland was a conspicuous gesture of support for an independent Ireland. As US chargé d'affaires Wainwright Abbott emphasized,

> The compliment paid on the Irish Free State by the visit of the Secretary on returning the visit of President Cosgrave to the United States is a milestone in the history of the Free State. It has not only been the first occasion that

the Free State has had the opportunity to receive so distinguished a guest and given the people of Dublin a chance to prove their sympathy for the United States, but it has emphasized in a concrete manner the autonomous status of the Free State in the British Commonwealth.[48]

This was a strong assertion that the visit to Ireland of Secretary Kellogg—then regarded as one of the world's leading statesmen—was a signal recognition of the Irish Free State as an independent member of the international community. As a result of the issues concerning the cruiser question, the Irish Free State consequently found itself on the edge of an Anglo-American international incident and the recipient of distinctive acknowledgment by the US government.(see appendix 4).

Epilogue

Ireland and America

The Irish American community, although sometimes divided over ideology or personalities, consistently supported some form of Irish self-government. The reunification of the Irish Parliamentary Party in 1900 and the growing prospect of home rule over the next decade provided the circumstances for enthusiastic support from a wide spectrum of Americans. This included substantial cash contributions, which kept the Irish Party able to meet election expenses and subsidize its members of parliament. The Ulster Revolt and the outbreak of World War I in 1914 eroded the prospects of home rule and opened a window of opportunity for the Clan na Gael to provide leadership and funds for the 1916 Rising. The British suppression of the Rising and the executions of its leading figures, together with the United States entering the war just a year later, created a new dynamic within the Irish American community. President Woodrow Wilson's statements that people had a right to live under governments of their own choice raised expectations in Ireland and America that this principle would clearly apply to Irish aspirations—the "Wilsonian moment." The Irish demand for change and for action was legitimized by the sweeping electoral victory of Sinn Féin in the 1918 general election and the meeting of Dáil Éireann in January 1919 that declared the independence of Ireland from Great Britain. These events set in motion an enormous effort by the Irish American community, through the creation of the American Commission on Irish Independence, to secure the recognition of an independent Ireland at the Paris Peace Conference. However, the failure of the conference to deal with the Irish question, despite the discreet efforts of President Wilson and Colonel House, disappointed and alienated many Irish Americans and contributed significantly to the defeat of the Versailles Treaty and US membership in the League of Nations. As the situation in Ireland deteriorated into the Anglo-Irish War, Irish Americans rallied in support of the Dáil government and the Irish people. Americans raised over one million dollars for the Irish Victory Fund in 1919, purchased almost six million dollars of Irish bond certificates in 1920 and 1921 to provide revenue for the running of the Irish government, and contributed over five million dollars to the American Committee for Relief in Ireland in 1921 for the destruction caused by the Anglo-Irish War. These were significant amounts of money, reaching a total of $11,820,634 (roughly $154,003,823 in today's dollars). Moreover, the public hearings by the American Commission on Conditions in Ireland focused attention on the suffering and disruption caused by British forces in Ireland and indicated the extensive support for Ireland in the United States. The hearings also generated unflattering public opinion about Britain, America's former ally. British anxiety about this capacity of the Irish American community to provide sustained support for the Dáil government and generate hostile public opinion were certainly major factors in the Lloyd George government's decision to open peace talks in the summer of 1921.

The role of the US government in the struggle for Irish self-government and independence was perhaps of even greater importance, although it was generally less public. Certainly, diplomatic convention at the time prohibited the government of one country to become involved in the internal affairs of another, unless it was prepared to go to war, and it was certainly never in the interests of the United States to consider war over the Irish question. However, American relations with both Britain and Ireland were unusual in diplomatic terms, because the United States had a large population of first- and second-generation Irish American citizens (over 4,000,000) and an enormous number of citizens of Irish descent (20,000,000), almost 21 percent of the total population. President Wilson was careful not to mention Irish issues in public, for which he has been criticized. However, he did speak about Irish matters privately, possibly to both A. J. Balfour and David Lloyd George. He clearly instructed his secretary of state, his ambassador in London, and his advisor Colonel House to raise the matter of an Irish settlement as a means of achieving a better working relationship with Britain during World War I. Arguably, the Irish Convention of 1917–18 was set in motion in part in response to the urgings of Wilson and other leading Americans, such as former president Theodore Roosevelt. Wilson also met with many Irish American groups and spokespersons, most notably in Paris, with the American Commission on Irish Independence. That these efforts did not produce results was probably less the fault of Wilson than of the leaders of the British government. President Warren G. Harding did publicly support the program for relief in Ireland in 1921, thereby giving a stamp of official approval to the raising of money for Ireland in 1921, a matter that provoked alarm in diplomatic circles. Harding's secretary of state, Charles Evans Hughes, also raised the Irish matter directly, in the context of a number of British-American issues, adding to the anxiety of the British government about the extent to which the Irish problem impinged on relations with the United States. Undoubtedly the American problem contributed to the British government's willingness to negotiate with Sinn Féin in 1921.

Once the Irish Free State came into existence in December 1922, William T. Cosgrave's government moved quickly to open diplomatic relations with the United States. Within just over a year and a half, the details were worked out, and on 7 October 1924, president Calvin Coolidge received Timothy A. Smiddy, the first Irish minister. This may seem unremarkable today, but it was in fact dramatic at the time, inasmuch as this was the first instance of the envoy of a Dominion of the British Commonwealth being accepted by a foreign power—Ireland's "first real diplomatic post," as Michael Kennedy has put it.[1] Diplomatic recognition by another sovereign state was a conventional definition in international law of an independent international legal person. Coolidge authorized the sending of a US minister to Dublin in 1927 and hosted President Cosgrave in the White House the following January. Secretary of State Frank B. Kellogg made an official visit to Dublin in 1928, at the very peak of his international celebrity status, after the dramatic signing of the Kellogg-Briand Pact in Paris, in which the Free State also participated. This marked public acceptance of the Irish Free State into the community of nations, as well as defiance of the view of a faction in Ireland that only with the de Valera government in 1932 or the new constitution in 1937 or neutrality in 1939 or the Republic of Ireland Act of 1948 that Ireland became truly an independent nation. It is significant that it was not until 1929 that other powers—France, Germany, and the Holy See—also extended recognition to the Free State.

The US Congress, while less capable than the executive branch of taking direct action, consistently offered a platform from which US sentiments about Ireland could be expressed. Many resolutions were introduced in both houses, but most noteworthy were the Senate resolutions on behalf of clemency for Roger Casement in 1916, for a hearing for the Irish delegation at the Paris Peace Conference in 1919, and for Irish self-determination and Irish membership in the League of Nations in 1920. Even more significant was the fact that both houses of Congress also invited President Cosgrave into their chambers in 1928.

These were dramatic acts and gestures by private citizens (Ireland's "exiled children in America") and by the US government (the White House, the State Department, and the Congress) in their support for Ireland in its long struggle for autonomous self-government and status as an independent sovereign nation. Of course, only the Irish themselves, through courage, persistence, and determination, were able to achieve the goal of independence. But would this have been possible without American money and support? Clearly, American aid not only provided enormous practical assistance to the successive Irish governments; it constituted something of an alarm bell, warning British governments that the Irish issues would have to be settled. Clearly the Irish government pursued American support and recognition among other channels of international status. Historian Jason Knirck has concluded, "Cumann na nGaedheal [the Cosgrave government] actually staked out a fairly aggressive foreign policy agenda," and United States diplomatic relations were a key element of that program.[2] Nicholas Mansergh's qualified assertion in 1940 and 1965 that American support was "not of decisive importance" may now be considered in a fresh context and effectively challenged.[3] It can be said with confidence—more in line with Joseph J. Lee's recent comment, "No America, no New York, no Easter Rising"—that, from 1916 to 1928, the United States contributed significantly to the making of an independent Ireland.[4]

ACKNOWLEDGMENTS

Every book is the result of the work of many hands, and this volume has enjoyed the interest and support of a great number of people and institutions. I am particularly indebted to Kevin Kenney, director of Glucksman Ireland House, and Miriam Nyhan Grey, director of graduate studies at Glucksman House, for their generous support and urging that I submit my manuscript to New York University Press. Several friends and colleagues read the manuscript and gave me valuable and insightful comments: Maureen O'Rourke Murphy, Hofstra University; Thomas E. Hachey, Boston College; and David R. Ringrose, University of California, San Diego. Libraries and archives provide the building materials for any historical work, and this book is the product of the rich resources that been made available so generously, as listed in the bibliography. Particularly helpful in obtaining documents by long distance were Sarah Horowitz, curator of rare books and manuscripts at the Haverford College Library; Craig G. Wright, supervisory archivist at the Herbert Hoover Presidential Library; the Digital Library of Villanova University; the Manuscripts Division of the Library of Congress; the Office of the Historian at the Department of State; the Manuscripts Division of the National Library of Ireland; archivist E. Hoare at the Eton College Library; and Sarah Williams, archives assistant at the Parliamentary Archives. Here at the University of Manitoba, both the St. John's College Library and the Elizabeth Dafoe Library have been enormously helpful, especially the interlibrary loan division, as has Michael Lachislaw of Information Services and Technology in preparing my photographs for publication. The thesis of this book has developed over a period of years, during which time I have been fortunate to test my ideas in a series of journals and books. Although the arguments in this book are more fully researched and strongly articulated than those in the earlier articles, I should like to thank the editors of the *New Hibernia Review*, the *Recorder: The Journal of the American Irish Historical*

Society, Eire-Ireland, Irish Studies in International Affairs, Irish Historical Studies, James Joyce and His Contemporaries, and the *Theodore Roosevelt Association Journal.* Let me offer my thanks to editor Clara Platter and associate editor Veronica Knutson of NYU Press for their advice and enthusiasm in bringing this project to life. I am particularly grateful also for the generous assistance of the University of Manitoba through Vice President Dr. Digvis S. Jaysas. Finally, my gratitude to Janet Foster Carroll for her continuing encouragement and support.

APPENDIX I

The Meeting of John Quinn's Delegation with A. J. Balfour on 4 May 1917

Typescript of the interview with Balfour by John Quinn, in MS 1751, John Quinn Papers, National Library of Ireland
New York, June 2, 1917

NOTES OF RECENT AMERICAN OPINION AND ACTION ON THE IRISH HOME RULE QUESTION

About six weeks ago it was intimated to me from very high official quarters, not the ambassador personally, that a cable by prominent Irish Americans direct to Lloyd George as to the importance of a prompt settlement of the Home Rule questions of all Irish parties and factions getting together to that end would be officially welcomed in England, and would be a good thing to do. It was no small job to get twenty-five or thirty American Irishmen to agree as to the language and substance of such a cable. It involved meetings, many of them at lunch and at dinners, and conferences. While the cable was under way and approaching its final revision, the British and French commissions arrived. Through Sir Horace Plunkett it was arranged that Mr. Balfour should receive a small deputation in Washington. The deputation was made up as follows: former presiding Justice of the Appellate Division of the Supreme Court, Morgan J. O'Brien, a conservative Irishman, highly respected, and one of the leading citizens of New York City and State, vice president of the last New York State Constitutional Convention and a man of prominence; Colonel Robert Temple Emmet, formerly of the United States regular army and a highly respected, influential man; Lawrence Godkin, Esq., a leading lawyer and public spirited citizen, whose father, the late Lawrence Godkin, was an Ulster Protestant of high literary attainments, a friend of James Russell Lowell and others, and for many years the editor and proprietor of the *New York Evening Post*, one of the most influential papers in America; former mayor John D. Fitzgerald of Boston, and John Quinn. The conference took place at the headquarters of the British Commission in Washington, DC, Friday, 4 May 1917. Mr. Balfour was there with his secretary Sir Eric Drummond, KCB, and Mr. Ian Malcolm. The conference lasted two hours. The entire Irish situation as it appeared to the members of the delegation was presented to Mr. Balfour. It was made plain that the overwhelming sentiment of people of Irish extraction in this country as well as that of other countries had all favored an early settlement of the Irish problem. It was further pointed out that men eminent in American public life favored it.

Mr. Balfour was very courteous and expressed great interest in the statements made. He expressed himself as being impressed by the representative character of the delegation and by the moderation of their views. He said that he had not come to America with any mandate upon the Irish question; that he did not know of the late developments of it except what he had read in the papers; that the cables he was getting from his government related to "ships and shells and not to Irish politics," but that he was in complete sympathy with the objects of the visitors.

It was impressed upon Mr. Balfour that the Parliamentary Party had largely lost its influence here because of the repeated postponements and evasions of the Home Rule question. I told him that the Americans might be provincial and all that, but that there was a strong and wide spread sentiment of fair play and that fair-minded people thought Ireland had won her innings and for one reason or another and by one evasion and another had been deprived of her hard-earned innings.

Former Mayor Fitzgerald told that at a meeting at Faneuil Hall in Boston four days before (Faneuil Hall is known in American history as the Cradle of Liberty), at which an American, in passing, had referred to the sinking by German submarines of 400,000 tons of ships in the week previous, and said that the meeting went wild, 99 people out of 100 in the audience cheered for three minutes. Fitzgerald gave that as one of several illustrations of the danger of letting the Irish sore fester in this country. He told how he had been a consistent supporter for twenty years of Redmond and the Parliamentary Party in this country; of how he had run for the United States Senate on the Democratic ticket a year ago against the Hon. Henry Cabot Lodge, whom Mr. Balfour knew well; how he was defeated by some 23,000, and how he was told by his supporters, after the election, that the great majority of votes against him was made up of irreconcilable and radical Irishmen in Massachusetts who were dissatisfied with the policy of the paper he owned and which had always supported Redmond; he told of two of his boys who had volunteered for service in France. He said that he could not understand why the Home Rule had not been granted to Ireland and that Americans generally could not understand; that he represented New England opinion upon the subject and that a settlement of the thing that would result in an undivided Ireland and would be welcomed and cut the ground from under the radicals who had lived upon predictions of betrayal which time after time had been fulfilled.

(I should have said above that of the delegation of five, former Judge O'Brien and former Mayor Fitzgerald of Boston are prominent Roman Catholics; Colonel Emmet and Mr. Godkin are Protestants; and John Quinn might be termed a "neutral." Mr. Fitzgerald was a member of Congress for six years and was mayor of Boston for six years.)

I will not attempt to summarize here all that was said during the course of the two-hour conference. I will add however that among other things I said: that the Irish question had now in a sense become an American question. That Americans generally would like to see it settled. That it was the one outstanding obstacle to complete and cordial relations between the people of this country, as distinguished from the administration and government officials, and Great Britain. That the Irish and the Germans had coalesced some years ago and that the Irish furnished the brains and the motive power and initiative, and that that combination had been productive of harm and might be productive of greater harm. I pointed out that if what is known as the McLemore resolution had been adopted in Congress, Americans would have been warned off and forbidden passports for traveling on belligerent ships and Germany might easily have taken the line that she would sink all belligerent ships but would make an exception of American ships; that she could easily have done that because American ships were comparatively negligible as to numbers, and that in that event we would not have been involved in war with Germany. The McLemore resolution was forced by German propaganda, and the brains of that German propaganda was supplied largely by the disaffected Irish Americans. I pointed that out to Mr. Balfour as just one occasion upon which that hostility might have been fatal.

I pointed out to him that the American people generally understood what I might call for short the Ulster game as excluding three to six counties in Ireland, and that if Home Rule were adopted and those counties excluded, it would be generally felt here that Ulster and Carson had won, that Carson was in the cabinet and that he had gained his point, and the American feeling would be sympathetic with radical Irishmen here who would denounce the Ulster-Carson victory as another "betrayal," and that any Home Rule settlement plastered over with that legend would be regarded by Americans as no satisfactory settlement from an Irish point of view, and Americans would say that if the Irish continued to be disaffected and hostile to England that they were not to blame and that England was to blame. That Americans could not understand why England was willing to allow Ireland generally to be disaffected, and to continue to have general disaffection here over three or four counties in the north of Ireland. That this war had put sacrifices upon everyone and that it was up to Ulster to submit to certain possible inconveniences in order to solve the question finally. I added that the radicals of this country had lived upon predictions of betrayal and selling out and incompetency on the part of Redmond, and that those predictions had time after time apparently been fulfilled, and that the radicals had lived upon those predictions and upon Redmond's failures and procrastinations and upon the alleged betrayals of England's pledges to Ireland. That more generous terms must be given now than would have been acceptable three years ago.

I pointed out to Mr. Balfour that I was not looking at this from a sentimental point of view and that I was trying to look at it from the point of view of British self-interest and from American opinion generally. I told him that the time for quibbling and for political refinements and for casualical [sic] arguments and the day for pettifogging and of "small things" in the Irish question had passed. That it had now become an international question, and that only a generous settlement on large lines, would in my opinion meet the situation.

I told him that in my opinion it was not so much a question of Ulster coming in as it was of the Sinn Féiners being satisfied. I added that

I thought that there should be an immediate general amnesty of Irish political prisoners and their return to Ireland, and that the influence of a man like John McNeill [Eoin MacNeill], would be of the very best in healing the breach between the Sinn Feiners on the one side and the Parliamentary Party and the Ulsterites on the other.

I told him if a settlement was made which would include a large part and the Sinn Feiners and not result in the division of Ireland, conservative Irishmen of prominence in this country would welcome it, applaud it, rejoice over it, and acclaim it as a solution of a great outstanding historical wrong; that it would remove the feeling of disfavor of England in this country; that it would result in general rejoicing; that there was machinery here by which a great wave of public approval and public favor could be started rolling in; that the cardinals and archbishops and bishops and prominent clergy of the Catholic Church would rejoice over Home Rule and an undivided Ireland. That prominent Irish Americans would rejoice over it and that Americans generally and President Wilson and former Presidents Roosevelt and Taft and other prominent Americans would welcome it, and that the tide would turn. But I pointed out to him that unless it was settled in a large and generous way, conservative Irish Americans, who were broad-minded and pro-Ally in their sympathies, and had been pro-Ally in their sympathies from the beginning of the war, would be helpless. I emphasized the fact that no bargain would be made with the radical Irish in this country; that intellectually and temperamentally one could not reason with them; that some of them thought that Germany was winning, or would win; others thought Ulster would not play fair, and that anything that was offered would have a string to it, others thought that Sinn Féin would sweep all before it, and that at the Peace Conference there would be an independent Irish Republic. But I did say that a countercurrent of public opinion could be started which would become so broad and extensive that thereafter Americans generally, as well as liberal Irish Americans, would be impatient with the claims of the irreconcilables and that they would be blanketed or pushed aside and made largely negligible.

Mr. Balfour spoke of all that had been done by England, of past historical wrongs, that they were the rule in those days, that they hoped they were forgotten and believed they generally were forgotten; spoke of what England had done for Ireland during the past twenty years; of the Land Acts, in which he had had a large part; of the Irish University Act, which under any American law would probably be unconstitutional; contrasted the condition of the Irish by the English in the last fifty years with the treatment of the Poles by the Germans. He repeated again that he had not come from his government to take up the Irish question here, but that no one could be more anxious than he and his associates and his government were that the question could be amicably settled. He said that he was not much impressed by the argument that Ulster would be economically ruined by Home Rule for the whole of Ireland, nor that Home Rule would be followed by religious bigotry and persecution, nor was he much impressed with guarantees. He said that he believed that if legislators acted with the right spirit that their sense of equity and fair play was a better protection than any constitutional guarantees. He laid aside those two arguments including Ulster, but he said that the argument really was a sentimental one; that Ulster was satisfied to remain where she was; that Ulster felt herself nearer to England and more a part of England than she was near to and a part of the rest of Ireland; that she had been loyal to England; that she was contented; and when Ulster said to England that she was loyal and contented and wanted to remain as she was and retain her present connections, that he felt it was hard for the English to say that Ulster should be put where she did not want to be put, under Home Rule, against her wishes. He added that certainly it seemed to him an unwise thing to use force to coerce Ulster in the midst of a war, when sons of Ulster were fighting for England on the field of battle.

I made the reply that Ulster should make a sacrifice even of [*sic*] her feelings and her sentiment if it was necessary to influence the opinion of America and the world, and above all it was necessary, as it seemed to me it was, to have a united Ireland.

I said to Mr. Balfour that I could send him editorials, many of them very long editorials, from substantially all of the great daily newspapers in the great cities of this country, urging upon England from various angles a settlement of the Irish question in a way that would satisfy Irish opinion generally in Ireland and this country. I told Mr. Balfour that I had literally hundreds of these editorials that had been sent to me by friends and that I had collected in the last six weeks.

There was nothing that might be called speech-making at the conference. It was a meeting of earnest men talking as friends over a perplexing and difficult question.

The five members of the deputation agreed not to make any statements about it. Sir Eric Drummond said that a very brief statement could be given out. A brief statement was given out from the embassy side. No member of the deputation made any statement.

At the end of the conference Mr. Balfour stood up, and, as he was surrounded by the members of the deputation and his secretaries, he repeated that he had been greatly impressed by the moderation of the statements made to him, and that he would cable to his government forthwith the fact of the interview and the substance of the statements made, and the views that were given to him, and he finished: "And, gentlemen, I will add that it is your private conviction that any compromise, resulting in the exclusion of a part of Ireland, or any Home Rule plan that leaves out even a part of Ulster, will not meet the situation; in short, will, in your judgment, be worse than useless."

Every member of the deputation felt that Mr. Balfour would do just as he said he would do. They felt that he might be the beginning of a new chapter in English and Irish history. But above all they felt that it would do more than anything else possibly could toward removing the one cause of friction or suspicion of Great Britain in the United States.

Of course this is only a very rough sketch, with many omissions, of what was said at the conference. As I have said, Mr. Balfour explicitly stated that he was not much impressed and never had been much impressed by the claim that to include Ulster in Home Rule would lead to the economic ruin of Ulster or to religious persecution in Ulster. He laid stress upon the sentimental feeling of Ulster. I pointed out to him that the argument that home rule would result in an orgy of legislation, in jobbery, and in financial ruin, was without any reasonable basis in fact. I pointed out that the old bogey of years ago that Home Rule would result in an Irish Tammany Hall was quite unsound. There were Irishmen in this country in municipal organizations and in the national congress and in state governments. Whereas the state governments and the national government were as free from scandal as any government in the world, there had been scandals in municipal organizations, the same as perhaps there had been scandals in the corporation of Dublin or the corporation of Belfast. I pointed out that the men who would go into the home rule parliament would be of a different breed and kind than those who have gone into the Dublin municipal corporation; that municipal corruption in this country in the past was not limited to the Irish; that in Philadelphia, Pennsylvania, for example, they had a corrupt municipal government and the Irish had never been in control there; that in Cleveland, Ohio, where the Irish were strong, there had never been municipal corruption; that Chicago, where the Irish were strong, had had reform mayors and no Tammany Hall, and that Tammany Hall was merely a bogey; that in the last twenty years the Republicans and anti-Tammany had held control of the City of New York for the majority of the time, and that businessmen felt that Tammany administration was the best administration that New York could have. It was then that Mr. Balfour said that he was not impressed with the argument of religious persecution or financial ruin of Ulster, and did refer to the sentimental argument.

At any rate, I am certain that Mr. Balfour felt that the deputation that went there and the moderate American Irishmen the deputation represented were not playing any selfish game; that they were sincere friends of Great Britain and the allied cause; that they were looking at the question from an American and English point of view; that America was now one of the Allies, even though there was no formal treaty or had been no formal treaty or pledge; and that whatever their interest and affiliations in the past had been, they felt that from an American and English point of view, as well as from a pro-Ally point of view, the sooner the Irish question were settled to the satisfaction of people in Ireland generally, and on a basis that pro-Ally, Irish Americans could openly proclaim a satisfactory solution, the better it would be for England and the pro-Ally cause, and the better it would be for America.[1]

APPENDIX 2

Documents Submitted and Witnesses at the Senate Foreign Relations Committee Hearings on the Treaty of Peace with Germany

Memorial to the Senate of the United States, presented by Patrick J. Lynch and signed by 189 concerned citizens from across the United States.

Extended remarks and text of Judge Daniel F. Cohalan, including the presentation of:

    Ireland's Declaration of Independence, Proclaimed by Dáil Éireann, January 21, 1919;[1]

    Ireland's Message to the Nations;[2]

    Ireland's Democratic Program, Proclaimed by Dáil Éireann;[3]

    Letter from the Irish Delegates appointed by Dáil Éireann to Present Ireland's Case, May 17, 1919, to M. Georges Clemenceau;

    Letter from the Irish Delegates appointed by Dáil Éireann to Present Ireland's Case, May 26, 1919, to M. Georges Clemenceau

    Letter from the Irish Delegates Appointed by Dáil Éireann to Present Ireland's Case, May 26, 1919, to Council of the League of Nations;

    Sean T. O'Kelly's Letter No. 1 to Premier George Clemenceau and all the Peace Conference Delegates, February 22, 1919;[4]

    Sean T. O'Kelly's Letter No. 2 to Premier George Clemenceau and all the Peace Conference Delegates, March 31, 1919; and

    Memorandum in Support of Ireland's Claim for Recognition as a Sovereign Independent State;

Correspondence in the Case of Ireland's Claim of Independence between American Commission on Irish Independence—American Commission to Negotiate Peace and Representatives of Other Governments;[5]

Report of Conditions in Ireland with Demand for Investigation by Peace Conference, Frank P. Walsh and E. F. Dunne, Paris, June 3, 1919;[6]

Interview between President Wilson and Messrs. Edward F. Dunne and Frank P. Walsh, at the President's House, 11 Place Des Etats Unis, Paris, Wednesday, June 11, 1919;[7]

Brief of Protest to the Foreign Relations Committee of the US Senate;

Statement by Rev. James Grattan Mythen, Assistant Minister, Christ Church, Norfolk, Virginia, as made to the Foreign Relations Committee, Saturday, August 30, 1919;

Statement by Former Congressman James F. O'Connell, Representing a Delegation of the Bench and Bar of Massachusetts Before the Senate Committee on Foreign Relations, August 31, 1919;

Statement by James E. Derry, Indianapolis, National President of the Ancient Order of Hibernians in America;

Statement of Rev F. X. McCabe, CM, LLD, President of DePaul University, Chicago, Illinois;

Statement of Mary F. McWhorter, National President of the Ladies' Auxiliary, Ancient Order of Hibernians in America;

Statement Submitted by District Attorney Joseph C. Pelletier, of Boston, Massachusetts, Supreme Advocate of the Knights of Columbus;

Statement of Judge O'Neill Ryan, of St. Louis, Missouri;

Statement of Daniel T. O'Connell, Director of the Irish National Bureau, Washington, DC;

Resolutions of Irish National Assembly, Expressing Thanks to the US Senate;

Statement of the Hon. Eugene F. Kinkead, Former Member of Congress and Former Major in the US Army;

Statement of Katherine Hughes, Secretary of the Irish National Bureau;

Statement of Patrick J. Lynch, of Indianapolis, Clerk of the Supreme and Appellate Courts of Indiana;

Joint Statement of Rev. John J. Moran, of Youngstown, Ohio, and Charles P. Mooney, of Cleveland, Ohio, Reporting on Behalf of the State Convention of the Ancient Order of Hibernians of Ohio;

Statement of Matthew Cummings, of Boston, Massachusetts, Ex-National President of the Ancient Order of Hibernians;

Statement Presented by the Advisory Committee of the Irish Victory Fund of Boston, Massachusetts;

Letter of Thomas F. Cooney and Others to the US Senate Committee on Foreign Relations;

Telegram to Congressman John I. Nolan Representing the Unanimous Sentiment of the Irish Societies of California against Section 10 of the League of Nations;

Joint Statement of Michael L. Fahey, Paul F. Spain, and Joseph Brennan, of Boston, Massachusetts;

Statement of Hugh O'Neill, of Chicago, Illinois, Speaking as a Representative of the Committee of One Hundred for an Irish Republic;

Statement of Richard W. Wolfe, of Chicago, Former President of the Cook County Real Estate Board of Chicago, on Behalf of the Committee of 100 for an Irish Republic;

Address of Shaemas O'Sheel, Representing the William Pearse Branch of the Friends of Irish Freedom and the William Rooney Society, both of New York;

Statement of R. E. O'Malley, of Kansas City, Missouri;

Resolution Unanimously Adopted by the Delegates to the Central Labor Union of Philadelphia, Pennsylvania, July 13, 1919, Presented by William J. Boyle;

Statement of Edward F. McSweeney of Boston, Massachusetts, Member of the Advisory Committee of the Irish Victory Fund and National Officer Friends of Irish Freedom.

Source: US Congress, Senate, Committee on Foreign Relations, *Treaty of Peace with Germany: Hearings* (Senate doc. no. 106, 66th Cong., 1st sess., 1919, 879–933).

APPENDIX 3

American Commission on Conditions in Ireland
Hearings and Witnesses before the Commission in Washington, DC

FIRST HEARING
Session One, 18 November 1920

Denis Morgan (Irish)
    Chairman of the Urban Council of Thurles
Rev. Michael M. English (US)
    Whitehall, Montana
John F. Martin (US)
    Attorney, Green Bay, Wisconsin
Rev. James M. Cotter (US)
    Clergyman and Editor, Ironton, Ohio

Session Two, 19 November 1920

John Durham (Irish)
    Town Councilor of Balbriggan
Mrs. Agnes B. King (US)
    Ironton, Ohio
Francis Hackett (US)
    Associate Editor of the *New Republic*, New York City, investigated conditions in Ireland for the *New York World*
Signe Toksvig (Mrs. F. Hackett) (US)
    Associate Editor of the *New Republic*, New York City

SECOND HEARING
Session One, 8 December 1920

Miss Mary MacSwiney (Irish)
    Sister of the late Lord Mayor of Cork

Session Two, 9 December 1920

Mrs. Muriel MacSwiney (Irish)
    Widow of the late Lord Mayor of Cork
Miss Mary MacSwiney (Irish)

Session Three, 10 December 1920

Miss Mary MacSwiney (Irish)
P.J. Guilfoil (US)
    Pittsburgh, Pennsylvania
Daniel Francis Crowley (Irish)
    Member of the Royal Irish Constabulary from November 1914 to June 1920
John Tangney (Irish)
    Member of the Royal Irish Constabulary from October 1913 to July 1920
Mrs. Anna Murphy (Irish)
    New York City (Husband an Irish citizen)
John Joseph Caddan (Irish)
    Member of the Royal Irish Constabulary from February to November 1920
Daniel Galvin (Irish)
    Member of the Royal Irish Constabulary from October 1907 to July 1920

THIRD HEARING
Session One, 15 December 1920

Miss Ruth Russell (US)
    Chicago, Illinois, investigated conditions in Ireland for the *Chicago Daily News*
Hon. Laurence Ginnell (Irish)
    Former Member of the British Parliament, Member of the Dáil Éireann and the Dáil government

Session Two, 16 December 1920

Miss Nellie Craven (US)
    Washington, DC, cousin of Michael Walsh, murdered Councilor of Galway
Paul J. Furnas (US)
    New York City, member of the Society of Friends

FOURTH HEARING
Session One, 21 December 1920

Mrs. Annot Erskine Robinson (British)
   Manchester, England, representative of the British Branch of the Women's International League
Miss Ellen C. Wilkinson (British)
   Manchester, England, representative of the British Branch of the Women's International League

Session Two, 22 December 1920

Miss Susanna Walsh (Irish)
   Sister-in-law of Alderman Thomas MacCurtain, late Lord Mayor of Cork
Miss Anna Walsh (Irish)
   Sister-in-law of Alderman Thomas MacCurtain, late Lord Mayor of Cork
Daniel J. Broderick (US)
   Chicago, Illinois

Session Three, 23 December 1920

Mrs. Michael Mohan (US)
   Corona, New York
John Charles Clarke (US)
   Corona, New York

FIFTH HEARING
Session One, 13 January 1921

Hon Daniel O'Callaghan (Irish)
   Lord Mayor of Cork

Session Two, 14 January 1921

Hon. Daniel O'Callaghan (Irish)
Thomas Nolan (Irish)
   Merchant, Galway
Emil Pezolt (US)
   Oakland, California, Junior Engineer on USS West Cannon
Henry Turk (US)
   San Francisco, California, Junior Engineer on USS West Cannon
Harold Johnson (US)
   Bucks County, Pennsylvania, sailor on USS West Cannon

Ralph Taylor (US)
  Scott Township, Pennsylvania, messman on the USS West Cannon
Peter J. MacSwiney (US)
  New York City, brother of the late Lord Mayor of Cork

SIXTH HEARING
Session One, 19 January 1921

Frank Dempsey (Irish)
  Chairman of the Urban Council of Mallow
J.J. Fawsitt (Irish)
  Consul-General of the Dáil Éireann government in New York

Session Two, 21 January 1921

Miss Louie Bennett (Irish)
  Dublin, secretary of the Irish Branch of the Women's International League
Miss Caroline Townshend (Irish)
  Bandon, County Cork, officer of the Gaelic League

Source: Albert Coyle, ed., *Evidence on Conditions in Ireland* (Washington, DC: American Commission on Conditions in Ireland, 1921).

APPENDIX 4

Report on Secretary of State Frank B. Kellogg's Visit to Dublin in August 1928

Dublin, September 6, 1928

The Honorable
The Secretary of State
Washington, DC

Sir:

I have the honor to report that the Secretary of State landed from the USS *Detroit* at Kingstown in the morning of August 30th on a visit to the Irish Free State. He was accompanied by Mrs. Kellogg and Mr. Cosgrave, President of the Executive Council of the Free State Government, who had been in Paris to sign for the Free State the Treaty for the Renunciation of War.

The Secretary was met by the Minister and Secretary of the Legation, Members of the Cabinet, the Chairman of the Dublin City Commissioners and the Chairman of the Reception Committee, who boarded the *Detroit* after formal salutes to the Irish Free State and United States' flags had been exchanged, and conducted the Secretary and his party and Mr. Cosgrave in a tender to the landing stage of the Royal Irish Yacht Club. In the club house the Town Clerk of Kingstown read an address of welcome on behalf of the four adjacent Urban Councils. The Secretary was then brought by motor car to Dublin, a mounted escort joining the motor cars at the old gates of the city. Arriving at the Mansion House a halt was made in order that Mr. Kellogg might be presented with the Freedom of the City of Dublin and inscribe his name on the roll of Freemen. Upon the conclusion of this ceremony the Secretary was driven, still accompanied by the mounted escort, to the legation where he was to remain during his visit as the guest of the Minister. All along the route, from the landing at Kingstown through Dublin to the Legation in Phoenix Park, the streets had been decorated and great crowds had assembled. The cheering and enthusiasm was vociferous and genuine; it was a great welcome.

At the request of the Secretary official functions and entertainment had been cut to a minimum. During the afternoon of the day of arrival the Secretary made his official call upon the Governor General, and in the evening with Mrs. Kellogg he attended a banquet given in his honor by the President and Members of the Executive Council, followed by a reception. On the following evening another dinner in his honor was tendered by the Governor General at the Vice Regal Lodge, after which he attended a reception and dance at the Legation. This concluded all official entertainment during the visit. Before leaving Dublin, however, Mr. and Mrs. Kellogg paid an informal call on Mr. and Mrs. Cosgrave at the private house of the latter in the suburbs of the city.

CONFIDENTIAL

The compliment paid the Irish Free State by the visit of the Secretary on returning the visit of President Cosgrave to the United States is a milestone in the history of the Free State. It has not only been the first occasion that the Free State has had the opportunity to receive so distinguished a guest and given the people of Dublin a chance to prove their sympathy for the United States, but it has emphasized in a concrete manner the autonomous status of the Free State in the British Commonwealth. The Irish Free State flag was saluted by a United States vessel of war on entering a Free State port, and as aptly put by the conservative *Irish Times*, a stanch supporter of the Treaty of 1921, "in her (the Free State's) official welcome to Mr. Kellogg she demonstrates her new rights and dignity to her own people on her own soil."

The abstention of all members of the Fianna Fail party, including Mr. de Valera, in the reception of the Secretary of State was very noticeable and, I have no doubt, will be much criticized in the United States. The Party in its blundering way sometimes recognizes the Constitution and yet again will not admit that the Free State is a British Dominion; and to prove this time that they have no connection with Great Britain they have offered a slight to Mr. Kellogg and to the United States. By taking this line of action they have only hurt themselves and in no way affected the great success of the visit.

Upon sailing on the *Detroit* from Dublin on Monday afternoon,

September 4th [sic], Mr. and Mrs. Kellogg were seen off at the dock by the Minister, Mr. and Mrs. Cosgrave and Members of the Cabinet in Dublin on that day.
Wainwright Abbott
Chargé d'Affaires *ad interim*

Source: Wainwright Abbott, chargé d'affaires, ad interim, United States Legation, Dublin, to the secretary of state, 6 September 1928, 711.002 Anti War/408.RG 59, State Department Records, NARA.

NOTES

PROLOGUE

1 For a discussion of the memory and commemoration of these historic anniversaries see Daly and O'Callaghan, *1916 in 1966*; and Grayson and McGarry, *Remembering 1916*.
2 J. J. Lee in Grey, "Introduction," in Grey, *Ireland's Allies*, 1.
3 McCaffrey, *Irish Diaspora in America*, 3–10 and 107–37.
4 Mansergh, *Irish Question*, 282. The original edition was published under the title *Ireland in the Age of Reform and Revolution* (London: George Allen & Unwin, 1940), and, although it also contains a good section called "American Reactions to the Irish Question," Mansergh did not make as strong an assertion of the American contribution to the Irish struggle then as he did in 1965.

1. AMERICA AND THE IRISH RISING OF 1916

1 Keogh to Redmond, 27 May 1912, John Redmond Papers, National Library of Ireland (NLI).
2 Cockran to Frewen, 25 March 1914, William Bourke Cockran Papers, Box 16, New York Public Library (NYPL).
3 See Ryan, *Phoenix Flame*; and Golway, *Irish Rebel*. The two sisters who ran the rooming house donated his valuable collection of papers to the National Library of Ireland.
4 Keating to Devoy, 14 January 1910, John Devoy Papers, Box RU-S, NLI.
5 See Edwards, "American Aspects of the Rising," in Edwards and Pyle, *1916*, 104–34; Ward, *Ireland and Anglo-American Relations*; and Carroll, *American Opinion and the Irish Question*.
6 O'Broin, *Revolutionary Underground*, 140.
7 See McCartan, *With DeValera in America*; Cronin, *McGarrity Papers*; Lynch, *IRB and the 1916 Insurrection*; and MacAtasney, "Tom Clarke's New York," 45–59.
8 O'Broin, *Revolutionary Underground*, 140–45.
9 Edwards, *Patrick Pearse*, 184–97; Greaves, *Life and Times of James Connolly*, 168–245.
10 See Reid, *Man from New York*; Tansill, *America and the Fight for Irish Freedom*; and Doorley, *Justice Daniel Cohalan*, 34–38.
11 Devoy to Cohalan, 29 November 1911, cited in Tansill, *America and the Fight for Irish Freedom*, 125–26.
12 Tierney, *Eoin MacNeill*, 97–141; McDiarmid, "Casement, New York, and the Easter Rising," 91–107. The Irish Volunteers numbered about 10,000 in January 1914, but by September may have reached 180,000.

13 McDiarmid, "Casement, New York, and the Easter Rising," 98; R. Willits, "Stereopticon," in 185–91. For the Roosevelt comment, see Roosevelt to Bainbridge Colby, 12 August 1914, Box 7, Misc. Correspondence, W. J. M. A. Maloney Collection, NYPL.
14 Devoy, *Recollections of an Irish Rebel*, 403.
15 Devoy, 405; Golway, "John Devoy and the Easter Rising," 25–27.
16 Doerries, *Prelude to the Easter Rising*, 3.
17 McDiarmid, "Casement, New York, and the Easter Rising," 99–105; Doorley, *Justice Daniel Cohalan*, 71–73.
18 Hobson, *Ireland Yesterday and Tomorrow*, 71.
19 Devoy, *Recollections of an Irish Rebel*, 458.
20 Doorley, *Justice Daniel Cohalan*, 76–84.
21 Doorley, *Irish-American Diaspora Nationalism*, 36–61; Casey, "Victor Herbert, Nationalism, and Musical Expression," in 168–70.
22 Golway, *Irish Rebel*, 228–29; Tierney, *Eoin MacNeill*, 196–227.
23 Walsh, *Bitter Freedom*, 12.
24 Leslie, *Irish Issue in Its American Aspect*, 189–90.

2. AMERICA, THE WAR CRISIS, AND THE IRISH PROBLEM, 1916–1918
1 Quinn to Gonne, 29 July 1916, in Londraville, *Too Long a Sacrifice*, 173.
2 *Christian Science Monitor*, 26 April 1916; *New York World*, 26 April 1919.
3 *New York Times*, 26 and 29 April 1916. For a more extensive analysis of American newspaper coverage of the Rising, see Schmuhl, "Bifocalism of US Press Coverage"; Tucker, "Some American Responses," 605–18; and Carroll, *American Opinion and the Irish Question*, 55–69.
4 *New York World*, 27 April 1916; *Chicago Tribune*, 26 April 1916; *Literary Digest*, 6 May 1916.
5 *Washington Post*, 7 May 1916; *New York World*, 13 May 1916.
6 *Nation*, 11 and 18 May 1916.
7 Quinn to Gonne, 29 July 1916, in Londraville, *Too Long a Sacrifice*, 170; Carroll, *American Opinion and the Irish Question*, 59–69.
8 Casey and Shevlin, "An American in Dublin," 307–15; O'Driscoll, "Remembering Diarmuid Lynch," 52–55; McGough, *Diarmuid Lynch*, 69–81.
9 Owen Dudley Edwards and Stephen Hartley argue that the consul intervened successfully in de Valera's case. See Edwards and Pyle, *1916*, 162; and Hartley, *Irish Question as a Problem*, 60–62. Alan Ward and, more recently, Robert Schmuhl conclude that by 10 May, when de Valera was sentenced to life in prison, the decision had been made to end the executions, except for the remaining signatories of the 1916 Proclamation (Ward, *Ireland and Anglo-American Relations*, 118; Schmuhl, *Ireland's Exiled Children*, 121–22). See also Whelan, *United States Foreign Policy and Ireland*, 103–7.
10 Troy, O'Connor, and Mulhern to Wilson, 19 May 1916; Phelan to Wilson, 22 May 1916; Wilson to Troy, 7 July 1916, File 6, No. 3152, Box 520, Woodrow Wilson Papers, Library of Congress (LC).

11 *Congressional Record*, 64th Cong., 1st sess., vol. 53, 12 May 1916, H. Res. 235, 7439 and 7899; H. Res. 244, 8358; H. Res. 245, 8427 (*Cong. Rec.*). None of these House Resolutions were reported out of committee or voted on by Congress.
12 *Cong. Rec.*, Appendix to, 64th Cong., 1st sess., vol. 54, 16 May 1916, 959.
13 *Cong. Rec.*, 64th Cong., 1st sess., vol. 53, 17 May 1916, S. Res. 196, 8140–41; 1 June 1916, 9026–27; 2 June 1916, 9150. See also Polk to Stone, 27 May 1916, Drawer 77, File 133, Frank L. Polk Papers, Yale University Library (YUL).
14 Doyle had represented Casement in a slander case in 1914 and had been active in Irish affairs (Devoy, *Recollections*, 404 and 477–78). Wilson to Tumulty, 2 May 1916, File 6, No. 3085, Box 520, Wilson Papers, LC; Polk to Doyle, 31 May 1916, Drawer 77, File 134, Polk Papers, YUL.
15 Memorandum of interview with Doyle, 17 June 1916, FO 800/86, National Archives, Kew (TNA); Grey to Samuel, 16 June 1916, FO 800/12, TNA.
16 Page wrote to the department: "I am privately informed that much information about him of an unspeakably filthy character was withheld from publicity," and the US government should have nothing to do with him. Page to secretary of state, 3 July 1916, Drawer 77, File 135, Polk Papers, YUL. Quinn's biographer notes that he "flew into a rage" at the charges of "degeneracy" against Casement (Reid, *Man From New York*, 236–37).
17 *Cong. Rec.*, 64th Cong., 1st sess., vol. 53, 20 June 1916, S. Res. 223, 10251–52.
18 *Cong. Rec.*, 64th Cong., 1st sess., vol. 53, 29 July 1916, S. Res. 241, 11770–83.
19 Polk to Page, nos. 3606 and 3608, 2 August 1916; Laughlin to Polk, 3 August 1916, *Foreign Relations of the United States, 1916, Supplement*, 870–71 (*FRUS*). See also Polk, "Memorandum on Casement Resolution," 17 August 1916, 841.00/23 ½, RG 59, State Department Records, National Archives and Records Administration (NARA); Hendrick, *Life and Letters of Walter H. Page*, vol. 2, 166–69; and Whelan, *United States Foreign Policy and Ireland*, 108–12. For the British decision, see Hartley, *Irish Question as a Problem in British Foreign Policy*, 90–92. In his biography of Asquith, Roy Jenkins concludes, "There can be few other examples of a Cabinet devoting large parts of four separate meetings to consider an individual sentence—and then arriving at the wrong decision" (*Asquith*, 453).
20 Grey to House, 28 August 1916, in Seymour, *Intimate Papers of Colonel House*, vol. 2, 317–18.
21 Bartlett, *Ireland*, 395–96; Grayson, "Beyond the Ulster Division," 112–37. See also Jeffery, *Ireland and the Great War*, 37–68; and Grayson, *Dublin's Great Wars*, 85–112.
22 Spring Rice to Grey, 4 May 1916, FO 800/86 [Grey], TNA. The ambassador wrote privately to Grey, "All are agreed that it will be dangerous to make Casement a martyr." Spring Rice to Grey, 19 May 1916, in Gwynn, *Letters and Friendships of Sir Cecil Spring Rice*, vol. 2, 331.
23 Reid, *Man From New York*, 235; Bhroiméil, "American Opinion," 210–11; Spring Rice to Grey, 26 and 29 July 1916, FO 800/86; Quinn to Spring Rice, 27 July 1916; Spring Rice to Grey, 28 July 1916, FO 371/2798; Quinn, Byrne, Crimmons, Crowninshield,

Cutcheon, Davies, Dawson et al. to Grey, 28 July 1916, CAB 37/152/32, TNA. See Quinn to Gonne, 29 July 1916, in Londraville, *Too Long a Sacrifice*, 171–72.
24 Bennett to the king of England, 14 July 1916, FO 371/2798; Lodge to Grey, July 29, 1916; Grey to Spring Rice, 2 August 1916, FO 800/86, and CAB 41/37/29, TNA.
25 Quinn, "Roger Casement," 1–4.
26 Spring Rice to Grey, 14 July 1916, in Gwynn, *Letters and Friendships of Sir Cecil Spring Rice*, vol. 2, 338.
27 McCormack to Mitchel, 12 May 1916, Box 10, John Purroy Mitchel Papers, LC; *New York Times*, 26 May 1916.
28 *Gaelic American*, 27 May and 3, 10, and 17 June 1916 ; Moore to Golden, 28 June 1916, MS 13,414, Peter Golden Papers, NLI.
29 O'Doherty, *Assignment-America*, 22–23; Page to secretary of state, 28 July 1916, 341.112k29/66, Box 2972, RG 59, State Department Records, NARA; Thompson to Campbell, 28 September 1916, FO 371/2795, TNA; Whelan, *United States Foreign Policy and Ireland*, 119.
30 Feighery, "Timely and Substantial Relief," 288–91; Wolf, "James Connolly's 'Good End,'" 319-27.
31 Feighery, 288–91.
32 Schumuhl, *Ireland's Exiled Children*, 74–117.
33 McGuire, *King, the Kaiser, and Irish Freedom*; McGuire, *What Germany Could Do for Ireland*.
34 *New York Times*, September 30, 1916; O'Leary, *My Political Trial and Experiences*, 45–47.
35 Wilson to O'Leary, 30 September 1916, in Link, *Papers of Woodrow Wilson (PWW)* vol. 38, 286; *New York Times*, 30 September 1916.
36 Roosevelt, *Fear God and Take Your Own Part*, 105 and 143–44.
37 Roosevelt, *Foes in Our Own Household*, 61 and 294.
38 Memorandum, 8 March 1917, Wiseman File, Edward M. House Papers, YUL.
39 Hartley, *Irish Question as a Problem in British Foreign Policy*, 113.
40 Wilson to Lansing, 10 April 1917, in *FRUS, Lansing Papers*, vol. 2, 4–5. Debates and the introduction of several resolutions can be found in *Cong. Rec.*, 65th Cong., 1st sess., vol. 55, 663, 1558, 2305, 2424, 5474, and 5532–33.
41 Wilson to Lansing, 10 April 1917, in *FRUS*.
42 Shannon, *Arthur J. Balfour and Ireland*, 33–225.
43 Page to the president, 18 April 1917, in Link, *PWW*, vol. 42, 93. See also Quinn to Gonne, 20 May 1917, in Londraville, *Too Long a Sacrifice*, 197.
44 Page to Wilson, 4 May 1917, in Hendrick, *Life and Letters of Walter H. Page*, vol. 2., 259–60.
45 Instructions, 10 April 1917, CAB 23/2, TNA.
46 Wilson to Tumulty, ca. 20 April 1917, in Tumulty, *Woodrow Wilson as I Know Him*, 399.
47 Balfour to War Cabinet, 1 May 1917, F60/2/13, David Lloyd George Papers, House of Lords Library. Balfour addressed both Houses of Congress. See *Cong. Rec.*, 65th

Cong., 2nd sess., vol. 55, part 2, 1879–80, and *Cong. Rec.: Appendix*, vol. 56, 104–6. Spring Rice had warned the Foreign Office of the certainty that Wilson "will speak of the Irish question." Spring Rice to Cecil, 13 April 1917, in Gwynn, *Letters and Friendships of Sir Cecil Spring Rice*, vol. 2, 392–93.
48 Lansing, *War Memoirs of Robert Lansing*, 276–77.
49 Balfour to Lloyd George, 23 June 1917, CAB 1/25(5), TNA.
50 Quinn to Roosevelt, 30 April 1917, Series 1, Box 331, Theodore Roosevelt Papers, LC. See also Plunkett diary, 24 April 1917, and Godkin to Plunkett, 1917, MS 42,222, Horace Plunkett Papers, NLI; Plunkett to Balfour, April 25, 1917, and Quinn to Drummond, May 1 and 2, 1917, FO 800/208 (Balfour), TNA.
51 Quinn, "Notes of Recent American Opinion," 2 June 1917, MS 1752, John Quinn Papers, NIL; Ní Bhroiméil, "American Opinion," 212–13; Reid, *Man from New York*, 328–29.
52 Balfour to prime minister, 5 May 1917, FO 371/3070, TNA.
53 Shannon, *Arthur J. Balfour and Ireland*, 232.
54 Balfour to Lloyd George, 23 June 1917, CAB 1/25(5), TNA; *Cong. Rec.: Appendix*, 65th Congress, 2nd sess., vol. 56, 104–6; Willert, *Road to Safety*, 75–77; Whelan, *United States Foreign Policy and Ireland*, 133–35; Shannon, *Arthur J. Balfour and Ireland*, 229–32.
55 *Cong. Rec.: Appendix*, 65th Cong., 1st sess., vol. 55, 30 April 1917, 161.
56 Brennon, Conboy, Crimmons, Cockran, Coyle, Robert E. Dowling, Victor J. Dowling et al. to Redmond, April 22, 1917, memorandum, Series 1/330, Roosevelt Papers, LC.
57 *Times of London*, 26 April 1917; Quinn to Roosevelt, 1 May 1917, Roosevelt Papers, LC.
58 *Times of London*, 26 April 1917.
59 *Times of London*, 27 April 1917.
60 Jordan to Redmond, 6 May 1917, Redmond Papers, NIL.
61 Leslie to Redmond, 6 May 1917, Redmond Papers, NIL. Leslie married Marjorie Ide, daughter of Henry Clay Ide, US minister to Spain and former governor-general of the Philippines, which made him a brother-in-law of congressman W. Bourke Cockran.
62 McDowell, *Irish Convention*, 76.
63 Leslie, *Irish Issue in Its American Aspect*, 206.
64 Plunkett to House, 28 September 1917, Seymour, *Intimate Papers of Colonel House*, vol. 3, 76–77; McDowell, *Irish Convention*.
65 *Times of London*, 26 April 1917.
66 Roosevelt to Russell, 6 August 1917, Roosevelt Papers, LC.
67 Russell, *Irish Home Rule Convention*. The title page listed "Thoughts on a Convention" by George Russell (Æ); "A Defence of the Convention," by the Right Hon. Sir Horace Plunkett; and "An American Opinion," by John Quinn. See also Carroll, "Theodore Roosevelt, John Quinn, and *The Irish Home Rule Convention*," 11-14.
68 Reid, *Man From New York*, 330–31.

69 Reid, 330.
70 Reid, 331.
71 Lloyd George to Plunkett, 25 February 1918, in *Report of the Proceedings of the Irish Convention* (Cd.9019), HC, 1918, 20; Lloyd George to Bonar Law, 12 January 1918, cited in Fanning, *Fatal Path*, 167–68.
72 From the Plunkett Papers, cited in Digby, *Horace Plunkett*, 231.
73 Digby, 230–37; McDowell, *Irish Convention*, 185–217.
74 Wilson to House, 3 April 1918, House Papers, YUL; Fowler, *British American Relations*, 159–60. The conscription issue was of such concern to Wilson that he sent Ray Stannard Baker to Ireland to assess the situation. Baker traveled to Dublin, the west of Ireland, and Ulster and conferred with figures such as Sir Horace Plunkett, John Dillon, and Sir George Clark. He found southern Irish defiant and no settlement acceptable under threat of conscription. He reported, "Leaders agree seriousness of situation can scarcely be exaggerated." Baker to Lansing, contained in a cable from Page to secretary of state, 841.00/80, RG 59, State Department Papers, NARA; Baker, *American Chronicle*, 335–37.
75 Brun, "Papers of Charles M. Hathaway," 18–19.

3. THE 1919 PARIS PEACE CONFERENCE, THE AMERICAN COMMISSION ON IRISH INDEPENDENCE, AND SELF-DETERMINATION FOR IRELAND

1 Address to a joint session of Congress, 8 January 1918, in Link, *PWW*, vol. 45, 534–39.
2 Address to a joint session of Congress, 11 February 1918, Link, *PWW*, vol. 46, 321. Dr. Patrick McCartan, the IRB envoy in the United States, wrote to Wilson in 1917 urging him to apply US war aims to Ireland. See McCartan to the US president and Congress, 18 June 1917, MS.18,105, Devoy Papers, NLI.
3 Lansing, *Peace Negotiations*, 97. See also Hannigan, *Great War and American Foreign Policy*, 208–10.
4 *Dáil Eireann, Minutes of the Proceedings, 1919–1921*, 9 May 1919, 84. See also Brindley, "Woodrow Wilson," 62–80; Hopkinson, *Irish War of Independence*, 165–66; and Manela, *Wilsonian Moment*, 3–17.
5 Creel, *War, the World, and Wilson*, 163.
6 US Congress, House of Representatives, Committee on Foreign Affairs, *The Irish Question*, Hearings on HJ Res. 357 (House Doc. No. 1832, 65th Cong., 3rd sess.), 1919; *Cong. Rec.*, 65th Cong., 3rd sess., vol. 57, 4 March 1919 (H. Cong. Res. 67), 2868, 3174, and 5026–57.
7 Carroll, *American Opinion and the Irish Question*, 121–28; Walsh to Wilson, 2 December 1918, and Wilson to Walsh, 3 December 1918, Box 190, Thomas J. Walsh Papers, LC; Wilson to Shahan, 3 December 1918, and McLaughlin to Wilson, 2 December 1918, Box 558, Wilson Papers, LC; *New York Times*, December 11, 14, and 16, 1918.
8 Wiseman to Balfour and Drummond (cable), 4 February 1918, in Fowler, *British-American Relations*, 259–62.
9 Quinn to Gonne, 17 July 1917, in Londraville, *Too Long a Sacrifice*, 204.

10 Tansill, *America and the Fight for Irish Freedom*, 278–83; Doorley, *Irish-American Diaspora Nationalism*, 84–86. New York State governor Charles S. Whitman served as temporary chairman and also spoke at length (Hopkinson, *Irish War of Independence*, 166).
11 *Dáil Éireann, Minutes of the Proceedings, 1919–1921*, 9–26.
12 Walsh, *Bitter Freedom*, 12.
13 *New Republic*, 1 March 1919.
14 Caniffe to Devoy, 26 November 1918, Box C-CA, Devoy Papers, NLI; *New York Times*, 11 December 1918; McCartan, *With De Valera in America*, 57–58 and 70–78. A Second Irish Race Convention was held in New York on 18 and 19 May 1918.
15 *Gaelic American*, 19 January and 1 March 1919; *Irish World*, 4 January and 1 March 1919; McCartan, *With De Valera in America*, 79–88.
16 *New York Times*, 1 March 1919; Splain, "Irish Movement in America," 234–35; Tumulty to Wilson, 1 March 1919, and Wilson to Tumulty, n.d., Box 3, Joseph Tumulty Papers, LC.
17 *New York Times*, 5 March 1919; Doorley, *Justice Daniel Cohalan*, 116–19. See also Splain, "Irish Movement in America," 234; *Gaelic American*, 8 March 1919; Kinkead to Wilson, 8 March 1919, Box 15, Wilson Papers, LC; and Doorley, *Irish-American Diaspora Nationalism*, 92–93.
18 Grayson diary, 4 March 1919, in Link, *PWW*, vol. 55, 411–12.
19 Baker, *American Chronicle*, 385–86; Miller, *Drafting of the Covenant*, vol. 1, 294; Bonsal, *Unfinished Business*, 149. See also Duff, "Versailles Treaty and the Irish-Americans," 582–98.
20 *Cong. Rec.*, 65th Congress, 3rd Session, vol. 57, 5042–57.
21 Walworth's information comes from a 31 March 1919 diary entry of Edith Benham, Mrs. Wilson's secretary. See Walworth, *Wilson and His Peacemakers*, 469. George W. Egerton notes that Wilson mentioned Irish home rule at a dinner meeting with Lord Robert Cecil on 18 March, although he regarded it as a domestic issue; no specific source is given (*Great Britain and the Creation*, 154). See also Ambrosius, *Woodrow Wilson and the American Diplomatic Tradition*, 143.
22 Tumulty to Wilson, 29 February 1919, Box 3, Tumulty Papers, LC; Creel, *Rebel at Large*, 215. See also O'Ceallaigh to Brugha, 7 March 1919, *Documents on Irish Foreign Policy*, vol. 1, 9 (*DIFP*).
23 Creel, *War, the World, and Wilson*, 182.
24 Creel to Wilson, 1 March 1919, Plunkett to Wilson, 2 March 1919, and Wilson to Plunkett, 26 March 1919, Box 15, Wilson Papers, LC; Creel, *Rebel at Large*, 220–21; John W. Davis, 4 March 1919, in Davis and Fleming, *Ambassadorial Diary of John W. Davis*, 67.
25 Creel, *Rebel at Large*, 220–21.
26 Walsh had worked closely with George Creel in Missouri politics. See Creel, *Rebel at Large*, 48–57.
27 Carroll, *American Commission on Irish Independence*, 8–20; Manning, *Frank P. Walsh and the Irish Question*, 28–32; Whelan, *United States Foreign Policy and Ireland*, 204–6.

28 Carroll, *American Commission on Irish Independence*; Carroll, commission diary, 2–15 April 1919, 33–38.
29 Carroll, commission diary, 15 April 1919, 38.
30 Walsh, Ryan, and Dunne to Wilson, 16 April 1919; Gilbert F. Close to Walsh, 17 April 1919, in Carroll, 91–92.
31 Carroll, commission diary, 17 April 1919, 41–42.
32 Carroll, commission diary, 17 April 1919, 40–45.
33 The circumstances surrounding the two weeks between the commission's initial contacts with the American authorities and their trip to Ireland are ambiguous. The papers of the major participants—Walsh, House, and Lloyd George—are contradictory in their accounts. Walsh and Dunne claimed that House told them de Valera *would* be granted safe conduct; House later said he thought de Valera *might* be granted safe conduct; Lloyd George said that he wanted to talk with Walsh simply to present the English case to the commission. There was also a similar disagreement about who wanted the commission to go to Ireland. Walsh, Ryan, and Dunne to Wilson, 20 May 1919, in Carroll, 93; Dunne, *What Dunne Saw in Ireland*, 6; House to Wilson, 9 May 1919, in Link, *PWW*, vol. 58, 585; "Notes on Conversation between Colonel House and Walsh, Dunne, and Ryan," 23 May 1919, and Lloyd George to House, 9 May 1919, House Papers, YUL. For one account, see Hodgson, *Woodrow Wilson's Right Hand*, 244–45.
34 *Times of London*, 5 May 1919.
35 *Manchester Guardian*, 5 May 1919; *Times of London*, 6–10 May 1919.
36 *Dáil Eireann, Minutes of the Proceedings, 1919–1921*, 9 May 1919, 99–108.
37 Sean T. O'Ceallaigh to Dublin, 24 May 1919, *DIFP*, vol. 1, 17–18; *Manchester Guardian*, 13, 14, and 19 May 1919.
38 *Morning Post*, 5 and 6 May 1919; *Times of London*, 6 and 7 May 1919; *Daily Mail*, 7 May 1919; *Globe*, 8 May 1919.
39 *Times of London*, 13 May 1919. The British Embassy, whose warnings about Irish matters were often discounted, reported in 1919 a dramatic rise in anti-British agitation in the United States, particularly among Irish and German communities. See *British Documents on Foreign Affairs: Confidential Prints, Part II, Series C, North America, 1919–1939, Vol. 7*, 2–9 (BDFA).
40 *Parliamentary Debates*, 5 (Commons), 14 May 1919, 115, cols. 1581–82 (*Parl. Deb.*).
41 *Parl. Deb.*, 5 (Lords), 22 May 1919, 34, cols. 795–800 and 804–8; War Cabinet 567A, 14 May 1919, CAB 23/15, TNA; Stamfordham to Lloyd George, 9 May 1919, F 33/2/62, Lloyd George Papers, House of Lords Records Office.
42 David Lloyd George to Edward M. House, 9 May 1919, House Papers, YUL. Lloyd George raised the matter of the American Commission on Irish Independence at a meeting of the Council of Four on 7 May, in which he said "it is impossible for me to meet them" because of their association in Ireland with "agitators of sedition." The minutes record no comment on this matter by Wilson, Clemenceau, or Orlando. Conversation between President Wilson and M. Clemenceau, Lloyd George, and Orlando, 7 May 1919, in Mantoux, *Deliberations of the Council of Four*, vol. 1, 500–501.

43 House to Lloyd George, 9 May 1919, House Papers, YUL. See also House diary, vol. 16, 10 and 20 May 1919, House Papers, YUL.
44 Lloyd George to House, 10 May 1919, House Papers, YUL.
45 *New York Times*, 14 and 15 May 1919.
46 For commentary, see Walsh, "Woodrow Wilson Historians," 55–66.
47 Walsh, Ryan, and Dunne to Lansing, 17 May 1919; Walsh, Ryan, and Dunne to Wilson, 20 May 1919; Lansing to Walsh, 24 May 1919, in Carroll, *American Commission on Irish Independence*, 92–93 and 97. Sean T. O'Ceallaigh, the Dáil envoy in Paris, reported that it was "certain" that the Irish delegation would not be allowed to come to the Peace Conference and that "the fight will have to be very vigorously pushed in the States." O'Ceallaigh to O'Brian, 24 May 1919, MS.8422, Art O'Brien Papers, NLI.
48 House diary, vol. 16, 23 May 1919, and "Notes on Conversation between E.M. House and Walsh, Dunne, and Ryan," House Papers, YUL; Walsh to Lansing, 26 and 27 May 1919, in Carroll, *American Commission on Irish Independence*, 98–99; White to Lodge, 29 May 1919, Henry Cabot Lodge Papers, Massachusetts Historical Society; Nevins, *Henry White*, 454.
49 Walsh to Wilson, 28 May 1919, Walsh and Dunne to Grew, 29 May 1919, and Grew to Walsh and Dunne, 31 May 1919, in Carroll, *American Commission on Irish Independence*, 102–5; Lansing, White, House, and Bliss to Wilson, 31 May 1919, House Papers, YUL.
50 Walsh and Dunne to Grew, 2 June 1919, in Carroll, *American Commission on Irish Independence*, 110.
51 "Notes of an Interview of Secretary Lansing with Frank P. Walsh," 6 June 1919, vol. 43, Robert Lansing Papers, LC; "Report on Conditions in Ireland," in Carroll, *American Commission on Irish Independence*, 137–49. Sean T. O'Ceallaigh recommended at this point that it would not be worthwhile for the Dáil delegation to come to Paris and that it would be more useful for de Valera to go to the US. See O'Ceallaigh to Dublin, 24 May 1919, *DIFP*, vol. 1, 17–18.
52 Baker, *American Chronicle*, 435.
53 Tumulty to Wilson (cable), 26 May 1919; Tumulty to Grayson, 9 June 1919; Wilson to Tumulty (cable), 9 June 1919, Box 3, Tumulty Papers, LC.
54 Wilson to Tumulty (cable), 9 June 1919; Tumulty to Wilson (cable), 9 June 1919, Box 3, Tumulty Papers, LC. Alan Ward doubts that Wilson had "cleared the way" for an Irish delegation (*Ireland and Anglo-American Relations*, 183).
55 Commission diary, 11 June 1919, in Carroll, *American Commission on Irish Independence*, 72–78. The diary passage quoted here is quite similar to the passage from the Wilson letter to Tumulty quoted in the preceding paragraph. Wilson's physician, Admiral Cary T. Grayson, also kept notes on what was said. Grayson's records do not contradict those of Walsh and Dunne. He quotes Wilson as saying, "I should be frank with you, and tell you that it is due to tactics which you yourselves pursued that the American Commission was unable to secure safe conducts and a hearing for those you have just mentioned to come here to Paris." From Grayson diary, 11 June 1919, in Link, *PWW*, vol. 60, 383–87.

56 Commission diary, 11 June 1919, in Carroll, *American Commission on Irish Independence*, 72–78; and US Congress, Senate, Committee on Foreign Relations, *Treaty of Peace with Germany: Hearings* (Senate doc. no. 106, 66th Cong., 1st sess.), 1919, 836–38. The vivid phrase "that it was you gentlemen who kicked over the apple cart" does not appear in the typescript diary of the commission nor in Grayson's account.

57 Commission diary, 11 June 1919, in Carroll, *American Commission on Irish Independence*, 75–78. Grayson's record of this comment by Wilson is as follows: "You cannot realize how difficult has been the task that has been set for me to do and how it has hurt me inside to realize that I have not been able to carry through to completion the entire program which I outlined" (Grayson diary, 11 June 1919, in Link, *PWW*, vol. 60, 387). Sean T. O'Cealliaigh reported that the meeting had not gone well, that Wilson considered Irish matters a British "domestic" issue, and that he was very defensive about his earlier references to self-determination and small nations, prompting an angry reply to Walsh that he "didn't give a d____." See O'Cealliagh to Dublin, 15 June 1919, *DIFP*, vol. 1, 29. O'Cealliagh had earlier concluded that "Wilson is not to be relied on as an enthusiastic supporter of ours." Cited in Brindley, "Woodrow Wilson," 78.

58 *Cong. Rec.*, 66th Cong., 1st sess., vol. 58, 6 June 1919, 729; Cohalan to Borah, 12 and 27 May 1919, and Borah to Cohalan, 14, 23, and 28 May 1919, Box 551, William E. Borah Papers, LC.

59 Ambrosius, *Woodrow Wilson and the American Diplomatic Tradition*, 143–44. The Dáil passed a resolution thanking the Senate for asking that the American delegation facilitate de Valera, Griffith, and Plunkett representing Ireland at the Peace Conference. *Dáil Éireann proc., 1919–21*, 17 June 1919, 113.

60 Walsh and Dunne to the American Commission to Negotiate Peace, 13, 17, 19, and 20 June 1919, and Grew to Walsh, 12 June 1919, in Carroll, *American Commission on Irish Independence*, 117, 124, 119, 127, and 130; minutes of the daily meetings of the commissioners plenipotentiary, 21 June 1919, 184.00101/93, *FFRUS, Paris Peace Conference*, vol. 11, 242.

61 Walsh and Dunne to Clemenceau, 27 June 1919, in Carroll, *American Commission on Irish Independence*, 132–33; *New York Times*, 28 June and 9 and 10 July 1919. See also Dunne, *What Dunne Saw in Ireland*, 6–7.

62 White to Lansing, 26 August 1919, vol. 46, Lansing Papers, LC.

63 White to Lodge, 4 September 1919, and Lodge to White, 2 October 1919, Lodge Papers, Massachusetts Historical Society. The Irish envoys in Paris felt that the commission and, particularly, Walsh were a great success. See Duffy to McCartan, 18 March 1919, Margaret Duffy to _____, 27 June 1919, and Duffy to Mac [Joseph McGarrity], ca. summer 1919, Ms. 17,449, Joseph McGarrity Papers, NIL; and O'Kelly to Devoy, 18 July 1919, Box N-OL, Devoy Papers, NIL.

64 Creel, *Ireland's Fight for Freedom*, xi–xii, 45, and 174.

65 *Cong. Rec.*, 66th Cong., 11th sess., vol. 58, 6 June 1919, 729.

66 Cohalan to Borah, 11 July 1919, and Borah to Cohalan, 14 July 1919, Box 551, Borah Papers, LC; Hopkinson, *Irish War of Independence*, 167.

67 US Congress, Senate, Committee on Foreign Relations, *Treaty of Peace with Germany: Hearings* (Senate doc. no. 106, 66th Cong., 1st sess.), 1919, 797–903: Doorley, *Justice Daniel Cohalan*, 124–26.
68 *Treaty of Peace with Germany*, 835–38. In an article titled "Coming Home to Roost," the *New Republic* said that what was presented at the hearings was the uncorroborated recollections of Walsh and Dunne after they had left Wilson (17 September 1919).
69 *Treaty of Peace with Germany*, 879–903 (quotation from 902).
70 *Treaty of Peace with Germany*, 903–33. The correspondence and report of the American Commission for Irish Independence were published as a separate document in *Cong. Rec.*, 66th Cong., 1st sess., vol. 58, 2 September 1919, 4611–19 and 4650–718. The correspondence and report can also be found in Carroll, *American Commission on Irish Independence*, 91–149. See also Walsh to O'Kelly, 17 September 1919, Box 124, Frank P. Walsh Papers, NYPL; Ambrosius, *Woodrow Wilson and the American Diplomatic Tradition*, 248–50; and Cooper Jr., *Breaking the Heart of the World*, 558.
71 "Address in the City Auditorium in Pueblo, Colorado," 25 September 1919, in Link, *PWW*, vol. 63, 500–513. See also Cooper Jr., *Woodrow Wilson*, 506–31.
72 Walsh to O'Ceallaigh, 17 September 1919, Box 124, Frank P. Walsh Papers, NYPL.
73 O'Connell to Borah, 13 November 1919, Box 550, Borah Papers, LC; *Cong. Rec.*, 66th Cong., 1st sess., vol. 58, 2 September 1919, 4611–19 and 4650–718. All of the testimony together with the submissions to the Senate committee were published in a Senate report. See US Congress, Senate, Committee on Foreign Relations, *Treaty of Peace with Germany: Hearings* (Senate doc. no. 106, 66th Cong., 1st sess.), 1919.
74 *Gaelic American*, 29 November 1919.
75 Cohalan to Borah, 19 November 1919; Borah to Cohalan, 22 November 1919, Box 551, Borah Papers, LC. Others singled out Cohalan as well, thanking him for leading the Irish American fight against the treaty. See McGarry to Cohalan, 7 January 1920, Daniel F. Cohalan Papers, American Irish Historical Society (AIHS).
76 *Cong. Rec.*, 66th Cong., 2nd sess., vol. 59, 17 March 1920, 4457.
77 *Cong. Rec.*, 66th Cong., 2nd sess., vol. 59, 18 March 1920, 4502–22.
78 See Carroll, *American Opinion and the Irish Question*, 143–48; Ambrosius, *Woodrow Wilson and the American Diplomatic Tradition*, 248–50; Canfield, *Presidency of Woodrow Wilson*, 265–58; Margulies, *Mild Reservationists*, 244–50; and Cooper Jr., *Breaking the Heart of the World*, 355–59.
79 *Dáil Éireann proc., 1919–21*, 17 June 1919, 113–14.
80 Creel, *Rebel at Large*, 215.
81 Keown, *First of the Small Nations*, 39–40.
82 Creel, *Rebel at Large*, 222.
83 Dodd to Alexander F. Whyte, 9 January 1921, in Link, *PWW*, vol. 67, 44. Dodd later served as US ambassador to Germany from 1933 to 1938. Keown points out that Irish republicans believed that they had been responsible for the rejection of the Versailles Treaty by the United States (*First of the Small Nations*, 84).

4. MONEY

1 *Dáil Éireann proc., 1919–21*, 1 and 2 April 1919, 33–34 and 36–37.
2 *Dáil Éireann proc., 1919–21*, 10 April 1919, and 19 June 1919, 47 and 132–34.
3 For more detailed accounts of the Dáil finances, see Carroll, *Money for Ireland*, 1–14; Fanning, *Irish Department of Finance*, 13–25; and Mitchell, *Revolutionary Government in Ireland*, 64–65.
4 *Dáil Eireann, proc, 1919–1921*, 10 April 1919, 47; O'Cealliagh to Dublin, 24 May 1919, *DIFP*, vol. 1, 18; McCartan, *With De Valera in America*, 116–17; Nunan, "President Éamon de Valera's Mission," 237.
5 *Dáil Eireann, proc, 1919–1921*, 17 June 1919, 114.
6 The standard biographies that focus on de Valera's American mission are: Earl of Longford and O'Neill, *Eamon de Valera*, 95–114; Dwyer, *Eamon de Valera*, 21–38; and Coogan, *De Valera*, 135–96. For a balanced assessment of Cohalan, see Doorley, *Justice Daniel Cohalan*, 128–59. See also Tansill, *America and the Fight for Irish Freedom*; Ward, *Ireland and Anglo-American Relations*; Carroll, *American Opinion and the Irish Question*; and Hannigan, *De Valera in America*.
7 *New York Times*, 24 and 25 June 1919; Maher, *Harry Boland*, 92–96; Hannigan, *De Valera in America*, 1–10. In the context of world events, it should be noted that also on 23 June the Germans, with only hours to spare, accepted the terms of the Versailles Treaty, which was signed on 28 June.
8 Carroll, *Money for Ireland*, 1–14; McCartan, *With De Valera in America*, 141; O'Doherty, *Assignment-America*, 41; *Dáil Eireann proc, 1919–1921*, 19 June 1919, and 19 August 1919, 132–34, 139, and 150.
9 De Valera to the cabinet, 10 March 1920, *DIFP*, vol. 1, 58; Doorley, *Justice Daniel Cohalan*, 132–34. De Valera's claim of inadequacy for the FOIF must be seen in the light of his conflict with Judge Cohalan and John Devoy. Dáil Éireann Report on Foreign Affairs, June 1920, *DIFP*, vol. 1, 72. See also Maher, *Harry Boland*, 84–91.
10 Carroll, *Money for Ireland*, 15–17. Michael Doorley has provided a detailed accounting of the disbursements from the Irish Victory Fund in *Irish-American Diaspora Nationalism*, 192–93.
11 Longford and O'Neill, *Eamon de Valera*, 100–101. The "certificate" that could later be exchanged for a "bond" may have been the idea of W. J. M. A. Maloney. President Roosevelt would later tell the story of his advising de Valera on the bond certificate matter to all of his Irish visitors. See Brennan, *Ireland Standing Firm*, 11.
12 Carroll, *Money for Ireland*, 17–19; McCartan, *With DeValera in America*. 142–43; Boland to McGuire, 11 September 1919, Cohalan Papers, AIHS; prospectus of the first issue of bond certificates authorized by Dáil Éireann, 1 October 1919, Devoy Papers, NLI; Longford and O'Neill, *DeValera*, 100.
13 For the argument that the legal objections were insincere, see O'Doherty, *Assignment-America*, 40–45; and McCartan, *With DeValera in America*, 141–43.
14 De Valera to Griffith, 13 July 1919, Eamon De Valera Papers, University College Dublin Archives (UCDA); De Valera to Griffith ,13 August 1919, *DIFP*, vol. 1, 39;

Walsh to Dunne, 12 August 1919, and Walsh to de Valera, 2 October 1919, Boxes 124 and 115, Frank P. Walsh Papers, NYPL; Manning, *Frank P. Walsh*, 70–73.

15 *New York Times*, 24 August 1919; Boland to Cockran, 20 November 1919, and instructions on organization for Irish Bond certificate campaign, n.d., Box 17, Cockran Papers, NYPL; Maher, *Harry Boland*, 98; Lavelle, *James O'Mara*, 141–47.

16 De Valera to Griffith, 21 August 1919, *DIFP*, vol. 1, 43–44; Montieth, *Casement's Last Adventure*, 239; McCartan, *With DeValera in America*, 142–45; Maher, *Harry Boland*, 105; Lavelle, *James O'Mara*, 143–47.

17 Longford and O'Neill, *DeValera*, 101–2; O'Doherty, *Assignment-America*, 70–74 and 93–112; Lavelle, *James O'Mara*, 144–46; Nunan, "President Éamon de Valera's Mission," 242.

18 Prospectus for the Irish bond issue, 1 October 1919, instructions on organization for Irish Bond certificate campaign, n.d., and Frank P. Walsh to all state and city chairmen, 8 December 1919, Box 17, Cockran Papers, NYPL.

19 Walsh, circular letter, 15 January 1920, Box 17, Cockran Papers, NYPL.

20 *New York Times*, 18, 19, and 20 January 1920; *Irish World*, 17, 24, and 31 January 1920; "Irish Bonds," *Literary Digest* 64, no. 6 (7 February 1920): 16; Nunan to Collins, 20 January 1920, *DIFP*, vol. 1, 49. See also O'Doherty, *Assignment-America*, 127–31; and Hannigan, *De Valera in America*, 105–14.

21 Hayes to Cockran, 17 January 1920, Box 17, Cockran Papers, NYPL.

22 De Valera to Griffith, 6 March 1920, *DIFP*, vol. 1, 56; Whelan, *United States Foreign Policy and Ireland*, 302.

23 Cited in Coogan, *De Valera*, 176. For a full discussion of these events, see Carroll, *Money for Ireland*; Doorley, *Irish-American Diaspora Nationalism*; and Hannigan, *De Valera in America*.

24 Splain to Walsh, 17 September 1920, Frank P. Walsh Papers, NYPL.

25 Slattery to Walsh, 3 January 1921, Frank P. Walsh Paper, NYPL.

26 Moore to Cockran, 8 February 1920, Box 17, Cockran Papers, NYPL; Mrs. Golden to Peter Golden, 16 February 1920, Golden Papers, NLI.

27 Hastings to Wilson, 19 December 1919, 841d.51/1, RG 59, State Department Records, NARA.

28 Glass to H. B. Hastings, 22 December 1919, 841d.51/1, RG 59, State Department Records, NARA.

29 Houston to Walsh, 7 February 1920, Box 125, Frank P. Walsh Papers, NYPL.

30 Walsh to all state and city chairmen, 8 December 1919, Box 17, Cockran Papers, NYPL.

31 De Valera to Walsh, September 1919, Box 124, Frank P. Walsh Papers, NYPL.

32 *New York Times*, 11 January 1920. Many non-Irish commentators were very critical of these instruments. The *Wall Street Journal* was particularly so: "Sold as bonds the de Valera issue is nothing more than a swindle" (4 February 1920).

33 As the US Bond certificate campaign was ending, authorities in Dublin Castle concluded that the Dáil government was running out of funds and that the election of Warren Harding as US president would make it difficult for the Irish Americans

to raise more money. See Sturgis diary, 4 November 1920, in Hopkinson, *Last Days of Dublin Castle*, 65. In fact, the Dáil never exhausted its financial resources.

34 In the course of introducing his motion, de Valera singled out Frank P. Walsh, the chairman of the American Commission on Irish Independence for his assistance in the Bond certificate drive (*Dáil Éireann rep., 1921–2*, 17 August 1921, 25–26).

35 Boland to de Valera, 20 July 1921, and memorandum from O'Mara to de Valera, 12 August 1921, *DIFP*, vol. 1, 172–74 and 190–92; De Valera to McGarrity, 9 December 1920, and Eamon de Valera to whom it may concern, 9 December 1920, in Cronin, *McGarrity Papers*, 91–92; Carroll, *Money for Ireland*, 24–25. See also De Valera to O'Mara, November 27 and 10 December 1920, MS 21, 548(4), James O'Mara Papers, NLI.

36 Boland to Brennan, 27 October 1921, *DIFP*, vol. 1, 203–4.

37 Boland to de Valera, 20 July 1921, and memorandum from O'Mara to de Valera, 12 August 1921, Boland to Brennan, 27 October 1921, *DIFP*, vol. 1, 173, 190–91, and 203–4.

38 *Dáil Eireann proc. 1919–21*, 182 and 289; *Dáil Eireann, tuairisc oifigiúil (official report)* [1921–22], 84–85; and *Iris Dhail Eireann*, 302–3.

39 *Dáil Éireann rep., 1921–2*, 28 February 1922, 113–15.

40 Sagarra, *Envoy Extraordinary*, 51–59; *Irish Free State, et al. v. Guaranty Safe Deposit Company, et al.*, 126 New York Miscellaneous Reports 584, 129 New York Miscellaneous Reports 551, and 222 New York Supplement 182. This tension is clearly explained in the report by Denis McCulough to George Gavan Duffy, 8 May 1922, *DIFP*, vol. 1, 452–53.

41 *Fogarty and others v. O'Donoghue and others*, [1926] Irish Reports 531.

42 *Fogarty and others v. O'Donoghue and others*, [1926] Irish Reports 531; Carroll, *Money for Ireland*, 41–45.

43 *Gaelic American* and *Irish World*, especially November 1925, May 1927, June 1931, and November 1931. See also Carroll to Cohalan, 20 January 1923, Drawer 1, Cohalan Papers, AIHS; and Hearn to Finerty, 13 December 1922, and Finerty to de Valera, 20 January 1923, Drawer 1, John F. Finerty Papers, University of Michigan Library.

44 *Irish Free State, et al. v. Guaranty Safe Deposit Company, et al.*, 129 New York Miscellaneous Reports 551; 222 New York Supplement 182; Carroll, *Money for Ireland*, 47–59.

45 This case was *Irish Free State v. Guaranty Safe Deposit Company, Friends of Irish Freedom, v. Brady et al.*, 233 New York (Supreme Court, Appellate Division) 835; and 251 New York Supplement 104. Efforts to have this decision overturned by the Court of Appeals of New York were unsuccessful.

46 This case was *Montague and others v. Cooney and others*, 147 New York Miscellaneous Reports 125. See also Carroll, *Money for Ireland*, 671–63 and 69–78.

47 Memorandum by the assistant secretary of state, 26 October 1927 and 27 January 1928; and memorandum by the solicitor for the State Department, 8 February 1928, *FRUS, 1928, Vol. III*, 83–89.

48 *Dáil Éireann deb.*, 60, cols. 609 and 2057. See also O'Brien, *De Valera*, 7–28 and 59–62.

5. IRELAND IN THE EYE OF PUBLIC OPINION

1 For a discussion of Irish activities in the United States, see Ward, *Ireland and Anglo-American Relations*, 16–236; Carroll, *American Opinion and the Irish Question*, 121–93; and Doorley. *Irish-American Diaspora Nationalism*, 122–37.
2 Dumont to secretary of state, 23 December 1919, 841d.00/115, RG 59, State Department Records, NARA.
3 The comparison with the Bryce Commission is not strictly correct, although the public may not have made that distinction. That body was authorized to investigate conditions in Belgium by the British government in late 1914 and its report was published as a command paper. See *Report of the Committee on Alleged German Outrages*, HC, 1915 [Cmd. 7894]. A closer parallel might have been the later work by Lord Bryce on behalf of the Armenians. Through entirely private, people who had travelled to Ottoman Turkey were interviewed. The documents were compiled and published by Lord Bryce and Arnold Toynbee in 1916 as *The Treatment of Armenians in the Ottoman Empire, 1915–1916: Documents Presented to Viscount Grey of Fallodon, Secretary of State for Foreign Affairs, by Viscount Bryce* (London: Sir Joseph Causton & Sons, 1916). A more recent and closer parallel is the "Russell Tribunal" to investigate the US war in Vietnam. See Duffert, *Against the Crime of Silence*.
4 Villard to Thomas, 29 March 1921, L. Hollingsworth Wood Papers, Haverford College; McCartan, *With DeValera in America*, 210–16 and 235–37; Villard, *Fighting Years*, 487–90; Whelan, *United States Foreign Policy and Ireland*, 254. Villard had been a founder of the Anti-Imperialist League and the National Association for the Advancement of Colored People. A pacifist, Villard attempted to walk the delicate line between opposing the Germany of the Kaiser and refusing to support the Allies, an awkward position after the United States entered the war in 1917.
5 *Nation*, 6 October 1920, 340 and 367; *Nation* to Walsh, 20 September 1920, File B, Box 170, Thomas J. Walsh Papers, LC.
6 Committee of One Hundred Fifty, list of members, 23 September 1920; and second list of members, 5 October 1920, Oswald Garrison Villard Papers, Harvard University Library (HUL).
7 Moore to Villard, 3 October 1920, Villard Papers, HUL.
8 Deegan, "Jane Addams and the American Commission," 29–37.
9 *Nation*, November 3, 1920, 500–501; Coyle, *Evidence on Conditions in Ireland*, vi–viii. The commission was initially to have been chaired by Joseph W. Folk, former governor of Missouri. However, Folk's legal work with Egyptian nationalists led him to withdraw from the commission lest his presence compromise its objectivity (Coyle, 3).
10 *Nation*, 13 October 1920; MacDonald to Villard, 27 October 1920, and speech by O. G. Villard, n.d., Villard Papers, HUL.
11 MacDonald to France, 20 October 1920; MacDonald to Villard, 21 October 1920, Villard Papers, HUL.
12 MacDonald to Villard, 6 November 1920; speech by O. G. Villard, n.d., Villard Papers, HUL.

13 Maloney's memorandum on Washington Commission on British Atrocities, in McCartan, *With DeValera in America*, 259–62.
14 Geddes to Foreign Office, 16 September 1920, FO 371/4552, TNA.
15 Geddes to Foreign Office, 29 September and 7 October 1920, FO 371/4552, TNA.
16 Craigie to MacDonald, 10 November 1920, cited in *American Commission on Conditions in Ireland*, 122.
17 Geddes to MacDonald, 23 October 1920, in *Nation*, November 3, 1920, 501.
18 Davis and Fleming, *Ambassadorial Diary of John W. Davis*, 370.
19 Howe to Villard, November 1920; Gleason to Villard, 24 November 1920, Villard Papers, HUL.
20 MacDonald to Geddes, 24 November 1920, cited in *Interim Report*, 123–24; Geddes to Foreign Office and minutes, 26 November 1920, FO 371/4554, TNA.
21 Walsh, France, LaFollette, Ransdell, Walsh, Gronna, Chamberlain et al. to Colby, 15 December 1920, 841.00/265, RG 59, State Department Records, NARA.
22 Davis to each senator, 11 January 1921, Thomas J. Walsh Papers, LC.
23 Walsh to Davis, 14 January 1921, Thomas J. Walsh Papers, LC.
24 Coyle, *Evidence on Conditions in Ireland*, 5.
25 Coyle. Manly and Malone were also members of the Committee of One Hundred Fifty.
26 Coyle, 6–52.
27 Coyle, 109–11.
28 Coyle, 137–81; McCartan, *With De Valera in America*, 222. The four other Americans were Rev. Michael M. English, John F. Martin, Rev. James H. Cotter, and Agnes B. King. The Hacketts, and their appreciation of conditions in Ireland, were highly praised by James G. Douglas, a Dublin Quaker active in the relief effort. Douglas to Wood, 20 March 1921, Wood Papers, Haverford College Library.
29 Coyle, *Evidence on Conditions in Ireland*, 223.
30 Villard, *Fighting Years*, 488. The British ambassador, Sir Auckland Geddes, downplayed the impact of the commission in his Annual Report for 1920. "On the whole it may be said that comparatively little public interest was taken in the proceedings of the commission, which was fairly generally regarded, outside Irish circles, as the work of self-appointed busybodies." Geddes to Curzon, 1 September 1921, Annual Report, 1920, *BDFA*, vol. 1, 56.
31 Coyle, *Evidence on Conditions in Ireland*, 265–302 (quotations from 297).
32 Coyle, 376–427.
33 *New York Times*, 13 December 1921.
34 Coyle, *Evidence on Conditions in Ireland*, 530–78 (quotation from 570–71).
35 Coyle, 624–25.
36 Coyle, 578–717.
37 Memorandum of conversation between Craigie and Davis, 31 January 1921, Norman Davis Papers, LC; memorandum dealing with lord mayor O'Callaghan by Flourney,

25 March 1921, and Nielsen to secretary of state, 29 March 1921, Fred K. Nielsen Papers, LC. See also Whelan, *United States Foreign Policy and Ireland*, 265–70.
38. Coyle, *Evidence on Conditions in Ireland*, 740.
39. Coyle, 830.
40. Coyle, 718–892. The four American seamen were Emil Pezolt, Henry Turk, Harold Johnson, and Ralph Taylor.
41. Coyle, 893–1052.
42. See the *Nation* from December 1920 to March 1921 for installments.
43. *American Commission on Conditions in Ireland*; McCartan, *With DeValera in America*, 235–37.
44. *Interim Report*, 13.
45. *Interim Report*, 15–19.
46. *New York Times*, 1 April 1921.
47. *Parl. Deb.*, Commons, 7 April 1921, vol. 140, cols. 465–66. Roughly two months later Oswald Mosley raised the matter for the prime minister, noting the distinguished people involved with the commission, and asking about government accountability for its agents "to slay, burn, and loot" and whether "the moral responsibility" for these crimes did not rest "on those who fashioned and used it." Neville Chamberlain, answering for the prime minister, also noted that the witnesses held "extreme views" and that the government did not "recognize the right of citizens of a foreign State to hold any inquiry into the conditions of any part of His Majesty's Dominions." *Parl. Deb.*, 6 June 1921, vol. 142, cols. 1505–6.
48. *New Republic*, 13 April 1921.
49. *Nation*, 6 April 1921, 498; Whelan, *United States Foreign Policy and Ireland*, 328.
50. Villard to Thomas, 29 March 1921, Wood Papers, Haverford College Library; Addams, *Second Twenty Years at Hull House*, 205–7. See also Geddes to Curzon, 8 December 1921, Annual Report, 1921, *BDFA*, vol. 1, 139–40.
51. Villard to Wood, 20 and 26 January and 25 March 1921, Villard Papers, HUL.
52. Wood to Walsh, 18 and 21 May 1921, Frank P. Walsh Papers, NYPL; McCartan, *With DeValera in America*, 236. The money Maloney "lent" to the commission may have been drawn from the Dáil funds in the United States.
53. Osborn, *John Sharp Williams*, 352; acting secretary Finch to the *Nation*, 11 September 1920, Papers of the Carnegie Endowment for International Peace, Columbia University Library; Neilson to Villard, 39 November 1920, Villard Papers, HUL.
54. Winslow to Villard, n.d., Wood Papers, Haverford College Library.
55. *New York Times*, 8 January 1921.
56. Ochs to Villard, 24 November 1920, Van Anda to Villard, 15 December 1920, Villard to Bassett, 14 December 1921, and Villard to Dunning, 13 April 1921, Villard Papers, HUL; *Nation*, 26 January 1921; Wreszin, *Oswald Garrison Villard*, 142; McCartan, *With DeValera in America*, 236–37.
57. *Gaelic American*, 2 October 1920, 4.
58. Moore to Villard, 3 October 1920, BMS Am. 1323 (1878), Villard Papers, HUL. The writer Lincoln Colcord, who had worked on the *Nation* in 1919 and 1920, wrote

to Maloney to say the commission's report was "an admirable document," and that Maloney had his "heartiest congratulations." Colcord to Maloney, Box 19, Maloney Collection, NYPL.
59 Wood to Walsh, 18 May 1921, Walsh Papers, NYPL. See also Villard, *Fighting Years*, 489–91.
60 Humes, *Oswald Garrison Villard*, 239.
61 Cabinet minutes, 24 December 1920, in Middlemass, *Thomas Jones*, vol. 3, 47–48.
62 Cabinet minutes, 30 January 1921, in Middlemass, 49.
63 Cabinet minutes, 12 May 1921, in Middlemass, 69.
64 Cited in Deegan, "Jane Addams and the American Commission," 35.
65 Thomas to Villard, 24 March 1937, Villard Papers, HUL.
66 Shaw to Villard, 17 October 1939, in Villard, *Fighting Years*, 490–91.

6. AMERICAN AID FOR IRELAND, 1920–1922

1 Nicholson to Pickett, in Pickett to Thomas, 13 November 1920, Ireland folder, 1920, American Friends Service Committee Archives (AFSC Archives). Pickett would eventually become the executive secretary of the AFSC.
2 Pickett to Norton, 15 November 1920, Ireland folder, 1920, AFSC Archives.
3 Norton to Pickett, 17 November 1920; Pickett to Norton, 19 November 1920; memorandum for executive board meeting, 23 November 1920, Ireland folder, 1920, AFSC Archives. By December the Irish Quakers were operating soup kitchens in several towns (Hatton, *Largest Amount of Good*, 243).
4 "Summons to Service," 2.
5 Thomas to Barlow, 31 December 1920, in Thomas to American Friends Service Committee, 3 February 1921, Ireland folder, 1921, AFSC Archives.
6 Barlow to Thomas, 29 January 1921, in Thomas to American Friends Service Committee, 3 February 1921, Ireland folder, 1921, AFSC Archives. See also Graveson to Pollard, 14 and 29 December 1920, Relief Work Papers, Friends Historical Library.
7 Thomas to Sloan, 29 January 1921; Thomas to Rhoads, 9 February 1921, Ireland folder, 1921, AFSC Archives. Thomas gave the same explanation to the State Department: "The American Friends Service Committee is sending some money for relief work in Ireland but is doing it though a group of English Friends." Thomas to State Department, 8 February 1921, 841d. 48/3, RG 59, State Department Records, NARA.
8 Graveson to Jones (chairman of the American Friends Service Committee), 30 March 1921, and Jones to Graveson, 19 April 1921, Relief Work Papers, Friends Historical Library; "Proceedings of the 1921 Friends Yearly Meeting," 100, Friends House Library. See also Jones, *Quakers in Action*, 156.
9 O'Callaghan to American Red Cross, 16 December 1920, 841d. 48/5, RG 59, State Department Records, NARA.
10 Davis to the president, 15 December 1920, 841d. 48/-a, RG 59, State Department Records, NARA; memorandum by Stanley (director of the joint committee of the

British Red Cross and the Knights of St. John of Jerusalem) to Foreign Office, 29 December 1920, FO 371/4613, TNA; Whelan, *United States Foreign Policy and Ireland*, 266.

11 American Red Cross to Mrs. Golden, 30 December 1920, and Mrs. Golden to American Red Cross, 1 January 1921, MS 13,141/2, Golden Papers, NLI; *Nation*, 12 January 1921; Gallivan to Colby, 14 December 1920, and Adee to Gallivan, 20 December 1920, 841d. 48/-, RG 59, State Department Records, NARA.

12 Carroll, *American Opinion and the Irish Question*, 78–80 and 165; Feighery, "Timely and Substantial Relief," 283–91; McCartan, *With De Valera in America*, 223–34.

13 *Nation*, December 29, 1920.

14 McCartan, *With DeValera in America*, 223–34. Doheny was the nephew of Michael Doheny, of the Young Ireland rebellion of 1848, and his enlistment into the Irish movement was very important. However, within just a few years he was implicated in the infamous "Tea Pot Dome" scandal.

15 McCartan, 225–27; *Report of the American Committee for Relief in Ireland*, 48; "Summons to Service," 2.

16 Attitude of American Relief Administration, Herbert Hoover Papers, Hoover Presidential Library. Hoover had organized the Commission for Relief in Belgium early in the war and then headed first the US Food Administration and then the American Relief Administration.

17 McCartan, *With De Valera in America*, 7, 51, and 225–27; Gaughan, *Memoirs of James G. Douglas*, 61. See also Quinn to Gonne, 20 June 1921, in Londraville, *Too Long a Sacrifice*, 230.

18 For descriptions of American relief operations in Belgium and elsewhere, see Gibson, *Journal from Our Legation in Belgium*; Gay, *Commission for Relief in Belgium*; Surface and Bland, *American Food in the World War*; Hoover, *American Epic*; and Weissman, *Herbert Hoover and Famine Relief*.

19 Thomas to Sloan, 29 January 1921; Thomas to State Department, 8 February 1921, Ireland folder, 1921, AFSC Archives. Thomas asked Judge Richard Campbell not to use the name of the Society of Friends in their promotional activities. Thomas to Hoover, 14 March 1921; Thomas to America Friends Service Committee, 15 March 1921, Ireland folder, 1921, AFSC Archives. See also Shaw to secretary of state, 17 March 1921, Herbert Hoover Papers, Hoover Presidential Library.

20 American Committee for Relief in Ireland, broadsheet, 30 January 1921, Thomas J. Walsh Papers, File B, Box 190, LC; McCartan, *With DeValera in America*, 225.

21 Report to the executive committee of the American Committee for Relief in Ireland, by France and McCoy, 16 March 1921, MS 21,549(3), O'Mara Papers, NLI. James Douglas, in a letter Hollingsworth Wood, put his finger exactly on the general's desire to "bring these people to their senses." Douglas said the British objected to relief efforts easing Irish suffering "when they [the British] meant to break the spirit of the people." Douglas to Wood, 31 March 1921, Wood Papers, Haverford College Library.

22 Sturgis diary, 14 and 16 February 1921, in Hopkinson, *Last Days of Dublin Castle*, 126 and 129.
23 Hopkinson, 126 and 129.
24 Douglas to O'Brien, 31 March 1921, Wood Papers, Haverford College Library; Gaughan, *Memoirs of Senator James G. Douglas*, 66.
25 Sturgis diary, 12 March 1921, in Hopkinson, *Last Days of Dublin Castle*, 140.
26 Report to the executive committee of the American Committee for Relief in Ireland, by France and McCoy, 16 March 1921, MS 21,549(3), O'Mara Papers, NLI; Williams, *Report of the Irish White Cross*, 125–40; Wood to Graveson, 8 June 1921, Relief Work Papers, Friends Historical Library; France and McCoy to the trustees of the Irish White Cross, 12 September 1921, Box 19, Maloney Papers, NYPL.
27 *Report of the American Committee for Relief in Ireland*, 62–67; minutes of the meeting of the advisory committee, 14 February 1921, Relief Work Papers, Friends Historical Library.
28 Hoover to secretary of state, 11 March 1921, 841d. 48/7, RG 59, State Department Records, NARA; *Report of the American Committee for Relief in Ireland*, 7; Campbell to Walsh, Thomas J. Walsh Papers, LC; McCartan, *With De Valera in America*, 228. See also Lucey to O'Brien, 25 March 1921, Hoover Papers, Hoover Presidential Library.
29 *Report of the American Committee for Relief in Ireland*, 8–15.
30 *Report of the American Committee for Relief in Ireland*, 20–41; "Suggested Plan for National Organization," 1–3.
31 Lucey to Hoover, 11 March 1921, Hoover Papers, Hoover Presidential Library.
32 *Nation*, 2 February 1921.
33 *Report of the American Committee for Relief in Ireland*, 50; " Summons to Service," 5–16.
34 Harding to O'Brien, 26 March 1921, Warren G. Harding Papers, Ohio Historical Society. For the request and subsequent thanks and assurances, see O'Brien to Harding, 23 and 29 March 1921, Harding Papers, Ohio Historical Society. The lord mayor of Dublin cabled thanks to the president: "The afflicted people of Ireland are sincerely grateful for your kind promise of financial support. America was always true to Ireland in her hour of trial. Fund urgently needed to restore destruction and relieve distress." O'Neill to Harding, 29 March 1921, 841d.48/17, RG 59, State Department Records, NARA. See also *Report of the American Committee for Relief in Ireland*, 6, 19, 50, and 59–60. Pamphlets and broadsheets were published for publicity purposes—for example, *Need for Relief in Ireland* (n.p., n.d.); McCoy, *Distress in Ireland*.
35 *Report of the American Committee for Relief in Ireland*, 6 and 19; *New York Times*, March 27, 1921. Vice President Coolidge said he was "in entire accord" with Harding's statement, and that the American people would be "especially responsive to a race which has contributed so much to the defense and greatness of our commonwealth."
36 *New York Times*, 31 March 1921.
37 *Report of the American Committee for Relief in Ireland*, 43–44 and 62–63.
38 Carroll, *American Opinion and the Irish Question*, 52–54.

39 *Report of the American Committee for Relief in Ireland*, 51–52 and 56–58; Campbell to Walsh, 8 January 1921, Thomas J. Walsh Papers, LC; memorandum of conversation between Parsons and Bicknell of the Red Cross and the third assistant secretary of state, 28 March 1921, 841d.48/19, RG 59, State Department Records, NARA. See also *White Cross News*, n.d., MS 10, 558, Col. Maurice Moore Papers, NLI; Gallagher to Frankhouse, 13 April 1921, Bishop Gallagher Papers, Archdiocese of Detroit, Archives; and Geddes to Curzon, 15 September 1921, Annual Report, 1920, *BDFA*, vol. 1, 56.

40 Lucey to Hoover, 8 March 1921; Hoover to Lucey, 9 March 1921, Herbert Hoover Papers, Hoover Presidential Library.

41 O'Brien, Lucey, Godkin, and Brady to Hoover, 10 March 1921, and Hoover to Lucey, 11 March 1921, Hoover Papers, Hoover Presidential Library; Thomas to Sloan, 29 January 1921, and Thomas to Rhoads, 9 February 1921, Ireland folder, 1921, AFSC Archives.

42 Hoover to Hughes, 11 March 1921, Hoover Papers, Hoover Presidential Library.

43 "Distress in Ireland," Report of Friends' Investigation Committee, December 1920 to March 1921, minutes of the committee on Ireland, 8 February 1921, and Wood to Douglas, 19 December 1920, Relief Work Papers, Friends Historical Library; Gaughan, *Memoirs of Senator James G. Douglas*, 9 and 62–33; *Report of the American Committee for Relief in Ireland*, 51–52 and 56–58; Williams, *Report of the Irish White Cross*, 34–40 and 110–12.

44 Douglas to Wood, 31 March 1921, Wood Papers, Haverford College Library.

45 Williams, *Report of the Irish White Cross*, 53–73.

46 Williams, 28–31.

47 *Report of the American Committee for Relief in Ireland*, 45.

48 Foreign Office to Geddes, 30 March 1921, and Geddes to Foreign Office, 31 March 1921, FO 371/5663, TNA.

49 Geddes to Foreign Office, 5 April 1921, FO 371/5663, TNA. Harry Boland wrote to de Valera with journalist Joseph Scott's report that he had met with the president and Harding had "urged the Ambassador [Geddes] to impress on the British Government the importance of settling the [Irish] question." Boland to de Valera, 20 July 1921, *DIFP, 1919–1922*, vol. 1, 174. Geddes reported more or less the opposite.

50 Memorandum of conversation with McCoy and Shaw, 21 April 1921; memorandum on Irish Relief by Shaw for secretary of state, 29 April 1921, 841d. 48/35 and -/38, RG 59, State Department Records, NARA.

51 *Parl. Deb.*, Commons, 7 April 1921, vol. 140, cols. 461–2.

52 Geddes to Foreign Office, no. 303, 5 May 1921, FO 371/5663, TNA.

53 Geddes to Foreign Office, no. 303, 5 May 1921, FO 371/5663, TNA.

54 Geddes to Foreign Office, no. 304, 5 May 1921, FO 371/5663, TNA.

55 Geddes to Cabinet, "Ireland and America," 9 May 1921, Cab. 24/123, TNA.

56 Cabinet minutes, 10 May 1921, Cab. 23/25, C. 36/21/4, TNA.

57 Curzon to Geddes, ca. 10 May 1921, FO 371/5663, TNA. See also Geddes to Curzon, 8 December 1921, Annual Report, 1921, *BDFA*, vol. 1, 139–45.

58 Memorandum of interview with the British ambassador, 23 May 1921, Box 125, Charles Evans Hughes Papers, LC.
59 Geddes to Foreign Office, 15 May 1921, FO 371/5663, TNA.
60 Whelan, *United States Foreign Policy and Ireland*, 321.
61 Dumont to secretary of state, 22 March 1921, 841d. 00/339, RG 59, State Department Records, NARA.
62 Dumont to secretary of state, 17 May 1921, 841d. 48/27; Dumont to secretary of state, 9 June 1921, 841d. 00/27, RG 59, State Department Records, NARA.
63 De Valera to Boland, 30 April 1921, cited in Whelan, *United States Foreign Policy and Ireland*, 325; minister of finance to president, 28 June 1921, DE 2/450, Department of Foreign Affairs Papers, National Archives of Ireland (NAI). See also Davis and Fleming, *Ambassador's Diary*, 359, 382–83, and 397.
64 Minutes of the Committee of Irish Friends Co-operating with a Committee of the Meeting for Sufferings, London, 9 May 1921, Relief Work Papers, Friends Historical Library,
65 Williams, *Report of the Irish White Cross*, 49–73; Gaughan, *Memoirs of Senator James G. Douglas*, 65. While not contradicting the reports of need for relief assistance in Ireland, it is interesting to note that the Dáil authorized sending £1,000 to Geneva for relief in Russia: "Ireland cannot remain unmoved by the knowledge of the terrible misery which afflicts so many millions of Russians." See Law to Griffith, 21 April 1921, DE 2/469, Department of Foreign Affairs Papers, NAI.
66 Harding to secretary of state, 20 April 1921, 841d. 00/392, RG 59, State Department Records, NARA.
67 Carr to Dumont (Dublin), Mitchell (Belfast), and Kent (Cork), 11 April 1921, 841d. 48/22a, -/22b, and -/22c, RG 59, State Department Records, NARA; Hughes to Dumont, 11 July 1921, 841d. 00/381, RG 59, State Department Records, NARA. Dumont had been in the consular service since 1911 and had served in several posts during the war, including Florence, before that had been a construction engineer for the Pennsylvania Railroad, so his remarks could not be dismissed as without some experience. See Keegan, *US Consular Representation since 1790*, 133.
68 Hoover to secretary of state, 11 March 1921, 841d. 48/7, RG 59; Shaw to secretary of state, 15 April 1921, 841d. 00/339, RG 59 ; British Embassy to Hughes, 17 June 1921, 841d. 00/379, RG 59, State Department Records, NARA. See also Herter (assistant to Hoover) to Shaw, 20 April 1921; and Herter to Hoover, 26 April 1921, Hoover Papers, Hoover Presidential Library.
69 See Ellis, *Republican Foreign Policy*, 93–103; Vinson, *Parchment Peace*, 21–31 and 97–114; and Buckley, *United States and the Washington Conference*, 29–34.
70 Northedge, *Troubled Giant*, 275–84; Roskill, *Naval Policy Between the Wars*, vol. 1, 196–99; Fry, *Illusions of Security*, 121–58. It should be noted that Mrs. Erskine Childers wrote to de Valera on 1 June 1921, pointing out to him the extent to which the Anglo-Japanese Alliance was a major problem for the United States and thus was an issue that could be turned to advantage by the Irish. See Mrs. Childers to de Valera, 1 June 1921, DE 2/526, NAI.

71 Memorandum of a conversation between the secretary and the British ambassador, 23 June 1921, *FRUS, 1921*, vol. 2, 315–16.
72 Geddes to Foreign Office, 5 May 1921, FO 371/5663, TNA.
73 Walsh to Duffy, 1 February 1921, MS 5582, Gavan Duffy Papers, NLI.
74 Cabinet minutes, 12 May 1921, in Middlemass, *Thomas Jones*, vol. 3, 69.
75 Roskill, *Naval Policy Between the Wars*, vol. 1, 293; Duroselle, *From Wilson to Roosevelt*, 158.
76 Pusey, *Charles Evans Hughes*, vol. 2, 492.
77 Ellis, *Republican Foreign Policy*, 94. Alan J. Ward does not link the relief effort or the pending congressional resolution with the Anglo-Japanese treaty, but he does argue that "Hughes forced the British to retreat" over the relief question by permitting funds to be distributed (*Ireland and Anglo-American Relations*, 245). Bernadette Whelan suggests that any bargaining strength Hughes might have had was undercut by the news that a shipment of Thompson machine guns intended for Ireland had been uncovered at the New Jersey docks on 13 June 1921 on a ship carrying relief supplies (*United States Foreign Policy and Ireland*, 341–43).
78 Whelan, 348. See also Hachey, "British Foreign Office," 3–13.
79 *Parl. Deb.*, Commons, 11 July 1921, vol. 144, cols. 914–18.
80 Cabinet minutes 30 January 1921; Middlemas, *Tom Jones, Whitehall Diary*, vol. 3, 49.
81 Wood to Douglas (cables), 10 and 11 August 1921, Wood Papers, Haverford College Library; Gaughan, *Memoirs of James G. Douglas*, 70–76. See also Collins to the president, 15 October and 9 November 1921, DE 2/450, Foreign Affairs Papers, NAI.
82 Cited in Monteith, *Casement's Last Adventure*, 246–47.
83 France to Maloney, 20 December 1921, Frank P. Walsh Papers, Box 112, NYPL. See also *Cong. Rec.*, 67th Cong., 2nd sess., vol. 62, 2143, House Joint Resolution 265, 3 February 1922; Plunkett diary, 8 February 1922, Plunkett Papers, NLI; and Carroll to Walsh, 20 December 1922, Box 111, Frank P. Walsh Papers, NYPL.
84 France and Douglas to O'Brien and Campbell, 19 January 1922; France to Maloney, 19 January 1922; Douglas to Ryan, 19 January 1922, Box 19, Maloney Papers, Maloney Collection, NYPL. See also France to Collins, 11 January 1922, Box 19, Maloney Papers, Maloney Collection, NYPL.
85 The mere fact that the committee attempted to use its influence to support the protreaty forces convinced some that the respectable, wealthy capitalists who made up the executive committee had betrayed the Irish revolution. See Monteith, *Casement's Last Adventure*, 248–49; and Williams, *Report of the Irish White Cross*, 139–40. The "personal relief" included the rebuilding of houses and barns and loans for small businesses up to £500.
86 Bernadette Whelan points out that the Harding administration took a much more activist role in dealing with distress in the Soviet Union and Anatolia, but then Russia and Turkey were not then major powers with whom cooperation was essential (*United States Foreign Policy and Ireland*, 348).
87 Griffith, Collins, Duffy, Barton, and Duggan to Campbell and Pulleyn, 29 October 1921, *Report of the American Committee for Relief in Ireland*, 56.

88 Cited in Maher, *Harry Boland*, 145.
89 O'Connell to Ryan, 19 December 1932, Frank P. Walsh Papers, NYPL. It is worth noting that Timothy A. Smiddy, the Dáil envoy to the United States, had a similar view of the forces that drew the British to make a settlement with the Irish. "This pact [the Four Power Treaty of 1921 negotiated at the Washington Naval Conference, which ended the Anglo-Japanese Alliance and reduced Anglo-American tensions] was vital to England, and to obtain it she was ready to make peace with Ireland." Smiddy to Gavan Duffy, 4 May 1922, *DIFP*, vol. 1, 449–50.

7. THE EMERGENCE OF THE IRISH FREE STATE AND AMERICAN DIPLOMATIC RECOGNITION, 1921–1927

1 War Cabinet 628(4), 4 October 1919, CAB 23/12; C.P. 56, 4 November 1919, first report of the cabinet committee on the Irish question, CAB 24/92; cabinet meeting 5/19(2), 11 November 1919, Cabinet meeting 12/19(10), 10 December 1919, cabinet meeting 16/19(9), 10 December 1919, CAB 23/18, TNA.
2 Memorandum by Duffy, "The Position of Ireland's 'Foreign Affairs' at the Date of the General Election, 1922 (Confidential)," 21 June 1922, *DIFP*, vol. 1, 468–77.
3 *Sinn Feiner*, July 9, 1921.
4 Geddes to Foreign Office, 29 November 1921, FO 371/5633, TNA.
5 *Gaelic American*, 26 February; 14 May; 2, 9, and 23 July; and 8 and 15 October 1921; Cohalan to Gallagher, 8 July 1921, Bishop Gallagher Papers, Archdiocese of Detroit, Archives. See also Lynch to members of the Senate, 9 August 1921, File B, Box 190, Thomas J. Walsh Papers, LC; McGrath to Williams, 30 October 1921, Box 56, John Sharp Williams Papers, LC; Lynch to FOIF branches, 13 September 1921, Bishop Thomas Shahan Papers, Catholic University of America Archives; and FOIF circular letter, 3 December 1921, Box 111, Frank P. Walsh Papers, NYPL.
6 McBarron to Walsh, 24 September 1921; Butte, Montana AARIR to Harding, 24 September 1921, File B, Box 190, Thomas J. Walsh Papers, LC.
7 *Cong. Rec.*, 67th Cong., 1st sess., vol. 61, 3917, 15 July 1921, House Resolution 150; MacSwiney to Cockran, 31 July 1921, and Cockran to MacSwiney, 11 August 1921, Box 18, Cockran Papers, NYPL.
8 Walsh to O'Flannagan, 15 November 1921, Box 111, Frank P. Walsh Papers, NYPL; Manly to Walsh, 19 November 1921, File B, Box 190, Thomas J. Walsh Papers, LC.
9 Manly to Walsh, 7 July 1921, Box 110, Frank P. Walsh Papers, NYPL.
10 Walsh to Daly, 4 October 1921, and Walsh to Scott, 19 October 1921, Box 111, Frank P. Walsh Papers, NYPL; Walsh to O'Brien, 4 October 1921, MS 8427, Art O'Brien Papers, NLI.
11 Walsh to Barron, 1 October 1921, File B, Box 190, Thomas J. Walsh Papers, LC.
12 Gallagher to de Valera, 16 August 1921; McGarry to de Valera, 16 August 1921, Drawer 1, Cohalan Papers, AIHS.
13 Boland to de Valera, 5 August 1921, *DIFP*, vol. 1, 178.
14 Executive committee of the Irish White Cross Society to Walsh, 27 August 1921, and France to Campbell, 2 September 1921, File B, Box 190, Thomas J. Walsh Papers, LC.

15 *Report of the American Committee for Relief in Ireland*, 45–46.
16 Walsh to Scott, 19 October 1921, Box 111, Frank P. Walsh Papers, NYPL.
17 Dumont to secretary of state, 21 June 1921, 841d.51/9, RG 59, State Department Records, NARA; Boland to de Valera, 20 July 1921, *DIFP*, vol. 1, 172–73. O'Mara was not confident about attempting to start a new bond certificate campaign in the autumn, but accepted that it was important to do so for political reasons. See O'Mara to de Valera, 12 August 1921, *DIFP*, vol. 1, 190–91.
18 *Dáil Éireann rep. 1921–2*, 26 August 1921, 84–85; *Dáil Éireann treaty deb.*, 7 January 1922, 302–3.
19 O'Mara, circular letter, Fall 1921, Box 17, Cockran Papers, NYPL. See also Peterson to Lord Curzon, 31 August 1921, FO 317/563; Sir A. Geddes to Foreign Office, 7 November 1921, and minutes, FO 317/5633, TNA.
20 O'Mara to Barrett, 31 October 1921, Box 17, Cockran Papers, NYPL.
21 Walsh to Lydon, 20 October 1921, Box 111, Frank P. Walsh Papers, NYPL; *Dáil Éireann treaty deb.*, 19 December 1921, 39.
22 Some $30,000 were raised in Washington and $552,000 in Illinois; other areas brought the total up to $622,720. *Dáil Éireann treaty deb.*, 7 January 1922, 303 and 335; R. F. Downing, "Men, Women, and Memories," 221; Lynch, *IRB and the 1916 Insurrection*, 216; O'Mara to Walsh, 29 October 1921, Box 111, Frank P. Walsh Papers, NYPL.
23 The actual title of the document signed was "Articles of Agreement for a Treaty between Great Britain and Ireland," but it has been known generally as the "Anglo-Irish Treaty."
24 Catholic Order of Foresters to Walsh, 21 December 1921, Legislation File, Box 272; Walsh to McCavin, 12 December 1921, File B, Box 190, Thomas J. Walsh Papers, LC.
25 For descriptions of the meeting, see Nevinson, *Last Changes, Last Chances*, 129–200; and Downing, "Men, Women, and Memories," 221. See also *Dáil Eireann treaty deb.*, 7 January 1922, 334–35.
26 Cited in Tansill, *America and the Fight for Irish Freedom*, 334–35. Doheny's satisfaction with the treaty was noted by the British Embassy as early as December 8, when Geddes reported to the Foreign Office that he was attempting to take credit for creating the conditions that made it possible. Sir A. Geddes to FO, 8 December 1921, FO 371/5715, TNA. It was also observed that since the signing of the treaty, James Farrell, the president of the United States Steel Corporation, who was regarded as having "strong Sinn Fein sympathies," spoke at a luncheon for Balfour." Kinkead to O'Mara, 17 January 1922, cited in Lavelle, *O'Mara*, 277.
27 Minutes of the national executive of the AARIR, 17 December 1921, Folder v, MS 13,141, Golden Papers, NLI; Downing, "Men, Women, and Memories," 221.
28 Walsh to France, 5 January 1922, Box 112, Frank P. Walsh Papers, NYPL.
29 Connolly to Department of Foreign Affairs, 16 January 1922, *DIFP*, vol. 1, 373–4.
30 Memorandum, "Why AARIR Should Be Maintained"; Manly to Lyons (national secretary), 14 December 1921, Box 112, Frank P. Walsh Papers, NYPL.

31 Downing, "Men, Women, and Memories," 221–22. See also Lyons to President Harding and members of Congress, 13 February 1922, Box 58, Williams Papers, LC; and appeal of state directorate to the national executive, AARIR, ca. May 1922, Box Misc., Devoy Papers, NLI.
32 *New York Times*, 14 February 1922.
33 Lyons to Doheny, 15 February 1922, MS 13,141, Folder v, Golden Papers, NLI.
34 Walsh to O'Mara, 17 March 1922, and Walsh to Boland, 12 February 1922, Box 115, Frank P. Walsh Papers, NYPL; Downing, "Men, Women, and Memories," 222, Monteith, *Casement's Last Adventure*, 248–49.
35 *Irish World*, 10, 17, and 31 December 1921; and 7 and 14 January 1922.
36 Cited in Tansill, *America and the Fight for Irish Freedom*, 437.
37 *Gaelic American*, 10 December 1921.
38 Lynch, *IRB and the 1916 Insurrection*, 214–15. See also *Cong. Rec.*, 67th Cong., 2nd sess., vol. 62, 3855 and 3907–10, 14 and 15 March 1922; correspondence concerning Williams's statements on Irish Americans, 14–31 March 1922, Boxes 58 and 59, Williams Papers, LC; "Declaration of Principles" by the national council of the FOIF, 10 and 11 December 1921, Shahan Papers, Catholic University of America Archives; and Cohalan to Bishop Gallagher, 21 December 1921, Drawer 3, Cohalan Papers, AIHS.
39 Splain, "Irish Movement in America," 253–54; *Gaelic American*, December 17, 1921; Geddes to Lord Curzon, 20 December 1921, FO 371/7265, TNA.
40 *Gaelic American*, 10, 24, and 31 December 1921; and 21 January 1922. The *Gaelic American* argued that de Valera was a charlatan quibbling about meaningless terms and that he had probably worked out the Dominion solution with Lloyd George during the summer but was attempting now to escape the responsibility for it.
41 Devoy to Collins, 16 February 1922, cited in Tansill, *America and the Fight for Irish Freedom*, 438–39.
42 *Gaelic American*, 4 March and 22 April 1922.
43 Cohalan to Cummings, 13 March 1922, Drawer 3, Cohalan Papers, AIHS; Cohalan to O'Connell, 13 March 1922, Drawer 1, Cohalan Papers, AIHS. See also Doorley, *Justice Daniel Cohalan*, 162–68.
44 *Gaelic American*, 18 March and 8 April 1922; declaration on the political situation in Ireland adopted by the national council of the FOIF, 28 March 1922, Shahan Papers, Catholic University of America Archive.
45 Collins to James O'Mara, 28 February 1922, cited in Lavelle, *O'Mara*, 278; Douglas to Maloney, 21 January 1922, Box 19, Maloney Papers, Maloney Collection, NYPL. See also Duffy to McCullough, 23 March 1911, *DIFP*, vol. 1, 411–2.
46 For descriptions of their arrival in New York on St. Patrick's Day, see *Irish World*, 25 March 1922; *Gaelic American*, 25 March 1922; and *New York Times*, 18 March 1922.
47 Hearn, Horgan, McGarrity, Walsh, O'Connor, Kelly, Griffin, and Harrigan to Collins and de Valera, 13 March 1922, Box 112, Frank P. Walsh Papers, NYPL.
48 Boland to Walsh, 28 February 1922, Frank P. Walsh Papers, NYPL.
49 *Irish World*, 1 and 15 April and and 6, 13, and 20 May 1922; *Gaelic American*, 25 March and 8 April 1922. For descriptions of the tours of the two delegations, see

Lavelle, *O'Mara*, 279–80; Marreco, *Rebel Countess*, 269–76; and Van Voris, *Constance Markievicz*, 310–12. See also Collins to Walsh, 12 April 1922; and memorandum of conversation between Walsh and O'Mara, 1 May 1922, Boxes 112 and 115, Frank P. Walsh Papers, NYPL.

50 *Gaelic American*, 22 April and 6 May 1922; *Irish World*, 6 and 14 January and 20 May 1922. Beginning in May, the *Irish World* almost always referred to the Irish Free State as the "Freak State."

51 *Gaelic American*, 8 July 1922.

52 Quinn to Hyde, 15 July, cited in Reid, *Man from New York*, 527–28.

53 *Gaelic American*, 30 September 1922; Armstrong to the foreign secretary, 11 September 1922, FO 371/7266, TNA; Curley to Cummings, 2 February 1923, cited in Tansill, *America and the Fight for Irish Freedom*, 440; Kelly to Ginnell, 6 August 1922, Drawer 2, Cohalan Papers, AIHS. See also Cohalan to Gallagher, 19 July 1922; Gavegan to Cohalan, 6 August 1922, Drawer 3, Cohalan Papers, AIHS; and O'Sullivan to Cohalan, 15 January 1923, Drawer 2, Cohalan Papers, AIHS.

54 Maloney, Memorandum on his part in attempting to reach a truce in August 1922, Box 20, Maloney Papers, Maloney Collection, NYPL. Maloney and Magennis met with General Mulcahy, Eoin MacNeill, and other members of the cabinet in Dublin on August 14 and later near Cork with Mary MacSwiney and one of her brothers for the republicans, but they were denied permission to consult with the republican commander in chief, Rory O'Connor, who was being held in Mountjoy Prison. The talks went no further. The Irish writer Louie Bennett attempted, through Jane Addams, to move the American Commission on Conditions in Ireland to arrange a truce, but that organization had ceased to exist. Bennett to Addams, 20 January 1923, Box 20, Maloney Papers, Maloney Collection, NYPL.

55 *Gaelic American*, 23 October 1922; Lynch, *IRB and the 1916 Insurrection*, 215.

56 *Gaelic American*, 2 and 16 December 1922. For examples of pro-republican anguish and dismay at the Civil War and the reprisals, see Joseph McGarrity's poems "To Ireland," "Erskine Childers," "For Liam Mellows," and "Rory O'Connor," in McGarrity, *Celtic Moods and Memories*, 44, 74, 90–91, and 99–100.

57 Murray to Finerty, 18 July 1922, Finerty to Murray, 3 August 1922, Murray to Finerty, 10 August 1922, Folder 6, Drawer 2, Finerty Papers, University of Michigan Library (UML); Manning. *Frank P. Walsh*, 75.

58 *Irish World*, 15 and 29 July and 25 November 1922. See also Armstrong to the foreign secretary, 2 September 1922, FO 371/7266, TNA.

59 *Irish World*, 23 September 1922 and 5 May 1923; draft of circular letter, 21 September 1922, and Walsh to Sheehy-Skeffington, 3 November 1922, Box 112, Frank P. Walsh Papers, NYPL; Finerty to de Valera, 19 February 1923, Folder 7, Drawer 1, Finerty Papers, UML.

60 De Valera to McGarrity, 10 September 1922, cited in Cronin, "Fenian Tradition." 12.

61 Armstrong to the foreign secretary, 22 September 1922, FO 371/7266, TNA.

62 McCann to Walsh, 27 November 1922, Walsh to McCann, 18 December 1922, Margaret Walsh to Walsh, 30 January 1923, Margaret Walsh to Walsh, 13 February

1923, Legislative File, Box 272, Thomas J. Walsh Papers, LC; Manly to Walsh, 14 December 1922, Box 112, Frank P. Walsh Papers, NYPL.
63 See "Irish Legation Circular," no. 1, January 1923; and Ginnell to de Valera, 6 January 1923, MS 8422, O'Brien Papers, NLI.
64 Ginnell to de Valera, 6 and 19 January and February 1923, Ginnell to O'Brien, 9 February and 2 March 1923, and Message from AARIR to Ireland, ca. 1 March 1923, MS 8422 and 8428, O'Brien Papers, NLI.; and "Irish Legation Circular," no. 6, 12 April 1923.
65 Smiddy to Department of External Affairs, 1 and 3 January 1923, and Smiddy to FitzGerald, 6 January 1923, *DIFP*, vol. 2, 24–25 and 28–29. See also Briscoe, *For the Life of Me*, 194–210; and *BDFA*, vol. 14, 7–8.
66 Finerty to Stack, 21 November 1922, Hearn (national treasurer of AARIR) to Lyons; 24 March 1923; Smithwick (Connecticut state president, AARIR) to Finerty, 2 April 1923; Hughes (New Jersey state president, AARIR) to Finerty, 5 April 1923, Drawer 1, Finerty Paper, UML.
67 See Mason, "Rebel Ireland"; Allen, "Brief for Irish Independence"; and Jones, *Eighteen Months*. Mason had been in Ireland during the Civil War and came back convinced that de Valera was right; Rev. Allen was an Episcopal clergyman with strong republican and anti-British sympathies.
68 *Irish World*, 9 June 1923; Davis, "Irish Civil War," 92–112.
69 *Gaelic American*, 5 May and 16 June 1923.
70 De Valera's mother appealed to President Coolidge for her son on the grounds that he was an "American born citizen." Wheelright to Coolidge, 22 September 1923, 841d.00/618, RG 59, State Department Records, NARA. See also Senator Neely to secretary of state, 27 September 1923; Lodge to secretary of state, 4 October 1923; Wheeler to secretary of state, 5 October 1923; Dixon to Coolidge, 12 October 1923; Walsh to Hughes, 22 February 1924; Walsh to Hughes, 23 February 1924; and Dickstein to secretary of state, 4 April 1924, 341D.1121 VALERA, EAMON DE /46–59, Box 4095, RG 59, State Department Records, NARA.
71 Hamill et al. to Walsh, 10 October 1923, and Walsh to Hamill, 10 October 1923, Box 272, Thomas J. Walsh Papers, LC; *Cong. Rec.*, 68th Cong., 1st sess., vol. 65, 679, 7 January 1924, House Joint Resolution 1925.
72 Finerty to Olds (American Red Cross, Paris), 24 October 1923; Payne (chairman, executive committee, national headquarters, American Red Cross) to Olds, 24 October 1923, Drawer 1, Finerty Papers, UML.
73 Letters cited in FitzGerald, *Voice of Ireland*, 120–21; Hughes to Geddes, 28 December 1922, cited in Whelan, "Recognition of the Irish Free State," 123.
74 Curtis to the Duke of Devonshire, 10 September 1923, CO 739/20, TNA.
75 See Kennedy, *Ireland and the League of Nations*,18–223; and Keown, *First of the Small Nations*, 105–35. In fact the Provisional Government was discussing an application to the league as early as July 22, 1922 and decided to do so on September 1, although this was not yet practical. See Meetings of the Provisional Government, 22 July and 1 September 1922, G 1/2, National Archives of Ireland (NAI).

76 Harkness, *Restless Dominion*, 87–134; McMahon, "Ireland, the Empire, and the Commonwealth," 221; Lowry, "Captive Dominion," 202–26. For an Irish External Affairs discussion of this process, see the memorandum by the Irish Free State delegation to the 1926 Imperial Conference, entitled "Existing Anomalies in the British Commonwealth of Nations (Secret)," 2 November 1926, *DIFP*, vol. 3, 73–76.
77 Castle to secretary of state, 15 August 1923, 841d.00/605, RG 59, State Department Records, NARA; Keown, *First of the Small Nations*, 118.
78 Annual Report, 1923, *BDFA, Vol. 14, Annual Reports, 1922–1924*, 144.
79 See Lauterpacht, *Recognition in International Law*, 38–78; Brierly, *Law of Nations*, 137–43; and De Visscher, *Theory and Reality*, 236–46.
80 Memorandum from legal advisor to [Canadian] prime minister, 19 September 1919; colonial secretary to [Canadian] governor-general, 28 October 1919, *Documents on Canadian External Relations, Volume 3, 1919–1925*, 6–10. See also Winter, "Establishment of the First Canadian Legation," 57–76.
81 Colonial secretary to [Canadian] governor-general, 22 April 1924; [Canadian] governor-general to colonial secretary, 26 April 1924, *Documents on Canadian External Relations, Volume 3, 1919–1925*, 40–43.
82 Smiddy to Fitzgerald, 7 March 1923, Desmond Fitzgerald Papers, UCDA; *New York Times*, 22 May 1923.
83 Sir Esme Howard went on to say, "My best course was to refuse to discuss the matter." Annual Report, 1924, in *BDFA*, vol. 14, 259.
84 O'Hegarty to MacNeill, 19 October 1923, *DIFP*, vol. 2, 203–4; Whelan, *United States Foreign Policy and Ireland*, 445–54; Davis, "Diplomacy as Propaganda," 117–29. For preliminary discussions about an Irish minister, see Curtis to Masterton Smith, 21 February 1923; Loughnane to Sturgis, 1 December 1923, CO 739/19; and Curtis to the Duke of Devonshire, 27 November 1923, CO 739/21, TNA. See also Hilliker, *Canada's Department of External Affairs*, vol. 1, 69–81.
85 Walshe to McNeill, 27 May 1924, *DIFP*, vol. 2, 296; *Parl. Deb., House of Lords, 1924*, vol. 57, 5th series, cols. 994–1009.
86 Hathaway to secretary of state, 17 June 1924, 841d.00/705, RG 59, State Department Records, NARA.
87 British ambassador (Howard) to secretary of state, 24 June 1924; secretary of state to British ambassador (Howard), 28 June 1924, *FRUS, 1924*, vol. 2, 246–48.
88 Hughes to Coolidge, 26 June 1924, Irish Free State File, Calvin Coolidge Papers, LC.
89 Healy to Thomas, 3 March 1924; Fitzgerald to Smiddy, 25 June 1924; Healy to Thomas, 8 July 1924, *DIFP*, vol. 2, 277–78, 309–10 and 317.
90 FitzGerald to Healy, 1 February 1923, *DIFP*, vol. 2, p. 40; Sagarra, *Envoy Extraordinary*, 27–64.
91 Smiddy to Duffy, 28 April 1922, cited in Whelan, "Recognition of the Irish Free State," 122–23.
92 Castle Jr. diary, 15 August 1923, cited in Whelan, 125; Lord Howard of Penrith, *Theatre of Life*, vol. 2, 515.

93 Howard to secretary of state, 24 June 1924, secretary of state to British ambassador, 28 June 1924, and Slemp (secretary to the president) to secretary of state, 7 October 1924, *FRUS, 1924*, vol. 2, 246–48; Sir E. Howard to Austen Chamberlain, 8 June 1925, Annual Report, 1924, *BDFA*, vol. 14, 258–59.
94 *New York Times*, October 8, 1924. Smiddy served in Washington until early 1929, when he became Irish high commissioner in London until 1933. He held several other public posts into the 1950s. Smiddy was not without his critics.
95 Walshe to minister of justice, 21 October 1924, *DIFP*, vol. 2, 360.
96 Kennedy, "Professor Smiddy," 129; Keown, *First of Small Nations*, 141. A University of Minnesota law professor published an article in early 1926, before the Imperial Conference and the Balfour Declaration, arguing that the Dominions were not international legal persons: "They were states, but not sovereign states," and the US willingness to receive an Irish minister did not "necessarily involve a recognition . . . of a full and complete international status for Ireland" (Allin, "Recent Developments," 120–22).
97 Whelan, *United States Foreign Policy and Ireland*, 447–50; Healy to secretary of state, Colonial Office, 16 May 1924; and Fitzgerald to Smiddy, 25 June 1924, CO 532/277, TNA; Healy to Amery, 19 February 1927, *DIFP*, vol. 3, 91. These ranks were further upgraded in 1950 to that of ambassador extraordinary and plenipotentiary.
98 Annual Report, 1924, *BDFA*, vol. 14, 259; Howard, *Theatre of Life*, vol. 2, 514–8.
99 *New York Times*, 8 October 1924; Howard to Chamberlain, 8 June 1925, Annual Report, 1924, FO 371/10651, TNA; Harkness, *Restless Dominion*, 63–67.
100 Davis, "Timothy Smiddy's Tenure," 131–35; Sagarra, *Envoy Extraordinary*, 68–83. Ambassador Howard reported to the Foreign Office in 1929 that Smiddy "had filled a difficult position with great tact, distinction and success. He had endeared himself to his colleagues and to the members of the United States Government, and there is no doubt that he did much towards securing for the Irish Free State the support of the larger number of Irish Americans in this country." *BDFA*, vol. 20, 44–46.
101 Sagarra, *Envoy Extraordinary*, 60.
102 Hughes to Coolidge, 7 October 1924, Irish Free State File, Coolidge Papers, LC. Charles Hathaway, who might have been promoted to minister, remained in Dublin until 1927, when he was transferred to Munich.
103 Whelan, *United States Foreign Policy and Ireland*, 482–83; Carr to Hathaway, 17 January 1927, and 28 April 1927, 841d.00/887 and /905, RG 59, State Department Records, NARA.
104 Carr to Hathaway, 17 January 1927, and 28 April 1927, 841d.00/887 and /905, RG 59, State Department Records, NARA; Keown, *First of the Small Nations*.
105 Secretary of state to ambassador (Houghton), 1 December 1926; British secretary of state for foreign affairs (Chamberlain) to the American chargé d'affaires (Sterling), 6 January 1927, *FRUS, 1927*, vol. 1, 481–83. See also US Congress, House of Representatives, Committee on Foreign Affairs, Hearings on H. Res. 3404, "To Provide Salaries of a Minister and Consuls to the Republic of Ireland," 66th Cong., 2nd sess., 1920, 4–59. For Canadian interests, see [Canadian] governor-general to colonial

secretary, [16] November 1926; British chargé d'affaires in the United States to secretary of state, 19 November 1926; and secretary of state to British chargé d'affaires, 20 November 1926, *Documents on Canadian External Relations, Volume 4, 1926–1930*, 13–16.

106 Secretary of the department of external affairs to secretary of the executive council, 13 April 1927, S 4/070, NAI; Whelan, *United States Foreign Policy and Ireland*, 477–82. Smiddy described him as "reserved, unostentatious and a gentleman" with a "sympathetic attitude" toward Ireland. William R. Castle Jr., sometimes Sterling's superior, wrote for a Harvard alumni magazine that Sterling was "immensely popular in Ireland." However, some of the Irish diplomatic correspondence would suggest that Sterling to either too reserved or too British oriented. See Smiddy to FitzGerald, 5 April 1927, *DIFP*, vol. 3, 104; Castle Jr., "Harvard Men in the Foreign Service," 17. Sterling left Dublin in 1933 and had subsequent postings in Bulgaria, Latvia, Estonia, and Sweden.

107 *Irish Times*, 26 July 1927; *New York Times*, 26 July 1927.

108 *Irish Times*, 27 July 1927; *New York Times*, 27 July 1927.

109 *Irish Times*, 27 July 1927; *New York Times*, 26 July 1927.

110 *Irish Times*, 26 July 1927; *New York Times*, 26 July 1927.

111 Sterling to Castle, 4 August 1927, Ireland File, William R. Castle Papers, Hoover Presidential Library; *Irish Times*, 28 July 1927. Later in the afternoon Sterling visited the government buildings and was introduced to members of Cosgrave's cabinet.

112 Phelan to FitzGerald, 18 February 1927, *DIFP*, vol. 3, 89.

113 *Irish Times*, 26 July 1927.

114 Hathaway to secretary of state, 30 July 1927, 841d.00/922, RG 59, State Department Records, NARA.

115 Sterling to Castle, 4 August 1927, Ireland File, Castle Papers, Hoover Presidential Library.

116 Secretary of the department of external affairs to secretary of the executive council, 13 April 1927, S 4/070, NAI; Whelan, *United States Foreign Policy and Ireland*, 483–84.

117 Carroll, *American Presence in Ulster*, 164. Wainwright Abbott was appointed consul general in Belfast from 1949 to 1951, at which point he retired from the Foreign Service and settled in Dublin.

118 Hathaway to secretary of state, 30 July 1927, 841d.00/922, RG 59, State Department Records, NARA.

8. PRESIDENT WILLIAM T. COSGRAVE COMES TO THE UNITED STATES, 1928

1 *Iris Dhail Éireann*, 32.

2 The acceptance of the Balfour formula in 1926 by Britain and the Commonwealth and the Statute of Westminster in 1931 ended any legislative supremacy that the British Parliament and government might have over the Dominion legislatures. The memo's concluding statement was: "The position of the Dominion Governments as defined

by the [Imperial] Conference is one of complete equality with Great Britain and hence with all other world states." Memorandum by the Department of External Affairs on the status of the Irish Free State, 1927, *DIFP*, vol. 3, 153–54; Harkness, *Restless Dominion*.

3 See Jordan, *W.T. Cosgrave,*. 9–142; and Lee, *Ireland*, 174. In his book about both W. T. Cosgrave and Liam Cosgrave, Stephen Collins in *The Cosgrave Legacy* makes no mention of these foreign policy matters.

4 Lee, *Ireland*, 150–57.

5 Sterling to secretary of state, 10 December 1927, 841d.00/937, RG 59, State Department Records, NARA.

6 Smiddy to Fitzgerald, 2 July 1925, S 4/529, NAI; Sagarra, *Envoy Extraordinary*, 74–76.

7 Hoover to Cullinan, 25 September 1925; Cullinan to Hoover, 28 September 1925, Hoover Papers, Hoover Presidential Library. The rest of the Irish party was made up by General Richard Mulcahy, minister of defense; Michael Hayes, speaker of the Dáil; Thomas Johnson, leader of the Irish Labor Party; and Gordon Campbell, secretary of industry and commerce.

8 Extract from memorandum from Walshe to O'Hegarty, 8 December 1927, *DIFP*, vol. 3, 162–63; "Ministerial Visit to America," 8 December 1927, P80/466, FitzGerald Papers, UCDA.

9 Extract from minutes of a meeting of the cabinet, 13 December 1927, *DIFP*, vol. 3, 163–64.

10 Whelan, *United States Foreign Policy and Ireland*, 566; Carroll, *American Opinion and the Irish Question*, 177–93.

11 Laffan, *Judging W. T. Cosgrave*, 267–78; Keown, "Creating the Template?," 139.

12 Aristide Briand, French premier and foreign minister, had come to Washington for the naval and Far Eastern treaty negotiations in 1921 and Arthur J. Balfour had visited the United States in 1917 and again in 1921, although as British foreign secretary not as prime minister. David Lloyd George, almost a year out of office, toured the United States and Canada in the autumn of 1923 and was also invited to lunch by President Coolidge and feted in New York City. The first British prime minister to make official visits to the United States was Ramsay MacDonald in 1929 and 1933.

13 Castle Jr. diary, 17 December 1927, vol. 11, MS AM 2021, William R. Castle Papers, HUL; Sterling to secretary of state, 2 January 1928, 033.41D 11/6, RG 59, and Sterling to secretary of state, 18 September 1929, 033.41d11/11, RG 59, State Department Papers, NARA.

14 Whelan, *United States Foreign Policy and Ireland*, 561; memorandum for Cooke, 20 December 1927, 033.41D 11/3 ½, RG 59, and Macaulay to Kellogg, 22 December 1927, 033.41d 11/5, RG 59, State Department Records, NARA; Smiddy to minister for external affairs, 9 January 1928, Department of the Taoiseach, S4529, NAI. The Jesuit weekly *America* reported the trips of both Cosgrave and de Valera in early 1928, but quite misleadingly stated that "these visits are not to be marked by any public celebrations." *America*, 7 January 1928, 307.

15 *Irish Times*, 6 January 1928; *Irish Independent*, 6 and 10 January 1928; *Gaelic American*, 31 December 1927; *America*, 21 January 1928, 355.

16 Quotation from the *New York Times*, 21 January 1928, *New York Evening Telegram*, 20 January 1928; and *New York Evening Post*, 20 January 1928. See also *New York American*, 20 January 1928; and *New York Herald-Tribune*, 20 January 1928. Prior to Cosgrave's arrival, the 15 January 1928 edition of the *New York Times* ran a feature article on Cosgrave, by Ralph Hayes entitled "Cosgrave to Tell Us of Free State Affairs."
17 Keown, "Creating the Template?," 140.
18 Speech of William T. Cosgrave at the Drake Hotel, Chicago, broadcast over national radio in the United States, 21 January 1928, *DIFP*, vol. 3, 174–80; Sagarra, *Envoy Extraordinary*, 74–75. The broadcast was also heard in parts of Ireland. See also Keown, *First of the Small Nations*, 186–87.
19 *Chicago Herald & Examiner*, 22 January 1928. The paper also printed the passage quoted above by Cosgrave that the Irish Free State was a sovereign state.
20 Smiddy to McGilligan, 9 and 13 January 1928, *DIFP*, vol. 3, 167–74; memorandum for Cooke, 20 December 1927, 033.41d 11/3 ½, RG 59, State Department Records, NARA; Macaulay to Gilbert, 4 January 1928, RG 59, State Department Records, NARA; program of visit to Washington of His Excellency, Mr. William T. Cosgrave, the President of the Executive Council of the Irish Free State, n.d., 033.41d 11/8 ½, RG 59, State Department Records, NARA.
21 *New York Herald-Tribune*, 24 January 1928; *Washington Post*, 25 January 1928.
22 *Irish Times*, 25 January 1928; *New York Herald-Tribune*, 25 January 1928; *Time Magazine*, 6 February 1928.
23 *New York Times*, 25 January 1928; *Irish Independent*, 25 January 1928.
24 Castle Jr. diary, 25 January 1928, vol. 11, MS AM 2021, Castle Papers, HUL.
25 Memorandum of conversation with Cosgrave, president of the executive council of the Irish Free State, on 27 January 1928, in Castle to Hackworth, 28 January 1928, 841d.51/140, RG 59, State Department Records, NARA; Castle Jr. diary., 6 and 27 January 1928, vol. 11, MS AM 2021, Castle Papers, HUL. See also memorandum of the solicitor of the State Department, 8 February 1928, *FRUS, 1928*, vol. 3, 86–89; and Carroll, *Money for Ireland*, 31–93.
26 *Cong. Rec.*, 70th Cong., 1st sess., vol. 69, part 11, 25 January 1928, 2041–42.
27 *Cong. Rec.*, 70th Cong., 1st sess., vol. 69, part 11, 25 January 1928, 2009: *New York Herald-Tribune*, 26 January 1928.
28 *With the President in America*, 36; *Washington Post*, 25 January 1928; *New York World*, 26 January 1928.
29 *Irish Times*, 25 January 1928; *Irish Independent*, 26 January 1928.
30 *New York Times*, 25 January 1928.
31 Discourse of Bishop Shahan, rector of the Catholic University of America, at the conferring of honorary degree of Doctor of Laws on His Excellency, William T. Cosgrave, President of the Irish Free State, January 26, 1928, Honorary Degree Reference Files, American Catholic History Research Center and University Archive (ACUA); *New York Herald-Tribune*, 27 January 1928.
32 Howard, *Theatre of Life*, vol. 2, 514–18.
33 *With the President in America*, 45–51; *New York Herald-Tribune*, 29 January 1928.

34 *Philadelphia Bulletin*, 27 January 1928.
35 *With the President in America*, 52–58. See also Carroll, "Official Visits," 176–90.
36 *New York Herald-Tribune*, 2 February 1928; *New York Times*, 3 February 1928; *Gaelic American*, 4 and 11 February 1928.
37 *Boston Globe*, cited in Doorley, *Justice Daniel Cohalan*, 188.
38 *New York American*, 2 and 4 February 1928; *Brooklyn Citizen*, 4 February 1928. Smiddy had to turn down invitations for Cosgrave to meet many other Irish organizations in the New York and Boston areas, as well as in Indiana, Illinois, Wisconsin, and Minnesota. See Smiddy to McGilligan, 9 January 1928, *DIFP*, vol. 3, 167–72.
39 *New York Times*, 21 January 1928
40 *New York American*, 2 February 1928.
41 *Boston Globe*, 4 February 1928.
42 President of the executive council of the Irish Free State to the president of the United States, 3 February 1928 (cable), 033.41d 11/9, RG 59, State Department Papers, NARA.
43 *Boston Globe*, 2 February 1928.
44 In his speech from the dock in 1803, Robert Emmet had said, "When my country takes her place among the nations of the earth, then and not until then, let my epitaph be written." Cosgrave and his party returned to Dublin on 11 February to a tumultuous welcome. Once again there were processions, flags, and speeches. The triumphs of the trip were made clear to the Irish public. See *Irish Independent*, 11 and 13 February 1928; and *Irish Times*, 11 February 1928.
45 *Irish Independent*, 24 January 1928.
46 Cosgrave to Smiddy, 5 March 1928; Smiddy to Cosgrave, 6 May 1928; memorandum on a visit to Chicago, 14 May 1928, *DIFP*, vol. 3, 182–94.
47 Memorandum by Cushendun, 27 August 1928, *Documents on British Foreign Policy (DBFP)*, series I, vol. 5, 803.
48 Howard to Chamberlain, 27 January 1928 and 9 February 1928, FO 371/12820, TNA; Annual Report, 1928, *BDFA*, vol. 20, 44.
49 Sterling to secretary of state, 13 February 1928, 033.41d 11/10, RG 59, State Department Records, NARA.
50 *Gaelic American*, 11 February 1928; *Commonweal*, 8 February 1928; *Catholic World*, vol. 126 (1927–28), 843–44.
51 *Irish Times*, 14 February 1928; *Irish Independent*, 13 February 1928.
52 *Irish World*, 14 January and 4 and 11 February 1928. By contrast, the *Irish World* ran the headline, "Thousands Cheer De Valera." De Valera stalwart Sean T. O Ceallaigh hoped to embarrass the government in the Dáil in February by asking how Cosgrave's trip was paid for, but Fianna Fáil really did not want to call attention to the actual success of the trip. *Irish Independent*, 4 February 1928; *Dáil Éireann, Parliamentary Debates, Official Report*, vol. 22, 22 February 1928, col. 104.
53 *America*, 4 February 1928, p. 401; and Walsh to O'Mara, 9 February 1928, MS. 21,551, O'Mara Papers, NLI. The *Irish Independent* concluded that "the great success of

President Cosgrave's tour in the United States is reflected in the vast amount of space which the American journals have devoted" to it. *Irish Independent*, 1 February 1928.
54 Smiddy to Cosgrave, 21 March 1928, S 4/529, NAI.
55 O'Brien, "Ireland in International Affairs," 104.
56 Meehan, *Cosgrave Party*, 152.
57 FitzGerald, "Significance of the Tour," in *With the President in America*, 8.

9. SECRETARY OF STATE FRANK B. KELLOGG COMES TO IRELAND, 1928
1 Bryn-Jones, *Frank B. Kellogg*, 269; memorandum by Lord Cushendun, Paris, 27 August 1928, *DBFP*, vol. 5, 803.
2 Houghton to Kellogg, 3 April 1928; Sterling to Kellogg, 26 April 1928, Frank B. Kellogg Papers, Minnesota Historical Society (MHS).
3 Cosgrave to Kellogg, 12 May 1928, Kellogg Papers, MHS.
4 Kellogg to Houghton, 14 April 1928; Kellogg to Sterling, 17 May 1928; Kellogg to Cosgrave, 2 June 1928, Kellogg Papers, MHS.
5 Kellogg to Sterling, 2 June 1928, Kellogg Papers, MHS.
6 Minister in Canada to secretary of state, 8 May 1928; secretary of state to minister in Canada, 9 May 1928, *FRUS, 1928*, vol. 1, 56–58.
7 Secretary of state for external affairs to Dominions secretary, 11 May 1928, *Documents on Canadian External Relations, 1926–1930*, vol. 4, 695–96; minister in Canada to secretary of state, 10 May 1928, *FRUS, 1928*, vol. 1, 60.
8 Telegram from McGilligan to Amery, 14 May 1928; extract from minutes from the cabinet, 17 May 1928, *DIFP*, vol. 3, 194 and 199.
9 British ambassador in to secretary of state, 19 May 1928 [containing the text of Austin Chamberlain to Alanson B. Houghton, 19 May 1928], *FRUS, 1928*, vol. 1, 69.
10 Extracts from a meeting of cabinet, 17 and 29 May 1928, *DIFP*, vol. 3, 199; secretary of state to British ambassador in Britain, 21 May 1928, *FRUS, 1928*, vol. 1, 69–70; US minister to secretary of state for external affairs, 22 May 1928, *Documents on Canadian External Relations, Volume 4, 1926–1930*, 699.
11 McGilligan to Sterling, 30 May 1928, *DIFP*, vol. 3, 199–200; minister in the Irish Free State to secretary of state, 30 May 1928, *FRUS, 1928*, vol. 1, 76; Whelan, *United States Foreign Policy and Ireland*, 551–52. Whether by design or not, Canada replied on 30 May 1928 also.
12 Sterling to secretary of state, 24 May 1928, 841d.00/942, RG 59, State Department Records, NARA.
13 See McGilligan to Amery, 12 July 1928, *DIFP*, vol. 3, 200; and Keown, *First of the Small Nations*, 189–91.
14 Miller, *Peace Pact of Paris*, 251.
15 McGilligan to Sterling, 14 July 1928, *DIFP*, vol. 3, 201; Ferrell, *Peace in Their Time*, 170–91; Miller, *Peace Pact of Paris*, 75–76, 101, 206, and 226.
16 Kellogg to Coolidge, 13 July 1928, Kellogg Papers, MHS. See also Kellogg to Mrs. Kellogg, 21 July 1928, Kellogg Papers, MHS. Kellogg was also convinced that his offer to go to Paris helped push the French to sign.

17 Sterling to Kellogg (cable), 22 July 1928, and Sterling to Kellogg, 22 July 1928, Kellogg Papers, MHS.
18 Bryn-Jones, *Frank B. Kellogg*, 269; memorandum by Cushendun, Paris, 27 August 1928, *DBFP*, vol. 5, 803. See also Kellogg to Mrs. Kellogg, 17 and 21 July 1928, Kellogg Papers, MHS.
19 McGilligan to Cosgrave, 14 August 1928, *DIFP*, vol. 3, 203–4. McGilligan closed his note to Cosgrave by saying, "Anyway be sure to go—it is a golden opportunity." See McGilligan to Amery, 17 August 1928, *DIFP*, vol. 3, p. 205.
20 Sterling to secretary of state, 9, 15, and 16 August 1928, 711.41d12/17, 711.0012/199, and /235, RG 59, State Department Records, NARA; Kellogg to American Legation, Dublin, 7 August 1928, and Kellogg to Houghton, 28 July 1928, Kellogg Papers, MHS.
21 Ellis, *Frank B. Kellogg and American Foreign Relations*, 157–92.
22 British chargé d'affaires (Chilton) to secretary of state, 31 July 1928; secretary of state to chargé d'affaires (Chilton), 2 August 1928, *FRUS, 1928*, vol. 1, 264–67; McKercher, *Second Baldwin Government*, 128–70. This crisis is downplayed in Roskill, *Naval Policy Between the Wars*, vol. 1, 456–49.
23 Ferrell, *Peace in Their Time*, 202–9. McKercher makes a plausible explanation for the manner in which this diplomatic faux pas unfolded. Chamberlain was ill and coming down with pneumonia while he was speaking in the House. He collapsed the next day and was sent to hospital, and was replaced for several months by Lord Cushendun as foreign secretary. Chamberlain's remarks in the House had not been authorized by cabinet and clearly in the circumstances he was not at his best. McKercher, *Second Baldwin Government*, 150.
24 Secretary of state to Coolidge, 3 August 1928; Coolidge to secretary of state, 3 August 1928, *FRUS, 1928*, vol. 1, 267–70. See also Coolidge's first reaction: "Please make no commitments concerning limitations of armaments." Coolidge to secretary of state (cable), 2 August 1928, *FRUS, 1928*, vol. 1, 267–70. In recording conversations with American diplomats, both R. L. Craigie and Lord Cushendun used the term "bombshell" to describe American reactions to the announcement of the Anglo-French agreement. Recorded by a conversation with Atherton, 7 August 1928, and Lord Cushendun to Chilton (Washington), 10 August 1928, *DBFP*, vol. 5, 785–86 and 791–93; Chilton to Earl of Birkenhead, 13 September 1928, *DBFP*, vol. 5, 815. Presumably Coolidge's provocative Armistice Day speech contained much of what he had wanted to say in the note.
25 Kellogg to Coolidge, 4 August 1928, Kellogg Papers, MHS.
26 Kellogg to Coolidge, 4 August 1928, Kellogg Papers, MHS; Ferrell, *Peace in Their Time*, 204–5. For the dating of the shift in plans, compare the unsent letter (Kellogg to Coolidge, 16 August 1928) to the letter sent (Kellogg to Coolidge, 17 August 1928, Kellogg Papers, MHS).
27 Kellogg to Coolidge, 17 August 1928, Kellogg Papers, MHS.
28 Kellogg to Coolidge, 17 August 1928, Kellogg Papers, MHS; O'Murchadha to Blythe, 16 August 1928, P 24/471, Ernest Blythe Papers, UCDA. It was not until

the *Île de France* stopped briefly at Plymouth to disembark passengers that reporters who came on board were told by Kellogg that he would not be coming to London. *Times of London*, 15 and 24 August 1928. See also Carter, *British Commonwealth and International Security*, 124–35; and McKercher, *Second Baldwin Government*, 166.
29 Eventually sixty-two countries, making up most of the international community, signed the treaty. Bryn-Jones, *Frank B. Kellogg*, 246–47; Miller, *Peace Pact of Paris*, 246–53.
30 For a revised argument about the lasting impact of the Kellogg-Briand Pact, see Hathaway and Shapiro, *Internationalists*.
31 *Irish Times*, 31 August 1928; *Irish Independent*, 31 August 1928; *New York Times*, 31 August 1928.
32 *Irish Times*, 31 August 1928; *Irish Independent*, 31 August 1928; *New York Times*, 31 August 1928; Bryn-Jones, *Frank B. Kellogg*, 271.
33 *New York Times*, 31 August 1928.
34 Bryn-Jones, *Frank B. Kellogg*, 271.
35 Bryn-Jones, 272.
36 *Irish Times*, 1 September 1928; *Irish Independent*, 1 September 1928; *New York Times*, 1 September 1928; Bryn-Jones, *Frank B. Kellogg*, 272.
37 *Irish Times*, 3 September 1928; *Irish Independent*, 3 September 1928; *New York Times*, 3 September 1928. Keown notes that no business was discussed during Kellogg's visit (*Firsts of the Small Nations*, 192–93).
38 *Irish Times*, 4 September 1928; *Irish Independent*, 4 September 1928; *New York Times*, 4 September 1928. Once at sea, Kellogg sent Cosgrave a very personal cable from the *Detroit*, thanking him for his hospitality during the visit. Kellogg to Cosgrave (cable), 3 September 1928, Kellogg Papers, MHS.
39 *New York Sun*, 31 August 1928.
40 *Chicago Tribune*, 31 August 1928; *New York Times*, 1 September 1928.
41 Carter, *British Commonwealth and International Security*, 124–25; Harkness, *Restless Dominion*, 140–41; Smiddy to McGilligan, 2 October 1928, *DIFP*, vol. 3, 219–22.
42 Abbott to secretary of state, 6 September 1928, 711.0012 Anti War/408, RG 59, State Department Records, NARA. Apart from Joseph P. Kennedy being given an honorary degree by the National University of Ireland in 1938 while ambassador to Britain, and several senior military figures and the unofficial and clandestine visit of Eleanor Roosevelt to her aunt, who was the wife of the American minister to Ireland during World War II, it was not until president John F. Kennedy visited Ireland in 1963 that Ireland had another such high prestige diplomatic visitor.
43 *Times of London*, 31 August 1928.
44 Toynbee, *Survey of International Affairs*, 74. Lord Cushendun recorded a conversation with Kellogg in Paris just hours before the signing of the Peace Pact. Kellogg was very friendly and dismissed the newspapers stories that he was not going to London "because the President did not want him to do so." "Who," Kellogg is quoted directly as saying, "can be the inventor of such absurdities." He would not have time to make a useful visit to London, whereas his trip to Dublin was a formal

return for Cosgrave's visit and "a couple of days would be sufficient." Memorandum by Cushendun, Paris, 27 August 1928, *DBFP*, vol. 5, 803–4.

45 Annual Report, 1928, *BDFA*, vol. 20, 30.

46 The connection between the naval controversy, the Irish visit, and MacKenzie King and Kellogg was pointed out by such newspapers as the *New York American*, 4 September 1928; and the *Philadelphia Public Ledger*, 4 September 1928. See also Craigie, 12 November 1928 memorandum, "Outstanding Problems affecting Anglo-American Relations," *DBFP*, vol. V, 862–63; and Watt, *Succeeding John Bull*, 56–57.

47 McGilligan to Cosgrave, 14 August 1928, *DIFP*, vol. 3, 203; McKercher, *Second Baldwin Government*, 150–99.

48 Abbott to secretary of state, 6 September 1928, 711.0012 Anti War/408, RG 59, State Department Records, NARA.

EPILOGUE

1 Kennedy, "Professor Smiddy," 129.
2 Knirck, *Aftermath of Revolution*, 212.
3 Mansergh, *Irish Questions*, 282.
4 Lee, in Grey, "Introduction," in Grey, *Ireland's Allies*, 1.

APPENDIX 1. THE MEETING OF JOHN QUINN'S DELEGATION WITH A. J. BALFOUR ON 4 MAY 1917

1 Quinn wrote to Maud Gonne on 2 June 1917 that he had read in the morning newspapers that George Russell was to be a member of the Irish Commission and decided to put down his recollections of the meeting with Balfour on 4 May and send them to him. He also sent a copy to Gonne. See Quinn to Gonne, 2 June 1917, in Londraville, *Too Long A Sacrifice*, 199.

APPENDIX 2. DOCUMENTS SUBMITTED AND WITNESSES AT THE SENATE FOREIGN RELATIONS COMMITTEE HEARINGS ON THE TREATY OF PEACE WITH GERMANY

1 Text also found in *Dáil Éireann proc., 1919–1921*, 21 January 1919, 14–6; and *Documents on Irish Foreign Policy, 1919–1922*, vol. 1, 1.
2 Text also found in *Dáil Éireann proc., 1919–1921*, 21 January 1919, 18–20; and *Documents on Irish Foreign Policy, 1919–1922*, vol. 1, 2.
3 Text also found in *Dáil Éireann proc., 1919–1921*, 21 January 1919, 21–24.
4 Text also found in *Documents on Irish Foreign Policy, 1919–1922*, 5–6.
5 Letters and report included in Carroll, *American Commission on Irish Independence*, 91–134.
6 Carroll, 137–49.
7 Carroll, 72–78.

BIBLIOGRAPHY

MANUSCRIPTS
Great Britain
House of Lords Records Office
   David Lloyd George Papers
Library and Archives of Friends House, London
   Proceedings of the 1921 Yearly Meeting
National Archives
   Cabinet Papers
      CAB 1
      CAB 23
      CAB 24
      CAB 37
      CAB 41
   Colonial Office Papers
      CO 739
   Dominion Office
      DO 35
   Foreign Office Papers
      FO 371 (US affairs)
      FO 800 (Private papers in the Foreign Office Collection)

Ireland
Friends Historical Library
   Relief Work Papers
National Archives of Ireland
   Department of Foreign Affairs Papers
      DE 2
   Department of the Taoiseach Papers
      S 4
National Library of Ireland
   John Devoy Papers
   George Gavan Duffy Papers
   Peter Golden Papers
   Joseph McGarrity Papers

    Col. Maurice Moore Papers
    Art O'Brien Papers
    James O'Mara Papers
    Sir Horace Plunkett Papers
    John Quinn Papers
    John Redmond Papers
University College Dublin Archives
    Ernest Blythe Papers
    Eamon de Valera Papers
    Desmond Fitzgerald Papers

United States
American Friends Service Committee Archives
    Ireland folders, 1920 and 1921
American Irish Historical Society
    Daniel F. Cohalan Papers
Archdiocese of Detroit Archives
    Bishop Michael J. Gallagher Papers
Catholic University of America Archives
    Bishop Thomas Shahan Papers
    Honorary Degree Reference File
Columbia University Library
    Papers of the Carnegie Endowment for International Peace
Haverford College Library
    L. Hollingsworth Wood Papers
Hoover Presidential Library
    Herbert Hoover Papers
    William R. Castle Jr. Papers
Houghton Library, Harvard University
    Oswald Garrison Villard Papers
    William R. Castle Jr. Papers
Library of Congress
    William A. Borah Papers
    Calvin Coolidge Papers
    Norman Davis Papers
    Charles Evans Hughes Papers
    Robert Lansing Papers
    John Purroy Mitchel Papers
    Fred K. Nielsen Papers
    Theodore Roosevelt Papers
    Joseph Tumulty Papers
    Thomas J. Walsh Papers

John Sharp Williams Papers
Woodrow Wilson Papers
Massachusetts Historical Society
    Henry Cabot Lodge Papers
Minnesota Historical Society
    Frank B. Kellogg Papers
National Archives and Records Administration of the US
    State Department Records, RG 59
New York Public Library
    William Bourke Cockran Papers
    W. J. M. A. Maloney Papers
    Frank P. Walsh Papers
Ohio Historical Society
    Warren G. Harding Papers
University of Michigan Library
    John F. Finerty Papers
Yale University Library
    Edward M. House Papers
    Frank L. Polk Papers

PUBLISHED DOCUMENTS
Canada
Documents on Canadian External Relations
    Volume 3, 1919–1925
    Volume 4, 1926–1930

Great Britain
Parliamentary Debates (Hansard)
    House of Lords
    House of Commons
Report of the Committee on Alleged German Outrages, HC 1915 [Cmd. 7894].
Report of the Proceedings of the Irish Convention HC 1918 [Cd. 9019].
Documents on British Foreign Policy, series 1a, vol. 5
British Documents on Foreign Affairs: Reports and Papers from the Foreign Office Confidential Prints, series C, North America, 1919–39, vols. 1, 7, 14, and 20.

Ireland
Dáil Eireann, Miontuairisc an Chead Dala, 1919–1921, Minutes of Proceedings of the First Parliament of the Republic of Ireland, 1919–1921, Official Record.
Dáil Eireann, Tuairsig Oifigiúil (official report) [1921–22].
Iris Dhail Éireann, tuairisq oifigiuil, díosbóireacht ar an gConnradh idir Éire agus Sasana do signigheadh I Lundain ar an 6adh lá de mhi ná Nodlag 1921: official report, debate

on the Treaty between Great Britain and Ireland signed in London on 6th December 1921 (Dublin: Stationary Office, n.d.),

Dáil Éireann . . . díosbóireachtai páirliminte (parliamentary debates); tuairisg oifigiúil (official report).

Documents on Irish Foreign Policy, edited by Ronan Fanning, Michael Kennedy, Dermot Keogh, and Eunan O'Halpin (Dublin: Royal Irish Academy 1998–2002).

United States

US Congress, Senate, Committee on Foreign Relations, *Treaty of Peace with Germany: Hearings* (Senate doc. No. 106, 66th Cong., 1st sess., 1919).

US Congress, House of Representatives, Committee on Foreign Affairs, *Hearings on H. Res. 3404, To provide salaries of a minister and consuls to the Republic of Ireland*, 66th Cong., 2nd sess., 1920.

Congressional Record

Foreign Relations of the United States
 1916–1928 and Supplements
 The Lansing Papers, 1914–1920
 Paris Peace Conference, 1919

COURT CASES CITED

Fogarty v. O'Donoghue [1926], Irish Reports, 531.

Irish Free State et al. v. Guaranty Safe Deposit Company et al., 126 New York Miscellaneous Reports, 584, 129 New York Miscellaneous Reports 551, and 222 New York Supplement 182.

Irish Free State v. Guaranty Safe Deposit Company, Friends of Irish Freedom v. Brady et al,. 233 New York (Supreme Court, Appellate Division) 835, 251 New York Supplement 104, 257 New York Reports 618, 178 Northwestern Reporter 819, and 148 New York Miscellaneous Reports 256.

Montague and others v. Cooney and others, 147 New York Miscellaneous Reports 125.

NEWSPAPERS AND JOURNALS

America
Boston Globe
Brooklyn Citizen
Catholic World
Chicago Herald & Examiner
Chicago Tribune
Christian Science Monitor
Commonweal
Gaelic American
Irish Independent
Irish Times
Literary Digest
Manchester Guardian

Morning Post
Nation
New Republic
New York American
New York Evening Post
New York Herald-Tribune
New York Times
New York World
Philadelphia Bulletin
Philadelphia Public Ledger
Sinn Feiner
Times of London
Wall Street Journal
Washington Post

MEMOIRS AND CONTEMPORARY WRITING

"A Summons to Service from the Women and Children of Ireland." American Committee for Relief in Ireland, n.d.
Addams, Jane. *The Second Twenty Years at Hull House*. New York: Macmillan, 1930.
Allen, Rev. Albert W. *Briefs for Irish Independence*. Chicago: American Calendar, 1923.
Allin, C. D. "Recent Developments in the Constitutional and International Status of the British Dominions." *Minnesota Law Review* 10, no. 2 (January 1926): 100–22.
American Commission on Conditions in Ireland: Interim Report. Chicago: Benjamin Franklin Bureau, 1921.
American Commission on Irish Independence, 1919: The Diary, Correspondence, and Report. Edited by F. M. Carroll. Dublin: Irish Manuscript Commission, 1985.
Baker, Ray Stannard. *American Chronicle*. New York: Charles Scribner's Sons, 1945.
Bonsal, Stephen. *Unfinished Business*. Garden City, NY: Doubleday, 1944.
Brennan, Robert. *Ireland Standing Firm and Eamon de Valera: A Memoir*. Dublin: University College Dublin Press, 2002.
Brindley, Ronan. "Woodrow Wilson, Self Determination and Ireland, 1918–1919: A View from the Irish Newspapers." *Éire-Ireland* 23, no. 4 (Winter 1988): 62–80.
Castle, William R., Jr. "Harvard Men in the Foreign Service of the United States." *Harvard Graduate* September 1929,14–23).
Coyle, Albert, ed. *Evidence on Conditions in Ireland*. Washington, DC: American Commission on Conditions in Ireland, 1921.
Creel, George. *Ireland's Fight for Freedom: Setting Forth the High Lights of Irish History*. New York: Harper & Brothers, 1919.
———. *Rebel at Large*. New York: G. P. Putnam's Sons, 1947.
———. *The War, the World, and Wilson*. New York: Harper & Brothers, 1920.
Cronin, Sean. *The McGarrity Papers*. Tralee: Anvil, 1972.
Davis, John W. *The Ambassadorial Diary of John W. Davis*. Edited by Julia Davis and Dolores A. Fleming. Morgantown: West Virginia University Press, 1993.

Devoy, John. *Recollections of an Irish Rebel*. New York: Chas. P. Young, 1929.
Downing, Rossa F. "Men, Women, and Memories." In FitzGerald, *Voice of Ireland*.
Douglas, James G. *Memoirs of Senator James G. Douglas (1887–1954): Concerned Citizen*. Edited by J. Anthony Gaughan. Dublin: University College Dublin Press, 1998.
Dunne, Edward F. *What Dunne Saw in Ireland*. New York: Friends of Irish Freedom, 1919.
FitzGerald, William G., ed. *The Voice of Ireland*. Dublin: John Haywood, 1924.
Gay, George L. *The Commission for Relief in Belgium: A Statistical Survey of Operations*. Stanford, CA: Stanford University Press, 1929.
Gibson, Hugh. *A Journal from Our Legation in Belgium*. Garden City, NY: Doubleday, Page, 1917.
Hobson, Bulmer. *Ireland Yesterday and Tomorrow*. Tralee: Anvil, 1968.
Hoover, Herbert. *An American Epic*. 3 vols. Chicago: Henry Regnery, 1959.
House, Edward M. *The Intimate Papers of Colonel House*. 4 vols. Edited by Charles Seymour. Boston: Houghton Mifflin, 1926–28.
Howard of Penrith, Lord. *The Theatre of Life: Life Seen from the Stalls*. London: Hodder & Stoughton, 1936.
Jones, J. *Eighteen Months with the Republicans in Ireland* (Brooklyn, NY: n.p., 1921).
Jones, Thomas. *Thomas Jones, Whitehall Diary, Ireland, 1918–1925*. 3 vols. Edited by Keith Middlemas. London: Oxford University Press, 1971.
Lansing, Robert. *The Peace Negotiations: A Personal Narrative*. Boston: Houghton Mifflin, 1921.
———. *War Memoirs of Robert Lansing*. Indianapolis: Bobbs-Merrill, 1935.
Leslie, Shane. *The Irish Issue in its American Aspect*. London: T. Fisher Unwin, 1918.
Lynch, Diarmuid. *The IRB and the 1916 Insurrection*. Cork: Mercier, 1957.
Mantoux, Paul, ed. *The Deliberations of the Council of Four (March 24—June 28, 1919)*. 2 vols. Princeton, NJ: Princeton University Press, 1992.
Mason, Redfern. *Rebel Ireland*. San Francisco: n.p., 1923.
McCartan, Patrick. *With De Valera in America*. Dublin: Fitzpatrick, 1932.
McGarrity, Joseph. *Celtic Moods and Memories*. Dublin: Talbot, n.d.
McGuire, James K. *The King, the Kaiser, and Irish Freedom*. New York: Devin-Adair, 1915.
———. *What Germany Could Do For Ireland*. New York: Wolfe Tone, 1916.
McCoy, S. D. *Distress in Ireland*. New York: American Committee for Relief in Ireland, 1921.
Miller, David Hunter. *The Drafting of the Covenant*. 2 vols. New York: G. P. Putnam's Sons, 1928.
Montieth. *Robert, Casement's Last Adventure*. Dublin: Michael F. Moynihan, 1953.
The Need for Relief in Ireland. N.p., n.d.
Nevinson, H. W. *Last Changes, Last Chances*. London: Nisbet, 1928.
Nunan, Sean. "President Éamon de Valera's Mission to the United States of America, 1919–1920." *Capuchin Annual* (1970): 236–49).
O'Leary, Jeremiah A. *My Political Trial and Experiences*. New York: Jefferson, 1919.
Osborn, George C. *John Sharp Williams*. Baton Rouge: Louisiana State University Press, 1943.

Page, Walter H. *The Life and Letters of Walter H. Page*. 3 vols. Edited by Burton K. Hendrick. London: William Heinemann, 1922.

Quinn, John. "Roger Casement, Martyr: Some Notes for as Chapter of History by a Friend Whose Guest He Was When the War Broke Out." *New York Times Magazine*, 13 August 1916, 1–4.

Report of the American Committee for Relief in Ireland. New York: American Committee for Relief in Ireland, 1922.

Roosevelt, Theodore. *Fear God and Take Your Own Part*. New York: George H. Doran, 1916.

———. *The Foes in Our Own Household*. New York: George H. Doran, 1917.

———. *The Letters of Theodore Roosevelt*. Vol. 8. Edited by Elting E. Morison. Cambridge, MA: Harvard University Press, 1954.

Russell, George W. The Right Hon. Sir Horace Plunkett, and John Quinn. *The Irish Home Rule Convention*. New York: Macmillan, 1917.

Splain, J. G. "The Irish Movement in America." In Fitz-Gerald, *Voice of Ireland*.

Spring Rice, Sir Cecil. *The Letters and Friendships of Sir Cecil Spring Rice: A Record*. 2 vols. Edited by Stephen Gwynn. London: Constable, 1929.

Sturgis, Mark. *The Last Days of Dublin Castle: The Mark Sturgis Diaries*. Edited by Michael Hopkinson. Dublin: Irish Academic Press, 1999.

"Suggested Plan for National Organization." (N.p.: American Committee for Relief in Ireland, n.d.).

The Treatment of Armenians in the Ottoman Empire, 1915–1916: Documents Presented to Viscount Grey of Fallodon, Secretary of State for Foreign Affairs, by Viscount Bryce. London: Sir Joseph Causton & Sons, 1916.

Tumulty, Joseph. *Woodrow Wilson as I Know Him*. Garden City, NY: Doubleday, Page, 1921.

Villard, Oswald Garrison. *Fighting Years: Memoirs of a Liberal Editor*. New York: Harcourt, Brace, 1939.

Willert, Arthur. *The Road to Safety: A Study in Anglo-American Relations*. London: Verschoyle, 1952.

Williams, W. J. *Report of the Irish White Cross to 31st August 1922*. Dublin: Martin Lester, 1922.

With the President in America: The Authorized Record of President Cosgrave's Tour in the United States and Canada. Dublin: O'Kennedy-Brindley, 1928.

Wilson, Woodrow. *The Papers of Woodrow Wilson*. Edited by Arthur S. Link. Princeton, NY: Princeton University Press, 1966.

LATER WORKS

Ambrosius, Lloyd E. *Woodrow Wilson and the American Diplomatic Tradition: The Treaty Fight in Perspective*. Cambridge: Cambridge University Press, 1987.

Bartlett, Thomas. *Ireland: A History*. Cambridge: Cambridge University Press, 2010.

Bhroiméil, Úna Ní. "An American Opinion: John Quinn and the Easter Rising." In Grey, *Ireland's Allies*, 201–13.

Brierly, J. L. *The Law of Nations: An Introduction to the International Law of Peace.* New York: Oxford University Press, 1963.
Bromage, Mary C. *De Valera and the March of a Nation.* New York: Noonday, 1956.
Brun, Christian. "The Papers of Charles M. Hathaway: A Diplomat's Experience in Ireland and Germany." *Soundings,* November 1970, 17–29.
Bryn-Jones, David. *Frank B. Kellogg: A Biography.* New York: G. P. Putnam's Sons, 1937.
Buckley, Thomas H. *The United States and the Washington Conference, 1921–1922.* Knoxville: University of Tennessee Press, 1970.
Butler, Stephen, ed. *The 1916 Rising: New York and Beyond.* New York: United Irish Counties Association of New York, 2016.
Canfield, Leon H. *The Presidency of Woodrow Wilson: Prelude to a World in Crisis.* Rutherford, NJ: Fairleigh Dickinson University Press, 1966.
Carroll, Francis M. *American Opinion and the Irish Question, 1910–1923: A Study in Opinion and Policy.* New York: St. Martin's, 1978.
———. *The American Presence in Ulster: A Diplomatic History, 1796–1996.* Washington, DC: Catholic University of America Press, 2005.
———. *Money for Ireland: Finance, Diplomacy, Politics, and the First Dáil Éireann Loans, 1919–1936.* Westport, CT: Praeger, 2002.
———. "Official Visits: President Cosgrave Comes to Ottawa." *Canadian Journal of Irish Studies* 36, no. 2 (Fall 2010): 177–90.
———. "Theodore Roosevelt, John Quinn, and *The Irish Home Rule Convention.*" *Theodore Roosevelt Association Journal* 6, no. 2 (Spring 1980): 11–14.
Carter, Gwendolen. *The British Commonwealth and International Security: The Role of the Dominions, 1919–1939.* Toronto: Ryerson, 1947.
Casey, Marion. "Victor Herbert, Nationalism, and Musical Expression." In Grey, *Ireland's Allies,* 165–82.
———, and Ed Shevlin. "An American in Dublin: John Killgallon's Rising." In Grey, *Ireland's Allies,* 305–17.
Collins, Stephen. *The Cosgrave Legacy.* Dublin: Blackwater, 1989.
Coogan, Tim Pat. *De Valera: Long Fellow, Long Shadow.* London: Random House, 1995.
Cooper, John Milton, Jr. *Breaking the Heart of the World: Woodrow Wilson and the Fight for the League of Nations.* Cambridge: Cambridge University Press, 2001.
———. *Woodrow Wilson: A Biography.* New York: Alfred A. Knopf, 2009.
Cronin, Sean. "The Fenian Tradition." *Irish Times,* 25 April 1965, 12.
Daly, Mary E., and Margaret O'Callaghan, eds., *1916 in 1966: Commemorating the Easter Rising.* Dublin: Royal Irish Academy, 2007.
Davis, Troy D. "Diplomacy as Propaganda: The Appointment of T. A. Smiddy as Irish Free State Minister to the United States." *Eire-Ireland* 31, nos. 3–4 (Fall/Winter 1996): 11–29.
———. "The Irish Civil War and the 'International Proposition' of 1922–23." *Eire-Ireland* 29, no. 2 (Summer 1994): 92–112.
———. "Timothy Smiddy's Tenure as Irish Free State Minister in the United States." *Irish Studies in International Affairs* 26 (2015): 131–35.

Deegan, Mary Jo. "Jane Addams and the American Commission on Conditions in Ireland, 1920–1922." *Sociological Origins* 5, no. 1 (Fall 2006): 29–37.
De Visscher, Charles. *Theory and Reality in Public International Law*. Princeton, NJ: Princeton University Press, 1968.
Digby, Margaret. *Horace Plunkett: An Anglo-American Irishman*. Oxford: Blackwell, 1949.
Doorley, Michael. *Irish-American Diaspora Nationalism: The Friends of Irish Freedom, 1916–1935*. Dublin: Four Courts, 2005.
———. *Justice Daniel Cohalan, 1865–1946: American Patriot and Irish-American Nationalist*. Cork: Cork University Press, 2019.
Dorries, Reinhart R. *Prelude to the Easter Rising: Sir Roger Casement in Imperial Germany*. London: Frank Cass, 2000.
Duff, John B. "The Versailles Treaty and the Irish-Americans." *Journal of American History* 55, no. 3 (December 1968): 582–98.
Duffert, J., ed. *Against the Crime of Silence: Proceedings of the Russell International War Crimes Tribunal, Stockholm-Copenhagen*. New York: Bertrand Russell Peace Foundation, 1969.
Duroselle, Jean-Baptiste. *From Wilson to Roosevelt: Foreign Policy of the United States, 1913–1945*. New York: Harper & Row, 1968.
Dwyer, T. Ryle. *Eamon de Valera*. Dublin: Gill & Macmillan, 1980.
Edwards, Owen Dudley. "American Aspects of the Rising." In Edwards and Pyle, *1916*, 153–80.
———, ed. *Conor Cruise O'Brien Introduces Ireland*. London: Andre Deutsch, 1969.
———, and Fergus Pyle, eds. *1916: The Easter Rising*. London: MacGibbon & Kee, 1968.
Edwards, Ruth Dudley. *Patrick Pearse: The Triumph of Failure*. Dublin: Poolbeg, 1990.
Egerton, George W. *Great Britain and the Creation of the League of Nations: Strategy, Politics, and International Organization, 1914–1919*. London: Scholar Press, 1979.
Ellis, L. Ethan. *Frank B. Kellogg and American Foreign Relations, 1925–1929*. Westport, CT: Greenwood, 1974.
———. *Republican Foreign Policy, 1921–1933*. New Brunswick, NJ: Rutgers University Press, 1968.
Fanning, Ronan. *Fatal Path: British Government and Irish Revolution, 1910–1922*. London: Faber & Faber, 2013.
———. *The Irish Department of Finance, 1922–58*. Dublin: Institute of Public Administration, 1978.
Ferrell, Robert H. *Peace in their Time: The Origins of the Kellogg-Briand Pact*. New York: W. W. Norton, 1969.
Feighery, Kate. "Timely and Substantial Relief: New York's Cardinal John Farley and the 1916 Easter Rising." In Grey, *Ireland's Allies*, 283–91.
Fowler, W. B. *British American Relations, 1917–1918: The Role of Sir William Wiseman*. Princeton, NJ: Princeton University Press, 1969.
Fry, Michael. *Illusions of Security: North Atlantic Diplomacy, 1918–22*. Toronto: University of Toronto Press, 1972.
Golway, Terry. *Irish Rebel: John Devoy and America's Fight for Ireland's Freedom*. New York: St. Martin's, 1998.

———. "John Devoy and the Easter Rising." In Grey, *Ireland's Allies*, 21–29.
Greaves, C. Desmond. *The Life and Times of James Connolly*. New York: International Press, 1971.
Grayson, Richard S. "Beyond the Ulster Division: West Belfast Members of the Ulster Volunteer Force and Service in the First World War." In Grayson and McGarry, *Remembering 1916*, 112–37.
———. *Dublin's Great Wars: The First World War, the Easter Rising, and the Irish Revolution*. Cambridge: Cambridge University Press, 2018.
———, and Fearghal McGarry, eds. *Remembering 1916: The Easter Rising, the Somme, and the Politics of Memory in Ireland*. Cambridge: Cambridge University Press, 2016.
Grey, Miriam Nyhan, ed. *Ireland's Allies: America and the Easter Rising*. Dublin: University College Dublin Press, 2016.
Hachey, Thomas E. "The British Foreign Office and New Perspectives on the Irish Issues in Anglo-American Relations, 1919–1921." *Eire-Ireland* 7, no. 2 (Summer 1972): 3–13.
Hannigan, Dave. *De Valera in America*. Basingstoke: Palgrave Macmillan, 2010.
Hannigan, Robert E. *The Great War and American Foreign Policy, 1914–24*. Philadelphia: University of Pennsylvania Press, 2017.
Harkness, David. *The Restless Dominion: The Irish Free State and the British Commonwealth of Nations, 1921–31*. New York: New York University Press, 1969.
Hartley, Stephen. *The Irish Question as a Problem in British Foreign Policy, 1914–18*. New York: St. Martin's, 1987.
Hathaway, Oona A., and Scott J. Shapiro. *The Internationalists: How a Radical Plan to Outlaw War Remade the World*. New York: Simon & Schuster, 2017.
Hatton, Helen E. *The Largest Amount of Good: Quaker Relief in Ireland, 1654–1921*. Kingston: McGill-Queen's University Press, 1993.
Hilliker, John. *Canada's Department of External Affairs*. 3 vols. Toronto: University of Toronto Press, 1990.
Hodgson, Godfrey. *Woodrow Wilson's Right Hand: The Life of Colonel Edward M. House*. New Haven, CT: Yale University Press, 2006.
Hopkinson, Michael. *The Irish War of Independence*. Kingston: McGill-Queens University Press, 2002.
Humes, D. Joyce. *Oswald Garrison Villard, Liberal of the 1920s*. Syracuse, NY: Syracuse University Press, 1960.
Jeffrey, Keith. *Ireland and the Great War*. Cambridge: Cambridge University Press, 2000.
Jenkins, Roy. *Asquith*. London: Collins, 1964.
Jones, Lester. *Quakers in Action: Recent Humanitarian and Reform Activities of the American Quakers*. New York: Macmillan, 1929.
Jordan, Anthony J. *W. T. Cosgrave, 1880–1965: Founder of Modern Ireland*. Dublin: Westport, 2009.
Keegan, Nicholas M. *US Consular Representation in Britain Since 1790*. London: Anthem, 2018.
Kennedy, Michael. *Ireland and the League of Nations, 1919–1946*. Dublin: Irish Academic Press, 1996.

———. "Professor Smiddy and the Development of the Irish Diplomatic Service." *Irish Studies in International Affairs* 26 (2015): 127–30.
Keown, Gerard. "Creating the Template? Reflections on the First Decade of Irish Diplomacy and the United States." *Irish Studies in International Affairs* 26 (2015): 137–45.
———. *First of the Small Nations: The Beginnings of Irish Foreign Policy in the Inter-War Years, 1919–1932*. Oxford: Oxford University Press, 2016.
Knirck, Jason. *Aftermath of Revolution: Cumann na nGaedheal and Irish Politics, 1922–1932*. Madison: University of Wisconsin Press, 2014.
Laffan, Michael. *Judging W. T. Cosgrave: The Foundation of the Irish State*. Dublin: Royal Irish Academy, 2014.
Lainer-Vos, Dan. *Sinews of the Nation: Constructing Irish and Zionist Bonds in the United States*. Cambridge: Polity, 2013.
Lauterpacht, Hersch. *Recognition in International Law*. Cambridge: Cambridge University Press, 1947.
Lavelle, Patricia. *James O'Mara: A Staunch Sinn Feiner*. Dublin: Clomore & Reynolds, 1961.
Lee, J. J. *Ireland, 1912–1985: Politics and Society*. Cambridge: Cambridge University Press, 1989.
Longford, Earl of, and Thomas P. O'Neill. *Eamon de Valera: A Biography*. Boston: Houghton Mifflin, 1971.
Lowry, Donal. "The Captive Dominion: Imperial Realities Behind Irish Diplomacy, 1922–49." *Irish Historical Studies* 36, no. 142 (November 2008): 202–26.
MacAtasney, Gerard. "Tom Clarke's New York: A Refuge (1880) and a Home (1899–1907)." In Grey, *Ireland's Allies*, 45-59.
McCaffrey, Lawrence J. *The Irish Diaspora in America*. Washington, DC: Catholic University of America Press, 1984.
McDiarmuid, Lucy. "Casement, New York, and the Easter Rising." In Grey, *Ireland's Allies*, 91–107.
McDowell, R. B. *The Irish Convention, 1917–18*. London: Routledge & Kegan Paul, 1970.
McGough, Eileen. *Diarmuid Lynch: A Forgotten Patriot*. Cork: Mercier, 2007.
McKercher, B. J. C. *The Second Baldwin Government and the United States, 1924–1929*. Cambridge: Cambridge University Press, 1984.
McMahon, Deidre. "Ireland, the Empire, and the Commonwealth." In *Ireland and the British Empire*, edited by Kevin Kenney, 182–219. New York: Oxford University Press, 2004.
Maher, Jim. *Harry Boland: A Biography*. Cork: Mercier, 1998.
Manela, Erez. *The Wilsonian Moment: Self-Determination and the International Origins of Anticolonial Nationalism*. New York: Oxford University Press, 2007.
Manning, Julie. *Frank P. Walsh and the Irish Question: An American Proposal*. Washington, DC: Georgetown University Press, 1989.
Mansergh, Nicholas. *Ireland in the Age of Reform and Revolution*. London: George Allen & Unwin, 1940.
———. *The Irish Question, 1840–1921*. London: George Allen & Unwin, 1965.

Margulies, Herbert F. *The Mild Reservationists and the League of Nations Controversy in the Senate.* Columbia: University of Missouri Press, 1989.

Marreco, Anne. *The Rebel Countess: The Life and Times of Constance Markieviez.* London: Corgi, 1969.

Meehan, Ciara. *The Cosgrave Party: A History of Cumann na nGaedheal, 1923–33.* Dublin: Royal Irish Academy, 2010.

Miller, David Hunter. *The Peace Pact of Paris: A Study of the Kellogg-Briand Treaty.* New York: G. P. Putnam's Sons, 1928.

Mitchell, Arthur. *Revolutionary Government in Ireland: Dáil Éireann 1919–22.* Dublin: Gill & Macmillan, 1995.

Nevins, Allan. *Henry White: Thirty Years of Diplomacy.* New York: Harper & Brothers, 1930.

Northedge, F. S. *The Troubled Giant.* New York: Praeger, 1966.

O'Brien, Conor Cruise. "Ireland in International Affairs." In Edwards, *Conor Cruise O'Brien Introduces Ireland*, 104–34.

O'Brien, Mark. *De Valera, Fianna Fail, and the* Irish Press*: Truth in the News.* Dublin: Academic Press, 2001.

O'Broin, Leon. *Revolutionary Underground: The Story of the Irish Republican Brotherhood, 1858–1924.* Dublin: Gill & Macmillan, 1976.

O'Doherty, Katherine. *Assignment-America: Eamon de Valera's Mission to the United States.* New York: De Tanko, 1957.

O'Driscoll, Mae. "Remembering Diarmuid Lynch." In Butler, *1916 Easter Rising*, 52–59.

Osborn, George C. *John Sharp Williams.* Baton Rouge: Louisiana State University, 1943.

Pusey, Merlo J. *Charles Evans Hughes.* 2 vols. New York: Macmillan, 1952.

Reid, B. L. *The Man From New York: John Quinn and His Friends.* New York: Oxford University Press, 1968.

Roskill, Stephen. *Naval Policy Between the Wars, 1919–1929.* 2 vols. London: Collins, 1968.

Ryan, Desmond. *The Phoenix Flame: A Study of Fenianism and John Devoy.* London: Arthur Barker, 1937.

Sagarra, Eda. *Envoy Extraordinary: Professor Smiddy of Cork.* Dublin: Institute of Public Administration, 2018.

Shannon, Catherine B. *Arthur J. Balfour and Ireland, 1874–1922.* Washington, DC: Catholic University of America Press, 1988.

Schmuhl, Robert. "Bifocalsim of US Press Coverage: The Easter Rising and Irish America." In Grey, *Ireland's Allies*, 269–81.

———. *Ireland's Exiled Children: America and the Easter Rising.* New York: Oxford University Press, 2016.

Surface, Frank M., and Raymond L. Bland. *American Food in the World War and Reconstruction Period.* Stanford, CA: Stanford University Press, 1931.

Tansill, Charles Callan. *America and the Fight for Irish Freedom, 1866–1922.* New York: Devin-Adair, 1957.

Tierney, Michael. *Eoin MacNeill: Scholar and Man of Action, 1867–1945.* Oxford: Oxford University Press, 1980.

Toynbee, Arnold J. *Survey of International Affairs.* London: Oxford University Press, 1929.
Tucker, D. M. "Some American Responses to the Easter Rebellion, 1916." *Historian* 29 (August 1967): 605–18.
Van Voris, Jacqueline. *Constance Markieviez: In the Cause of Ireland.* Amherst: University of Massachusetts Press, 1967.
Vinson, John Chalmers. *The Parchment Peace.* Athens: University of Georgia Press, 1955.
Walsh, James A. "Woodrow Wilson Historians vs. the Irish." *Eire-Ireland* 2, no. 2 (Summer 1967): 55–66.
Walsh, Maurice. *Bitter Freedom: Ireland in a Revolutionary World.* New York: Liveright, 2015.
Walworth, Arthur. *Wilson and His Peacemakers: American Diplomacy at the Peace Conference, 1919.* New York: W. W. Norton, 1986.
Ward, Alan J. *Ireland and Anglo-American Relations, 1899–1921.* London: Weidenfeld & Nicolson, 1969.
Watt, D. Cameron. *Succeeding John Bull: America in Britain's Place.* Cambridge: Cambridge University Press, 1984.
Weissman, Benjamin M. *Herbert Hoover and Famine Relief to Soviet Russia, 1921–23.* Stanford, CA: Hoover Institute, 1974.
Whelan, Bernadette. "Recognition of the Irish Free State, 1924: The Diplomatic Context of the Appointment of Timothy Smiddy as the First Irish Minister to the U.S." *Irish Studies in International Affairs* 26 (2015): 121–25.
———. *United States Foreign Policy and Ireland: From Empire to Independence, 1913–29.* Dublin: Four Courts, 2006.
Willits, R. Bryan. "The Stereopticon: German and Irish Propaganda of Deed and Word and the 1916 Easter Rising." In Grey, *Ireland's Allies*, 185–99.
Winter, Carl G. "The Establishment of the First Canadian Legation." *Historian* 15, no. 1 (Autumn 1952): 57–75.
Wolf, Daphne Dyer. "James Connolly's 'Good End,' The Irish Relief Fund Bazaar Poster." In Grey, *Ireland's Allies*, 319–27.
Wreszin, Michael. *Oswald Garrison Villard: Pacifist at War.* Bloomington: Indiana University Press, 1965.

INDEX

Page numbers in *italics* indicate photos

AARIR. *See* American Association for the Recognition of the Irish Republic
Abbott, Wainwright, 161, 163, 195, 196–97, 255n117
Addams, Jane, *85*, 92–93, 108, *109*
American Aid for Ireland (1920–1922), 117–18, 124, 141; American Friends Service Committee, 111–13; American Red Cross and, 112–14; Anglo-Japanese Alliance, 134–37, 246n70, 247n77, 248n89; British government unfavorable views of, 129; Harding support of, 122–23, 125, 128, 201; Henry on lack of need for, 129; Hoover support and, 115, 125, 128, 134; Irish White Cross and, 119, 120, 126–27, 129, 132, 137–39, 247n85; Maloney relief operation, 114–16; relief appeal, 122–23; relief distribution, 126, 129. *See also* American Committee for Relief in Ireland
American Association for the Recognition of the Irish Republic (AARIR): Anglo-Irish Treaty and, 145–47; bond certificate purchases by, 72; Civil War and, 150; division in, 151; Finerty of, 150; inactivity of, 143; Irish Republic Defense Fund of, 146
American Commission on Conditions in Ireland (1920–1921), 110–11, 199, 200, 251n54; Addams of, *85*, 92–93, 108, *109*; on atrocities, 89–90, 98, 100–103; Boland funding and, 95; British government committee members travel refusal, 96–97; British witnesses testimony, 100–101; controversies of, 107–8; Dempsey testimony at, 103; Derham and Morgan testimony to, 98; de Valera funding, 94; *Evidence on Conditions in Ireland* final report, 106–7; finance problems for, 94–95, 106–7; Greenwood delegation denial, 96; Hackett and Toksvig testimony to, 98; Howe of, 92, 96; *Interim Report*, 104–6; Irish origins of, 95; MacSwiney, Muriel, and MacSwiney, Mary, testimony, 99; Maloney and, 90, 94–95; Maurer of, *85*, 93, 96; Newman of, *85*, 93, 96; Norris of, 93; O'Callaghan testimony at, 102; Plunkett, H., testimony and, 96; second hearings of, 99–100; secretariat of, 94; Thomas, N., of, 93, 96; US public hearings, 97–98; US testimony at, 101–3; Villard criticism of, 107; Walsh, D., of, *85*, 93; witness legal counsel for, 97–98; Wood of, *85*, 92, 106–7
The American Commission on Conditions in Ireland: Interim Report, 104–6
American Commission on Irish Independence, 201; bond certificate support, 65; Creel on, 59, 62; de Valera meeting with, 46, *84*; Dublin strong reaction to, 47; FOIF financing of, 68; Great Britain press reaction to, 48; impressive record of, 61; Ireland trip of, 46–50;

277

American Commission on Irish Independence (*cont.*)
Lansing letter for termination of, 50; Lloyd George and, 45–48, 61–62, 232n42; at Paris Peace Conference, 42–46, 235n70; Senate Foreign Relations Committee testimony, 57; Sinn Féin meeting with, 46; Wilson meeting with, 52–54. *See also* Dunne, Edward; Ryan, Michael J.; Walsh, Frank P.

American Commission to Negotiate Peace, 44, 54, 55, 56

American Committee for Relief in Ireland, 86, 200, 242n34; American Friends Service Committee and, 117, 125; Boland on reconstruction funds of, 144; British government rejection of, 131–32; Catholic Church funding, 124; delegation of, 115–20; Douglas on funds of, 133–34, 241n21; France, C., on, 144; funding of, 111; Geddes on, 129–30; Irish Free State support by, 138; Irish White Cross payments, 137–38; on job creation and placement, 139; Maloney on politics of, 128; on reconstruction, 120, 144; on relief finances needed, 123–24; Sinn Féin and Dumont on funds, 133; success of, 139–40

American Consulate, 35; advice to American delegation, 117–18; dismissal of need for aid, 132–34; Easter Rising, 15; elevation to consulate general, 158–59; proposal of consulate general, 138. *See also* Dumont, Frederick T. F.; Hathaway, Charles M., Jr.

American Friends Service Committee, 111–13; American Committee for Relief in Ireland affiliation, 117, 125; Macready and Anderson relief reservations, 118–19; northern Ireland tour by, 118

American Legation, 159, 193; on Kellogg Ireland trip, 195; under Sterling, 160–63

American Peace Commissioners: Irish self-government hearing and, 51; Walsh, F., Dunne and Ryan and, 51, 52, 232n33

American Quaker Relief Mission, 118

American Red Cross, 117; relief assistance caution by, 112–14

Anderson, John (Sir), 117, 118–19

Anglo-American relations, 23–26, 134–37, 140, 189–91; Hoover and, 196

Anglo-Irish Treaty (1921), 75, 138, 142, 249n23; AARIR and, 145–47; Boland and O'Mara, S., criticism of, 145, 148; Cohalan on, 143, 148; Collins on, 165; Dáil Éireann and Sinn Féin split after, 76–77; de Valera disapproval of, 146; FOIF and Clan reactions to, 147–48; Second Dáil negotiation of, 79; Shahan and Cockran support of, 145; support for, 169; Walsh, F., concerns, 146; Walsh, T., support of, 145; War of Independence end and, 76

Anglo-Irish War. *See* War of Independence

Anglo-Japanese Alliance, 134–37, 246n70, 247n77, 248n89

Armistice, WWI, 36–38

Ash, Thomas, 5

Baker, John C., 86, 116

Baker, Ray Stannard, 40, 44, 230n74

Balfour, Arthur J., 83, 262n1; deputation of, 26–28, 205, 211–12; on Great Britain positives for Ireland, 209–10; Irish Americans deputation meeting with, 26–28; on Irish conscription, 34; on Irish self-government, 24–28, 200; Lansing meeting with, 25–26; Leslie meeting with, 26, 28; Plunkett, H., meeting with, 26; Quinn delegation meeting with, 26–27, 205–12; US Congress address by, 28; Wilson meetings with, 25–26

Balfour Declaration (1926), 152, 165, 255n2
Barlow, John H., 101, 112
Barrett, A. J., 144–45
Bartlett, Thomas, 18
Beaslai, Piaras, 148
Black and Tans British force, 100, 102, 103, 109, 111
Boland, Harry, 41, 66, 69–70, 74, 77, 133, 245n49; American Commission on Conditions in Ireland funding, 95; on American Committee for Relief in Ireland reconstruction funds, 144; Anglo-Irish Treaty criticism, 145, 148; bond certificate sales, 65; Smiddy and, 156
bond certificate sales (1919–1921), 64, 84, 124, 200; AARIR purchase of, 72; American Commission on Irish Independence support of, 65; Boland and, 65; Clan na Gael and FOIF concerns, 69; Cohalan legal concerns for, 68; Dáil Éireann gratitude for US, 74, 76; de Valera campaign, 68–70, 238n34; de Valera on *Irish Press* and, 80–81; loan claims for, 77–80; loan trustees for, 74, 77; Maloney, W., on, 236n11; O'Mara, J., and campaign for, 70; organization instructions on, 237n18; public campaign for, 71–74; Roosevelt, F., and, 68, 236n11; Second Loan campaign for, 74–75; Sinn Féin, 65; symbolic significance of, 75–76; US government obstacles for, 73–74; Walsh, F., support of, 65, 69–70, 73–74, 238n34; Walsh-Ryan-Dunne Commission campaign for, 69–70
Borah, William E., 16, 54, 59–60, 66
Borah Senate resolution: Clemenceau receipt of, 54, 55, 56; Senate passage of, 54, 56
Brett, George H., 32
Briand, Aristide, 191–92, 256n12
Brindley, Ronan, 37

British Commonwealth, Irish Free State membership in, 152–53, 157, 164
British government: American Commission on Conditions in Ireland members travel refusal by, 96–97; American Committee for Relief in Ireland rejection by, 131–32; American relief unfavorable views, 129; Carson and Smith, F., promotion in, 19; de Valera negotiations with, 144; Hobson on insurrection against, 8–9; *Interim Report* response, 106; Irish Free State diplomatic recognition support, 156–57; Irish White Cross unfavorable view by, 129
Bryce Commission on Atrocities in Belgium, 89–90, 108, 239n3
Butler, Nicholas Murray, 14, 29

Campbell, Richard, 114, 115
Canada: Cosgrave trip to, 165–83, 201, 256n14, 258n38; diplomatic recognition for, 154, 157–58, 160; Kellogg-Briand Pact and, 186–87; Mackenzie King of, 154, 186, 196; Smiddy trips to, 154
Carson, Edward (Sir), 6, 13, 19, 25
Casement, Roger (Sir), 5, 82, 227n14, 227n16; arrest of, 9–10, 13; execution of, 17–18; Germany contact by, 8; Great Britain treason charges on, 16–17, 19; Irish Volunteers and, 6–7; private efforts to save, 18–19; Quinn, J., on clemency of, 18–19; US support of, 16–18, 202
Castle, William R., Jr., 156–57, 170, 255n106
Catholic Church: American Committee for Relief in Ireland funding by, 124; on Home Rule, 209; Irish Americans Irish relief, 20–21; Irish conscription and, 34–35
Ceannt, Éamonn, 12
Chamberlain, Austin (Sir), 190, 260n23
Chicago visit, of Cosgrave, 168, 169, 172–73

Churchill, Winston, 29, 109, 136
Civil War, ix, 142; AARIR and, 150; deaths in, 149; end of, 151–52; FOIF denouncement of, 149
Clan na Gael, 38; Anglo-Irish Treaty reaction, 147–48; bond sales concerns, 69; Devoy leadership of, 3–4; Easter Rising funding by, 199; FOIF and, 10, 39, 69; inactivity of, 143; IRB support by, 4–5; as Irish American secret society, 3; Irish organizations support by, 5, 7; Irish Volunteer funds by, 6; representatives, 4–5; Third Irish Race Convention and, 39
Clark, George (Sir), 230n74
Clark, J. Reuben, 191
Clarke, Thomas J., x, 4, 11–12
Clemenceau, Georges, 51; Borah Senate resolution sent to, 54, 55, 56
Cockran, William Bourke, 3, 14, 58, 72, 143, 145, 229n61
Cohalan, Daniel F., 5, 7, 40, 59–60, 67; on Anglo-Irish Treaty, 143, 148; bond sales legal concerns of, 68; de Valera conflict with, 236n9; FOIF organization by, 10; host to Cosgrave in New York, 171, 179; Irish Free State support, 169; Paris Peace Conference and, 54; Versailles Treaty testimony, 57, 235n75
Collins, Michael, 41, 74, 76, 77, 133; on Anglo-Irish Treaty, 165; death of, 166; in Finance from Home Affairs, 64; as Irish White Cross officer, 119
Committee of One Hundred Fifty, 91, 107, 108–9
Congress, US: Balfour address to, 28; Borah Senate resolution, 54, 55, 56; Cosgrave meeting with, 175–76, 202; on Easter Rising court-martials, 16–18; *The Irish Question* transcript, 37–38; Irish Republic recognition by, 135–36; Irish self-government support by, 28–29, 41; Senate Foreign Relations Committee and, 56–58
Connolly, James, x, 5, 11–12, 146
constitutive theory, for diplomatic recognition, 153
Coolidge, Calvin, xi, 123, 157, 159, 161, 162; Cosgrave meeting with, 170, 174; de Valera arrest and, 151–52, 252n70; Kellogg and Ireland approval, 184–85, 188; on naval arms limitation agreement, 189–90; Smiddy and, 201
Cope, A. W. "Andy," 118
Cosgrave, William T., 46, 80–81, 87, 88, 221–23; background of, 166; Chicago visit of, 168, 169, 172–73; Coolidge meeting with, 170, 174; *Gaelic American* support of, 151; Hayes meeting with, 171; on Irish Free State progress, 172–73; Kellogg-Briand Peace Pact signing, 188–89; Kellogg formal dinner with, 176; Kellogg meeting with, 173–74; New York City visit of, 178–79; Smiddy on US trip of, 180–83, 258n38; Sterling and, 167; US and Canada trip of, 165–83, 201, 256n14, 258n38; US Congress meeting with, 175–76, 202; US trip summary, 180–82; Walshe on US speaking engagements of, 168–69; in Washington D.C., 173–77; Whelan on government of, 170
Coyle, Albert, 94, 106
Creel, George, 45, 56, 231n26; on American Commission on Irish Independence, 59, 62; Lloyd George meeting with, 41–42; on Wilson and Peace Conference, 37, 62
Cullen, Edgar M., 29

Dáil Éireann government, x, xii, 37, 200, 237n33; Anglo-Irish Treaty and, 76–77, 138; bond sale target, 67; Cosgrove as executive council president, 165; declaration of independence, 39,

57, 64, 199; de Valera, Griffith, and Plunkett, G., as Paris Peace Conference representatives of, 43–44, 49–50, 52–54, 62, 234n59; de Valera as prime minister of, 64; France, C., on split in, 138; internal loan for, 65; loan monies custody of, 77–78; O'Ceallaigh gratitude for US bond sales, 76; Paris Peace Conference representatives of, 43–44; reorganization of, 64; Russian aid from, 246n65; Second Loan campaign of, 74–75; Sinn Féin Party split with, 76–77; Walsh, F., Dunne and Ryan meeting with, 47
Dáil Éireann Loans and Funds Act, 80
Dáil External Loan, 144–45
Davis, John W., 96, 117
Dawes, Charles G., 172, 174–76
declaration of independence, of Dáil Éireann government, 39, 57, 64, 199
declaratory theory, for diplomatic recognition, 153
"A Defence of the Convention" (Plunkett, H.), 32
Dempsey, Frank, 103
deputation, of Balfour, 26–28, 205, 211–12
Derham, John, 98
de Valera, Edward Eamon, ix, 15, 35, 133, 140–41, 149; American Commission on Conditions in Ireland funding, 94; American Commission on Irish Independence meeting with, 46, 84; Anglo-Irish Treaty disapproval, 146; arrest of, 151–52, 226n9, 252n70; bond certificate sales campaign, 68–70, 238n34; British government negotiations, 144; Cohalan and Devoy conflict with, 236n9; as Dáil Éireann prime minister, 64; Fianna Fáil political party formed by, 80, 166–67, 222; *Gaelic American* on Irish Republic betrayal by, 143, 147–48; as internal loan trustee, 65; Irish American nationalists split and, 66–67, 72–73; on *Irish Press* and bond certificates, 80–81; *The Irish World* backing of, 169; 1918 British election victory by, 38–39; as Paris Peace Conference representative, 43–44, 49–50, 52–54, 62, 234n59; public bond campaign and, 71–74; on self-determination, 37; US bond sales mission of, 65–67, 167, 169; US failure to support Irish Republic and, 66–67

Devoy, John, 7, 11, 67, 82; as Clan leader, 3–4; de Valera conflict with, 236n9; Easter Rising information to, 9; *Gaelic American* founding by, 4; greeted by Cosgrave in New York, 178; Irish Free State support, 169; Pearse and, 3, 5
diplomatic recognition: for Canada, 154, 157–58, 160; constitutive theory for, 153; declaratory theory for, 153; of Irish Free State by US, x, xii, 153–58, 201; US response to, 155–56, 201; Walshe on, 155, 157
Dodd, William E., 62, 235n83
Doheny, Edward L., 72, 145–46; Irish Free State support, 169; relief funding by, 114–15
Dominions, 240n47, 254n96, 255n2; Kellogg-Briand Pact and, 185–87; Mackenzie King and, 186; Versailles Treaty signing, 165
Doorley, Michael, 57, 236n10
Douglas, James G., 112, 113, 115, 138, 170; on American Committee for Relief in Ireland funds, 133–34, 241n21; on Irish White Cross, 119, 126–27
Doyle, Michael Francis, 9, 16–17, 97–98, 227n14
Duffy, George Gavan, 17, 44, 62; as Anglo-Irish Treaty negotiator, 142; Irish foreign policy report of, 142–43
Dumont, Frederick T. F., 246n67; France, C., and McCoy meeting with, 117–18; on Ireland lack of relief need, 132–34

Dunne, Edward F.: of American Commission on Irish Independence, 43, *84*; American Peace Commission and, 51, 52, 232n33; bond sales support, 65; Dáil Éireann government meeting with, 47; Ireland meetings of, 46–47; Ireland trip report by, 52; Versailles Treaty testimony of, 57–58; Wilson meeting with, 52–54

Easter Rising (1916), ix, 2–8, 90; British execution of leaders of, 14–15, 199; civilian casualties in, x; Clan na Gael funds for, 199; Devoy informed of, 9; fundraising after, 111; Germany arms for, 9; Irish Americans support of, 11; one-hundredth anniversary of, ix; Plunkett, J., and, 11–12; prisoners, US intervention for, 15–18; problems with, 1; Quinn on executions, 14–15; secret activities of, 10–11; signatories of, x, 11–12; US backing of, x; US Congress on court-martials after, 16–18; US newspapers condemnation of, 13–14, 225n4; Wilson on prisoners of, 15
Emmet, Robert Temple, 12, 27, 205, 258n44
Evidence on Conditions in Ireland final report, 106–7

Fianna Fáil, 258n52; de Valera formation of, 80, 166–67, 222
Finerty, John F., 150, 152, 182
FitzGerald, Desmond, 162, 168, 169, 183
Fitzgerald, John F., 27; on Balfour deputation, 205; McLemore resolution and, 207–8; on Redmond support, 206–7; on Sinn Féin, 208–9
The Foes of Our Own Household (Roosevelt, T.), 23
Fogarty, Michael, 46, 65
Fogarty and Others v. O'Donoghue and Others (1924), 77

FOIF. *See* Friends of Irish Freedom
Fourteen Points speech, of Wilson, 36, 57
France, Clemens J., *86*, 116, 117; on American Committee for Relief in Ireland funds, 144; on Dáil Éireann split, 138
France, Royal W., 94
Friends of Irish Freedom (FOIF), 11, 236n9; Anglo-Irish Treaty reaction by, 147–48; bond sales concerns, 69; Civil War denouncement by, 149; Clan members of, 10; Cohalan organization of, 10; funding by, 124; Herbert as president of, 10; inactivity of, 143; Irish Victory Fund termination, 67–68; loan claims and, 79–80; Third Irish Race Convention and, 39; US bond sales objections, 67; Versailles Treaty opposition by, 59
funding: of American Committee for Relief in Ireland, 111, 124, 133–34, 144, 241n21; Boland American Commission on Conditions in Ireland, 95; Clan na Gael, 6, 199; de Valera American Commission on Conditions in Ireland, 94; Doheny relief funding, 114–15; early relief, 111; by FOIF, 124. *See also* Irish Victory Fund

Gaelic American, 108; on Anglo-Irish Treaty, 147–48; Cosgrave support by, 151; on de Valera and Dominion solution, 250n40; on de Valera civil war encouragement, 149; on de Valera Irish Republic betrayal, 143, 147–48; Devoy founding of, 4
Geddes, Auckland (Sir), 95–96, 126, 240n30, 245n49; on American Committee for Relief in Ireland, 129–30; Hughes meeting with, 128, 131–32; *Interim Report* dismissal, 105
General Council, of Irish White Cross, 126–27

General Post Office (GPO) building, Irish Volunteers and Irish Citizen Army seizure of, 1
General Treaty for the Renunciation of War. *See* Kellogg-Briand Peace Pact
German Americans, Irish Americans support of, 7
Germany: Casement contact with, 8; Easter Rising arms from, 9; Irish self-government support by, 7–8; US relations deterioration with, 13; WWI submarine warfare, 23
Gerry, Peter C., 60
Gibbons, James (Cardinal), 18, 29, 66, 123
Godkin, Lawrence, 27, 205
Golden, Peter, 70, 73, 113
Gonne, Maud, 5, 13, 262n1
Government of Ireland Act (1920), 77–78, 79, 142
GPO. *See* General Post Office
Great Britain: American Commission for Irish Independence press reaction by, 48; Balfour on Ireland positives from, 209–10; British atrocities witness testimonies, 100–101; Casement treason charges by, 16–17; de Valera 1918 election victory, 38–39; Kellogg cancelled trip to, 191, 195–96; Kellogg trip to, 189; naval arms limitation agreement with France and, 190, 196; US relationship with, xi; US WWI alignment with, 23. *See also* British government
Greenwood, Hamar (Sir), 96, 117
Grew, Joseph C., 51, 55
Grey, Edward (Sir), 16–17, 19, 227n22
Griffith, Arthur, 66, 84, 166; as Irish White Cross officer, 119; as Paris Peace Conference representative, 43–44, 49–50, 52–54, 62, 234n59

Hackett, Francis, 98
Harding, Warren G., xi, 141, 237n33; Irish Free State congratulations, 152; relief committee support, 122–23, 125, 128, 201; Whelan on, 247n86
Hathaway, Charles M., Jr., 35, 118, 159, 161, 254n102
Hayes, Patrick J., 72, 171
Healy, James A., 121, 161, 170
Healy, Matthew Garth, 77
Healy, T. M., 87, 161
Hearn, John J., 74, 78
Hearn Committee, on Irish Republic and Irish Free State loan claims, 78–79
Henry, Charles (Sir): *Interim Report* dismissal, 105; on lack of relief need, 129
Herbert, Victor, 10
Hobson, Bulmer, 4, 5, 8–9, 11
Holland, John P., 21
Home Rule Bill, 2; Catholic Church on, 209; Clan opposition to, 3; Fitzgerald and, 207–8; passage of, 3, 4, 8
Hoover, Herbert, 62, 113–14, 123, 168, 241n16; Anglo-American relations and, 196; Irish relief support and, 115, 125, 128, 134; National Council and, 120–22
Hopkinson, Michael, 37
Houghton, Alanson B., 185
House, Edward M., 17, 20, 23, 46; Irish conscription and, 34; Lloyd George correspondence with, 49, 200; Walsh, F., meeting with, 44
Houston, David F., 73
Howard, Esmé (Sir), 156, 158, 177, 181
Howe, Frederick C.: of American Commission on Conditions in Ireland, 85, 92, 96; on US public hearings, 97–98
Hughes, Charles Evans, 125, 201, 247n77; on diplomatic recognition, 156; Europe trip of, 184; Geddes meeting with, 128, 131–32; on naval arms limitations, 137
Hulbert, Murray, 16
hyphenates immigrant groups, 21; Roosevelt, T., on, 22–23; Wilson on, 58–59

independent Ireland. *See* Irish self-government
Interim Report. See The American Commission on Conditions in Ireland: Interim Report
international diplomacy, 191–92, 200–201; in 1920s, xi–xii
IRB. *See* Irish Republican Brotherhood
Ireland: American Commission on Irish Independence trip to, 46–50; American Friends Service Committee northern tour, 118; Black and Tans British force removal from, 109; constitution, 30; fundraising relief 1916, 20–21; Kellogg trip to, 184–97; Sinn Féin 1918 election victories, 38–39, 41–42, 142, 199; US consulates reorganization, 158–60; US gestures of support for, 163–64; Walsh, F., and Dunne report, 52; Walsh, F., Dunne, and Ryan meetings in, 46–47
Ireland (Hackett), 98
Ireland nationalists: Irish Americans support of, 2–3; Irish Convention and, 33; Senate Foreign Relations Committee position at, 57–58
Ireland's Fight for Freedom (Creel), 56
Irish American nationalists: on British and Irish forces truce, 143; de Valera and split in, 66–67, 72–73; Maloney activities with, 90; split between, 89
Irish Americans, 181–82; Anglo-Saxon and Protestant culture of, xi; Balfour deputation meeting with, 26–28; Catholic churches Irish relief, 20–21; Easter Rising support by, 11; financial support after Easter Rising by, 30; German Americans support of, 7; Ireland election finance by, 2–3; Ireland nationalist activities support by, 2–3; Irish Free State and Irish Republic factions, 148–49; Irish Race Convention meeting of, 10; Irish self-government support, 199; McCaffrey on, xi; population of, 200; Redmond lack of support by, 3; statistics on, 2; street protests, 85; Versailles Treaty opposition by, 57–58, 62–63; Wilson and, 21, 200–201; WWI Britain-US alignment and, 23; WWI experience of, 36

Irish Citizen Army, x, 1, 5, 11
Irish conscription, WWI: Balfour to House on, 34; Catholic Church and, 34–35; Wilson and, 34–35, 230n74
Irish Convention (1917–1918), 32; Irish nationalists and, 33; for Irish self-government, 30, 200–201; McDowell, R., on, 30–31; Russell, G., secretariat at, 31; Sinn Féin and labor attendance refusal, 30
Irish Fellowship Club of Chicago, Cosgrave and McGilligan invitation to, 168, 169, 172
Irish foreign policy report, of Duffy, 142–43
Irish Free State (1921–1927), ix; American Committee for Relief in Ireland support of, 138; British Commonwealth membership, 152–53, 157, 164; as British Dominion, 78; British government diplomatic recognition support, 156–57; Cosgrave on progress of, 172–73; Cosgrave US visit and international status of, 182–83; Devoy, Cohalan, and Doheny support of, 169; election majority for, 149; emergence of, 142–64; Harding congratulations on, 152; League of Nations membership, 152–53, 157, 164, 165; loan claim by, 77–79; 1923 establishment of, 152, 201; reprisals by, 150–51; Smiddy and diplomatic recognition of, 153, 154, 156–58; Sterling as minister to, 160–64; US diplomatic recognition of, x, xii, 153–58, 201
Irish Free State, et al. v. Guaranty Safe Deposit Company, et al. (1927), 79, 238n45

Irish Free State Legation, 157–58
Irish-German collusion, WWI, 34–35
The Irish Home Rule Convention, 32–33
Irish Ministry of External Affairs, 165
Irish National Aid Association, 20
Irish organizations, Clan support of, 5, 7
Irish Parliamentary Party, 2, 3, 38–39, 41, 199
Irish Press, de Valera on bond certificates and, 80–81
Irish Problem (1916–1918), 13; Easter Rising prisoners, US and, 15–18; Irish conscription, 34–35, 230n74; Irish Convention, 30–33, 200–201; Roosevelt, T., and, 7, 14, 26–27, 29–33, 169, 201; Wilson and, 15, 21–26. *See also* Irish self-government
Irish Progressive League, 113; on self-determination, 38
Irish Quakers, aid request, 112
The Irish Question transcript, 37–38
Irish Race Convention, 10, 67; subcommittee at Paris Peace Conference, 42–46; Wilson meeting with committee of, 39–42
Irish Relief Fund Bazaar, 21, 111
Irish Relief Fund Committee, 20–21
Irish Republic, 148–49; Congress on recognition of, 135–36; de Valera US government support failure, 66–67; Irish Free State loan claim opposition, 77–79; *The Irish World* on, 150; Pearse creation announcement, 1; Sinn Féin declaration of, 64. *See also* American Association for the Recognition of the Irish Republic
Irish Republican Army. *See* Irish Volunteers
Irish Republican Brotherhood (IRB), x, 1; Clan support of, 4–5; Easter Rising and, 11
Irish Republican Soldiers and Prisoners Dependent's Fund, 150

Irish Republic Defense Fund, of AARIR, 146
Irish self-government, 50; American Peace Commissioners hearing and, 51; Balfour on, 24–28, 200; Churchill on, 109; Germany support of, 7–8; Irish Americans support of, 199; Irish Convention for, 30, 200–201; Lansing on, 23–26; League of Nations and, 40, 199–200; Lloyd George on, 24–25, 27–28, 200; *Nation* support of, 90, 107–8; Page on, 23–25; Roosevelt, T., on, 29, 31–33, 201; Ulster Unionists obstruction of, 27; US Congress support of, 28–29, 41; Wilson on, 23–24, 45, 228n47
Irish University Act, 210
Irish Victory Fund, 39, 80, 124, 200; Doorley on disbursements of, 236n10; FOIF termination of, 67–68
Irish Volunteer Dependents' Fund, 20, 111
Irish Volunteers, x, 1, 6–9, 11, 89, 225n12
Irish White Cross, 137–39, 247n85; British government unfavorable view of, 129; Collins and Griffth as officers of, 119; Douglas on, 119, 126–27; exploitation accusation for, 132; General Council of, 126–27; Macready relief reservations, 119; for relief distribution, 126–27; *Report of the Irish White Cross*, 120, 139
The Irish World, 108; AARIR and, 147; on Civil War end, 151; de Valera backing by, 169; Irish Republic defense, 150

Johnson, Hiram H., 91
Jordan, Michael J., 29–30

Kahn, Otto, 20
Keating, John T., 4
Kellock, Harold, 94
Kellogg, Frank B., *88*; Coolidge Ireland approval, 184–85, 188; Cosgrave celebration with, 192–94; Cosgrave

formal dinner with, 176; Cosgrave meeting with, 170, 173–74; on Cosgrave US trip, 181; Great Britain cancelled trip, 191, 195–96; Great Britain trip of, 189; Ireland trip of, 184–97, 201; report on Dublin visit of, 221–32; as secretary of state, 160; Smiddy on Ireland trip of, 195

Kellogg-Briand Peace Pact, 88, 184, 201, 221, 259n16, 261n29, 261n44; Cosgrave signing of, 188–89, 191; Dominions signing of, 185–87; Ireland inclusion in, 192

Kelly, Thomas Hughes, 10, 20
Kennedy, John F., 261n52
Kennedy, Joseph P., 261n42
Kennedy, Michael, 201
Kenney, John, 9
Keogh, Martin J., 3
Kern, John W., 16
Kerr, Philip, 44
The King, the Kaiser, and Irish Freedom (McGuire), 21–22
Knirck, Jason, 202

LaFollette, Robert M., 91
Lansing, Robert, 83; Balfour and Irish self-government, 23–26; Europe visit by, 184; letter for termination of American Commission on Irish Independence, 50; on self-determination, 36
Law, Andrew Bonar, 33, 48–49, 109, 137
League of Nations, 37, 56, 57; Irish Free State membership in, 152–53, 157, 164, 165; Irish self-government and, 40, 199–200; Preparatory Commission for the Disarmament Conference, 190; Wilson on Irish self-government, 45
Lee, Joseph J., x, 202
Lemass, Seán, 171
Leslie, Shane, 12, 29–30, 229n61; Balfour meeting with, 26, 28

Lloyd George, David, 140, 256n12; American Commission on Irish Independence meeting with, 45–48, 61–62, 232n42; Creel meeting with, 41–42; on de Valera meeting and settlement, 109; on Far Eastern affairs, 137; House correspondence with, 49, 200; on Irish Convention, 30; on Irish self-government, 24–25, 27–28, 200; Wilson talk with, 41

loan claims: FOIF and, 79–80; Hearn Committee on, 78–79; by Irish Free State, 77–79; Irish Republic opposition to Irish Free State, 77–79; Noonan Committee on, 78–79; Walsh, F., and Ryan bondholders committee, 80

Lodge, Henry Cabot, 19, 54–56
London Quakers, 111–13
Longstreth, Walter C., 116
Longworth, Nicholas, 174
Lover, Samuel, 10
Lovert, Robert Morss, 91, 96
Lowell, A. Lawrence, 14
Lucey, John F., 121, 122, 125, 134
Lynch, Jeremiah Diarmuid, 4, 11, 147; bond sales, 65; as Easter Rising prisoner, 15
Lyndon, W. P., 182

MacCaoilte, Sean, 148
MacCurtain, Thomas, 99, 100
Mac Diarmada, Seán, x, 4–5, 11–12
MacDonagh, Thomas, 12, 96
MacDonald, William, 90, 94, 95–96
Mackenzie King, William Lyon, 154, 186, 196
MacNéill, Eóin, 6, 11, 154–55, 209, 251n54
Macready, Neville (Sir), 117–18
MacSwiney, Mary, 99, 143, 251n54
MacSwiney, Muriel, 95, 99–100, 150
MacSwiney, Peter J., 103
MacSwiney, Terence, 99–100
Malone, Dudley Field, 97–98

Maloney, W. J. M. A., 107, 146, 251n54; American Commission on Conditions in Ireland and, 90, 94–95; on American Committee for Relief in Ireland politics, 128; on bond certificate sales, 236n11; relief operation, 114–16
Manela, Erez, 37, 199
Manly, Basil M., 97–98, 144, 151
Mansergh, Nicholas, xi–xii, 202, 225n4 (prologue)
Markievicz, Constance, 46, 76, 148
Martine, James E., 17
Mason, George, 26
Maurer, James A., 85, 93, 96
McCaffrey, Lawrence J., xi
McCartan, Patrick, 4, 11, 70, 104, 230n2; American Commission on Conditions in Ireland funding, 95; bond sales, 65
McCarthy, Charles, 14
McCormack, John, 20, 124
McCoy, Samuel Duff, 86, 116, 117, 129
McCullough, Denis, 4, 11, 148
McDowell, R. B., 30–31
McDowell, W. W., 58
McGarrity, Joseph, 4, 5, 6, 11, 66–67, 74, 146
McGilligan, Patrick, 168, 186, 188–89, 196
McGuiness, Joseph, 46
McGuire, James K., 21–22
McKim, Charles Follen, 90
McKim, Margaret, 90
McLemore resolution, 207–8
McNeill, James, 193
Meehan, Ciara, 183
Mellows, Liam, 65
Miller, David Hunter, 40–41
Mitchel, John Purroy, 20, 29
Mitchell, Arthur, 65
Monroe Doctrine, 57
Montieth, Robert, 70
Moore, John D., 10, 73, 92, 108
Morgan, Denis, 98
Mosley, Oswald, 240n47

Mulcahy, Richard, 77, 251n54
Muldoon, Peter, 40
Murray, James E. "Red," 150

Nation: American Commission on Conditions in Ireland and, 94, 103–4; on Committee of One Hundred Fifty, 91; Irish self-government support, 90, 107–8
National Council, for Ireland relief, 120–22, 124
National Volunteers, Irish Volunteers secession from, 7
National War Labor Board, Walsh, F., on, 42–43
naval arms limitation agreement, 256n12; Coolidge on, 189–90; Great Britain and France tentative, 190, 196
Newman, Oliver P., 85, 93, 96
New York City: bond certificate campaign, 71–72; Cosgrave visit, 178–79
Noonan Committee, on Irish Republic and Irish Free State loan claims, 78–79
Norris, George W., 93
Northern Ireland Boundary Commission, 166
Norton, James A., 111–12
Nunan, Sean, 70, 74

O'Brien, Morgan J., 5, 26–27, 115; on American Friends Service Committee, 125; on Balfour deputation, 205; on Irish White Cross, 119
O'Broin, Leon, 4
O'Callaghan, Donal, 102
O'Ceallaigh, Sean T., 44, 48, 59, 65–66, 233n47, 234n57, 258n52
O'Connell, Daniel T., 59
O'Connell, Kathleen, 141
O'Connell, William (Cardinal), 38
O'Connor, T. P., 2, 9, 106, 129
O'Doherty, Joseph, 150

O'Donoghue, Daithi, 77
O'Flaherty, Daniel C., 58
O'Hannigan, Michael, 84
O'Hegarty, Diarmuid, 154–55, 161, 169
O'Higgins, Kevin, 157, 166, 185
O'Kelly, J. J., 148, 150
O'Leary, Jeremiah A., 7, 22
O'Mara, James, 148; bond certificate sales campaign and, 70; as internal loan trustee, 65
O'Mara, Stephen, 74, 77, 78; Anglo-Irish Treaty criticism, 145, 148; Dáil External Loan and, 144–45
O'Neill, Laurence, 84, 124, 244n34
O'Reilly, Joseph, 169
O'Sheel, Shaemus, 7
O'Sullivan, J. C., 161

Page, Walter Hines, 16, 23–25
Paris Peace Conference (1919), x, xii, 233n47; American Commission on Irish Independence at, 42–46, 235n70; Borah Senate resolution and, 54, 55, 56; Dáil Éireann representatives at, 43–44; de Valera, Griffith, and Plunkett, G., as representatives to, 43–44, 49–50, 52–54, 62, 234n59; Ireland trip of American Commission on Irish Independence, 46–50; Irish Americans opposition to Versailles Treaty, 57–58, 62–63; Irish Race Convention meeting with Wilson, 39–42; Irish self-government discussion removal from, 50; Lloyd George meeting with American Commission on Irish Independence, 45–48, 61–62, 232n42; Sinn Féin 1918 election victories, 38–39, 41–42, 142, 199; Versailles Treaty defeat, 62–63, 199, 235n83; Wilson on post WWI self-determination rights, 36–37, 53, 57–58; WWI Armistice, 36–38
Pearse, Patrick, x, 1, 3, 5, 11–12

Plunkett, George Noble, 84; as Paris Peace Conference representative, 43–44, 49–50, 52–54, 62, 234n59
Plunkett, Horace (Sir), 32, 96, 205, 230n74; Balfour meeting with, 26; Irish Convention chairmanship, 30–31; Roosevelt, T., and, 30, 31
Plunkett, Joseph Mary, x, 9; Easter Rising and, 11–12
Preparatory Commission for the Disarmament Conference, of League of Nations, 190
Price, William, 86, 116

Quinn, John, 5, 7, 13, 29, 38–39; Balfour meeting with delegation of, 26–27, 205–12; on Casement clemency, 18–19; on Easter Rising executions, 14–15; Roosevelt, T., and, 31–32; WWI Allies support by, 19, 23

Redmond, John, 2, 7, 28; Clan opposition to, 3; constitutional convention support, 30; endorsement of, 13–14; Fitzgerald support of, 206–7; Irish Americans' lack of support for, 3; Jordan letter to, 29–30
Report of the Irish White Cross, 120, 139
Robinson, Annot Erskine, 100–101
Rockefeller, John D., Jr., 42
Roosevelt, Franklin D., 68, 236n11
Roosevelt, Theodore, 7, 14, 26–27, 169; on hyphenates immigrant groups, 22–23; Irish affairs interest, 22–23; on Irish self-government, 29, 31–33, 201; Plunkett, H., and, 30, 31; Quinn and, 31–32; Spring-Rice and, 31
Roskill, Stephen, 136
Russell, George, 31, 178, 262n1
Russia, Dáil Éireann aid to, 246n65
Ryan, Michael J.: of American Commission on Irish Independence, 43, 84; American Peace Commissioners and,

51, 52, 232n33; Ireland meetings of, 46–47; on loan claim bondholder committee, 80; Versailles Treat testimony of, 57–58

Samuel, Herbert (Sir), 16–17
Schmuhl, Robert, 13
Second Loan campaign, 74–75
self-determination: de Valera on, 37; Lansing on, 36; O'Connell, W., on, 38; Versailles Treaty Gerry reservation on, 60; Wilson on post WWI, 36–37, 53, 57–58, 199, 234n57
"Self-Determination for Ireland Week," 38
Senate Foreign Relations Committee: American Commission on Irish Independence testimony, 57; Irish nationalists position at, 57–58; Versailles Treaty and, 56–57
Shahan, Thomas, 257n31; Anglo-Irish Treaty support by, 145; on Cosgrave US visit, 176–77
Shannon, Catherine, 28
Shannon Electrification Scheme, 172
Shaw, Albert, 109
Shaw, G. Howland, 129, 134
Sheehy-Skeffington, Francis, 5
Sheehy-Skeffington, Hannah, 150
Sinn Féin, ix, 5; American Commission on Irish Independence meeting with, 46; bond sales, 65; Dáil Éireann split after Anglo-Irish Treaty, 76–77; Dumont on American Committee for Relief in Ireland funds and, 133; figures, arrest of, 34–35; Fitzgerald on, 208–9; Ireland 1918 election victories, 38–39, 41–42, 142, 199; Irish Convention attendance refusal, 30; Irish Republic declaration, 64
Slattery, W. P., 73
Smiddy, Timothy A., 77, 86, 88, 171, 254n100; Boland and, 156; on Cosgrave US trip, 180–83, 258n38; Irish Free State diplomatic recognition, 153, 154, 156–58; on Kellogg Ireland trip, 195; on US official visit, 167–68, 201
Smith, Alfred E., 72
Smith, F. E., 19
Spicer, R. Barclay, 86, 116
Spring-Rice, Cecil (Sir), 18, 31, 227n22, 228n47
Stack, Austin, 148
Statute of Westminster (1931), 152
Steffens, Lincoln, 44
Sterling, Frederick A., 88, 193, 255n106; American Legation under, 160–63; Cosgrave and, 167; on Cosgrave US trip, 170, 181, 201, 256n14, 258n38; as Irish Free State minister, 160–64; on Kellogg Ireland trip, 185; reception of, 161–62; as representative to Dublin, 87
Stone, William J., 17
Straight, Willard, 14
Stresemann, Gustav, 191
Strickland, Peter (Sir), 118
Sturgis, Mark, 118–19
Sullivan, A. M., 17
Survey of International Affairs (Toynbee), 195

Taft, William Howard, 29, 43, 169, 174
Tammany Hall, 211–12
Third Irish Race Convention, Clan, FOIF and, 39
Thomas, Norman M.: of American Commission on Conditions in Ireland, 93, 96; *Interim Report* and, 106
Thomas, Wilbur K., 112; Lucey meeting with, 125
Thompson, William Hale "Big Bill," 172
Thoughts for a Convention (Russell, G.), 31
Toksvig, Signe, 98
Tone, Wolfe, 13
Toynbee, Arnold J., 195
Tumulty, Joseph, 25, 29, 39–40, 52, 233n55

UIL. *See* United Irish League
Ulster Revolt (1914), 14, 199
Ulster Unionists, 6; Irish Convention and, 30; Irish self-government obstruction by, 27
United Irish League (UIL) of America, 2, 3, 7
United Kingdom. *See* Great Britain
United States (US), xi; American Commission on Conditions in Ireland public hearings, 97–98; American Commission on Conditions in Ireland testimony, 101–3; bond certificate sales obstacles in, 73–74; Casement support by, 16–18, 202; Cosgrave trip to, 165–83; Dáil Éireann gratitude for bond sales in, 74, 76; de Valera bond sales mission to, 65–67, 167, 169; Easter Rising backing by, x; Easter Rising condemnation of, 13–14, 225n4; on Easter Rising court-martials, 16–18; Easter Rising prisoners intervention by, 15–18; FOIF bond sales objections, 67; German relations deterioration with, 13; Great Britain WWI alignment with, 23; Ireland gestures of support, 163–64; Irish Free State diplomatic recognition by, x, xii, 153–58, 201; 1916 election campaign, 21–22; Smiddy on official visit to, 167–68, 201. *See also* American Consulate; American Legation; Congress, US

Versailles Treaty (1919), 194, 236n7; Cohalan testimony on, 57, 235n75; defeat of, 62–63, 199, 235n83; Dominions signing of, 165; Dunne, Ryan and Walsh, F., testimony, 57–58; FOIF opposition to, 59; Gerry self-determination reservation and, 60; Irish Americans opposition to, 57–58, 62–63; Senate Foreign Relations Committee on, 56–57; Wilson support appeals for, 58–59

Villard, Oswald Garrison, 90, 122; American Commission on Conditions in Ireland criticism, 107; on *Interim Report*, 106; support of, 109–10

Walker, James J., 71, *87*, 178
Walsh, David A., *85*, 93
Walsh, Frank P., 40, 59, 97–98, 136, 151, 231n26; as American Commission on Irish Independence leader, 42–43, *84*; American Peace Commissioners and, 51, 52, 232n33; Anglo-Irish Treaty concerns, 146; bond sales support, 65, 69–70, 73–74, 238n34; Dáil Éireann government meeting with, 47; on de Valera British government negotiations, 144; House meeting with, 44; Ireland meetings of, 46–47; Ireland trip report by, 52; on loan claim bondholder committee, 80; as National War Labor Board joint chairman, 42–43; Versailles Treaty testimony of, 57–58; Wilson meeting with, 45, 52–54; Wilson relationship with, 42–43
Walsh, Maurice, 12, 39
Walsh, Thomas J., 38; Anglo-Irish Treaty support by, 145; on de Valera arrest, 151–52; on de Valera British government negotiations, 144
Walshe, Joseph, 155, 157, 161, 168–69
Walsh-Ryan-Dunne Commission, 232n33; for bond certificate sales campaign, 69–70
War Labor Conference Board, Walsh, F., on, 43
War of Independence (Anglo-Irish War), ix, 62, 64, 75, 89, 137, 200; Anglo-Irish Treaty and end of, 76
Washington D.C., Cosgrave in, 173–77
What Dunne Saw in Ireland (Dunne), 55
What Germany Could Do for Ireland (McGuire), 21–22

Whelan, Bernadette, 20, 132, 247n77; on Cosgrave government, 170; on Harding, 247n86
White, Henry, 51, 52, 55
Wilber, Oren B., 86, 116
Wilkinson, Ellen C., 100–101
Wilson, Woodrow, 14, 209, 233n55; American Commission of Irish Independence meeting with, 52–54; Balfour meetings with, 25–26; Creel on Peace Conference and, 37, 62; on Easter Rising prisoners, 15; Fourteen Points speech of, 36, 57; on hyphenates immigrant groups, 58–59; Irish Americans and, 21, 200–201; Irish conscription and, 34–35, 230n74; Irish Race Convention committee meeting with, 39–42; on Irish self-government, 23–24, 45, 228n47; on League of Nations and Irish self-government, 45; Lloyd George talk with, 41; O'Leary challenge to, 22; on post WWI self-determination rights, 36–37, 53, 57–58, 199, 234n57; Spring-Rice on, 228n47; stroke of, 59, 63; Versailles Treaty support appeals, 58–59; Walsh, F., meeting with, 45, 52–54; Walsh, F., relationship with, 42–43; WWI declaration of war, 23–24

"Wilsonian Moment," Manela on, 37, 199
Wiseman, William (Sir), 38, 46
Women's International League, 100, 101, 103
Wood, L. Hollingsworth, 103–4, 112, 114; of American Commission on Conditions in Ireland, 85, 92, 106–7
World War I (WWI), 7, 33, 199; Armistice, 36–38; Germany submarine warfare in, 23; Irish Americans and, 23, 36; Irish conscription, 34–35, 230n74; Irish-German collusion in, 34–35; Quinn, J., Allies support in, 19, 23; US alignment with Great Britain, 23; Wilson declaration of war, 23–24; Wilson on self-determination rights post, 36–37, 53, 57–58, 199, 234n57

Yeats, William Butler, ix, 1, 5

ABOUT THE AUTHOR

Francis M. Carroll is Professor Emeritus at the University of Manitoba, and the author and editor of thirteen books, including *The American Presence in Ulster, 1796–1996* (2005) and *Money for Ireland: Finance, Diplomacy, Politics, and the First Dáil Éireann Loans, 1919–1936* (2002). He has held visiting chairs at Boston College, the University of St. Thomas, and University College Dublin.

www.ingramcontent.com/pod-product-compliance
Lightning Source LLC
Chambersburg PA
CBHW021846090426

42811CB00033B/2156/J